Critical Issues on Violence Against Women

Violence against women is a global problem and despite a wealth of knowledge and inspiring action around the globe, it continues unabated. Bringing together the very best in international scholarship with a rich variety of pedagogical features, this innovative new textbook on violence against women is specifically designed to provoke debate, interrogate assumptions, and encourage critical thinking about this global issue.

This book presents a range of critical reflections on the strengths and limitations of responses to violent crimes against women and how they have evolved to date. Each section is introduced with an overview of a particular topic by an expert in the field, followed by thoughtful reflections by researchers, practitioners, or advocates that incorporate new research findings, a new initiative, or innovative ideas for reform. Themes covered include:

- advances in measurement of violence against women;
- justice system responses to intimate partner violence and sexual assault;
- victim crisis and advocacy;
- behavior change programs for abusers; and
- prevention of violence against women.

Each section is supplemented with learning objectives, critical thinking questions, and lists of further reading and resources to encourage discussion and to help students to appreciate the contested nature of policy. The innovative structure will bring debate alive in the classroom or seminar and makes the book perfect reading for courses on violence against women, gender and crime, victimology, and crime prevention.

Holly Johnson's primary research interests are the effectiveness of criminal justice and societal responses to violence against women, primary prevention, and improving the measurement of violence and other gendered experiences. She was principal investigator on Canada's first national survey on violence against women and co-investigator of the International Violence Against Women Survey, and is the author of numerous publications in this area.

Bonnie S. Fisher's primary research focuses on the measurement and predictors of violence against college women, recurrent victimization, and the evaluation of bystander interventions. She has authored numerous publications spanning the field of victimology, with emphasis on measurement issues, and recently served on the National Academy of Sciences Panel on Measuring Rape and Sexual Assault.

Véronique Jaquier has trained in psychology and criminology in Switzerland and the United States. Her program of research examines the interrelations of women's victimization and use of aggression as it impacts mental health and risk behaviors, with emphasis on understanding how criminal justice and social institutions impact life trajectories.

"This is a timely and extremely valuable edited collection on violence against women (VAW). The contributions provide insight into and promote debate about many of the assumptions underlying responses to VAW, as well as outlining some inspiring approaches for tackling [it]. The collection's innovative structure, including learning objectives, questions, and readings for each section, make it essential for all courses and people interested in violence against women."

Dr Miranda Horvath, Reader in Forensic Psychology and Deputy Director of Forensic Psychological Services, Middlesex University, UK

"Violence against women is a universal and now recognized problem, as this volume attests. For over three decades research has addressed some key forms of violence women face around the globe. I recommend that in the first instance young scholars start here with this volume, and think creatively about how to move forward our initiatives and challenges to violence against women. In this volume researchers share their insight, the state of the art in thinking about confronting violence against women."

Professor Betsy Stanko OBE, Head of Evidence and Insight, Mayor's Office for Policing and Crime, London and Emeritus Professor of Criminology, Royal Holloway, University of London, UK

Critical Issues on Violence Against Women

International perspectives and promising strategies

Edited by Holly Johnson,
Bonnie S. Fisher, and
Véronique Jaquier

Routledge
Taylor & Francis Group
LONDON AND NEW YORK

Reprint 2019

First published 2015
by Routledge
2 Park Square, Milton Park, Abingdon, Oxon OX14 4RN

and by Routledge
711 Third Avenue, New York, NY 10017

Routledge is an imprint of the Taylor & Francis Group, an informa business

British Library Cataloguing-in-Publication Data
A catalogue record for this book is available from the British Library

Library of Congress Cataloging-in-Publication Data
Critical issues on violence against women : international perspectives and promising strategies / edited by Holly Johnson, Bonnie S. Fisher, Véronique Jaquier. — First Edition.
pages cm. — (Global issues in crime and justice; 3)
1. Women — Crimes against. I. Johnson, Holly, editor of compilation. II. Fisher, Bonnie, editor of compilation. III. Jaquier, Véronique, editor of compilation.
HV6250.4.W65C765 2014
362.88082—dc23 2014021433

ISBN: 978-0-367-24202-2 (pbk)
ISBN: 978-0-203-72780-5 (ebk)

Typeset in Times New Roman
by Keystroke, Station Road, Codsall, Wolverhampton

Printed and bound in India

For sale in India, Pakistan, Nepal, Bhutan, Bangladesh and Sri Lanka only.

Dedication

To all those whose energy, courage, and creativity are helping to build and sustain a world where women and girls have the right to live free of violence.

Contents

List of figures *xi*
List of tables *xiii*
List of contributors *xv*
Acknowledgments *xxi*
Abbreviations *xxiii*

Introduction 1
HOLLY JOHNSON, BONNIE S. FISHER, AND VÉRONIQUE JAQUIER

SECTION I
Measurement of violence against women 5

1 **Measurement innovations: overview of methodological progress and challenges** 7
HOLLY JOHNSON, BONNIE S. FISHER, AND VÉRONIQUE JAQUIER

2 **We are making progress in measuring sexual violence against women** 19
RONET BACHMAN

3 **Innovations in prevalence research: the case of the 28-country survey by the European Union Agency for Fundamental Rights** 31
SAMI NEVALA

SECTION II
Justice system responses to intimate partner violence 45

4 **Overview of current policies on arrest, prosecution, and protection by the police and the justice system as responses to domestic violence** 47
CAROL HAGEMANN-WHITE, CATHY HUMPHREYS, LESLIE M. TUTTY, AND KRISTIN DIEMER

5 **Pie in the sky? The use of criminal justice policies and practices for intimate partner violence** 66
AMANDA L. ROBINSON

6 **Perils of using law: a critique of protection orders to respond to intimate partner violence** 77
HEATHER DOUGLAS AND HEATHER NANCARROW

SECTION III
Justice system responses to sexual violence 91

7 **Policing and prosecuting sexual assault: assessing the pathways to justice** 93
CASSIA SPOHN, KATHARINE TELLIS, AND ERYN NICOLE O'NEAL

8 **The long and winding road: improving police responses to women's rape allegations** 104
JAN JORDAN

9 **Victim lawyers in Norway** 117
HEGE SALOMON

SECTION IV
Victim crisis and advocacy 129

10 **Breaking down barriers: new developments in multi-agency responses to domestic violence** 131
NICKY STANLEY

11 **Providing services to minority women and women with disabilities** 142
RAVI K. THIARA

12 **A culturally integrative model of domestic violence response for immigrant and newcomer families of collectivist backgrounds** 154
MOHAMMED BAOBAID, NICOLE KOVACS, LAURA MACDIARMID, AND EUGENE TREMBLAY

SECTION V
Behavior change programs for abusers 169

13 **Behavior change programs for intimate partner violence abusers: a means to promote the safety of women and children?** 171
DONNA CHUNG

14 **New approaches to assessing effectiveness and outcomes of domestic violence perpetrator programs** 183
LIZ KELLY AND NICOLE WESTMARLAND

15 **What do we mean by domestic violence? Mandatory prosecution and the impact on partner assault response programs** 195
MARK HOLMES

SECTION VI
Preventing male violence against women 207

16 **Current practices to preventing sexual and intimate partner violence** 209
MICHAEL FLOOD

17 **New approaches to violence prevention through bystander intervention** 221
ANN L. COKER AND EMILY R. CLEAR

18 **Engaging men in prevention of violence against women** 233
JACKSON KATZ

19 **A feminist "epistemic community" reshaping public policy: a case study of the End Violence Against Women Coalition** 244
MADDY COY, LIZ KELLY, AND HOLLY DUSTIN

Index 258

List of figures

12.1 Safe Integration Process 160
12.2 Four Aspects Screening Tool (FAST) 162

List of tables

2.1 Screening questions used to measure rape and sexual assault victimizations for the National Crime Victimization Survey and the National Intimate Partner and Sexual Violence Survey. 21
3.1 Percentage of women experiencing violent victimization, by type and EU member state. 33
3.2 Survey questions concerning experiences of sexual harassment. 36
3.3 Survey questions concerning experiences of stalking. 36
3.4 Percentage of women experiencing sexual harassment, sexual forms of cyberharassment, stalking, and cyberstalking since the age of 15, by EU member state. 37

Contributors

Ronet Bachman is Professor in the Department of Sociology and Criminal Justice at the University of Delaware. She is co-author of *Statistical Methods for Criminology and Criminal Justice*, *The Practice of Research in Criminology and Criminal Justice*, and *Violence: The Enduring Problem.* Her primary research interests revolve around violent victimization and offending.

Mohammed Baobaid, PhD, earned his doctoral degree from the Institute of Psychology at the University of Erlangen Nurnberg in Germany. He is the founder and the Executive Director of the Muslim Resource Centre for Social Support and Integration in Canada and works on innovative culturally integrative family violence responses.

Donna Chung is Professor of Social Work at Curtin University, Western Australia. Her work in gendered violence has spanned over 20 years, involving research, program evaluation, and policy advice. Areas of interest include intimate partner violence and women's employment, women's homelessness following violence, dating violence, and perpetrator programs for men.

Emily R. Clear, MPH, CHES, is a research coordinator in the Department of Obstetrics and Gynecology at the University of Kentucky. Her research interests include dating and sexual violence among adolescents, as well as health effects of various forms of violence against women.

Ann L. Coker, PhD, MPH, is Professor and Verizon Wireless Endowed Chair in the Department of Obstetrics and Gynecology, College of Medicine and the Department of Epidemiology, College of Public Health at the University of Kentucky. Her current research focuses on prevention interventions to reduce the impact of violence against women.

Maddy Coy is Deputy Director of the Child and Woman Abuse Studies Unit (CWASU) at London Metropolitan University and a Reader in Sexual Exploitation and Gender Inequality. Maddy has worked closely with the End Violence Against Women Coalition on research that evidences the value of an integrated approach to violence against women and girls.

Kristin Diemer has held a Senior Research Fellow position at the University of Melbourne, Department of Social Work, for six years. With a background in Sociology, she has spent 20 years working in the public, private, and academic sectors as a research specialist on violence against women and children.

Heather Douglas is a Professor in the TC Beirne School of Law at The University of Queensland. Heather's research explores the way the law impacts on and constructs women. Heather has published widely around justice issues and domestic violence. She is the lead researcher on the Australian Feminist Judgments Project.

Holly Dustin is Director of the End Violence Against Women Coalition, United Kingdom, which she helped found in 2005, and has secured major successes, including UK governments publishing violence against women and girls strategies, giving evidence to the Leveson Inquiry, and securing political action on girls' safety in schools.

Bonnie S. Fisher's primary research focuses on the measurement and predictors of violence against college women, recurrent victimization, and the evaluation of bystander interventions. She has authored numerous publications spanning the field of victimology and recently served on the National Academy of Sciences Panel on Measuring Rape and Sexual Assault.

Michael Flood is a researcher, educator, and activist. His research focuses on the primary prevention of violence against women, men and gender, and young men's heterosexual relations. Dr. Flood has had a long involvement in men's anti-violence work and pro-feminist activism.

Carol Hagemann-White (BA Harvard 1964, DPhil Berlin 1970), full Professor of Gender Studies and Educational Theory, has directed policy-related empirical studies on gender-based violence and evaluated intervention since 1977. She led an EU research network and has monitored the implementation of European policy recommendations on violence since 2002.

Mark Holmes has worked with men who have used abusive behavior, since 1985. He was appointed to the Government of Ontario's Domestic Violence Advisory Council in 2007 and traveled to Russia in 2010 to train Russian social service workers in domestic violence issues. He is currently interested in developing a differential treatment response based on Michael Johnson's typologies.

Cathy Humphreys has a driving interest in the interventions that are effective in promoting the safety and protection of women and their children from abuse. She has a strong focus on children and child protection issues in her work, which has spanned research in the United Kingdom, Europe, and Australia.

Véronique Jaquier has trained in psychology and criminology in Switzerland and the United States. Her program of research examines the interrelations of women's victimization and use of aggression as it impacts mental health and risk behaviors, with emphasis on understanding how criminal justice and social institutions impact life trajectories.

Holly Johnson's primary research interests are the effectiveness of criminal justice and societal responses to violence against women, primary prevention, and improving the measurement of violence and other gendered experiences. She has led national and international surveys on violence against women and is the author of numerous publications in this area.

Jan Jordan is an Associate Professor at the Institute of Criminology, Victoria University of Wellington, New Zealand. Dr. Jordan has over 20 years' experience teaching and researching in the area of women as victim/survivors of sexual violence and is a regular presenter on police adult sexual assault investigation training courses.

Jackson Katz, PhD, is an educator, author, and internationally acclaimed lecturer. He cofounded Mentors in Violence Prevention (MVP), created the films *Tough Guise* and *Tough Guise 2*, and authored *The Macho Paradox* and *Leading Men*. He lectures widely in the United States and around the world on violence, media, and masculinities.

Liz Kelly holds the Roddick Chair on Violence Against Women at London Metropolitan University, where she is also Director of the Child and Woman Abuse Studies Unit. Her research interests are sexual violence, intimate partner violence, trafficking and sexual exploitation, and state responses to violence against women.

Nicole Kovacs is the founder of Kovacs Group Inc., a consulting firm that collaborates with purpose-driven organizations to develop evidence-informed strategies and innovative solutions to address complex social challenges. Nicole holds a Master's degree in Business and is passionate about helping organizations change their corner of the world.

Laura MacDiarmid is a Senior Consultant at Kovacs Group Inc. Laura obtained her Honor's BA with a specialization in Sociology and a major in Criminology from Western University in 2009 and her Master's in Criminology from the University of Ontario Institute of Technology in 2011.

Heather Nancarrow is CEO of Australia's National Research Organisation for Women's Safety Ltd, established by Australian governments to provide evidence for future policy and practice to reduce violence against women and their children. Heather has extensive experience in this field, including research on justice responses and Indigenous family violence.

Sami Nevala is Head of Sector for Statistics and Surveys in the European Union Agency for Fundamental Rights (FRA). He has worked on a number of comparative, multi-country surveys both in his current position as well as at HEUNI (Finland) and as a consultant for UNODC, UNICRI, and OHCHR.

Eryn Nicole O'Neal is a doctoral student and research assistant in the School of Criminology and Criminal Justice at Arizona State University. Her research interests include intimate partner sexual assault, arrest and charging decisions in sexual assault and intimate partner violence cases, poststructural approaches in feminist theory, and qualitative methods.

Amanda L. Robinson received her PhD from Michigan State University and has worked as a criminologist at Cardiff University since 2001. During her career Dr. Robinson has undertaken a number of research projects on responses to violence, which have informed the development of service provision across the UK and Europe.

Hege Salomon works as a victim lawyer in the law firm Salomon Johansen in Oslo. In 2004 she received the DIXI award for her work for rape victims. From 2006 to 2008 she was a member of a public committee on rape (Voldtektsutvalget). She is active in the public debate concerning the rights of victims of rape and domestic violence.

Cassia Spohn is a Foundation Professor and Director of the School of Criminology and Criminal Justice at Arizona State University. Her research interests include prosecutorial and judicial decision making and sexual assault case-processing decisions. In 2013 she was selected as a Fellow of the American Society of Criminology.

Nicky Stanley is Professor of Social Work at the University of Central Lancashire, UK. She researches on domestic violence, child protection, and parents' and children's mental health. Her current studies address interventions for children experiencing domestic violence and service responses to trafficking. Recent studies examined interventions for abusive men.

Katharine Tellis's publications include books and scholarly articles about various aspects of sexual victimization. Dr. Tellis was co-principal investigator of a study funded by the National Institute of Justice (NIJ) in LA that led the Los Angeles Police Department to create a specialized sexual assault school, and the Los Angeles Sheriff's Department to centralize all rape investigations. NIJ supported a replication of the study in six jurisdictions.

Ravi K. Thiara is Principal Research Fellow in the Centre for the Study of Safety and Well-being, University of Warwick. Dr. Thiara has worked in the violence against women and children field at national and international levels since the late 1980s. She has published widely, sits on numerous advisory/expert panels, and supervises PhD students.

Eugene Tremblay, MSW, is a retired Child Welfare Supervisor who has worked in the area of multicultural practice for the past 40 years in two provinces in Canada. He has advanced training in family and group therapy. He is the Program Director at the Muslim Resource Centre for Social Support and Integration in London, Ontario.

Leslie M. Tutty, PhD, is a Professor Emerita with the Faculty of Social Work, University of Calgary, Alberta, Canada. Her research focuses on prevention and intervention for sexual abuse and intimate partner violence, including evaluations of shelters, groups for abused women and abusive batterers, and the criminal justice response to IPV.

Nicole Westmarland is Professor of Criminology and Co-Director of Durham University Research Centre for Research into Violence and Abuse. Her interests are all areas of male violence against women, particularly rape, sexual violence, and partner violence. She leads the Durham University Project Mirabal team.

Acknowledgments

This volume could not have been completed without the help and support of many. We thank Tom Sutton at Routledge Books for his enthusiastic support of our idea for the content and organization of this edited volume from the start. We are also grateful to Nicola Hartley and Heidi Lee at Routledge Books for answering our endless questions promptly and professionally and for seeing this project through to completion. We thank our colleagues and the hundreds of students at our respective universities who were compelled to listen and help reflect on our ideas concerning violence against women and concerns about policy failures. Over the years, your questions and feedback have fueled our thinking and our activism and have contributed in no small measure to this volume.

Edited volumes are a team effort and we are grateful to each contributor who was not only willing to share their insights and expertise with an international audience but who also responded graciously to our editorial suggestions and to what may have seemed at times unreasonable deadlines. We hope you will agree it was time and effort well spent. You all are in very good company indeed. We would also like to thank the European Union Agency for Fundamental Rights for permitting us to reproduce data from their publication 'Violence against women: an EU-wide survey' in Chapter 3.

Finally, our heartfelt appreciation goes to partners John, Nick, and Luc for their everlasting support, and to daughters, Laura, Olivia, Camille, and newest arrival Maxine. These girls and young women energize and stimulate our thinking through their questions and insights about growing up female in an unequal world. They are an inspiration and our hope for the future and are the reason we dedicate our personal and professional energies to ending gender-based violence.

Abbreviations

ACT	Australian Capital Territory
AFL	Australian Football League
AIAN	American Indian and Alaskan Native
ALRC/NSWLRC	Australian Law Reform Commission and New South Wales Law Reform Commission
ATSWTFV	Aboriginal and Torres Strait Islander Women's Taskforce on Violence (Queensland, Australia)
BJS	Bureau of Justice Statistics (US)
BME	black and minority ethnic
CAADA	Co-ordinated Action Against Domestic Abuse (UK)
CAFCASS	Children and Family Court Advisory and Support Service (UK)
CBIM	Coaching Boys Into Men (CBIM) program
CBT	cognitive behavioral therapy
CDC	Centers for Disease Control and Prevention (US)
CEDAW	Convention on the Elimination of Discrimination against Women Against Women
CIFSR	Culturally Integrative Family Safety Response
CJS	criminal justice system
CMC	Crime and Misconduct Commission (Queensland, Australia)
CORT	Coordinated Organization Response Team (MRCSSI, London ON, Canada)
CTS	Conflict Tactics Scales
DAIP	Duluth Abuse Intervention Program
DHS	Demographic and Health Surveys
DV	domestic violence
DVC	domestic violence court
DVO	domestic violence order
DVPP	domestic violence perpetrator program
EC	European Commission
EHRC	Equality and Human Rights Commission (UK)

EO	exclusion order
ESM	experience sampling methods
EU	European Union
EVAW	End Violence Against Women Coalition (UK)
FAST	Four Aspects Screening Tool (MRCSSI, London ON, Canada)
FRA	European Union Agency for Fundamental Rights
GLA	Greater London Authority (UK)
IAFN	International Association of Forensic Nurses
IMAGES	International Men and Gender Equality Survey
IPSA	intimate partner sexual assault cases
IPV	intimate partner violence
IRIS	Identification and Referral to Improve Safety program (UK)
ISS	integrated support services
LSHTM	London School of Hygiene and Tropical Medicine
MARAC	Multi-Agency Risk Assessment Conference (UK)
MOST	Men of Strength (MOST) program
MRCSSI	Muslim Resource Centre for Social Support and Integration (London ON, Canada)
MVP	Mentors in Violence Prevention
NCRVAWC	National Plan to Reduce Violence against Women and their Children (Australia)
NCS	National Crime Survey
NCVS	National Crime Victimization Survey
NGO	non-governmental organization
NIJ	National Institute of Justice (US)
NISVS	National Intimate Partner and Sexual Violence Survey
NOU	Norges offentlige utredninger (Norway)
NTDPP	Northern Territory Office of the Director of Public Prosecutions (Australia)
NVAWS	National Violence Against Women Survey
NWS	National Women's Study
OMB	Office of Management and Budget (US)
OWP	Office of Women's Policy (Queensland, Australia)
PAR	Partner Assault Response (PAR) program
PB	police ban
PFVO	police family violence order (Australia)
PO	protection order
PTSD	post-raumatic stress disorder
RDD	random digit dialing
SANE	Sexual Assault Nurse Examiner
SCREAM	Students Challenging Realities and Educating Against Myths (SCREAM) Theater

SEEDS	Students Educating and Empowering to Develop Safety
SES	Sexual Experiences Survey
SIP	Safe Integration Program (MRCSSI, London ON, Canada)
SV	sexual violence
TBP	Towards Better Practice (Australian Study)
TRO	temporary restraining order
UK	United Kingdom
UN	United Nations
US	United States
VAW	violence against women
VAWA	Violence Against Women Act (US)
VAWG	violence against women and girls
WAG	Welsh Assembly Government (UK)
WHO	World Health Organization
WNC	Women's National Commission (UK)
WWD	women with disabilities

Introduction

Holly Johnson, Bonnie S. Fisher, and Véronique Jaquier

Since the birth of the battered women's and rape crisis movements in the 1970s, grassroots women's organizations, researchers, governments, and international organizations have dedicated time and energy to finding effective strategies to support victims, hold perpetrators accountable, and prevent the multiple manifestations of male violence against women (VAW). Looking back over 40 years, our collective progress is undeniable. Thanks to new and evolving research tools, there is conclusive evidence that women throughout the world are targets of a vast array of lethal and non-lethal violence and abuse, and suffer harmful and enduring impacts. The negative toll is acutely felt by large proportions of women in each and every country of the world.

VAW crosses inter- and intra-national divides; there is no group of women who are immune from the threat of such violence and abuse. Thanks to the dedication and persistence of grassroots women's organizations, shelters, rape crisis centers, medical, legal and housing supports and other counseling are mainstays of a comprehensive coordinated response to these crimes in many countries. Community and state-level responses have proliferated and criminal and civil justice systems are challenged to modify their approaches to crimes that were previously hidden and that are uniquely intimate in nature. History has revealed that success in eliminating this violence depends on broad structural change at the societal level—not individualized victim-blaming approaches—and on reforming institutions that entrench and reinforce gender inequality and violate women's legal and human rights.

A virtual explosion of media—textbooks, academic journals, electronic mailing lists, websites, blogs, and tweets—is daily cataloguing a wide variety of viewpoints, real-time events, new initiatives, theories, research, debates, and controversies on the topic of VAW. So why is another volume on this topic needed in the growing collection? A quick Internet or library search will identify copious texts profiling diverse aspects of this widespread social problem from the perspective of multiple disciplines. Many investigate a particular aspect of the problem, such as sexual violence or intimate partner violence or femicide; some integrate or critically question research, theory, and policy responses. Some explore issues cross-nationally; many more narrowly focus on a particular country. After 40 years of activity addressing violence against women without having achieved the results we justifiably anticipated, this volume inserts a pause and a chance to reflect critically on where our efforts have taken us, to identify policies or programs that achieved positive outcomes and others that have failed to live up to their promise—in many cases causing direct harm—and to imagine where the future could and should lead.

The 19 chapters that comprise this volume collectively take stock of the progress made in addressing VAW, provide critical reflections on aspects of current responses, and feature some innovative new ideas. Many social and legal responses implemented with good intentions have resulted in unintended consequences, while others address the needs of some populations but not of others. Many responses remain deeply entrenched even though evaluations are equivocal; very few are evaluated at all, despite the investment of vast resources and anecdotal evidence they may be harming the women they were designed to help. The intent of this volume is to stimulate critical thinking and discussion about the elements of effective responses by introducing readers to different viewpoints and research from authors who have multiple disciplinary perspectives and live and work in different sociocultural contexts. The topics and debates are international in focus and scope. The contributors include university and community researchers, practitioners and advocates from around the world who critically reflect on their work and how they are reorienting the questions they ask, the programs they design and implement, and the methods they use to respond to new challenges.

We now know that VAW is a global problem, and although it may take subtly different forms, the root causes are remarkably similar at individual and societal levels. We also know that despite the wealth of knowledge that has been amassed and the inspiring action at all levels to prevent this violence and provide redress to victims, it continues unabated. The pervasiveness, assumed inevitability, and refusal of state actors to seriously commit to the structural changes needed to eradicate the root cause—gender inequality—speak to its function as a mechanism of male power and social control over women. It is clear that tinkering around the margins with policies that neatly fit into existing power structures and fail to seriously challenge dominant assumptions is no longer good enough for lasting change to occur.

Furthermore, rapid globalization and migration are presenting challenges that are comparable in many ways for policy makers and frontline service providers in all countries of the world. We therefore have much to learn by sharing outside our national boundaries and narrow disciplines. Globalization, forced migration resulting from war and conflict, and rapidly changing technology affect women uniquely as they become increasingly vulnerable to crimes of sexual exploitation, harassment, and violence. The impacts of this violence deepen women's marginalization and poverty. Social change is rapid, whereas, once entrenched, policies and practices are very slow to evolve, particularly those embedded within conventional socio-legal structures and institutions. Policy makers and service providers are constantly challenged to re-think one-size-fits-all responses and to address complex and diverse realities in culturally competent ways. The aim of this volume is to help share ideas among researchers, policy makers, practitioners, abused women and their advocates and to challenge traditional thinking and assumptions.

This volume contains six sections, each addressing a particular type of response: (1) measuring violence against women; (2) justice system responses to intimate partner violence; (3) justice system responses to sexual violence; (4) victim crisis and advocacy; (5) behavior change programs for abusers; and (6) preventing male violence against women. Sections are introduced by an overview of contemporary practices and how they evolved, authored by leading researchers. Researchers, practitioners, or advocates in each of the topic areas then reflect on the response by presenting an empirically grounded critique or a novel initiative or innovative idea for future direction on that topic. The objective is to inspire critical thinking among readers by presenting different viewpoints and research from multiple perspectives.

Our objective was more ambitious than what we were able to realize, which perhaps is to be expected in a project of this nature. Our ambition was to make this a truly international conversation by inviting contributors from South America, Africa, and Asia as well as from the primarily English-speaking countries which we were able to secure. There is a great deal of important pioneering work and many fine contributors we had hoped would be able to participate but were not able and with whom we wish to be able to engage in other fora in the future. We hope that we succeed in stimulating conversations and ideas that will continue beyond this text and into other disciplines and domains. It is our hope that these conversations will eventually encourage decision makers to reorient their efforts in ways that will better address not only the needs and aspirations of abused women but the structural barriers to gender inequality and justice for all women worldwide as well.

We were also constrained in the topics we were able to include. Violence against women is broad and expanding, and covers a vast array of behaviors including but not limited to trafficking for sexual exploitation, female genital mutilation, female foeticide, child marriage, forced marriage, bride burning, rape in war and conflict situations, and others that extend beyond the "mainstream" acts of violence addressed in this text. Researchers and decision makers struggle to recognize, count, analyze, and respond to violations and exploitation of women as they are exposed to public awareness. Through the work of activists internationally the world is awakening to the extent of everyday atrocities and mundane violence in the lives of women, to which governments and non-governmental organizations must respond. This text offers critical analyses of responses to but a select sample of women's experiences.

The breadth of responses to violence is also far broader than what can be contained in this collection. Activists and scholars are engaged every day with tackling the problem from a perspective of human rights abuses, sexism and androcentric biases within legal codes and the administration of the law, national action plans and other policies and legislation that hold governments accountable, and critiques of policies and practices that compound the difficulties in leaving violent partners and securing safety for women and their children. These are essential activities that demand the same level of critique and debate but, due to space restrictions, could not be included in this volume. So, we leave these topics for others to compile in future texts.

While we remain convinced of the importance of international collaborations and breaking down the Anglo American ethnocentrism that has dominated the violence-against-women field, we also recognize the problems associated with policy transfer due to vast differences in legal codes and structures, histories, cultures, and resources. The very different legal context provided by inquisitorial court systems as compared to adversarial systems is one example. An innovation providing support to victims in the former may appear so utterly foreign to those used to operating within the latter as to be deemed not worthy of consideration. But the problem may lie with a tendency to dismiss out of hand cultures that we perceive to be vastly different to our own rather than the impossibility of the task, and this entrenchment in ways of knowing and doing results in our missing out on opportunities to learn about the effective elements that may in fact be adaptable. While we admit there are legitimate questions and challenges to transferability, this should not foreclose opportunities to look seriously at approaches that are situated within contexts that *prima facie* appear unlike our own. If we are honest, we may have to admit that our reluctance has more to do with intransigence grounded in unexamined assumptions and biases than with truly insurmountable structural impediments. We hope the contributions to this text can help expose the assumptions at the basis of many of our longest-standing responses to violence against women so that we may commit to putting women's safety and freedom from violence at the center of all that we say and do.

SECTION I

Measurement of violence against women

Learning objectives

In reading this section, you will be able to:

1. Compare methods of measuring violence against women and identify the ones that produce the most reliable estimates.
2. Discuss how and why the definitions of violence against women, operationalizations of violent acts, and differences in the placement or wording of survey questions affect estimates of violence.
3. Recognize the challenges that rapid social and technological change present to survey researchers with respect to the content of surveys, the methods of recruiting and interviewing participants, and ensuring participants' safety.
4. Outline the contributions of feminist researchers toward developing and strengthening techniques for measuring women's experiences of violence.
5. Understand the important role survey findings play as tools for policy makers, service providers, researchers, and advocates.

Chapter 1

Measurement innovations

Overview of methodological progress and challenges

Holly Johnson, Bonnie S. Fisher, and Véronique Jaquier

> It is one thing to say violence against women is a multifaceted, multilevel social problem rooted in multinational histories of oppression and colonization and quite another to operationalize that statement—by either quantitative or qualitative standards.
>
> (Campbell 2011: 159)

This insight sums up where researchers are today. While innovations in the measurement of male violence against women (VAW) have expanded at an accelerated rate over the past 40 years, meeting the demands for measurement tools to keep pace with an ever-increasing complexity in theoretical understandings of VAW is an ongoing challenge.

Since the late 1970s, feminist researchers and advocates have successfully challenged androcentric methodologies. Their creativity produced some of the most important innovations in social science research since the advent of self-report surveys through the development and use of women-centered and respondent-sensitive data-collection practices. Influential methodological innovations—which include behaviorally specific questions, special training for and debriefing with interviewers, safety precautions for respondents and interviewers, and referrals to local legal and social service supports—are now accepted "best" methodological practice. These innovations have been refined over time by those who aim to more reliably document the full range of violence, stalking, and other coercive behaviors women are subjected to in private and public spaces and the interconnections among these experiences (Johnson 2013).

This chapter documents the progress made to improve methods of measuring the scope and dimensions of women's experiences of male violence. We conclude that sustained collaborations globally, coupled with critical self-reflection informed by theory, research, and practice, are essential for addressing limitations of the current state of VAW measurement.

Early developments

Contributions and limitations of criminal victimization surveys

Crime victimization surveys have developed into a primary source for estimating the scope of certain crimes among the general population and were considered a major breakthrough over once having to rely solely on police tallying reported crimes. The basic orientation and structure of these "omnibus" surveys is to ask a representative sample to recall different types of criminal victimizations experienced within a specified time, typically the previous 6 or 12 months. Respondents are expected to interpret questions unambiguously, accurately draw from memory, and willingly and candidly disclose their experiences by selecting from close-ended responses.

The shortcomings of early omnibus surveys for measuring VAW are well known (Jaquier *et al.* 2010 for a review). Typically, sexual violence was defined narrowly as rape and no thought was given to sensitively framing the questions or avoiding stigmatizing terms. Questions did not cue respondents to include dating or intimate partners and, as a result, stranger violence was disclosed disproportionately. Interviewers were not trained specifically to approach questions with sensitivity or to incorporate safety measures (Walby and Myhill 2001). Overall, the basic orientation and structure of these surveys present important measurement limitations if the goal is to stimulate recall and encourage disclosure of sensitive and potentially traumatic experiences. Further, the comparatively low rates of sexual and intimate partner violence (IPV) generated by these surveys helped reinforce the popular (mis)conceptions that these crimes are rare and attributable to a few dangerous men.

Family conflict surveys

Surveys designed to measure conflict in couples emerged in the 1970s and rely on the Conflict Tactics Scales (CTS, Straus 1979) and, later, the revised version of theses scales (Straus *et al.* 1996). Studies using the CTS produce the controversial findings that IPV is perpetrated equally by men and women. This gender symmetry is accepted uncritically by many researchers, policy makers, and the media and has contributed to a gradual erasure of gendered structural analysis in public discourse and policy. The limitations of the conflict approach are well documented: It does not measure context, motivations, or consequences of violence; it omits coercive controlling behaviors; less severe acts of violence are given equal weight to more severe acts; and, it does not capture ongoing patterns of abuse, escalation, or violence in previous relationships (e.g., Kimmel 2002).

Later on, the incorporation of emotional and verbal abuse into feminist-inspired surveys, both as forms of violence and as tactics designed to control female partners, contributed to a better understanding of the dynamics and gendered nature of IPV. Multivariate analysis portrays what simple frequencies do not: Severe and chronic constellations of violence, control, verbal abuse, and serious psychosocial consequences are inflicted by men on women and not the reverse (Ansara and Hindin 2011). This is one category of IPV that Kelly and Johnson (2008) identify as coercive controlling violence, which is qualitatively different than violent resistance (typically perpetrated by women defending themselves against a coercively controlling partner), situational couple violence, and separation-instigated violence (bi-directional or gender-neutral).

Early feminist contributions

A fundamental starting point for feminists is that, rather than unrelated discrete acts, women experience male violence as a continuum of threats, coercion, and assaults that are underlined by similar motives (Kelly 1988). The feminist perspective was also instrumental in bringing to attention the intimate context in which much of this violence occurs and the complex challenges this presents for studying and quantifying these experiences in the detail needed for developing interventions, prevention, and support for victims. Out of concern for the negative impacts that underestimations of VAW have had on public discourse and public policy, feminist researchers seized the opportunity to develop innovative survey questions that included explicit behaviorally descriptive wording and improvements to survey administration. Knowledge acquired about rape and IPV from smaller, community samples—including among culturally and ethnically diverse populations and sexual minorities—and through qualitative research capturing women's narratives, contributed critical insights into how women experience and interpret violence and coercion as well as into the social norms that hold women accountable and downplay the harms (Meloy and Miller 2011).

Two of the most influential feminist researchers to directly challenge the methods and outcomes of government-sponsored surveys were Americans Diana Russell and Mary Koss. In the first of many challenges to traditional social science large-scale survey methods, Russell conducted in-person interviews with a probability sample of women in San Francisco in 1978 to estimate the prevalence and incidence of rape and other forms of sexual assault. Through her work as an activist, she was able to incorporate women's lived experiences in multiple ways that addressed many of the limitations inherent in methods widely used at the time. She crafted explicitly worded questions including questions related to inability to consent (e.g., while drugged or unconscious) and the use or threat of force, and recognized that careful selection and training of female interviewers would improve disclosure (Russell 1982). These questions and protocols produced an incidence rate seven times higher than the 1974 National Crime Survey (NCS).

Koss' Sexual Experiences Survey (SES) reflected a growing feminist consciousness that women experience unwanted sexual acts along a continuum (Koss and Oros 1982). The SES is comprised of behaviorally specific questions that explicitly describe a broad range of unwanted sexual acts, coercion, attempted rape, and rape. When comparing the specific subset of SES questions that are comparable to the definition of rape used by the NCS (penile–vaginal intercourse), the rape victimization rate produced by the SES in a national probability sample of college women was 10 to 15 times higher than that produced by the NCS for women aged 16 to 24 (Koss *et al.* 1987). What is more, the SES captured disquieting realities masked in previous studies: A substantial proportion of women had experienced not only rape but other forms of sexual victimization; male college students known to the victims were perpetrating sexual violence in large numbers; and, most sexual victimizations had been hidden from public view and from official crime statistics due to non-reporting. Ongoing reliability and validity testing, primarily among college students in the United States, produced revisions of the SES in 1985 and 2007 designed to increase clarity and revise wording for assessing consent, alcohol-related incidents, and unwanted sexual acts (Koss *et al.* 2007).

A major scholarly contribution of Russell and Koss was to demonstrate how methodological choices—definitions, question wording and framing, and interviewer selection and training—affect disclosures, and subsequently public discourse and policy formation. As a direct result, government surveys came under growing pressure to expand and improve question wording and protocols, beginning with the redesign of the NCS and following quickly by varieties of modifications in other countries (e.g., British Crime Survey, Statistics Canada's General Social Survey). Equally important, feminist and social justice researchers began challenging the dominant and largely unquestioned androcentric understandings of "truth" and "objectivity" and urging reflection on how ways of knowing and the political perspective researchers bring to their work influence the choice of research techniques and outcomes (Leckenby 2007).

Methodological progress throughout the 1990s

Dedicated violence against women surveys

The 1992 National Women's Study's (NWS) survey in the US and Statistics Canada's dedicated Violence Against Women Survey in 1993 were among the first attempts to address methodological limitations inherent in large-scale surveys. The NWS focused exclusively on forcible rape and developed "provocative, personal questions in order to leave no doubt or confusion as to the definition of forcible rape" (Kilpatrick *et al.* 1992: 15). Modules of questions developed for the Canadian survey extended to sexual harassment and psychological and emotional abuse, in addition to sexual assault and IPV, thus reflecting the broader continuum of violence. Both incorporated behaviorally specific questions and computer-assisted telephone interviewing by trained interviewers. Dedicated surveys are now commonplace and have been fielded at the city or national level in over 90 countries (for review, Ellsberg and Heise 2005: 13–15) and among specific populations such as college women (e.g., Fisher *et al.* 2000).

Cross-national comparisons using standardized surveys

As survey research techniques improved and the demand for accurate estimates grew, so did an interest in cross-national comparisons. At least four internationally comparative VAW surveys have been conducted employing probability samples, standardized questionnaires translated into native languages, and identical criteria for selecting respondents and training interviewers (see García-Moreno *et al.* 2005; Hindin *et al.* 2008; Johnson *et al.* 2008; Nevala, this volume). Standardization is expected to reduce measurement error and allow for valid comparison across countries, which is considered an improvement over attempting to establish content validity post hoc across country-specific surveys (see Jaquier and Fisher 2009). In the interests of facilitating international comparisons, agencies of the United Nations (UN) have made available a model survey module and extensive manuals and guidelines that draw upon the experience of survey researchers in a wide variety of settings.[1]

While most international comparative projects are one-time snapshots, the Demographic and Health Surveys (DHS) program is unique with its large samples (up to 30,000 households) and five-year data-collection cycle. The DHS collects and disseminates health-related indicators in 25 countries and contains a module of questions on IPV; 23 countries gather indicators of the prevalence and attitudes toward female genital mutilation/cutting (Hindin *et al.* 2008). Together this body of internationally comparative work portrays VAW as a worldwide societal-level problem and finds considerable consistency among correlates and harmful impacts.

Assumptions underlying cross-cultural comparative surveys—that standardized instrument and protocols can accurately capture the experiences of women across disparate cultures—have not been rigorously tested. It is important to question the extent to which Western biases in definitions and methods may be imposed, and important forms of violence, reactions, or coping strategies may be missed. It is common practice to reapply instruments without in-depth qualitative or cognitive testing with diverse groups of women and to assume that these are applicable universally even though terminology, definitions, and social norms may vary considerably (for exceptions, see National Intimate Partner and Sexual Violence Survey [NISVS] Black *et al.* 2011 and Nevala, this volume).

Contemporary challenges

Salient among contemporary challenges are those responding to emerging debates about definitions, developing dynamic understandings of violence, expanding on risk and protective factors, and bringing in the perspective of male perpetrators.

Emerging debates over definitions

Understanding the multiple ways that women suffer physical, sexual, and emotional harm continues to evolve and pose measurement challenges. Typically, surveys focus on measuring distinct incidents of physical and sexual violence, impacts, and the number of women affected. Over time, definitions have evolved to include psychological and emotional violence and coercive control, stalking and other harassing behaviors, and more recently facilitation of these behaviors through new technologies and social media. Surveys have also addressed specific topics such as drug- and alcohol-facilitated and -enabled rape (see Kilpatrick *et al.* 2007, Krebs *et al.* 2007: 26–27). With social media rapidly becoming a primary site of interaction, harassment, stalking, and violence either perpetrated or recorded by digital technology means that the effects on victims can be public and endure long past the original incident. Enumerating these experiences calls for creativity as researchers are faced with ever-expanding definitions and modes of violence.

While some have questioned whether to include psychological aggression because it may be "more normative and not harmful" (Follingstad and Rogers 2013: 149), Evan Stark (2007) mounts a powerful argument against over-emphasizing injuries as a measure of severity because women face dangers by the "entrapment" that results from coercive control even in the absence of physical violence. Entrapment refers to a gender-specific feature of male IPV where, within the context of a gender-inequitable society, men can appropriate gender norms to strictly enforce stereotypical female roles without ever using physical violence or causing injury (Stark 2007: 105). A framework that emphasizes coercive control shifts claims for justice from the traumatizing effects of violence to the links between structural inequality and women's oppression in relationships, a very different interpretation demanding very different policy responses. How to capture "entrapment" in survey or interview questions requires collaborative experimentation among advocates, service providers, and researchers.

Dynamic understandings of violence

Whereas prevalence and incidence data are critical for understanding the span of violence, static counting of acts or incidents does not expand understanding of how victimization experiences unfold within a particular situational context, the dynamics of the interaction, or perpetrators' motivations. Methodologies are needed to capture women's daily, lived experiences of a broader continuum of threats and violent victimization as well as dynamics, contexts, and factors that contribute to an escalation and de-escalation of violence both within an incident and across time. In one example of creativity in a quantitative research design, Winstok (2013) modified the CTS to better understand dynamic interactions between intimate partners that escalate to violence. The results use the very instrument that produces gender symmetry to challenge existing paradigms.

Risk and protective factors

A shortcoming of existing research is the limited nature of data collected on risk and protective factors, in other words, the lack of "independent variables."

Although risks associated with the social location of victims and perpetrators, such as age, race/ethnicity, education, employment, and income have been informative, these correlates are well established. As well, analysis is often limited to bivariate statistics which can neither provide satisfactory explanations for the interconnections among these social locations nor determine whether the nature of the relationship is simply correlational, directly or indirectly causal, or spurious. Often, samples are too small to examine between- or within-group differences. What is more, a singular focus on factors associated with victim vulnerability leads to victim-blaming and prevention strategies that encourage subgroups of women to alter their behavior to reduce their exposure to would-be offenders.

There is also a lack of known protective factors in VAW research, such as questions pertaining to resilience or self-efficacy that can help identify why some women who are apparently at high risk are able to avoid victimization, while others with none or few risk factors are not. Perhaps even more daunting is the challenge to situate women's experiences into a broader social context of gender and racial inequalities, inadequate supports for women, weak condemnation of violence, and generalized misogyny that silences women and grants impunity to perpetrators (see the ecological framework, Heise 1998). Despite broad agreement that VAW is multifaceted and rooted in longstanding oppressions, it is challenging to operationalize and measure concepts at the levels that can be incorporated into quantitative, qualitative, or mixed methods research.

Multilevel models for examining the effects of the social ecology on individual experiences are emerging, however. Benson *et al.* (2003) found that in Chicago IPV against women is more common in disadvantaged neighborhoods, even when controlling for prior violence and individual- and couple-level attributes; this was the result of both structural (i.e., neighborhood features) and compositional effects (i.e., factors related to the composition of resident populations). Others have shown that IPV is associated with high neighborhood disadvantage and low collective efficacy, net of the effects of individual-level correlates (e.g., Wright & Benson 2010). In contrast, Kiss *et al.* (2012) found that in Sao Paulo, Brazil, individual-level characteristics were more important than neighborhood-level characteristics in predicting IPV, suggesting that generalizations across cultures should be avoided. The task of separating structural from compositional effects is complex, and research examining multi-level effects (e.g., family, neighborhood) remains scarce, in part due to barriers to accessing aggregate-level data that can be linked to respondent-level data.

First-hand knowledge from perpetrators

Effective public policy designed to prevent VAW and develop effective interventions calls for improving the knowledge base on motivations for perpetration among general populations of men, specific subgroups, and within diverse settings (Jewkes 2012). Recent progress has been rapid, with two internationally comparative studies. The International Men and Gender Equality

Survey (IMAGES), a household survey of men and women in seven countries (Brazil, Chile, Croatia, India, Mexico, Rwanda, and South Africa) in 2009–2010, broke new ground by making available data on men's gender equality attitudes and behaviors (as well as women's reports of men's behaviors) for the purposes of engaging men in gender-equality initiatives (Barker *et al.* 2011).

Fulu *et al.* (2013) conducted a separate survey in six Asian countries (Papua New Guinea, Indonesia, China, Cambodia, Sri Lanka, and Bangladesh). Men were interviewed by trained male interviewers and women by female interviewers, but sensitive questions related to the use of violence were self-completed on audio-enhanced personal digital assistants. In both studies, researchers followed practices that have become standard in surveys interviewing women, such as using behaviorally specific questions and adhering to ethical guidelines. Although rates varied across countries, overall the prevalence of IPV victimization reported by women on both surveys was comparable to or lower than men's disclosures, providing important validation that men will report these personal and negative behaviors if special precautions are taken. These results also provide a point of validation of women's survey disclosures.

Innovative methodologies and techniques

Innovative methodologies and techniques are prompted by counter-intuitive interpretations of findings, creativity of researchers, and new forms of victimization that evolve from changing social norms or new technologies. But innovation is relative: A technique might be novel for one researcher and familiar for another. This should not come as a surprise, given the various disciplines that are tackling VAW from multiple theoretical and methodological frameworks. Being innovative requires researchers to steer away from their own routines and comfort positions—it is about daring to be innovative. Just like we have been socialized into a certain methodological thinking, we can be "re-socialized" into other frameworks.

Whether it is about promoting methodological diversity, balancing the weaknesses of a specific data-collection strategy, or integrating qualitative and quantitative approaches in mixed methods designs, the objectives are the same: To improve the accuracy of estimates and to provide policy-relevant data that reflects the diversity of women's experiences. Breaking down methodological divides could mean greater access to rich data that potentially could stimulate new ideas for survey content or protocols. For example, photovoice, a completely different approach to large-scale surveys, is a type of participatory research that engages individuals in recording and critically reflecting on their everyday lives. Commonly used in women's safety studies (e.g., McIntyre 2003), it has recently been used in IPV research in the US to document individual, family, community, and societal factors related to these experiences through photographs, journals, field notes, and focus group transcripts (Haymore *et al.* 2012).

Unconventional approaches are necessary to overcome the limitations of past research. For instance, few prevalence studies address sexual harassment, even though its impacts affect lifestyle as well as psychological well-being. Between the time of Canada's national VAW survey in 1993 and the multi-country survey conducted by the European Union Agency for Fundamental Rights in 2012 (Nevala, this volume), sexual harassment and its links to other forms of VAW received little empirical attention. Among unique initiatives, the activists' network *hollaback!* provides an alternative data source by documenting and mapping women's experiences of street harassment in cities around the world. Studies conducted in Croatia, Poland, Istanbul, and Ottawa showing the pervasiveness and impacts of harassment offer insights that can be incorporated into surveys.[2]

Researchers are also gathering more comprehensive information through innovations to micro-longitudinal approaches such as the Experience Sampling Method (ESM), which captures data frequently and in near real-time (e.g., using telephone data collection) so that within-person, proximal relationships among study variables can be examined. ESM appears promising for examining repeat victimization experiences and could improve understanding of causal factors for violence. For example, Sullivan *et al.* (2012) used ESM to examine the daily co-occurrence of psychological, physical, and sexual IPV; preliminary evidence demonstrates that ESM can be used safely and effectively.

Improving data collection also involves continually working to increase participation rates. Innovative methods combining new technology and sampling design have been recently introduced into large-scale surveys, such as using mobile phones and web-based methods of recruitment. The recent NISVS employed a dual sampling design that included both mobile and landline phone numbers, and 55 percent of respondents were interviewed using mobile phones, which illustrates the critical importance of revisiting sampling frames in light of new technologies. Internet-based VAW surveys have been implemented among college populations using easily accessible web-based survey design tools (e.g., Coker *et al.* 2011) and more are likely on the horizon.

A more inclusive research agenda is essential in a rapidly changing world. Promising avenues for expanding beyond high-level generalizations include, for example, disproportionate sampling of multiethnic groups and within-group analyses to capture the heterogeneity of respondents and their victimization experiences, and development of refined mixed methods designs that allow for more nuanced understandings how race, class, and culture affect the nature, circumstances, and consequences of VAW. Similarly, White *et al.* (2013: 227) view the use of community-based participatory research principles as a practical solution "to balance the goals of standardization and cultural relevance in measurement." In working equitably together, community members and researchers share decision-making and ownership, thus co-constructing instruments sensitive to both between- and within-group differences. Violence, social norms, and reactions to violence are culture- and context-specific, thus ethnocultural community involvement is warranted at each step of the research process, from study conceptualization and recruitment and retention of participants to training for interviewers and interpretation of findings (Mechanic and Pole 2013).

Concluding thoughts

It is unlikely that a single measurement tool or set of survey questions will capture the variety and complex circumstances surrounding VAW. Innovative measurement depends on unconventional thinking, collaborations among disciplines, and an environment where new research questions are welcomed. Sustained collaboration among researchers, data users, service providers, and advocates are essential for continually improving the measurement of VAW and addressing inequalities that contribute to the culture of VAW.

Notes

1 See UN Economic Commission for Europe, www1.unece.org/stat/platform/display/VAW/Survey+module+for+measuring+violence+against+women (accessed 16 July 2014); and UN Statistics Division http//:unstats.un.org/unsd/genderstatmanual/violence-against-women-surveys.ashx (accessed 16 July 2014).
2 For references, see *hollaback!* Website: www.ihollaback.org (accessed 16 July 2014).

References

Ansara, D.L. and Hindin, M.J. (2011) 'Psychosocial consequences of intimate partner violence for women and men in Canada', *Journal of Interpersonal Violence*, 26: 1628–45.

Barker, G., Contreras, J.M., Heilman, B., Singh, A.K., Verma, R.K. and Nascimento, M. (2011) *Evolving Men: Initial Results from the International Men and Gender Equality Survey (IMAGES)*, Washington, DC: International Center for Research on Women, and Rio de Janeiro, Brazil: Instituto Promundo.

Benson, M., Fox, G., DeMaris, A. and Van Wyk, J. (2003) 'Neighborhood disadvantage, individual economic distress and violence against women in intimate relationships', *Journal of Quantitative Criminology*, 19: 207–35.

Black, M.C., Basile, K.C., Breiding, M.J., Smith, S.G., Walters, M.L., Merrick, M.T., Chen, J. and Stevens, M.R. (2011) *The National Intimate Partner and Sexual Violence Survey (NISVS): 2010 Summary Report*, Atlanta, GA: Centers for Disease Control and Prevention.

Campbell, R. (2011) 'Guest editor's introduction: Part I: methodological advances in recruitment and assessment', *Violence Against Women*, 17: 159–62.

Coker, A.L., Cook-Craig, P.G., Williams, C.M., Fisher, B.S., Clear, E.R., Garcia, L.S. and Hegge, L.M. (2011) 'Evaluation of green dot: an active bystander intervention to reduce sexual violence on college campuses', *Violence Against Women*, 17: 777–96.

Ellsberg, M. and Heise, L. (2005) *Researching Violence Against Women: A Practical Guide for Researchers and Activists*, Geneva: World Health Organization.

Fisher, B.S., Cullen, F.C. and Turner, M.G. (2000) *The Sexual Victimization of College Women*, Washington, DC: National Institute of Justice.

Follingstad, D. and Rogers, M.J. (2013) 'Validity concerns in the measurement of women's and men's report of intimate partner violence', *Sex Roles*, 69: 149–67.

Fulu, I., Warner, X., Meidema, S., Jewkes, R., Roselli, T., and Lang, J. (2013) *Why Do Some Men Use Violence Against Women and How Can We Prevent It? Quantitative Findings from the UN Multi-country Study on Men and Violence in Asia and the Pacific*, Bangkok: UNDP, UNFPA, UN Women and UNV.

Garcia-Moreno, C., Jansen, H.A., Ellsberg, M., Heise, L., and Watts, C. (2005) *WHO Multi-Country Study on Women's Health and Domestic Violence Against Women*, Geneva: World Health Organization.

Haymore, L., Morgan, M., Murray, C., Strack, R., Trivette, L. and Hall Smith, P. (2012) 'Through the eyes of a survivor: a pilot study to examine the use of a photovoice-based support group for women survivors of family-based interpersonal violence', *Family violence, Prevention, and Health Practice*, 12. Online. Available at http://www.futureswithoutviolence.org/health/ejournal (accessed 25 May 2014).

Heise, L.L. (1998) 'Violence against women: an integrated, ecological framework', *Violence Against Women*, 4: 262–90.

Hindin, M.J., Kishor, S. and Ansara, D.L. (2008) *Intimate Partner Violence Among Couples in 10 DHS Countries: Predictors and Health Outcomes*, Calverton, MD: Macro International Inc.

Jaquier, V. and Fisher, B.S. (2009) 'Establishing the content validity of threats, physical violence and rape against women across two national surveys', *International Journal of Comparative and Applied Criminal Justice*, 33: 249–71.

Jaquier, V., Johnson, H. and Fisher, B.S. (2010) 'Research methods, measures and ethics', in C.M. Renzetti, J. Edleson and R. Kennedy Bergen (eds.), *Sourcebook on Violence Against Women*, 2nd edn., Thousand Oaks, CA: Sage, 23–48.

Jewkes, R. (2012) *Rape Perpetration: A Review*, Pretoria, South Africa: Sexual Violence Research Initiative.

Johnson, H. (2013) 'Gendered violence against women: an international focus', in C. Renzetti, S.L. Miller and A.R. Gover (eds.), *Routledge International Handbook of Gender and Crime Studies*, New York: Routledge, 91–114.

Johnson, H., Ollus, N. and Nevala, S. (2008) *Violence Against Women: An International Perspective*, New York: Springer.

Kelly, J.B. and Johnson, M.P. (2008) 'Partner violence: research update and implications for interventions', *Family Court Review*, 46: 476–99.

Kelly, L. (1988) *Surviving Sexual Violence*, Cambridge, UK: Polity.

Kilpatrick, D.G., Edmunds, C.N. and Seymour, A.K. (eds.) (1992) *Rape in America: A Report to the Nation*, Arlington, VA: National Victim Center.

Kilpatrick, D.G., Resnick, H.S., Ruggiero, K.J., Conoscenti, L.M. and McCauley, J. (2007) *Drug-Facilitated, Incapacitated, and Forcible Rape: A National Study*, Charleston, SC: MUSC, National Crime Victims Research and Treatment Center.

Kimmel, M.S. (2002) 'Gender symmetry in domestic violence: a substantive and methodological research review', *Violence Against Women*, 8: 1332–63.

Kiss, L., Schraiber, L.B., Heise, L., Zimmerman, C., Gouveia, N. and Watts, C. (2012) 'Gender-based violence and socioeconomic inequalities: does living in more deprived neighbourhoods increase women's risk of intimate partner violence?', *Social Science & Medicine*, 74: 1172–79.

Koss, M.P. and Oros, C. (1982) 'Sexual Experiences Survey: a research instrument investigating sexual aggression and victimization', *Journal of Consulting and Clinical Psychology*, 50: 455–57.

Koss, M.P., Abbey, A., Campbell, R., Cook, S., Norris, J., Testa, M., Ullman, S., West, C. and White, J. (2007) 'Revising the SES: a collaborative process to improve assessment of sexual aggression and victimization', *Psychology of Women Quarterly*, 31: 357–70.

Koss, M.P., Gidycz, C.A. and Wisniewski, N. (1987) 'The scope of rape: incidence and prevalence of sexual aggression and victimization in a national sample of higher education students', *Journal of Consulting and Clinical Psychology*, 55: 162–70.

Krebs, C.P., Lindquist, C.H., Warner, T.D., Fisher, B.S. and Martin, S.L. (2007) *The Campus Sexual Assault (CSA) Study*, Washington, DC: US Department of Justice, National Institute of Justice.

Leckenby, D. (2007) 'Feminist empiricism: challenging gender bias and setting the record straight', in S.N. Hesse-Biber and P.L. Leavy (eds.), *Feminist Research Practice*, Thousand Oaks, CA: Sage, 27–52.

McIntyre, A. (2003) 'Through the eyes of women: photovoice and participatory research as tools for reimagining place', *Gender, Place & Culture*, 10: 47–66.

Mechanic, M. and Pole, N. (2013) 'Methodological considerations in conducting ethnoculturally sensitive research on intimate partner abuse and its multidimensional consequences', *Sex Roles*, 69: 205–25.

Meloy, M.L. and Miller, S.L. (2011) *The Victimization of Women: Law, Policies, and Politics*, Oxford, UK: Oxford University Press.

Russell, D.E.H. (1982) 'The prevalence and incidence of forcible rape and attempted rape of females', *Victimology: An International Journal*, 7: 81–93.

Stark, E. (2007) *Coercive Control: How Men Entrap Women in Personal Life.* Oxford, UK: Oxford University Press.

Straus, M.A. (1979) 'Measuring intrafamily conflict and violence: the Conflict Tactics Scales', *Journal of Marriage and the Family*, 41: 75–88.

Straus, M.A., Hamby, S.L., Boney-McCoy, S. and Sugarman, D.B. (1996) 'The revised Conflict Tactics Scales (CTS2): development and preliminary psychometric data', *Journal of Family Issues*, 17: 283–316.

Sullivan, T.P., McPartland, T.S., Armeli, S., Jaquier, V. and Tennen, H. (2012) 'Is it the exception or the rule? Daily co-occurrence of physical, sexual, and psychological victimization in a 90-day study of community women', *Psychology of Violence*, 2: 154–64.

Tjaden, P. and Thoennes, N. (2000) *Full Report of the Prevalence, Incidence, and Consequences of Violence Against Women: Findings from the National Violence Against Women Survey*, Atlanta, GA: Centers for Disease Control and Prevention.

Ullman, S.E. (2011) 'Longitudinal tracking methods in a study of adult women sexual assault survivors', *Violence Against Women*, 17: 189–200.

Walby, S. and Myhill, A. (2001) 'New survey methodologies in researching violence against women', *British Journal of Criminology*, 41: 502–22.

White, J., Yuan, N., Cook, S. and Abbey, A. (2013) 'Ethnic minority women's experiences with intimate partner violence: using community-based participatory research to ask the right questions', *Sex Roles*, 69: 226–36.

Winstok, Z. (2013) 'From a static to a dynamic approach to the study of partner violence', *Sex Roles*, 69: 193–204.

Wright, E.M. and Benson, M.L. (2010) 'Clarifying the effects of neighborhood context on violence behind closed doors', *Justice Quarterly*, 28: 775–98.

Chapter 2

We are making progress in measuring sexual violence against women

Ronet Bachman

At this writing, I am feeling renewed enthusiasm and confidence for the basic tenet of science that assumes knowledge will evolve and improve by continually building on the work of others. There is now general agreement that estimating the incidence of sexual violence (SV) using official police report data does not capture the true magnitude of these victimizations because the majority are never reported to the police. Because of the deficiency in police reports, most now agree that victimization surveys from a random sample of the general population are the method of choice if the goal is to estimate the prevalence of SV. However, despite the fact that it has been almost 30 years since the first Sexual Experiences Survey (SES) was developed by Mary Koss, and there is still no accepted universal standard for measuring the magnitude of violence against women (VAW), researchers have been making progress. After witnessing heated debates in the late 1980s between practitioners and researchers, I can unequivocally say that measurement of VAW has come a long way. Still, the inevitable glacial pace of change has left behind the largest ongoing federally funded survey in the United States that measures victimization, the National Crime Victimization Survey (NCVS). In this chapter, my goal is to highlight a few of the major differences that place estimates of SV obtained from the NCVS behind those of other surveys.

What are we measuring?

Conceptually, there is not a great deal of variation in how surveys define SV. Taking rape as an example, the World Health Organization's (WHO) definition of rape is "physically forced or otherwise coerced penetration of the vulva or anus with a penis or other body part or object" (World Health Organization/London School of Hygiene and Tropical Medicine 2010: 11). The National Intimate Partner and Sexual Violence Survey (NISVS), sponsored by the Centers for Disease Control and Prevention (CDC) along with the National Institute of Justice, defines rape as "completed or attempted unwanted vaginal (for women), oral, or anal penetration through the use of physical force or threats to physically harm and includes times when the victim was drunk, high, drugged, or passed out and unable to consent" (Black *et al.* 2011: 17). And the NCVS defines rape as "forced sexual intercourse including both psychological coercion as well as physical force. Forced sexual intercourse means vaginal, anal, or oral penetration by the offender(s). This category also includes incidents where the penetration is from a foreign object such as a bottle. It includes attempted rapes, male as well as female victims, and both heterosexual and homosexual rape. Attempted rape includes verbal threats of rape."[1] The main difference between these definitions of rape is that the NISVS explicitly includes incidents that occur when the victim was drunk, high, drugged, or passed out and unable to consent. Besides the SES conducted by Koss and colleagues (1987), the NISVS has been the only national survey to do this, despite the fact that this form of victimization meets the legal definition of rape in virtually every state in the US. Except for this difference, these conceptual definitions are quite similar. However, exactly how each of these surveys measures rape and other forms of sexual violence is very different.

Imagine filling out a questionnaire in person or taking a survey over the telephone. Many things will affect the way you answer the questions, including how the survey is introduced, how comfortable you feel answering the questions, and how the questions are asked. The first issue this chapter will address is question wording.

Question wording

Conceptualization, that is, defining what we intend to measure, is the first step in measurement. The next step is the operationalization process, which involves the development of procedures to measure what we intend to measure (Bachman and Schutt 2014), and herein lies one of the main differences between the NISVS and NCVS. The screening questions used to ask respondents about previous victimizations are very different for these two surveys. The exact wording for questions used in each survey is provided in Table 1. To measure rape and sexual assaults, the NCVS uses broad cues of "attacked or threatened" and also direct reference to "forced or unwanted sexual contact," and "any rapes or attempted rapes." It also provides cues to many locations (e.g., school, parties, work) and categories of offenders (e.g., someone at work or school, a relative or family member). However, unlike the NISVS, the NCVS does not ask questions with behaviorally specific language (e.g., "meaning that they put their penis in your mouth"), nor asks specifically about all forms of intercourse (e.g., oral, anal, vaginal) that legally constitute rape, including incidents when the victim was incapacitated in any way (e.g., drunk, high, passed out). However, the NCVS includes incidents that were "threatened" or "attempted," which the NISVS does not, even though these are not included in estimates of "completed rape."

Do differences in question wording matter? To validly compare the effect of question wording on estimates, a study would actually have to begin with that research question in mind. This opportunity presented itself when Bonnie Fisher and colleagues (2000) began investigating victimization of college women. This project was designed to represent a quasi-experiment in which two nationally

Table 2.1 Screening questions used to measure rape and sexual assault victimizations for the National Crime Victimization Survey and the National Intimate Partner and Sexual Violence Survey

National Crime Victimization Survey	*National Intimate Partner and Sexual Violence Survey*
Since [end date for 6-month reference period] were you attacked or threatened OR did you have something stolen from you: a. at home including the porch or yard, b. at or near a friend's, relative's, or neighbor's home, c. at work or school, d. in places such as a storage shed or laundry room, a shopping mall, restaurant, bank, or airport, e. while riding in any vehicle, f. on the street or in a parking lot, g. at such places as a party, theater, gym, picnic area, bowling lanes, or while fishing or hunting, or h. did anyone attempt to attack or attempt to steal anything that belongs to you from any of these places. Other than any incidents already mentioned, has anyone attacked or threatened you in any of these ways: a. with any weapon, for instance, a gun or knife, b. with anything like a baseball bat, frying pan, scissors, or stick, c. by something thrown, such as a rock or bottle, d. include any grabbing, punching, or choking, e. any rape, attempted rape, or other type of sexual attack,	Preamble: Sometimes sex happens when a person is unable to consent to it or stop it from happening because they were drunk, high, drugged, or passed out from alcohol, drugs, or medications. This can include times when they voluntarily consumed alcohol or drugs or they were given drugs or alcohol without their knowledge or consent. When you were drunk, high, drugged, or passed out and unable to consent, how many people ever ... • had vaginal sex with you? By vaginal sex, we mean that [if female: a man or boy put his penis in your vagina] [if male: a women or girl made you put your penis in her vagina] • [if male] made you perform anal sex, meaning that they made you put your penis into their anus? • made you receive anal sex, meaning they put their penis into your anus? • made you perform oral sex, meaning that they put their penis in your mouth or made you penetrate their vagina or anus with your mouth? • made you receive oral sex, meaning that they put their mouth on your [if male: penis] [if female: vagina] or anus? How many people have ever used physical force or threats to physically harm you to make you ... • have vaginal sex? • [if male] perform anal sex? • receive anal sex? • make you perform oral sex? • make you receive oral sex? • put their fingers or an object in your [if female: vagina or] anus?

(Continued)

Table 2.1 (Continued)

National Crime Victimization Survey	*National Intimate Partner and Sexual Violence Survey*
f. any face-to-face threats, or g. any attack or threat or use of force by anyone at all? Please mention it even if you are not certain it was a crime. Incidents involving forced or unwanted sexual acts are often difficult to talk about. Have you been forced or coerced to engage in unwanted sexual activity by: a. someone you didn't know before b. a casual acquaintance? or c. someone you know well? If respondents reply yes to one of these questions, they are asked in the subsequent incident report, "Do you mean forced or coerced sexual intercourse?" To be classified as rape victims, respondents must reply affirmative. All other sexual attacks are classified as other sexual assaults.	How many people have ever used physical force or threats of physical harm to . . . • [if male] try to make you have vaginal sex with them, but sex did not happen? • try to have [if female: vaginal] oral, or anal sex with you, but sex did not happen? How many people have you had vaginal, oral, or anal sex with after they pressured you by . . . • doing things like telling you lies, making promises about the future they knew were untrue, threatening to end your relationship, or threatening to spread rumors about you? • wearing you down by repeatedly asking for sex, or showing they were unhappy? • using their authority over you, for example, your boss or your teacher? How many of your romantic or sexual partners have ever . . . • slapped you? • pushed or shoved you? • hit you with a fist or something hard? • kicked you? • slammed you against something? • tried to hurt you by choking or suffocating you? • beaten you? • burned you on purpose? • used a knife or gun on you?

Source: The NCVS victimization screen questions can be found online: *NCVS Basic Screen Questionnaire*, available at www.bjs.gov/index.cfm?ty=dcdetail&iid=245#Questionnaires (accessed 16 July 2014). The NISVS sexual violence questions can be found online, *Appendix C*, available at www.cdc.gov/violenceprevention/pdf/nisvs_report2010-a.pdf (accessed 16 July 2014).

representative samples of college students were given two different versions of a screening instrument (see Fisher 2009 for details). One version used wording identical to the NCVS, while the other used graphic behaviorally specific screening questions consistent with the NISVS. Besides these differences, the two surveys were virtually identical in other methodological respects, including their sampling frames and designs, sample sizes (each over 4,000), interviewing context (female interviewers using computer-assisted telephone interviewing), administration period (Spring 1997), and reference period (since Fall 1996). As such, this study represents a measurement experiment and the most sophisticated study to date that has examined whether question wording affects rape estimates. Using the NCVS wording 0.16 percent of women reported experiencing a completed rape compared to 1.1 percent of women using the behaviorally specific wording. A similar differential was found for attempted rapes. Thus, behaviorally specific wording produced estimates over ten times larger than NCVS questions. Because all other methods were essentially identical, the only difference that could account for this disparity in estimates is the question wording.

In sum, there is now evidence to suggest that question wording affects the number of victimizations obtained from surveys. Another factor that may affect the NCVS estimates is how it calculates rates of victimization when respondents experience multiple victimizations of the same kind within the same reference period. These are called series victimizations by the NCVS and they will be discussed next.

Counting a series of victimizations

The NCVS generally reports incidence rates of victimization, which indicate how many new victimizations occurred during a specified period (e.g., annually), which are then calculated on a base number of women (e.g., per 1,000 women). Historically, a series victimization was defined as six or more similar but separate incidents, which the victim was unable to recall individually or describe in detail. When a respondent reports a series victimization, they are asked to indicate the number of times this victimization occurred and provide detailed information for the most recent victimization only. Because of concerns about the measurement error that may be associated with series victimizations, including whether all in a series occurred within the reference period and whether the characteristics of the most recent event actually reflect the characteristics of the other events in the series, until recently the Bureau of Justice Statistics (BJS) has excluded series victimizations from annual estimates. However, after examining the effects of including series victimizations in annual estimates (Lauritsen *et al.* 2012), the most recent NCVS estimates (2010) incorporated a new technique for including these high-volume repeat victimizations: Series incidents are now counted as the number reported by the victim, but are capped at ten incidents (Truman 2011). As expected, the estimate of violent victimization increased when series victimizations were included within annual estimates; however, the general trends in violent crime were not affected. An analysis of series victimizations revealed that they have declined in number and proportion over time; this perhaps is due to a "test-retest" effect or fatigue inherent in a panel study design. Violent series victimizations primarily consist of intimate partner violence (IPV), school violence, and work-related violence. Regarding BJS's decision to include series victimization, Lauritsen *et al.* (2012: iii) explain, "The strategy for counting series victimizations balances the desire to estimate national rates and account for the experiences of persons with repeated victimizations while noting that some estimation errors exist in the number of times these victimizations occurred."

This strategy will undoubtedly increase rates of rape and sexual assault in future estimates, but the cap at ten incidents still deflates the estimates compared to other surveys that report incidence rates but do *not* cap the number. For example, the National Violence Against Women Survey (NVAWS) reported that the average number of rapes reported by female victims was 2.9 (Tjaden and Thoennes 2006); however, the highest number was 24 (Bachman 2000). Clearly, large numbers such as this have the potential to affect incidence rates. Importantly, outliers such as this are not unlikely. For example, Koss and colleagues reported that 143 women indicated a total of 236 incidents of attempted intercourse where a man gave them alcohol or drugs, and 63 women experienced a total of 98 incidents of intercourse by threat or force (Koss *et al.* 1987: 168). As noted earlier, the NISVS 2010 report did not publish incidence rates of rape and sexual assault victimizations, only lifetime and 12-month prevalence rates, which are based on the number of women affected, not the total number of incidents. Still, it is important to keep this measurement difference in mind when making comparisons of estimates across surveys.

Survey context

Once again imagine that you are being asked to participate in a survey. Before agreeing to participate, all interviewers must tell respondents what the survey is about and who is sponsoring it. As the name implies, the NCVS is a clear indicator to respondents that interviewers are interested in "crimes" they have experienced. Despite the screening instrument asking questions that use short cues to facilitate recall of victimizations by many different perpetrators and in many different locations, all respondents have been primed with the notion that this is, in fact, a crime survey. The first screening question begins, "I'm going to read some examples that will give you an idea of the kinds of crimes the study covers" (Rand and Rennison 2005: 273). In contrast, the NISVS is presented to respondents as a survey interested in health-related issues. As the 2010 report notes, "Interviewers ask a series of health-related questions at the outset of the survey to establish rapport and establish a health context for the survey" (Black *et al.* 2011: 8). These contextual differences across surveys may lead some respondents in "health"-and/or "safety"-related surveys to report victimizations that may not be reported by respondents in "crime"-related surveys like the NCVS. Thus, even though both surveys are attempting to measure the same types of victimization, respondents are being primed to think about what they are being asked in very different ways.

Sampling frames, reference periods, and estimation procedures

The NCVS remains the only victimization survey of the general population that obtains its sample through a multi-stage cluster sampling design of US households.

The NCVS sample is drawn from the decennial census and is representative of the total US population that resides in non-institutionalized housing (e.g., excluding prisons, nursing homes) but includes boarding houses and college residence halls. This sampling frame includes residences regardless of a landline or mobile phone being present in the household. In contrast, the NISVS relied on the probability sampling method of random digit dialing (RDD). It relied on two target population lists—landline and mobile phone frames—from which potential respondents were randomly selected.

Eligible respondents for the NISVS were individuals age 18 or older, while the NCVS includes individuals age 12 and older. Individuals in the early stage of adolescence tend to have lower rates of victimization compared to those in older adolescence (beginning at around 17 and peaking in the late 20s), which provides useful data for policy purposes but may affect the overall rate.

The reference periods used across surveys are also different. As noted above, the NCVS currently asks respondents to report victimizations occurring in the six months prior to the interview. The selection of this six-month reference period was the result of research indicating that compared to longer reference periods, the six-month window resulted in less measurement error. The NISVS asked about victimizations that occurred "in your lifetime," and if respondents reported a victimization, they were then asked whether it occurred within the "previous 12 months." This method allows surveys to estimate both lifetime and 12-month prevalence estimates. Based on research examining reference periods (Cantor and Lynch 2000), this methodological difference may serve to increase estimates obtained by the NCVS compared to other surveys, because respondents have a greater likelihood of remembering incidents closer in time. However, the trauma associated with a rape or sexual assault is extremely salient and may serve to nullify this effect since salient events are significantly less likely to be forgotten.

And finally, the two-stage process of classifying incidents into crime categories used by the NCVS is different than the estimation procedures used in all other surveys, with the exception of the two surveys in Fisher (2009). As Rand and Rennison (2005: 272) note, "In lieu of explicit questions, NCVS uses extensive and detailed screen questions which promote recall of a broad range of victimizations across many contexts." As noted above, these screening questions ask respondents directly about rape, attempted rape, and other types of sexual attacks, with behaviorally specific questions involving "forced or unwanted sexual attacks," and other questions providing short cues to specific types of locations (e.g., school, home, work), offenders (e.g., a family member, someone you know well), and actions that could be associated with a victimization (e.g., face-to-face threats). Affirmative responses to any of these screening questions trigger an incident report that probes for details about what occurred and whether the act in question should be classified as a victimization, and if so, which type.

In contrast, other surveys have used the screening questions alone to classify incidents. If respondents reply yes to a particular question, say one measuring completed rape, they are counted as completed-rape victims. Some contend that unless respondents are further probed on what actually happened, some incidents may erroneously be classified as rapes when their experiences did not qualify (Fisher *et al.* 2010). The NCVS incident report asking respondents to clarify their experiences in several ways, including the question "Do you mean forced or coerced sexual intercourse?", mitigates this potential. To incorporate the best methods across all surveys, Fisher and colleagues (2010) employed both behaviorally specific screening questions and a two-stage process to classify victimizations with an incident report after the screening questions were asked. Evidence from their study suggests that the two-stage process did screen out incidents that would have been classified as rape had a one-stage process been used. For example, Fisher (2009: 144) explains, "of the 325 incidents that screened in on the rape screen questions, 21 of them could not ultimately be classified because the respondent could not recall enough detail in the incident report; 59 were then classified as "undetermined" because the respondent refused to answer questions or answered "don't know" to one or more questions in the incident report that would have allowed the incident to be categorized as rape; 155 were classified as a type of sexual victimization other than rape; and 90 were classified as rape."

In sum, each of these differences in measurement affects the victimization rates obtained across surveys. The issue of protecting respondents that will be discussed at the close of this chapter affects the extent to which respondents feel comfortable in disclosing their victimizations to interviewers; more importantly, it helps ensure their safety.

Measuring violence for small subgroups of the population

Johnson *et al.* (this volume) have highlighted the issues inherent in measuring violence cross-nationally. I would like to add a note regarding measuring violence against small subgroups of the population, including American Indian and Alaskan Native (AIAN) women. Measuring low base-rate crimes like rape and sexual assault for small subgroups of the population, including race/ethnic groups and different age groups, requires a large representative sample and quality screening questions. During the early 2000s, budget cuts to the NCVS were occurring at a time when Congress was demanding more efforts to measure violence against these subgroups of women. For example, the Violence Against Women Act of 2005 called for reliable estimates of violence against women of color, with specific attention focused on AIAN women. Other federal statutes have called for the monitoring of victimizations against the elderly and against individuals with developmental disabilities. Monitoring violence against subgroups of the population, including AIAN women, should continue, as well as efforts to more validly measure violence against other vulnerable populations like elderly women. These goals cannot be achieved without sufficient funding for both the development and administration of surveys tailored to these populations.

Protecting respondents

The NISVS and the NCVS have very different approaches to the protection of human subjects. Perhaps because the NISVS was conducted by the CDC, it reflects a public health approach in its implementation that followed the dictates of other public health organizations, including the WHO. The WHO has been a leader in delineating guidelines to the field of epidemiology when studying VAW. As Ellsberg and Heise (2005: 38) note, "The primary ethical concern related to researching VAW is the potential for inflicting harm to respondents through their participation in the study." Because many IPV perpetrators use control as a form of abuse, a respondent may suffer physical harm if an abuser finds out that she disclosed information to an interviewer about their relationship.

Guidelines to prevent this from happening include interviewing only one person in the household, and using a graduated informed-consent process to begin the interview. For example, the NISVS used a two-stage consent process: When a household was called, the initial person who answered the telephone was provided only general information about the survey topic (e.g., on health-related issues). Only after a respondent was selected were they told about the specific topics that would be covered (e.g., violent victimizations). Interviewers also reminded respondents that they could stop the interview at any time if they felt uncomfortable, or if someone else walked into the room while the respondent was on the telephone. During such an event, safety plans should be established between interviewers and respondents. For example, NISVS interviewers suggested that respondents answer questions in a private setting and instructed them to just say "goodbye" if they felt unsafe or someone threatening entered the room.

Finally, minimizing respondents' distress caused by reliving victimization events and providing them with information on services and resources that can help their situation are necessary. For example, the NISVS provided telephone numbers for the National Domestic Violence Hotline and the Rape, Abuse, and Incest National Network at the end of interviews. Clearly, respondent protection is even more complicated when asking about victimizations against minor children, as the NCVS does (e.g., it interviews individuals aged 12 or older). Currently, researchers do not fall under the purview of "mandatory reporters" according to most state statutes, and WHO claims there is no consensus internationally about how to handle cases of child abuse (Ellsberg and Heise 2005). This is true for cases of elder abuse that are reported by respondents as well. Even though statutes do not explicitly list researchers as mandatory reporters, interviewers should certainly be required to develop protocols to act in the best interests of a child or an elderly person when cases of these forms of abuse are revealed.

Conclusions and recommendations

As a society, our conceptions of VAW have significantly evolved during the past several decades, as have our methods to study this violence. We have made much progress and researchers appear to be moving toward consensus. For example, when the former National Crime Survey was being redesigned into the NCVS in the late 1980s, the Office of Management and Budget (OMB) was reluctant to allow a survey conducted by a federal agency to use graphic language such as "penis" and "anal intercourse." Today, the OMB fully supports the wording of the CDC-sponsored NISVS. Moreover, Fisher and colleagues (2010: 18) stated after their quasi-experimental design testing different question wording to measure rape, "The challenge in science is to probe for a study's potential weaknesses so as to illuminate the next set of investigations that might more fully calibrate ways of studying the phenomenon." Their results should leave little doubt that using behaviorally specific language is superior to other forms of eliciting recall for respondents, including that used by the NCVS.

Congress gave BJS a clear mandate for the NCVS to be the national resource of crime victimization independent of official reports to law enforcement. Because it is conducted in an ongoing manner, the NCVS is the best mechanism by which trends in victimization and emerging patterns can be illuminated. As such, it is necessary for BJS move forward regarding the measurement of VAW in general, and rape and sexual assault in particular. The behaviorally specific language that has been used in all other national surveys and internationally in the Crime Survey for England and Wales should be incorporated into the NCVS screening instrument. Importantly, amending the NCVS wording to conform to this standard will increase recall from respondents by cueing them to report events they may not have thought of. In addition, to be in compliance with most state rape and sexual assault statutes, questions should also ask about victimizations that occurred when respondents were not able to consent (e.g., when drunk, high on drugs, or otherwise incapacitated). Further, the two-stage estimation process for classifying victimizations after the screening questions should continue to be used to avoid the potential error associated with the classifying incidents based on screening questions alone (Fisher *et al.* 2010). And finally, the NCVS should be in compliance with standards that have already been adopted by the CDC for protecting respondents.

At this writing, the National Academy of Sciences just released its review of the methods used by the NCVS to measure rape, concluding, among other things, that the survey "does not measure the low incidence of events of rape and sexual assault with the precision needed for policy and research purposes" (Kruttschnitt *et al.* 2013). Hopefully, this will compel movement for the largest government-sponsored victimization survey to catch up with measurement standards that have already been tested and proven valid and reliable by other federally funded research and research in other nations.

Note

1 See Bureau of Justice Statistics, *Terms and Definitions: Victims*. Online. Available at www.bjs.gov/index.cfm?ty=tdtp&tid=9 (accessed 25 May 2014).

References

Bachman, R. (2000) 'A comparison of annual incidence rates and contextual characteristics of intimate partner violence against women from the National Crime Victimization Survey (NCVS) and the National Violence Against Women Survey (NVAWS)', *Violence Against Women*, 6: 839–67.

Bachman, R. and Schutt, R. (2014) *The Practice of Research in Criminology and Criminal Justice* (5th edition), Thousand Oaks, CA: Sage.

Black, M.C., Basile, K.C., Breiding, M.J., Smith, S.G., Walters, M.L., Merrick, M.T., Chen, J. and Stevens, M.R. (2011) *The National Intimate Partner and Sexual Violence Survey (NISVS): 2010 Summary Report*, Atlanta, GA: Centers for Disease Control and Prevention.

BJS, Bureau of Justice Statistics (2013) *NCVS Basic Screen Questionnaire, 2012*. Online. Available at www.bjs.gov/content/pub/pdf/ncvs1_2012.pdf (accessed 25 May 2014).

Cantor, D. and Lynch, J.P. (2000) 'Self-report surveys as measures of crime and criminal victimization', in *Measurement and Analysis of Crime and Justice, Criminal Justice 2000*, Volume 4, Washington, DC: US Department of Justice, Office of Justice Programs, 85–138.

Ellsberg, M. and Heise, L. (2005), *Researching Violence Against Women: A Practical Guide for Researchers and Activists*, Washington, DC: World Health Organization.

Fisher, B.S. (2009) 'The effects of survey question wording on rape estimates: evidence from a quasi-experimental design', *Violence Against Women*, 15: 133–47.

Fisher, B.S., Daigle, L.E. and Cullen, F.T. (2010) *Unsafe in the Ivory Tower: The Sexual Victimization of College Women*, Thousand Oaks, CA: Sage.

Groves, R.M. and Cork, D.L. (2008) *Surveying Victims: Options for Conducting the National Crime Victimization Survey*, Washington, DC: National Research Council.

Koss, M.P., Gidycz, C.A. and Wisniewski, N. (1987) 'The scope of rape: incidence and prevalence of sexual aggression and victimization in a national sample of higher education students', *Journal of Counseling and Clinical Psychology*, 55: 162–70.

Kruttschnitt, C., Kalsbeek, W.D. and House, C.C. (2013) *Estimating the Incidence of Rape and Sexual Assault*, Panel on Measuring Rape and Sexual Assault in Bureau of Justice Statistics Household Surveys: Committee on National Statistics; Division on Behavioral and Social Sciences and Education; National Research Council.

Lauritsen, J.L., Gatewood Owens, J., Planty, M., Rand, M.R. and Truman, J.L. (2012) *Methods for Counting High-Frequency Repeat Victimizations in the National Crime Victimization Survey*, Washington, DC: US Department of Justice, Bureau of Justice Statistics.

Rand, M.R. and Rennison, C.M. (2005) 'Bigger is not necessarily better: an analysis of violence against women estimates from the National Crime Victimization Survey and the National Violence Against Women Survey', *Journal of Quantitative Criminology*, 21: 267–91.

Tjaden, T. and Thoennes, N. (2006) *Full Report of the Prevalence, Incidence, and Consequences of Violence Against Women: Findings From the National Violence Against Women Survey*, Washington, DC: National Institute of Justice, and Atlanta, GA: Centers for Disease Control and Prevention.

Truman, J.L. (2011) *Criminal Victimization, 2010*, Washington, DC: US Department of Justice, Bureau of Justice Statistics.

World Health Organization and London School of Hygiene and Tropical Medicine (2010) *Preventing Intimate Partner and Sexual Violence Against Women: Taking Action and Generating Evidence*, Geneva: World Health Organization.

Chapter 3

Innovations in prevalence research

The case of the 28-country survey by the European Union Agency for Fundamental Rights

Sami Nevala[1]

The measurement of violence against women (VAW) has evolved significantly over the years (see Johnson *et al.*, this volume). This has led to a broad acceptance of using behaviorally specific questions to collect information about women's experience of violence, a better understanding of the correlates of violence, and an ever-increasing number of countries for which prevalence data are available. In parallel, the Council of Europe Convention on preventing and combating VAW and domestic violence (the Istanbul Convention) addresses forms of VAW that have not been included in many existing prevalence surveys. The Convention is an important milestone as the first legally binding instrument on the European level concerning VAW and creates new challenges not only in terms of legislation but also for data collection. This chapter provides a cross-national overview of the 28-country survey conducted by the European Union Agency for Fundamental Rights (FRA)—including all European Union (EU) member states—which examines multiple forms of VAW.

Challenges of comparing surveys across countries

The many challenges facing the designers of population surveys measuring women's experiences of violence and making cross-country comparisons are well documented (Martinez *et al.* 2007; UN 2013). In parallel to the recent developments in internationally comparative research that uses common questionnaires and protocols, other researchers have sought to build an overview of the extent of VAW using meta-analysis based on existing survey research (Alhabib *et al.* 2009; Jaquier *et al.* 2006; WHO *et al.* 2013), and extrapolating the available estimates on the extent of violence into regional estimates. These results have reconfirmed that VAW is present in all countries. However, while estimates derived from many existing VAW surveys are based on similar questions measuring violent acts, conducting comparisons across surveys remains difficult if one wants to go beyond overall rates of victimization.

Whereas the global estimates produced through meta-analysis provided a much needed idea of the extent of VAW in societies, many surveys also collect data—albeit in various ways—on the state response to violence. This comprises the police and other components of the criminal justice system, health care services, and social services. Without survey data, policy makers and service providers are struggling to develop these responses from a victim-centered perspective, taking into account not only the persons who contact and benefit from existing responses, but also to address their needs, which may have gone unmet or which have not been brought to the attention of the service providers. Indeed, at the same time as victimization surveys document high levels of unreported and unrecorded incidents of violence, service providers are often not prepared to tackle the full scale of the problem due to inadequacy of resources available to them. This results in a difficult balancing act between taking the best possible care of those who have stepped forward to seek assistance and reaching out to potentially many more victims of violence.

One measurement challenge facing survey researchers relates to the expanding definition of violence. For example, some forms of VAW that are specifically addressed in the Istanbul Convention are difficult to cover in surveys that are designed to produce estimates of the prevalence of VAW in the population. Such forms of violence include for example forced marriage, female genital mutilation, forced abortion and forced sterilization, and so-called "honor crimes." Because these forms of violence may affect disproportionally small subpopulations in Europe, samples drawn from the general population typically are not large enough to reliably measure the extent of these forms of violence. In addition, there are measurement challenges related to the growing diversity of populations, such as the need to arrange for interviews in a number of languages when addressing recent immigrants, and the need to create trust in the communities to collect data while at the same time ensuring confidentiality. The Istanbul Convention also requires state parties to criminalize forms of violence such as psychological violence and stalking, and to ensure that sexual harassment is subject to criminal or other legal sanctions. These forms of violence can potentially affect all women, but at the same time they have been covered to a limited extent in many existing VAW surveys. For example, a study published by the European Commission (EC) concluded that out of the 28 EU member states only four (the Netherlands, Poland, Sweden, and the United Kingdom) are able to present national estimates on the extent of stalking (EC 2010: 70). The same report also notes the dearth of data concerning the prevalence of sexual harassment (EC 2010: 60).

The prevalence of violence against women in the EU

In 2014, FRA released the results of its EU-wide survey on VAW, based on face-to-face interviews with a total of 42,000 women in the 28 member states. The interviews were carried out by female interviewers who had received dedicated in-person training to carry out interviews in a sensitive manner while ensuring the safety of both the respondent and the interviewer and the confidentiality of the collected information. The interviews took place in respondents' homes or in another safe location chosen by respondents. At the end of the interviews respondents were offered information about available support services. These measures follow the recommendations on good survey practice for measuring VAW (e.g., Martinez *et al*, 2007, WHO 2001, and most recently UN 2013).

Survey results show that one in three women (33 percent) had experienced physical and/or sexual violence since the age of 15, and one in five women (22 percent) had experienced these types of violence in a relationship (see Table 3.1). Overall, 43 percent of women who have a current or previous partner indicated that they had experienced one or more forms of psychological violence by a partner. One in three women also said that they had experienced physical, sexual and/or psychological violence before they were 15 years old by an adult perpetrator (FRA 2014a).

Table 3.1 Percentage of women experiencing violent victimization, by type and EU member state

	Physical and/or sexual violence since the age of 15			*Psychological violence since the age of 15 by any partner (current or previous)*	*Physical, sexual, or psychological violence before the age of 15 by an adult perpetrator*
	Any partner (current or previous)[a]	*Non-partner*[b]	*Any partner or non-partner*		
Austria	13	12	20	38	31
Belgium	24	25	36	44	30
Bulgaria	23	14	28	39	30
Croatia	13	13	21	42	31
Cyprus	15	12	22	39	15
Czech Republic	21	21	32	47	34
Denmark	32	40	52	60	46
Estonia	20	22	33	50	50
Finland	30	33	47	53	53
France	26	33	44	47	47
Germany	22	24	35	50	44
Greece	19	10	25	33	25
Hungary	21	14	28	49	27
Ireland	15	19	26	31	27
Italy	19	17	27	38	33
Latvia	32	17	39	60	34
Lithuania	24	16	31	51	20
Luxembourg	22	25	38	49	44

(Continued)

Table 3.1 (Continued)

	Physical and/or sexual violence since the age of 15			*Psychological violence since the age of 15 by any partner (current or previous)*	*Physical, sexual, or psychological violence before the age of 15 by an adult perpetrator*
	Any partner (current or previous)[a]	*Non-partner*[b]	*Any partner or non-partner*		
Malta	15	15	22	37	23
Netherlands	25	35	45	50	35
Poland	13	11	19	37	18
Portugal	19	10	24	36	27
Romania	24	14	30	39	24
Slovakia	23	22	34	47	36
Slovenia	13	15	22	34	16
Spain	13	16	22	33	30
Sweden	28	34	46	51	44
United Kingdom	29	30	44	46	40
EU-28	**22**	**22**	**33**	**43**	**35**

Source: Adapted from Tables 2.1, 4.2, and 7.1 (FRA 2014a).

Notes:

a Partners include persons with whom women were married, living together without being married, or involved in a relationship without living together at the time of the interview or any time in the past.

b Non-partners include all perpetrators other than women's current or previous partners.

Sexual harassment as a context for violence

Lori Heise's (1998) ecological framework of gender-based violence identified the risk factors of violence at various levels—individual, relationship, community, and the wider society—but prevalence surveys have been slow to adopt this model, to consider the risk factors in a comprehensive way across different levels, and to respond to the interconnectedness of various forms of violence. Rather, many surveys have adopted a very narrow definition of VAW, which has come at the expense of understanding the broader context in which violence is embedded. Several surveys, of both national and international scope, have measured forms of non-partner violence as another dimension of VAW, in addition to violence perpetrated by a partner. At the same time, as noted by Johnson and colleagues (this volume), sexual harassment has not received similar attention in survey research, despite the fact that it provides the societal context in which discrimination of women—and VAW as one of the forms of this discrimination—continues to be tolerated.

The FRA survey is the first to collect comparable data on the extent, nature, and consequences of various forms of VAW across the 28 EU member states. The survey has built on earlier cross-national prevalence surveys such as the International Violence Against Women Survey (Johnson *et al.* 2008) and the WHO's Multi-Country Study on Women's Health and Domestic Violence (Garcia-Moreno *et al.* 2005), particularly in regards to the measurement of physical, sexual, and psychological violence. However, neither of these international surveys included modules measuring women's experiences of sexual harassment or stalking. This may partly be due to the global scope of these projects and the need to adopt standardized measurement tools that can be used in starkly different cultural contexts.

The EU legislation recognizes sexual harassment as a form of discrimination against women (EU 2006). Therefore, it was important for FRA to include sexual harassment as a specific form of violence in its survey (FRA 2014a). While for some countries the FRA survey has been the first effort to collect nationally representative data on VAW, it also has gone beyond the scope of some existing national surveys by measuring violence perpetrated by partners and non-partners, covering forms of violence such as stalking and sexual harassment, and documenting both physical and psychological consequences of violence in a way that allows policy makers, both at the EU and member-state level, to reassess the adequacy of existing policy measures, based on the needs of the victims. These data—and the methods developed to collect them—are of particular importance as EU member states prepare to ratify and implement the Istanbul Convention, which addresses comprehensively a number of forms of VAW, including psychological violence, sexual harassment, and stalking.

Questions[2] concerning sexual harassment and stalking were based on existing national surveys, and they were further developed in expert consultations. To ensure that the new modules could be used in a multi-country context they were part of a survey pre-test study, which was carried out in 2011 before the full-scale survey (FRA 2014b). The pre-test was carried out in six countries (Finland, Germany, Hungary, Italy, Poland, and Spain) using a combination of quantitative and qualitative methods: A structured survey interview was followed by a cognitive interview to collect further information concerning the understanding respondents had of the key research concepts. The data-collection process was further documented through behavior coding and feedback collected from the interviewers (for an overview of different pre-test methods see e.g., Campanelli 2008). The final survey questions concerning experiences of sexual harassment and stalking are presented in Table 3.2 and Table 3.3.

According to the survey results, 55 percent of women in the EU have experienced one or more forms of sexual harassment since the age of 15, and 21 percent have experienced sexual harassment in the 12 months before the interview (see Table 3.4). In addition, across the 28 EU member states 18 percent of women have experienced one or more incidents of stalking since the age of 15, and 5 percent had been stalked in the 12 months before the interview.

Table 3.2 Survey questions concerning experiences of sexual harassment

At times you may have experienced people acting toward you in a way that you felt was unwanted and offensive. How often have you experienced any of the following? How often has this happened to you in the past 12 months?

Unwelcome touching, hugging, or kissing?
Sexually suggestive comments or jokes that made you feel offended?
Inappropriate invitations to go out on dates?
Intrusive questions about your private life that made you feel offended?
Intrusive comments about your physical appearance that made you feel offended?
Inappropriate staring or leering that made you feel intimidated?
Somebody sending or showing you sexually explicit pictures, photos, or gifts that made you feel offended?
Somebody indecently exposing themselves to you?
Somebody made you watch or look at pornographic material against your wishes?
Unwanted sexually explicit emails or SMS messages that offended you?[a]
Inappropriate advances that offended you on social networking websites such as Facebook, or in internet chat rooms?[a]

Source: Adapted from Box 6.1 (FRA 2014a).

Note:
a Items that can be examined as forms of cyberharassment.

Table 3.3 Survey questions concerning experiences of stalking

You may have been in a situation where the same person has been repeatedly offensive or threatening towards you. For the next questions, I would like to ask you to think about both your current and previous partners as well as other people. Since you were 15 years old until now/in the past 12 months, has the same person repeatedly done one or more of the following things to you:

Sent you emails, text messages (SMS), or instant messages that were offensive or threatening?[a]
Sent you letters or cards that were offensive or threatening?
Made offensive, threatening, or silent phone calls to you?
Posted offensive comments about you on the Internet?[a]
Shared intimate photos or videos of you, on the Internet or by mobile phone?[a]
Loitered or waited for you outside your home, workplace, or school without a legitimate reason?
Deliberately followed you around?
Deliberately interfered with or damaged your property?

Source: Adapted from Box 5.1 (FRA 2014a).

Note:
a Items that can be examined as forms of cyberstalking.

Table 3.4 Percentage of women experiencing sexual harassment, sexual forms of cyberharassment, stalking, and cyberstalking since the age of 15, by EU member state

	Sexual harassment[a]	*Sexual forms of cyberharassment*	*Stalking*[b]	*Cyberstalking*
Austria	35	8	15	4
Belgium	60	13	24	8
Bulgaria	24	8	10	2
Croatia	41	12	13	4
Cyprus	36	7	11	4
Czech Republic	51	7	9	4
Denmark	80	18	24	9
Estonia	53	11	13	7
Finland	71	14	24	8
France	75	15	29	7
Germany	60	13	24	6
Greece	43	8	12	4
Hungary	42	7	12	4
Ireland	48	10	12	5
Italy	51	10	18	6
Latvia	47	11	14	6
Lithuania	35	6	8	3
Luxembourg	67	12	30	8
Malta	50	8	26	5
Netherlands	73	17	26	6
Poland	32	7	9	4
Portugal	32	6	9	3
Romania	32	5	8	3
Slovakia	49	17	16	8
Slovenia	44	7	14	3
Spain	50	10	11	2
Sweden	81	18	33	13
United Kingdom	68	13	19	6
EU-28	**55**	**11**	**18**	**5**

Source: Adapted from Tables 4 and 5.1, Figures 6.2 and 6.7 (FRA 2014a).

Notes:

a Includes all forms of sexual harassment on the survey, including sexual forms of cyberharassment.

b Includes all forms of stalking on the survey, including cyberstalking.

It would not be possible to measure sexual harassment and stalking comprehensively without paying attention to the emerging role of new technologies. Indeed, the FRA survey shows that the use of tools such as mobile phones and the Internet play a significant role in the sexual harassment and stalking of young women living in the EU, and this is a trend which over time can become more and more influential for women of all ages. For example, half of women aged 18–29 years who had experienced stalking since the age of 15 indicated that this had involved some form of cyberstalking, while the proportion of cyberstalking out of all stalking experiences decreases with age (FRA 2014a: 87). While sexual harassment and stalking also are perpetrated in the absence of the new technologies, the challenge now is to ensure that women have quick and effective ways to report such abuse to the service providers who should help to put an end to it. In the FRA survey, 23 percent of women who had experienced stalking said that, as a result of the most serious incident, they had had to change their email address or telephone number in an effort to put an end to the unwanted, repeated contacts. Service providers should help to put the onus on the perpetrators to stop the unwanted contacts, instead of the victims having to limit their use of the services. Another measure to make the perpetrators accountable could involve providers of communication services assisting victims to collect and present evidence in legal proceedings when their services have been used for abusive purposes.

Conclusions

VAW surveys are not exempt from challenges that concern survey research more generally, such as declining response rates, pressures to reduce costs, and the resulting move toward multi-mode survey designs—that is, the use of a combination of data-collection modes such as self-completion questionnaires administered online or postal questionnaires, and interviewer-administered modes such as telephone or face-to-face interviews (including self-completion modules in the presence of an interviewer) in the course of a single survey.[3] The impact of survey mode on the results is the subject of intensive research among survey methodologists due to the increasing number of mixed mode surveys,[4] while evidence from FRA and WHO surveys suggest that this effect may also be small, or at least it may differ from country to country (FRA 2014a: 323, 135; Garcia-Moreno *et al.* 2005: 50). The results of multi-country surveys and differences between participating countries offer a number of interpretations on the direction of the differences and the underlying mechanism. There is the scope for further analysis of the existing data to examine these results and to use them for a critical analysis of national policies that are aimed at preventing violence and protecting the victims. Forms of violence which up until now have not been systematically addressed in VAW surveys need further attention in the area of measurement and questionnaire design, including pre-tests of items to establish their reliability and validity, particularly in cross-cultural surveys.

While the results of multi-country surveys such as the one carried out by the FRA should serve as a wake-up call for policy makers—both at the EU and national level—there is a continued need to develop data on VAW, including administrative statistics (improving data on police-recorded incidents and administrative data collection in other services, such as the health care sector) as well as population-based victimization surveys. Whereas a growing number of countries have carried out prevalence research on VAW, in only a few countries have surveys been repeated,[5] and in fewer still have surveys been adopted as a part of a national program of statistics.[6] In most cases prevalence surveys continue to be carried out with ad hoc funding, without commitment of the state to support the surveys on a sustained basis, either as a part of their annual data collection or less frequently. The UN Guidelines for Producing Statistics on Violence against Women (UN 2013) is an encouraging development, suggesting that prevalence surveys are ready to be integrated as a part of the activities of national statistical agencies, but it remains to be seen to what extent the guidelines are able to convince national statistical agencies to commit to collecting these data, or relevant government ministries or agencies to assign funds to carry out this much needed task. Among its many provisions, Article 11 of the Istanbul Convention calls for the parties to the Convention to conduct population-based surveys at regular intervals—addressing all forms of violence covered by the Convention—and countries are also requested to provide such information for the purpose of international benchmarking to the group of experts that will be established as a monitoring mechanism (Article 66—Group of experts on action against VAW and domestic violence). Comprehensive and comparable data on all forms of VAW is a pre-requisite for the group of experts to fulfil its mandate, monitoring the implementation of the Convention.

Notes

1 The author is the Head of Sector for Statistics and Surveys at the European Union Agency for Fundamental Rights (FRA). Views expressed in this chapter are the author's alone.

2 The full FRA survey questionnaire is available—together with FRA reports on the results—at http://fra.europa.eu/en/publication/2014/vawsurveymainresults.

3 For more information concerning the use of different interview modes in victimization survey research, see UN 2010: 908.

4 See for example an overview of a number of mixed mode surveys in Dex and Gumy (2011).

5 Some examples of violence against women surveys which have been repeated over time include the Crime Survey for England and Wales (formerly the British Crime Survey) which includes questions on violence against women (Office for National Statistics 2014); surveys in Spain that were repeated four times in 1999–2011 (Ministerio de Sanidad, Servicios Sociales e Igualdad 2012); and the Finnish survey on violence against women, first carried out in 1997 and repeated in 2005 (Piispa *et al.* 2006).

6 As an example the Crime Survey for England and Wales, carried out by the Office of National Statistics on a regular basis.

References

Alhabib, S., Nur, U. and Jones, R. (2009) 'Domestic violence against women: systematic review of prevalence studies', *Journal on Family Violence*, 25: 369–82.

Campanelli, P. (2008) 'Testing survey questions', in E.D. de Leeuw, J.J. Hox and D.A. Dillman (eds.), *International Handbook of Survey Methodology*, New York: Lawrence Erlbaum Associates: 176–200.

Council of Europe (2011) *Convention on Preventing and Combating Violence Against Women and Domestic Violence*. Online. Available at www.coe.int/t/dghl/standardsetting/convention-violence/about_en.asp (accessed 25 May 2014).

Dex, S. and Gumy, J. (2011) *On the Experience and Evidence about Mixing Modes of Data Collection in Large-scale Surveys Where the Web is Used as One of the Modes in Data Collection*, National Centre for Research Methods Review Paper. Online. Available at http://eprints.ncrm.ac.uk/2041/1/mixing_modes_of_data_collection_in_large_surveys.pdf (accessed 25 May 2014).

EC, European Commission (2010) *Feasibility Study to Assess the Possibilities, Opportunities and Needs to Standardise National Legislation on Violence Against Women, Violence Against Children and Sexual Orientation Violence*, Luxembourg: Publications Office of the European Union.

EU, European Union (2006) 'Directive 2006/54/EC of the European Parliament and of the Council of 5 July 2006 on the implementation of the principle of equal opportunities and equal treatment of men and women in matters of employment and occupation (recast)', *Official Journal of the European Union*, L: 204336.

FRA, European Union Agency for Fundamental Rights (2014a) *Violence Against Women: An EU-wide Survey*, Luxembourg: Publications Office of the European Union.

FRA, European Union Agency for Fundamental Rights (2014b) *Violence Against women: An EU-wide Survey—Survey Methodology, Sample and Fieldwork*. Technical report, Luxembourg: Publications Office of the European Union.

Garcia-Moreno, C., Jansen, H.A., Ellsberg, M., Heise, L. and Watts, C. (2005) *WHO Multi-Country Study on Women's Health and Domestic Violence Against Women*, Geneva: WHO.

Heise, L.L. (1998) 'Violence against women: an integrated, ecological framework', *Violence Against Women*, 4: 262–90.

Jaquier, V., Fisher, B.S. and Killias, M. (2006) 'Cross-national survey designs: equating the National Violence Against Women Survey and the Swiss International Violence Against Women Survey', *Journal of Contemporary Criminal Justice*, 22: 90–112.

Johnson, H., Ollus, N. and Nevala, S. (2008) *Violence Against Women: An International Perspective*, New York: Springer.

Martinez, M., Schröttle, M., Condon, S., Springer-Kremser, M., May-Chahal, C., Penhale, B., Lenz, H.J., Brzank, P., Jaspard, M., Piispa, M., Reingardiene, J. and Hagemann-White, C. (2007) *Perspectives and Standards for Good Practice in Data Collection on Interpersonal Violence at European Level*. Online. Available at www.cahrv.uni-osnabrueck.de/reddot/FINAL_REPORT__29-10-2007_.pdf (accessed 25 May 2014).

Ministerio de Sanidad, Servicios Sociales e Igualdad (2012) *Macroencuesta de violencia de género 2011* [Gender Violence Survey 2011]. Online. Available at www.observatorioviolencia.org/upload_images/File/DOC1329745747_macroencuesta2011_principales_resultados-1.pdf (accessed 25 May 2014).

Office for National Statistics (2014) *Crime Statistics, Focus on Violent Crime and Sexual Offences, 2012/13, Chapter 4—Intimate Personal Violence and Partner Abuse*. Online. Available at www.ons.gov.uk/ons/dcp171776_352362.pdf (accessed 25 May 2014).

Piispa, M., Heiskanen, M., Kääriäinen, J. and Sirén, R. (2006) *Naisiin kohdistunut väkivalta 2005* [Violence Against Women in 2005], Helsinki: National Institute for Legal Policy and Research & European Institute for Crime Prevention and Control, affiliated with the UN.

UN, United Nations (2013) *Guidelines for Producing Statistics on Violence against Women*, Geneva: UN Publications.

UN, United Nations (2010) *Manual for Victimization Surveys*, Geneva: UN Publications.

WHO, World Health Organization (2001) *Putting Women First: Ethical and Safety Recommendations for Research on Domestic Violence Against Women*, Geneva: WHO.

WHO, World Health Organization, London School of Hygiene and Tropical Medicine, and South African Medical Research Council (2013) *Global and Regional Estimates of Violence Against Women: Prevalence and Health Effects of Intimate Partner Violence and Non-partner Sexual Violence*, Geneva: WHO.

Section I: Measurement of violence against women

Questions for critical thought

1. Violence against women occurs between individuals but plays out within broader economic, social, and cultural contexts of gender inequality. Suggest sources of data that are needed to describe and measure the contexts in which this violence takes place. Explain your reasoning for each source of data.
2. Why is it important to include sexual harassment on surveys measuring women's experiences of violence?
3. List the benefits of cross-country comparative surveys for policy makers, service providers, researchers, and advocates. Explain the methodological challenges researchers face when designing and implementing violence against women surveys in multiple countries.
4. Most violence against women surveys are conducted by telephone (landline and mobile) or in person. Do you think it is feasible to obtain reliable data through Internet-based surveys? List some of the strengths and drawbacks of these three modes of data collection.

Further reading

Campbell, R. (ed.) (2011) 'Special issue: methodological innovations in violence against women research', *Violence against Women*, 17: 159–425.

Ellsberg, M. and Heise, L. (2005) *Researching violence against women: a practical guide for researchers and activists*, Geneva: WHO.

Hamby, S. (2014) 'Intimate partner and sexual violence research: scientific progress, scientific challenges, and gender', *Trauma, Violence, & Abuse*, 15: 149–158.

National Research Council (2014) *Estimating the Incidence of Rape and Sexual Assault*, Washington, DC: The National Academies Press.

WHO, World Health Organization (2001) *Putting women first: ethical and safety recommendations for research on domestic violence against women*, Geneva: WHO.

Websites

Centers of Disease Control and Prevention: Statistics and references on intimate partner and sexual violence and their impact on health, including compendium of violence definitions and measures and prevention initiatives and material.
www.cdc.gov/ncipc/pub-res/IPV_Compendium.pdf
www.cdc.gov/violenceprevention/pdf/sv_surveillance_definitionsl-2009-a.pdf

European Union Agency for Fundamental Rights Survey data explorer: Detailed results of the EU-wide survey on violence against women can be browsed using the interactive data explorer tool.
http://fra.europa.eu/DVS/DVT/vaw.php

Gender, Violence and Health Centre at London School of Hygiene and Tropical Medicine: Multi-disciplinary cross-departmental research group that collaborates with partners around the world to conduct action-oriented, intervention-based research on gender-based violence and health.
http://genderviolence.lshtm.ac.uk

United Nations Women compilation of violence against women surveys: Compilation of violence against women prevalence data by country.
www.endvawnow.org/uploads/browser/files/vawprevalence_matrix_june2013.pdf

Woman Stats Project: Comprehensive compilation of qualitative and quantitative indicators on the status of women in 175 countries, with emphasis on understanding the linkage between the situation of women and the security of nation states.
www.womanstats.org

SECTION II

Justice system responses to intimate partner violence

Learning objectives

In reading this section, you will be able to:

1. Understand how the criminal justice system's focus on single discrete incidents presents challenges when responding to a crime like intimate partner violence, which typically is characterized by ongoing violence and abuse.
2. Recognize that victims of intimate partner violence play a minimal role in criminal justice proceedings, despite recent enhancements to protections for victims.
3. Critically assess the disconnect between victims' goals when they report to the police and the criminal justice system's goals when called upon to respond to intimate partner violence cases.
4. Discuss the role of civil protection orders in intimate partner violence cases and their shortcomings.
5. Contrast the experiences of different populations in relation to intimate partner violence and criminal and civil justice system responses, using the experiences of Australian Indigenous people as an example.

Chapter 4

Overview of current policies on arrest, prosecution, and protection by the police and the justice system as responses to domestic violence

Carol Hagemann-White, Cathy Humphreys, Leslie M. Tutty, and Kristin Diemer

In the global struggle to end violence against women (VAW), impunity has been a key concern, and prosecution and punishment are proposed to reduce the likelihood of men's violence. In addition, criminal sanctions are expected to change social attitudes condoning violence, and to ensure women full and equal access to justice. Police, prosecutors, and the courts can also act to prevent and protect through the use of their unique coercive powers.

This chapter reviews policies that promote law enforcement and prosecution responses to domestic violence (DV) through procedures and regulations that impose sanctions on offenders. The focus is on violence by someone who was or is an intimate partner, regardless of whether there was ever a shared residence. Most laws and policy documents refer to either "domestic violence" or "family violence," underlining that justice holds sway in the home/in the family.[1]

A key challenge to legal measures is posed by long-term patterns of coercive control, since the justice system is geared to single acts. Policies thus generally involve different domains of law and must be seen in a broader context, within which different packages of measures evolve. There is considerable variety both in such policies and their implementation. They may prescribe police and justice intervention without the victim's consent, on the premise that the state has a responsibility to hold offenders accountable, or they may give the victim a voice in decisions.

This chapter reviews policies and practices in North America, Europe, and Australia. Each continent has multiple levels of governance, and thus shows considerable internal diversity in their legislation, legal responses, and implementation. The United States, Canada, and Australia are federations, while the European Union comprises 28 national states, of which a number also are internally federal, and the Council of Europe (47 members) sets standards but has no lawmaking powers. States, provinces, or partially autonomous regions may each issue DV legislation and regulate prosecutors, courts, and police. The past two decades have seen efforts to achieve more consistent responses across each continent, so that a picture can be drawn of trends toward adopting a characteristic or preferred overall approach.

Historical perspectives

Following the global spread of a feminist movement after 1973, police were seen as "gatekeepers" whose failure to intervene against battering meant that the vast majority of cases never reached the prosecutor or the courts. Guidelines classifying DV as a private matter (Schechter 1982: 157; Hagemann-White *et al.* 1981: 114–9) were challenged and police training improved, but progress was slow and uneven.

In the US, police and criminal justice system responses were framed as women's right to "equal protection under the law."[2] Successful class actions suits against police departments in 1976 and a high-profile liability case in 1984 (Schechter 1982: 160) dramatically raised awareness of the potential cost of non-intervention. In 1984, as well, research results were widely publicized, suggesting that arrest is the strongest deterrent to future violence and should be the preferred police response (Buzawa *et al.* 2012: 149–65). Police departments across the country thus moved to treating DV as a crime, while the media and women's advocacy groups demanded mandatory arrest policies. Today, 22 of the 50 states and the District of Columbia have statutes with mandatory arrest provisions for DV, six have preferred arrest statues, and all others authorize police by law to arrest on probable cause of DV (Hirschel 2008).

Buzawa, Buzawa, and Stark (2012) locate the pro-arrest consensus in the context of growing expectations in the early 1980s that government should be "tough on crime." Arrest, because of its immediacy and visibility, came to be considered in itself a sanction that would deter the arrested person as well as potential abusers from committing DV. Efforts toward effective prosecution came a decade later, pushed forward by the federal Violence Against Women Act of 1994 (VAWA). Although all states in the US now expect prosecution services to pursue sanctions, in reality the vast majority of cases seem to be dealt with as misdemeanors through plea bargaining. The evidence on whether this pattern of sanctions reduces the risk of repeat violence or the overall level of DV seems inconclusive (Buzawa *et al.* 2012: 168–73, 256–65).

Overall, specific conditions underlie the policy development in the US:

1. A predominant consensus that the best way to fight crime is to reduce police discretion and expand police power to arrest and shame presumed offenders.
2. Primacy of an equal-rights framing over framings centered on victim's needs and empowerment.
3. A broad coalition of advocacy and women's rights groups with policy makers on criminalization, in the belief that punishment is effective in changing behavior, and using pressure strategies such as civil liability suits.

4. A widespread belief that victims, while often reluctant to cooperate with prosecution (interpreted as a survival strategy), have a need for retribution.
5. Discretionary prosecution in combination with the widespread use of plea bargaining.

Legislating arrest as a sanction and deterrent is not characteristic for any of the countries under review here, although it was initially adopted, but soon modified in Canada. In a broader sense the US criminal justice approach, including the development of specialized prosecution units and specialist courts as well as victim's advocate services to provide support during proceedings, has influenced policy internationally, but with a variety of outcomes. This must be seen against the background of diverse conditions: Legal systems vary considerably with respect to the structural mechanisms involved in imposing sanctions.

Diverse legal systems

Generally, adversarial systems of justice (based on common law) include the right to a jury trial (except for minor offenses); the prosecutor argues for conviction against the defense, and the judge acts as referee. In investigative systems (with codified law), prosecutors have the duty to seek evidence for guilt or innocence equally and decide on the charge, and one or more judges hear all evidence to reach a verdict. Both systems have been modified and sometimes mixed over time. Beyond this, however, legal systems differ in whether the police and/or the public prosecutor and/or an investigative judge has discretion over whether or not to arrest, or to prosecute, even in cases of a "public interest" or "ex officio" offense, and in the extent to which any authority is legally able to instruct or require them to take such action as a policy. The role of the police varies, as does the responsibility for collecting evidence.

Legal systems further differ in whether they distinguish general categories of offenses (such as "misdemeanor" vs. "felony," "summary" vs. "indictable offenses," or "crime" vs. "administrative offense") with consequences for how cases are handled. Alternatively legal systems may penalize all offenses against the person in a unitary criminal code that foresees graded sanctions. There are also differences in the admissibility of diversion, the use of low-level sanctions such as "warnings" or "peace bonds," and in whether conditions can be imposed on the perpetrator before or only after sentencing. There are differences in the types of courts that exist, and at what level specialized courts are legally possible. Such structural aspects of law enforcement and justice are generally taken for granted when drafting policies or regulatory measures, and cannot be explored in this overview.

Since a wide range of differing legal concepts are operative, the next section offers terms and definitions for comparative discussion. We then trace the emergence of more active roles for police and justice systems in response to DV in Australia, Canada, and Europe. The discussion also will consider (civil) protection orders (as their breach can be penalized), specialized prosecution units and specialized courts, and further coercive and supportive police powers to protect victims. The final section summarizes the different responses in a comparative view.

Concepts and definitions

Offenses

Both common law and codified law systems differentiate levels of severity for intentional acts that may or do cause harm to another person. These levels determine whether there should be a police or justice reaction at all, whether the victim must report, request, or lay a complaint, and what kind of court will adjudicate, as well as the penalty if the accused is found guilty. In order to avoid generalizing legal concepts from one system that have no relevance in another, we will speak of "minor" or "low-level" violence on the one hand, and "major" or "more severe" violence on the other. The "more severe" category corresponds approximately to "indictable offenses," "felonies" or "ex officio" crimes, but the criteria differ by legal system. It can depend on the minimum prison sentence, the use of a weapon, the number of days that injuries require to heal, whether the act was done with malice, or on specific provisions. Generally, low-level or minor offenses can be dismissed from legal proceedings; depending on the legal system, the power to dismiss a case or declare there has been no crime may be in the hands of the police, the public prosecutor, or the court.

Police measures

In the core definition across legal systems, *arrest* means taking a person into police custody where necessary to ensure criminal proceedings for a prosecutable offense. In common law, police could only arrest without a court warrant if they actually saw the crime being committed; in all legal systems the arrested person can only be held for a limited period of time. The first step in the US and the UK was to make warrantless arrest possible on probable cause. A further step was to broaden the power to arrest, for example to protect a vulnerable person (UK); this does not remove, but may dilute the core function of arrest as intake into the criminal justice system.

Pro-arrest and no-drop prosecution policies were developed in the US to overcome the failure of sanctions within a legal system that allows both police and prosecutors a high degree of discretion. Whereas *mandatory arrest* statutes require police to arrest whenever an officer has probable cause to believe that an assault, or more broadly an act of DV has occurred, *no-drop prosecution* policies do not call for prosecution of every reported case, but declare that cases will not be dropped merely because the victims do not cooperate with the prosecution of their abusers. Thus, strong pro-arrest policies tend to remove police discretion, while no-drop policies circumscribe, but still maintain prosecutorial discretion. The latter aim to spur methods of gathering evidence that permit prosecution without a victim's testimony, but also may include screening to eliminate cases where the evidence base is weak (Smith and Davis 2004). In both types of policy, the state decides on sanctions, taking away or reducing the onus of victim's responsibility, but also her voice in the decision.

Outside the US, other preventive coercive measures have been developed; their primary rationale is not to bring offenders to justice, but to protect citizens, to ensure public safety or to avert danger. These measures rest on police power to direct or detain individuals who pose a danger, either by taking them temporarily into custody without a criminal charge *(detention)*, or, on the contrary, by ordering them to leave a place and stay away for a set period of time *(exclusion)*. Based on probable danger, the restrictions extend only until the immediate risk is over, after which the victim can decide what further steps she will take.

Penalization

Prosecution requires a formal accusation in which the suspect is *charged* with an illegal act.[3] In British common law, the police formerly could both charge and prosecute offenders, and this is still the case in Australia. Today, in England and Canada the Crown prosecutor decides on a formal charge to the court, but only after the police investigation ends with an initial charge. In most European codified law systems, all cases go to the public prosecutor, who examines the evidence of guilt or of innocence and assesses the appropriate charge.

Courts

Most legal systems have a simplified type of *lower-level court* with a single judge or magistrate to dispose of minor offenses; these are gaining significance as specialized DV courts are introduced. In the adversarial system, prosecutors can suggest that the defendant admit to a lesser offense in exchange for a lower penalty *(plea bargain)* to dispose of cases rapidly; the court then proceeds directly to sentencing, so that the events giving rise to prosecution are not adjudicated. In codified law systems, levels of courts differ only by the composition of the bench; the prosecutor decides on the charge and thereby on the court to which the case will go. All evidence must be presented to the court, even where forms of plea bargain have been introduced to reduce court case loads. Both convictions and acquittals can be appealed.

Protection

Growing importance accrues to injunctions on an aggressor, to protect victims from danger. Numerous concepts are in use, differing between and within countries. Orders of any type may, for example, prohibit someone from harassing, threatening, or making contact with the victim or close family members, or define a "no-go" area that the aggressor may not enter. These orders differ with respect to procedures, duration, and sanctions. In some countries they constitute an alternative to the punitive approach, while in others, the value of injunctions lies precisely in the relative ease with which the breach of an order can be prosecuted.

For clarity, we use the term *"police ban"* (PB) for temporary restraints imposed directly by police without a judicial decision (but sometimes requiring approval by the prosecutor). A police ban aims to secure immediate physical distance between victim and aggressor to avert the threat of harm, and is limited in duration (such as ten days). It can be issued on request of the victim, or on police authority and their assessment of danger regardless of the victim's wishes.

A *"temporary restraining order"* (TRO) (sometimes called an emergency protection order) in this chapter shall mean all judicial injunctions, whether by a civil or a criminal court or a specialized court, imposing restrictions for a set period of time on the behavior of the person deemed to pose a danger. A TRO can be issued *ex parte*, that is without presence or counsel of the defendant, and often does not pre-suppose a criminal charge, although such a charge may be pressed in addition. Like the police ban, it is an emergency measure, but is less immediate, as it requires a court decision. Sanctions for breach of a court order may be higher than for a police ban.

The term *"protection order"* (PO) will be used to cover all forms of judicial orders imposing restrictions on the aggressor for a longer period of time *after* a court hearing. They may, for example, be valid for six months, a year, or until a divorce settlement is concluded. *"Exclusion orders"* (EO) are possible within any or all of the above measures, but deserve special mention because they grant the victim of DV exclusive use of the joint residence, regardless of the rights that the aggressor may claim based on ownership or rental contract.

Police and justice responses in Australia

The influence of international trends in DV intervention has shifted DV from a preoccupation of the specialist women's sector to an issue in the mainstream of police and justice responses, a position reflected in all Australian jurisdictions. Australia is a federated state in which each state and territory has its own criminal code, administration of justice, and policy guidance for DV intervention. Wide variations between Australian states could lead to arguments that states are characterized more by difference than by similarity across legislation, policy, funding regimes, court, and police culture. However, there are some common directions in policy which are now underpinned by a national action plan, *Time for Action*, a plan which was endorsed by all the states through state/federal governance mechanisms and which, amongst other objectives, aims to address the variation in legislation and policy (Commonwealth of Australia 2009).

Particular issues that characterize the current justice response in Australia include: the balance between criminal prosecution and civil protection; the development of legislation and legal responses which support "safe at home" strategies; and a range of specialist responses being piloted in different states and territories. As with other countries, there are also the problems of differential access to justice for women with special needs (e.g., women with disabilities; minority ethnic women; Aboriginal and Torres Strait Islander women) and women living in remote and rural areas.

A problem in understanding the trends in policing and justice in Australia lies with the difficulties in tracking the criminal justice response. Without a specific criminal offense of DV, or a system of "tagging" DV cases through the courts, it is difficult to ascertain prosecution and conviction rates. Thus, while the number of arrests can be identified through police data, following these arrests in the court process can be lost in states without a tagging system.

Civil protection orders

Criminal prosecution and civil protection orders have different functions: The former addresses offenses which have already been committed, while the latter are designed for protection from future offenses. In Australia, there is a major pre-occupation with the development of the civil protection order as a means of combating DV (see Douglas and Nancarrow this volume). This trend has its roots in major Task Force recommendations on DV in the 1980s (Murray and Powell 2011) which prioritize the civil justice response. It also may be associated with the ability of police in most jurisdictions in Australia to act as third-party applicants to the court for protection orders (Kaye and Humphreys 1997). In Tasmania, an enhancement lies with Police Family Violence Orders (PFVOs), lasting up to 12 months, which can be issued immediately by senior police who are at the level of sergeant or above (Wilcox 2010). There are a number of advantages to the third-party process, particularly that it is free for the woman and it allows a third party to take the matter to court on her behalf at a time when she may feel particularly vulnerable. However, there are concerns that this police power may override women's self-determination and full control of the conditions on the order. There also may be a temptation (and an actuality in some states) that more offenders then become prosecuted for contempt of court for breaching a protection order rather than facing the more serious offenses against the person. The Australian Capital Territory (ACT) has found a compromise by providing easy and immediate access to full legal aid and victim support provided through the court process, thus side-stepping the need for third-party police applications.

Interestingly, in the Australian context the shift in the proportion of third-party applications by police for protection orders is often associated with an increase in more general police action on DV. In the state of Victoria, subsequent to police emphasis on third-party intervention orders from 2004 onwards, the courts have reported a notable increase, from approximately 20 to 50 percent, of such orders initiated by police (Diemer 2012: 61). In addition, police have recorded an increase in charging, from 25 to 35 percent over a four-year period

(Victoria Police 2012). Tasmania has similar focus and legislation and has experienced similar increases. By contrast, there is evidence that in Queensland a similar rise in police third-party protection applications has seen a dip in the number of arrests and prosecutions (Douglas and Godden 2002).

Police safety strategies

A strong trend in most Australian states and territories lies in attempting to keep more women and children safe in their own homes by an exclusion order removing the perpetrator (McFerran 2007). Not all women will choose this strategy; some will prefer a place of safety away from where they experienced abuse, while other women will have no choice but to leave their home as the abuser is too dangerous and safety cannot be guaranteed by police and court responses. Nevertheless, as elsewhere, there is growing recognition of the right of victims to remain in their homes rather than being forced out by the abusive perpetrators.

Policy, policing, and legislative developments are required to support "safe at home" strategies. These strategies are more effective when responses are integrated and formal intervention is actively supported by informal networks (Edwards 2011). Several states use "police holding powers" whereby police may detain a perpetrator in custody for around six hours (time may vary by state) while a protection order and other safety strategies such as changing locks can be put in place. Further legislation, such as the Victorian Police Family Violence Safety Notices (Family Violence Protection Act 2008) strengthen the after-hours police response, allowing them to issue a protective "safety notice" including particular conditions such as excluding the offender from the home prior to court orders (police ban).

Specialist pilot projects in different states

There is a culture in Australia of "looking across the borders" to see what programs or legislative changes have been made or are being considered.[4] The development of guidance for police, specialist services, and the courts, as well as legislation enhancements, can be piloted in one state and picked up by another. For instance, the ACT integrated response of police, specialist courts, and victim support services exemplified a strategy for increasing the criminal prosecution and conviction rates (Humphreys and Holder 2002) and has been picked up strongly in Tasmania (Murray and Powell 2011). Specialist DV courts where there is a consistent, specially trained magistrate and specific listing of DV cases now have exemplars in most states, but are not an option for the majority of DV matters. Geographic distance, a lack of clear evidence that this is an effective response, and constrained resources in the justice system combine to undermine widespread development. In addition, court-ordered attendance at men's behavior-change programs for perpetrators of DV is being tried in varying ways within most states and territories, and much of this strategy is tied to the specialist courts.

In concluding the discussion of the Australian approach to arrest, protection, and justice, it is clear that some issues characterize the response. The strong development of civil justice responses and the diversity between states are simultaneously strengths and weaknesses in the development of accountability and safety through the justice system in Australia.

Police and justice response in Canada

Canada is a federated state with one Criminal Code, which is administered by the provinces and territories. While often influenced by its influential neighbor, the US, Canada's legal system is based on British common law.

Criminal justice

In Canada, the police lay initial Criminal Charges, while Crown prosecutors review and make the decision to prosecute, with authority to alter the charges. Although police departments respond to numerous complaints yearly, the proportion of female victims of DV who actually call the police is low, an estimated 30 percent in 2009, down from 36 percent in 2004 (Statistics Canada 2011: 5).

Criminal justice policies in Canada were influenced by the movement in the US to institute pro-arrest policies but soon shifted to a focus on charging, capturing a wider range of cases, although—as in the United Kingdom—legislation has also given police clearer power to arrest when there are grounds to do so. While arrests are common, in cases when the safety of the victim seems secure and the nature of the charges warrant it, the accused can be released on their own recognizance at the scene. Nonetheless, these less severe charges are prosecuted with the same rigor as cases resulting in arrest.

All provinces have adopted pro-charge and pro-prosecution policies which were first seen in the 1980s. An early study in one city provides impressive support for the policy change showing an increase from 3 percent charging to 89 percent over a ten-year period (Jaffe *et al.* 1991). When victims are asked their opinions about pro-charging policies, most are supportive even if, in their own cases, they did not want the abuser charged (Barata 2007). Although most victims supported this, they wanted a system that would stop the immediate violence and provide them some influence in whether or not their partners would be prosecuted (Barata 2007; Brown 2000). An additional concern is that pro-charging has resulted in an increase in counter- or dual charges when the police perceive both partners to have committed criminally chargeable violent acts. Police officers may not have been trained to understand the dynamics of DV, and so they charge women who may simply be protecting themselves or their children (Snider 2008). Another concern is that an aggressive criminal justice response to

DV particularly disadvantages marginalized victims such as immigrant minorities or Aboriginal women (Martin and Mosher 1995).

Specialized DV courts are a recent innovation in the justice system and have become relatively common across Canada. Their aim is to more effectively address DV by holding offenders accountable and improving safety for victims. Specialized courts entail more than a court system. Most involve a coordinated community process that includes agencies that offer batterer intervention programs coordinating with the efforts of (sometimes) specialized police units, Crown prosecutors, victim advocates, and probation officers. Special consideration is often given to first time accused, and vigorous prosecution is used with serial or serious offenders (Tutty *et al.* 2011).

Evaluations of specialized DV courts show lower recidivism rates, a speedier criminal justice process, and more effective prosecution (Tutty *et al.* 2011; Ursel and Hagyard 2008). Other researchers focused on the perspectives of victims regarding specialized courts (Dawson and Dinovitzer 2008), concluding that cooperative victims were seven times more likely to have the cases prosecuted than victims who are reluctant to cooperate, raising questions about the extent to which the dual goals of victim safety and offender accountability can be attained.

Civil protection orders

In addition to Criminal Code provisions for protection orders, nine of the 13 provinces and territories in Canada have proclaimed civil DV legislation that allows for the provision of emergency protection orders. An evaluation in the province of Alberta supported the effectiveness of their civil legislation in principle (Tutty *et al.* 2005). However, two concerns remained: Some women seek but cannot access protection orders, and others are granted orders, but the offender breaches the conditions. Protection orders are only as good as the extent to which breaches are addressed. According to Statistics Canada (2011: 12):

> One in ten victims of spousal violence (10%) stated that they obtained a restraining or protective order against their abuser. Of those who had obtained a restraining or protective order, nearly one-third of victims (30%) reported that their abuser violated its terms. Over two-thirds (67%) of these victims stated that they reported this violation to the police.

Victims are reportedly highly supportive of such legislation, appreciating the immediacy of the protection afforded, as well as conditions such as exclusive occupation of their homes and temporary custody of their children (the Ad Hoc Federal-Provincial-Territorial Working Group Reviewing Spousal Abuse Policies and Legislation 2003). Nonetheless, knowledge of and access to emergency protection orders remains a problem. For example, in Alberta, a province with one of the highest rates of DV—156,000 victims of self-reported spousal violence in a five-year period from 1999 to 2004 (Statistics Canada 2011)—only a very small number of orders (about 800) were applied for and granted in a three-year period from 2001 to 2004 (Tutty *et al.* 2005).

In summary, although civil legislation is in place in the majority of Canadian provinces and territories, the criminal justice system is more commonly used by victims. Despite innovations to better address DV and support victims, research with women from the province of Ontario concluded that a number felt "further traumatized by ambivalent or discriminatory attitudes and practices prevalent within the system" (Gillis *et al.* 2006: 1150), especially women of non-Caucasian origins who were not fluent in English or French. Clearly, more consideration and evaluations are needed to both criminal and civil processes to achieve the goal of better supporting women abused by intimate partners.

Police and justice responses in Europe

Legal and institutional traditions in Europe are very diverse, but in general, criminal sanctions for DV have not been a priority, and concern for penalization is oriented to protecting victims from harm. The main tools that have emerged are:

1. Broader definitions of DV as public interest offenses, increasing the odds that cases may be prosecuted.
2. Police bans that expel a person posing a danger from the residence for a set period, coupled with pro-active counseling and support for victims.
3. Specialized, fast-track DV (magistrate) courts that both impose penalties and issue protective measures.
4. Multi-agency cooperation systems, some including risk assessment conferences, with a focus on victims' safety.
5. Specialized prosecution and/or police units with training on DV.
6. Comprehensive laws on DV, covering police, justice, and protection measures as well as victims' rights.

With the emergence of a global human rights framework, articulated in the UN in 1993, and the independence of new democracies from the former state socialist bloc, the spatial and political context for the obligation of states to stop VAW doubled in size and was transformed in its social constituency.[5] In the "old" Europe, by 1990 the feminist action projects had become more professional and ready to engage with multi-institutional cooperation, while many former activists had moved into government positions with equal-opportunity responsibilities. In the "new" Europe local initiatives, new women's rights organizations, state efforts to be good Europeans (Kriszan and Popa 2010) and international donors combined with activists and trainers from the West to increase interest in criminalization and prosecution.

In 2002 the Council of Europe issued comprehensive recommendations on "the protection of women against violence," including all forms of VAW, and calling for all measures to focus on the needs of victims, their maximum safety and empowerment. While not binding, the follow-up—monitoring (Hagemann-White 2008), a Europe-wide campaign, and seminars for exchange of good practice—gave this document considerable influence on country-level policies. It led up to a legally binding “Convention on Preventing and Combating Violence Against Women and Domestic Violence” opened for signature in May 2011.[6] While underlining criminalization and “due diligence” in prosecution, the Convention retains the focus on victim safety and empowerment, adding specific obligations of prevention.

Criminal justice

At present, no country in Europe has mandatory arrest, nor is arrest considered a sanction; however, the power to arrest may be used to provide the victim a (brief) period of safety. Prosecution of DV cases is legally independent of a victim’s request or complaint in the majority of countries, but the intent to prosecute regardless of the victim’s wishes has not been anchored in law, nor consistently sustained in practice.

Overall the criminal justice response to DV in Europe follows one of three pathways (Hagemann-White 2009): (1) eliminating exceptions within existing criminal law (via procedural law or guidelines) to establish that it is the *same* crime when the victim is an intimate partner; (2) declaring unlawful acts of violence to be a *more serious* offense if committed against a close person; or (3) introducing a specific, named offense into criminal law, suggesting that acts of violence within the family are a *different* crime. These approaches may be combined (e.g., introducing a specific offense may cite the family context as an aggravating circumstance). Some new offenses fill specific gaps in existing law, as when repeated violence (e.g., Austria, Sweden) or stalking (e.g., Germany, UK) is criminalized. Only Spain, Sweden, and more recently Portugal and France have introduced named offenses of gender-based violence within a relationship.

Unsurprisingly, within Europe the UK comes closest to adopting the pro-arrest and pro-prosecution policies favored in the US,[7] but these rest on a foundation of support for local multi-agency co-ordination to provide services (Matczak *et al.* 2011). The Domestic Violence, Crime and Victims Act in 2004 made breach of a protection order a crime and common assault an arrestable offense; the intent to prosecute regardless of the wishes of the victim was widely publicized. Concurrently specialist DV courts were introduced countrywide, based on specific training and multi-agency cooperation; Independent Domestic Violent Advisors were funded to support the victim (Robinson 2008). While prosecution is always discretionary in the UK, policy has aimed to raise the conviction rate, and sentencing guidelines were issued, but there is no distinct criminal offense of domestic violence. Since 2008 the focus has shifted toward multi-agency risk-assessment conferences to protect high-risk victims.

Specific laws

While a number of European Union countries now have legislation on DV—the first being a law on family violence in (Greek) Cyprus in 1994[8]—many of these do not focus on criminal prosecution, and most are gender neutral and family based. The 2004 Spanish law on "gender violence"[9] is highly regarded; it covers all acts of physical and psychological violence exercised against women by their present or former spouses or by men with whom they have had analogous affective relations, with or without cohabitation. The law explicitly defines such violence as "an expression of discrimination, the situation of inequality and the power relations prevailing between the sexes" (Article 1). Explicitly included are offenses against sexual liberty, threats, coercion, and the arbitrary deprivation of liberty. It is thus almost unique in Europe in criminalizing gender-based domestic violence both specifically and broadly.

The law establishes specialized DV courts, and all offenses are transferred to these courts if, at any point in the proceedings, intimate partner and gender aspects emerge. Cases are brought before the courts very quickly, often within 24 hours. Penalties for gender violence (by a man to a woman) are higher than for the same acts in other contexts. Suspended prison sentences are the rule (no fines), accompanied by protection measures, such as the prohibition of any attempt to contact the victim, and no right to possess a weapon for five years. While women are urged to report and cooperate in prosecution, there is a strong focus on victims' rights (to employment, legal residency, housing). Thus, prosecution is central, but punishment is not emphasized.

Police safety strategies

A contrasting and innovative approach was developed in Austria in a working group of activists and ministries (Federal Chancellery 2008). The police ban or expulsion order in conjunction with a proactive offer of advice and support[10] has had considerable impact on European policies. A key to its success was the disconnect from criminal justice, allowing police action to ensure safety from threat of violence regardless of evidence of a crime. The ban is independent of the wishes of the victim, based on the police duty to protect citizens from harm, and prohibits the return of the person expelled to the residence for two weeks; it can be extended if the victim applies for *ex parte* issuance of a civil protection order. Breach of the order is a criminal offense.

This model was adopted in a number of other countries, including Germany, Switzerland, Lichtenstein, Luxembourg, the Czech Republic, Slovakia, the Netherlands, and the UK (Kelly *et al.* 2011). It is popularized by slogans such as "Who hits out, goes out," and has been welcomed by police because the clear action paradigm fits with their role, while enabling them to refer the victim to a social worker/psychologist. Imposing non-contact is seen to give the woman a longer period of safety and time to sort out her future than would arrest, which requires releasing the man within a very short time. The measure presumes that men will usually obey a police order, and in fact, evaluations have found that the majority of them do so (e.g., Dearing and Haller 2005). Reactions to the idea of expelling a man from his home (and assessment of the probability of his complying) were much more skeptical in Scandinavia, where police bans were introduced but rarely used. In Sweden, for example, the Act on Restraining Orders (2003) requires sufficient evidence for criminal prosecution. Evaluation found that orders expelling the perpetrator were not only often denied, but almost never issued (only 2 percent of all exclusion orders) when the woman was living with the perpetrator—that is, he was only banned from returning if he had already left (Brå 2007). This suggests that police safety strategies are highly dependent on mainstream culture.

Innovation and experiments are still going on. In France, where a 1994 provision that violence against a spouse or partner constitutes an aggravating circumstance was found ineffective, a specific offense of violence against a partner was introduced in 2010 that includes psychological violence. With the 2011 "Law against VAW, violence within the couple relationship and its effects on children," criminal justice became secondary to victim safety: Civil protection orders issued by the family court are the basis, and most other measures follow from this.

Seen as a whole, European legislation and practice has been exploring ways to deploy the coercive powers of the police, specialized units in police, prosecution, or courts, sanctions and the threat of sanctions to ensure more safety and empowerment for victims of DV. Legal and sociocultural traditions continue to generate considerable diversity with regard to the practices that are accepted and effective.

Comparative assessment

Comparing approaches in a global perspective with case studies and looking beyond the variety of legal systems, it can be seen that the complex challenge to justice presented by DV is met by setting implicit priorities among the potential intervention duties of statutory agencies. These may be based in criminal law, in administrative and police law, or in civil (and more specifically, tort) law. A more detailed study would reveal considerable variety within each federally organized state or continent under discussion, as well as local models of coordinated multi-level practice.

The move in the US to mandatory arrest, followed later by no-drop prosecution, rests on a priority of immediate, visible sanctions and a presumption of their deterrent effect, yet case screening and plea bargaining limit the extent of actual penalization. While models of multi-agency co-operation in the US have had a great influence internationally, they generally do not have a foundation in law (as they increasingly do in Europe) and are not seen as the duty of the state, but rather as a choice of the community.

In Canada, legally based presumptive arrest is directly linked to police charging, so that arrest is not the sanction, but functions as intake into the criminal justice system. Debates thus focus on whether the police lay appropriate charges in DV cases. Criminal prosecution has been the policy priority, and legislation broadening the range of available protection measures is recent. As in the US, civil protection measures depend on the victim's initiative and are not directly linked to policing or other state intervention powers.

In Australia, police powers are broader and comprise, along with arrest where appropriate, both initiating prosecution and requesting civil protection orders from the court. Police "holding powers" or extended detention of DV perpetrators can cover the period until a protection order is in place, and expulsion orders increasingly follow the "safe at home" principle. Generally, police intervention and civil law measures are thus oriented to victim safety. Current debates focus on how equal levels of safety can be provided to women in diverse circumstances.

European policy sets empowerment of women and victim safety as its overall priority. Specialized DV courts have been successful in England and Wales and in Spain, but they require significant resources and training, as well as a legal basis for rapid action comprising both criminal and civil measures. The police ban—exclusion from the residence with a no-contact provision—has become a recognized intervention. Providing victims with advice and support toward longer-term civil law measures is understood to follow from the due diligence principle derived from the human rights framework for understanding VAW generally. Punishment receives less attention, and deterrent effects are expected from psycho-educational programs for violent men.

Tracing the evolution of DV policies for police and criminal justice comparatively, we see that they are typically driven by concern about failures specific to the legal and institutional system. In general, these comprise the failure to protect victims from continuing or imminent violence despite recognizable danger, the failure to call individual perpetrators to account and to stop their exercise of coercive control, and the failure to demonstrate a sustained and unambiguous political will to make such violence unacceptable. Implicitly these critiques define two very different points of reference for improving legal responses: the safety and well-being of the women exposed to violence by a (former) partner on the one hand, and the rule of law and quality of governance as they affect all citizens on the other.

Police and criminal justice reforms are necessarily based on country-specific knowledge of the powers and duties of agencies and their interaction, and these differ. Where the police power to lay (initial) charges is crucial to further legal action, as in Canada and the UK, encouraging arrest and/or charging became a policy focus. Where the police additionally have the power to prosecute and thus have direct access to the courts, as in Australia, third-party protection orders for victim safety were a logical step. Where all cases go to the public prosecutor for decision, as in most of Europe, specialist prosecution units took on more significance, and regulating police intervention tended to focus on the power to direct, detain, and protect. Additionally, cultural understandings of the proper role of the state and its agents, the proper response to crime, and the best way to change antisocial behavior influence the choice of measures.

The comparative review presented in this chapter underlines the need to limit or provide legally binding guidance to the discretion that the agents of law enforcement and criminal justice may have in dealing with DV, as the available research suggests that old habits of discounting its seriousness and preferring non-intervention tend to resurface after reforms are in place. At the same time, an exclusively punitive approach may not be effective in keeping women safe from further violence. Overall the evidence suggests that a clear and decisive response by statutory agencies, condemning violence, along with good protection measures, is a more effective deterrent of re-offending than either arrest or incarceration alone.

Across differing legal traditions and institutional cultures there have been significant innovations in the use of police coercive powers additional to, or instead of arrest. Regardless of policy priorities and legal systems, in actual practice prosecution and punishment seem to be limited to high-risk or easily proven cases. This may be due to court case overloads (e.g., US), skepticism as to its usefulness (e.g., Europe) or victim unwillingness to cooperate. Whatever the source of the attrition in the prosecution and punishment process, the path leading to potentially dissuasive penalties for the large majority of DV cases seems to be a "leaky pipeline." There is no single model for balancing the safety needs of victims with the obligation of state actors to signal that assaults are not acceptable and will not be tolerated, while taking account of the differing roles and functions of institutions within each system.

Notes

1 These laws may both narrow (household only, family only) and broaden (any member) the scope of acts falling under their purview, but often these terms are understood to refer to violence against an adult partner, and that is how the term will be used here.
2 An equal rights framing focuses on whether women are treated the same as men in comparable circumstances, while a needs and empowerment framing may be centred on the broader context of women's lives.
3 This is independent of a possible arrest. In all countries, suspects can be arrested but not charged, or charged but not arrested.
4 See www.austdvclearinghouse.unsw.edu.au.
5 Between 1990 and 2004, the Council of Europe, set up to promote democracy and protect human rights and the rule of law, expanded from 23 member states to 46 (now 47) and the European Union, based on treaties to regulate economic cooperation but with broadening competencies, from 12 to 25 member states (now 28).
6 Ratification processes take time, but the Convention is expected to come into force by late 2013 or 2014; see www.coe.int/t/dghl/standardsetting/convention-violence/about_en.asp.
7 The absence of pro-arrest policies elsewhere might be explained by the fact that most legal systems on the European Continent have rather restrictive rules for arrest,

requiring that custody can only be quite brief unless there are, for example, grounds for concern that the person will disappear or will try to conceal evidence—conditions unlikely to apply to domestic violence.

8 Law on Prevention of Domestic Violence and Protection of Victims N.47(I)/1994. Drafted by the Association of Women Lawyers, it aimed at ensuring *ex officio* prosecution, even making the victim a compellable witness if a child is in the home; provisions to protect victims are to be issued when the judge deems them necessary.

9 See www.isotita.gr/var/uploads/NOMOTHESIA/VIOLENCE/SPANISH%20LAW%20Organic%20Act%201_28-12-04%20on%20Violence.pdf.

10 Federal Act on Protection Against Domestic Violence, in force since May 1997, was amended several times to remove restrictions and extend duration of protection measures.

References

Ad Hoc Federal-Provincial-Territorial Working Group Reviewing Spousal Abuse Policies and Legislation (2003) *Spousal Abuse Policies and Legislation*, Ottawa, ON: Department of Justice Canada. Online. Available at www.justice.gc.ca/eng/rp-pr/cj-jp/fv-vf/pol/spo_e-con_a.pdf (accessed 25 May 2014).

Barata, P.C. (2007) 'Abused women's perspectives on the criminal justice system's response to domestic violence', *Psychology of Women Quarterly*, 31: 202–15.

Brå, Brottsförebyggande rådet (2007) *Restraining Orders in Sweden: An Evaluation of the Law, the New Regulations, their Implementation and Effects—English Summary*, Stockholm: Brå.

Brown, T. (2000) *Charging and Prosecution Policies in Cases of Spousal Assault: A Synthesis of Research, Academic, and Judicial Responses*, Ottawa, ON: Department of Justice Canada.

Buzawa, E.S., Buzawa, C.G. and Stark, E. (2012) *Responding to Domestic Violence. The Integration of Criminal Justice and Human Services*, 4th edn., Los Angeles, CA: Sage.

Commonwealth of Australia (2009) *Time for Action: The National Council's Plan for Australia to Reduce Violence against Women and their Children, 2009–2021*, Canberra: Australian Government.

Dawson, M. and Dinovitzer, R. (2008) 'Specialized justice: from prosecution to sentencing in a Toronto domestic violence court', in J. Ursel, L. Tutty and J. LeMaistre (eds.), *What's Law Got to Do with It? The Law, Specialized Courts and Domestic Violence in Canada*, Toronto, ON: Cormorant Press, 120–47.

Dearing, A. and Haller, B. (2005) *Schutz vor Gewalt in der Familie: Das österreichische Gewaltschutzgesetz*, Wien: Juristische Schriftenreihe Band, 210.

Diemer, K. (2012) *Measuring Family Violence in Victoria: Victorian Family Violence Database Volume 5*, Melbourne: Victims Support Agency, Victorian Government Department of Justice.

Douglas, H. and Godden, L. (2002) 'The decriminalization of domestic violence: possibilities for reform', paper presented at Expanding our Horizons: Understanding the Complexities of Violence against Women, University of Sydney.

Edwards, R. (2011) *Staying Home Leaving Violence: Listening to Women's Experiences*, Sydney: University of New South Wales, Social Policy Research Centre.

Federal Chancellery (2008) *Ten Years of Austrian Anti-violence Legislation, Documentation: International Conference in the Context of the Council of Europe*

Campaign to Combat Violence Against Women including Domestic Violence, Vienna: Federal Minister for Women and Civil Service.

Gillis, J.R., Diamond, S.L., Jebely, P., Orekhovsky, V., Ostovich, E.M., MacIsaac, K., Sagati, S. and Mandell, D. (2006) 'Systemic obstacles to battered women's participation in the judicial system: when will the status quo change?', *Violence Against Women*, 12: 1159–68.

Hagemann-White, C. (2009) *Typology of domestic violence laws in Council of Europe member states—a preliminary overview*. Online. Available at www.coe.int/t/dghl/standardsetting/convention-violence/CAHVIO/CAHVIO%20_2009_13%20%20e.pdf (accessed 25 May 2014).

Hagemann-White, C. (2008) 'Measuring progress in addressing violence against women across Europe', *International Journal of Comparative and Applied Criminal Justice*, 32: 149–72.

Hagemann-White, C., Kavemann, B., Kootz, J., Weinmann, U, Wildt, C.C., Burgard, R. and Scheu, U. (1981) *Hilfen für misshandelte Frauen*, Schriftenreihe des Bundesministeriums für Jugend, Familie und Gesundheit, Band 124, Stuttgart: Kohlhammer.

Hirschel D. (2008) *Domestic Violence Cases: What Research Shows About Arrest and Dual Arrest Rates*, Washington, DC: National Institute of Justice.

Humphreys, C. and Holder, R. (2002) 'An integrated criminal justice response to domestic violence: it's challenging, but it's not rocket science', *SAFE The Domestic Abuse Quarterly*, 3: 16–19.

Jaffe, P., Reitzel, D., Hastings, E. and Austin, G. (1991) *Wife Assault as a Crime: The Perspectives of Victims and Police Officers on a Charging Policy in London*, Ontario from 1980-1990. London, ON: London Family Court Clinic.

Kaye, M. and Humphreys, C. (1997) 'Third party applications for protection orders: opportunities, ambiguities and traps', *Journal of Social Welfare and Family Law*, 19: 403–21.

Kelly, L., Hagemann-White, C., Meysen, T. and Römkens, R. (2011) *Realizing Rights? Case Studies on State Responses to Violence Against Women and Children in Europe*, London: London Metropolitan University.

Kriszan, A. and Popa, R. (2010) 'Europeanization in making policies against domestic violence in Central and Eastern Europe', *Social Politics*, 17: 379–406.

Martin, D. L. and Mosher, J. E. (1995) 'Unkept promises: Experiences of immigrant women with the neo-criminalization of wife abuse', *The Canadian Journal of Women and the Law*, 8: 3–43.

Matczak, A., Hatzidimitriadou, E. and Lindsay, J. (2011) *Review of Domestic Violence Policies in England and Wales*, London: Kingston University and St George's University of London.

McFerran, L. (2007) *Taking back the Castle: How Australia Is Making the Home Safer for Women and Children,* Sydney: University of New South Wales, Australian Domestic and Family Violence Clearinghouse.

Murray, S. and Powell, A. (2011) *Domestic Violence: Australian Public Policy*, Melbourne: Australian Scholarly Press.

Robinson, A. (2008) 'Measuring what matters in specialist domestic violence courts', *Cardiff School of Social Sciences Working Papers*, 102. Online. Available at www.cardiff.ac.uk/socsi/resources/wp102.pdf (accessed 25 May 2014).

Schechter, S. (1982) *Women and Male Violence. The Visions and Struggles of the Battered Women's Movement*, Boston, MA: South End Press.

Smith, B.E. and Davis, R.C. (2004) *An Evaluation of Efforts to Implement No-Drop Policies: Two Central Values in Conflict*, Washington, DC: US Department of Justice.

Snider, L. (2008) 'Criminalising violence against women: solution or dead end?', *Criminal Justice Matters*, 74: 38–39.

Statistics Canada (2011) *Family Violence in Canada: A Statistical Profile*, Ottawa, ON: Canadian Centre for Justice Statistics.

Tutty, L. M., Koshan, J., Jesso, D. and Nixon, K. (2005) *Alberta's Protection Against Family Violence Act: A Summative Evaluation*, Calgary, AB: RESOLVE Alberta. Online. Available at www.child.alberta.ca/home/images/familyviolence/Summative_Evaluation.pdf (accessed 25 May 2014).

Tutty, L.M., Koshan, J., Jesso, J., Ogden, C., and Warrell, J.G. (2011) *Evaluation of the Calgary Specialized Domestic Violence Trial Court & Monitoring the First Appearance Court: Final Report to National Crime Prevention and the Alberta Law Foundation*, Calgary, AB: RESOLVE Alberta. Online. Available at www.ucalgary.ca/resolve-static/reports/2011/2011-01.pdf (accessed 25 May 2014).

Ursel, E.J. and Hagyard, C. (2008) 'The Winnipeg Family Violence Court', in J. Ursel, L. Tutty and J. LeMaistre (eds.), *What's Law Got to Do with It? The Law, Specialized Courts and Domestic Violence in Canada*, Toronto, ON: Cormorant Press, 95–119.

Victoria Police (2012) *Victoria Police Family Incident Reports 2007 to 2012*, Melbourne: Victoria Police. Online. Available at www.police.vic.gov.au/content.asp?a=internetBridgingPage&Media_ID=84497 (accessed 25 May 2014).

Wilcox, K. (2010) 'Connecting systems, protecting victims: toward vertical coordination of Australia's response to domestic and family violence', *The University of New South Wales Law Journal*, 33: 1013–17.

Chapter 5

Pie in the sky? The use of criminal justice policies and practices for intimate partner violence

Amanda L. Robinson

Hagemann-White and colleagues (this volume) provide a discussion of contemporary police, prosecution, and protection strategies, including specialized domestic violence (DV) courts, to address intimate partner violence (IPV). They conclude that "overall the evidence suggests that a clear and decisive response by statutory agencies, condemning violence, along with good protection measures, is a more effective deterrent of re-offending than either arrest or incarceration alone" (see p. 62). The chapter describes some of the benefits that are possible from a more proactive, coordinated criminal justice response.

The aim of this chapter is to critically reflect on these developments in criminal justice policy and practice. In so doing, a discussion of several intractable dilemmas for criminal justice approaches to IPV is provided. The use of the term "intractable" is deliberate, as it is far from certain if or how these dilemmas could be fully resolved. Rather than abandoning criminal justice policies and practices for addressing IPV, this chapter underlines the importance of using criminal justice in combination with other approaches as the preferred way forward.

The rise of the criminal justice paradigm

> We govern through crime to the extent to which crime and punishment become the occasions and the institutional contexts in which we undertake to guide the conduct of others (or even of ourselves).
>
> (Simon 1997: 173)

The non-interventionist or "do-nothing" response of yesteryear's criminal justice system was, by all accounts, indefensible. Over time, in most Western countries, a more proactive, interventionist, and legalistic approach to IPV developed to take its place. The rise of the criminal justice paradigm has been heralded by many victim advocates, criminal justice officials, politicians, and scholars (including me) as progressive. Some have even described the increased involvement of the criminal justice system in IPV since the 1970s as a "revolution" (Stark 2007). A formal response invoked by the enforcement of the criminal law on behalf of victims is seen to reinforce the message that IPV is a crime that will not be tolerated by society. As the preeminent system for dealing with crime, criminal justice action (or inaction) can be seen to send those who perpetrate IPV "either a green light or a red light for the continuation of their violent actions" (Dobash 2003: 316). Criminalizing IPV encourages the legal system to treat violence between intimates in the same manner as violence between strangers. As a result, more offenders are held accountable and more victims are afforded protection.

It is important to recognize that the enhancement of the criminal justice "apparatus of control" for IPV is not unique, but rather part of a wider development in recent decades. The contemporary crime-control landscape is seen to include: a reduced focus on rehabilitation in favor of other penal goals such as retribution, incapacitation, and the management of risk; political discourse on crime which is more openly punitive and emotional; a zero-sum game where concern for offenders is seen to retract from the rights of victims; an increased demand for public protection by the state; a narrowing of the range of crime policy proposals; and an ever expanding infrastructure to address crime and social disorder, to name but a few (Garland 2001). There are implications for harnessing the power of the law and criminal justice to a particular issue, both wide ranging and sometimes unforeseen. When we create a crime problem out of a problem that has not previously been defined as such, as with the case of IPV, then some consequences arise that might not have otherwise. Focus and funding are placed on particular strategies, perhaps at the expense of others. Legalistic, formal, and bureaucratic approaches can crowd out other styles of handling problems. Simon's (1997) notion of "governing through crime" (quoted above) seems particularly apropos for describing the dominant governmental approaches to IPV in most Western countries. Simon argued, however, that "governing through crime" is problematic for several reasons: It is too costly; makes communities less governable through alternative strategies; is corrosive of democracy; and does not work (because criminal justice processing does not reduce the offending rate). It is necessary to critically reflect on how contemporary approaches to crime generally are shaped by, and continue to shape, the approaches taken to IPV specifically.

The unknown figure of crime

> Our observations can only refer to a certain number of known and tried offences, out of the unknown sum total of crimes committed. Since this sum total of crime committed will probably ever continue unknown, all the reasoning of which it is the basis will be more or less defective.
>
> (Quetelet 1842)

The fact that many, if not most, crimes remain unknown to police and other state authorities has been acknowledged and empirically verified for more than a century. The implications of this are truly profound, even if one does not accept that "if we do not know the true rate of crime, all our theories are built on quicksand" (Young 2004: 18). Official statistics can only describe a partial, and undoubtedly biased group, of incidents that people have chosen (for one reason or another) to a) identify as a "crime" and b) report to police. Some time ago, Skogan (1977) noted that this body of unreported crime has several consequences for the criminal justice system: It limits its deterrent capability; contributes to the misallocation of police resources; renders victims ineligible for public and private benefits; affects insurance costs; and helps to (mis)shape the police role in society.

Further complicating matters is that the unknown figure of crime varies across crime types. In every country that can provide some (imperfect) measure of this "unknown figure of crime" by, for example, comparing police statistics with those from self-report victimization surveys, it is clear that IPV goes mostly unreported. For example, in 1985, the United Kingdom's Women's National Commission revealed that only 2 percent of incidents of "marital violence" were reported to the police. Nearly 30 years later, with increased public awareness of the issue and a less restrictive definition, UK statistics show that less than one-quarter of IPV victims choose to report their experience to the police (Britton 2012). This proportion remains under one-third even when victims are being supported by specialist trained support workers who provide them with advice and information about the criminal justice process (CAADA 2012).

Many factors influence a victim's willingness to report, including age, gender, ethnicity, income, prior victimization, perceptions of police effectualness, sense of their own culpability, and incident-specific factors such as seriousness of the crime, perceived threat, and when it occurred (MacDonald 2002; Maguire 2012). Overcoming the independent effects of such a huge array of factors, let alone the interactions between them, is impossible even if it were unquestionably desirable. The unknown figure of crime thus presents an intractable dilemma in that criminal justice will only ever be responding to a small, biased, subsample of cases. Undoubtedly these "known" cases continue to shape our impression of the problem at large and the best way to address it, but anything flowing from this will be inherently flawed to some degree, as Adolphe Quetelet noted 172 years ago.

Nevertheless, the rise of the criminal justice paradigm has involved many new initiatives and approaches that have been designed to improve its performance and capability with respect to IPV. This has been an extensive and costly exercise, and one taken to greater or lesser extent in every country that has a criminal justice system and recognizes IPV as a crime. In addition to the dilemmas posed by the multidimensional and repetitive nature of IPV, and the fact that most cases will never come to the attention of the criminal justice system, a further dilemma is posed by the structure of the criminal justice system itself.

Tinkering with adversarialism

Recognition of these shortcomings has resulted in an increasing pre-occupation with how the conventional criminal justice response might do

> better. It is those responses that I have chosen to call "tinkering with adversarialism," since it is the adversarial system of justice itself that is frequently the barrier to the ultimate success or failure of the kinds of policy initiatives to be discussed here.
>
> (Walklate 2007: 111)

The adversarial system of justice creates its own set of barriers to the effective deployment of new policies and practices. Systems of justice underpinned by adversarial (rather than, say, inquisitorial) principles are especially ill suited to dealing with IPV. This model of criminal justice has as its central aim the proper functioning of the criminal trial. This model is structured around a case being brought against a defendant, and ensuring the defendant's rights are upheld. The response of such a system to IPV creates a number of dilemmas. For example, a substantial volume of research produced over time has rendered in a detailed way the multi-dimensional nature of IPV. Not only does this phenomenon include aspects beyond physical violence (e.g., psychological abuse, financial control), but it also tends to manifest as a pattern of behaviors rather than as discrete or isolated incidents. Consequently, a criminal justice focus on incidents can contradict the lived reality of victimization, which is often experienced as a process in people's everyday life (Walklate 2007). An equally significant dilemma is that victims only feature as "triggers" of state action. The conventional model of adversarial criminal justice posits that victims have a minimal role apart from as witnesses for the prosecution. This has been predicated on the assumption that giving victims a marginal role will help safeguard defendants' rights. Although the conventional adversarial structure has little place for the "victim's voice," this has been an area of substantial tinkering in recent years, by a range of policy and political actors.

As noted by Hagemman-White *et al.* (this volume), legal and policy instruments have explicitly attempted to re-orient the criminal justice system toward a more "victim-centered model." In many countries there have been new initiatives designed to achieve these aims, envisioned as "rights" or "codes of practice" which include, for example: The right to receive information about the crime within specified time scales; notification of eligibility for compensation; provision of victim advice and support services; enhanced services or adjustments for vulnerable or intimidated victims, etc. (see e.g., UK Code of Practice for Victims of Crime, 2006).[1] While these are largely seen as welcome initiatives, they do not do more than "tinker" with a system that is structurally designed to ensure the victim is peripheral, rather than central, to the case. Additionally, the decision to prosecute within adversarial systems is taken on behalf of the "public interest," which may or may not simultaneously meet people's (different) perceptions of their own interests. Finally, this system is predicated on black and white notions of guilt and innocence, which do not always easily map onto the lived reality of IPV. The dichotomous conceptualization of people as victims or offenders can be seen as both false and fruitless, leading some to argue that "violence that occurs in an intimate relationship is not conducive to a paradigm that assigns all the blame to one party while wholly exonerating the other" (Mills 2003: 31). The notion of joint responsibility continues to influence the perspectives of many professionals confronted with incidents of IPV.

A certain ideological caution

> Police officers over the last century have developed a certain ideological caution, which still persists today . . . that the police should not interfere in disputes between husband and wife unless it cannot be avoided; that both parties may turn upon the officers concerned; and that the police should only intervene when serious injury has occurred, or is imminent, or that matter has spilled out into the public domain.
>
> (Bourlet 1990: 15–17)

Along with ample research over the past 40 years, the quote above reveals the ideological basis that supports the avoidance of formal intervention in cases of IPV. Maintaining the "unity of the spouses" was traditionally the overriding concern of police, who were explicitly advised against taking action that could turn a bad situation worse (House of Commons Select Committee on Violence in Marriage 1975). The occupational reluctance of police flowed from a more general societal reluctance to intervene in the private business of family life. It would not be contentious to suggest that this reluctance—within the police occupational subculture as well as societal culture more generally—has dissipated over time, but by no means has it been erased (Buzawa *et al.* 2012). Reluctance to "see" IPV as a crime requiring the enforcement of the criminal law is still a pressing issue, even among police officers who are trained, and even in police agencies that have pro- or mandatory-arrest policies to structure their use of discretion. A recent study in the United States indicates that several police investigative actions that are optional rather than mandated (e.g., more evidence collection, listing additional charges on the police report) increase the probability of prosecution and conviction; however, these activities are not routinely undertaken and may be easily subverted "in the absence of a personal drive to investigative excellence" (Nelson 2013: 545). In short, it is still possible, and in many cases will be acceptable, for police to exhibit little more than minimalist effort when investigating IPV cases.

While there is a wide range of criminal justice policies and practices in place to address IPV, particularly within Western developed countries, the scientific community is only now beginning to understand the limits and benefits of these efforts. Research found that arrests may deter future IPV incidents to a statistically significant degree, but this effect is modest (Maxwell *et al.* 2002). Furthermore, the deterrent effect of arrest for IPV does not work equally well for all offenders, and varies across settings (Garner *et al.* 1995). Such research contrasted more proactive and legalistic policing with the status quo, which was to do nothing. It could be argued that, regardless of the empirical findings, such responses should be encouraged because the alternative (to do nothing) is unacceptable. But it is worth remembering that "the process by which such deterrence works (e.g., self-control and recognition of future consequences of actions) is assumed rather than studied" (Manning 1993: 637). In other words, even if such policing practices "work," researchers have little understanding of *why* they work.

More recently, the research focus has shifted to other components of the criminal justice system, such as prosecution, conviction, and sanctioning of offenders, to determine how these decisions influence the subsequent rate of repeat IPV. Unfortunately, this body of research does not allow us to formulate a definitive conclusion about the effectiveness of these approaches, and it certainly should encourage us to take a cautionary pause before recommending them. For example, in their review of 31 studies conducted in the United States and Canada, Maxwell and Garner (2012: 485) concluded that "the most frequent outcome is that criminal justice sanctions that follow an arrest for IPV have no effect, in either a positive or negative direction, on the pattern of subsequent offending." Their analysis showed that 65 percent of the 144 comparison tests produced no significant differences in the rates of recidivism. Research based on a more narrow focus on specialized DV courts by Cissner *et al.* (2013) also reported mixed findings in terms of recidivism outcomes from nine quasi-experimental evaluations: Five of the 12 data analyses indicated significantly lower IPV recidivism rates; six indicated no difference in recidivism rates; and one indicated a significant increase in recidivism. A review of 21 studies assessing the relationship between restraining orders and IPV recidivism found only mixed support for their effectiveness, as 43 comparison tests produced only 15 statistically significant results. The most prevalent finding was that there is no difference in the rates of recidivism between those with and those without a restraining order (Maxwell and Robinson 2013). A recent analysis of all DV-related arrests in one US state found that penalties, at least as set at the current levels, do not deter future arrests and convictions (Sloan *et al.* 2013).

Even if it could be conclusively demonstrated that criminal justice approaches were effective in reducing recidivism, it is unlikely this effect is constant and uniform across various types of victims, offenders, and communities. Several studies indicate that caution is required before drawing any conclusions about what might "work," or not, as sanctions work in different ways for different people, in different local contexts (Kingsnorth 2006; Visher *et al.* 2008). Indeed, some might produce the opposite effect from the one intended. Taken together, these studies question the utility of a one-size-fits-all criminal justice approach for IPV. Furthermore, it is doubtful we could envision these approaches always coinciding with what every victim desires and expects from criminal justice.

Trying to preserve what they value

> They are deeply conflicted about how to address the abuse while trying to preserve what they value in their relationships.
>
> (Mills 2003: 30)

Extant research compellingly reveals the difficulty of using the criminal law and the criminal justice system to address problems between people who have once had, or who continue to have, an intimate relationship. There is now increased awareness that victims may use the criminal justice system to satisfy several different goals (e.g. protection, prevention, reform, and justice) and that these goals often change over time (Lewis *et al.* 2000). Research has shown that what the majority of victims (80 percent) want from outside intervention is to be safe, but they have different ideas about how this might be achieved, and less than one-quarter linked criminal justice involvement to enhanced safety (Robinson 2005). Victims of IPV are negotiating a complex and ill-suited system that often does not fully recognize that their decisions may stem from an understandable desire to preserve what they value in their relationships. This does not mean that all victims want to stay with their perpetrators, but it is unhelpful fantasy to ignore that some victims will want to continue their relationships. Furthermore, when children are involved, it is likely that many victims will expect that a relationship with the perpetrator will need to continue, even if it changes form. Trying to manage this concern can put victims at odds with the criminal justice system and the demands that are placed upon participants in a criminal case.

Early US research illustrated the frequent disconnect between the goals of victims and those of the criminal justice system, revealing that women called the police to help them manage the violence against them, but after this immediate goal was satisfied, they often disengaged from the system (e.g., dropped the charges) (Ford 1991). Research from many countries has subsequently reinforced this observation, showing that the decisions of victims to stop participating in the investigation or to withdraw participation from the prosecution are taken in the context of a range of pressures, many of which derive from the actions of perpetrators, including: Fear of the perpetrator and/or repercussions from his family, her own family and/or the community; the extent and nature of her injuries; fear of damaging family status and honour; social isolation; fear of losing children; a lack of information about and fear of criminal and civil processes, particularly for women who do not speak or read the dominant language; lack of information about, and delays to, the progress of their case; whether the defendant offers an initial plea of guilty; changes to bail conditions; and immigration status (Holder, 2006; Robinson and Cook 2006). Many of these concerns are not under the direct control of criminal justice employees, yet they are directly relevant to the victims, and therefore rightly inform their attempts to keep themselves and their children safe.

Safety must be central to the development of criminal justice interventions, and new policies and practices must be aligned with protection measures that assist in keeping victims safe (Robinson 2008; Römkens 2006). Otherwise, the law, as well as criminal justice policies and practices, will be seen to be paternalistic, unhelpful, or even dangerous if it overrides a victim's autonomy, ignores her support needs, or conflicts with what she wishes to achieve from criminal justice (Hester 2009; Mills 2003). Exposure to criminal justice policies and procedures that negate or undermine women's safety is counterproductive, to put it mildly. Instead, victims want to have their stories listened to and believed by respectful and well-trained professionals; they want to receive timely information about the progression of their case; and they want the violence/abuse to cease (Cook *et al.* 2004). Research shows that more empowering experiences in the court predicted improvement in depression and quality of life, in addition to stronger intention to use the system in the future if needed (Cattaneo and Goodman 2010). Although issues related to court *outcomes*, such as case disposition and enforcement, have been shown to be important to victims' evaluations of helpfulness, they more frequently mentioned court *processes*, including treatment by staff, process length, and public disclosure (Bell *et al.* 2011). Listening to victims indicates that there may be important benefits from the criminalization of IPV that have less to do with the hard measures of success traditionally sought after (e.g., arrests, convictions) and more to do with approaches that give victims a "voice" and respond to their needs as individuals.

Do you want to prevent crimes?

> It is better to prevent crimes than to punish them. This is the ultimate end of every good legislation . . . Do you want to prevent crimes? . . . the surest but most difficult way to prevent crimes is by perfecting education . . . .
>
> (Beccaria 1764: 15)

Although Cesare Beccaria was not writing about IPV specifically, and he was writing more than 200 years ago, his reflection is relevant here. He suggested several methods to achieve crime prevention, including: The implementation of clear and simple laws; the accompaniment of liberty with enlightenment; hiring a scrupulous magistracy; rewarding virtue; and perfecting education. Regardless of our preferred method to prevent crime, Beccaria's advice reminds us that violence is not inevitable and we should try to not only respond effectively to it when it does happen, but to also try to prevent it happening in the first place.

Policy decisions about how to prevent, or respond to, IPV can be understood as a discourse about its underlying causes. Favoring a criminal justice approach implies that individual or situational explanations are more valid, whereas those calling for more prevention, awareness raising, and education are implying that a structural, societal explanation is at the root of IPV. An over-reliance on criminal justice policies and procedures can be seen to be problematic because it obfuscates the "underlying social, legal, and political structures that underpin male privilege and use of violence" (Miller and Meloy 2006: 108).

In spite, or perhaps because of, the surge of attention given to criminal justice approaches over the past two decades, today there is a call for more preventive approaches to IPV. Such approaches may include education in schools on "healthy relationships," public awareness campaigns, and stricter controls over forms of media that influence young people's attitudes toward sex and relationships.

Criminal justice policies and practices should only ever be considered one part of a wider social response to IPV that must also include community-based, rehabilitative, and preventative strategies (Lewis 2004). It would be foolish to argue against efforts to achieve primary prevention, as this is a noble goal. Unfortunately, however, we are not very far down the track to understanding which interventions successfully prevent IPV, be they criminal justice or other types of interventions.

Correcting the imbalance

> It is time to correct the imbalance between the criminal justice response and other responses to intimate partner violence.
>
> (Peterson 2008: 542)

Several serious dilemmas that confront criminal justice approaches to IPV have been discussed in this chapter. The problems associated with "governing through crime" are worrying and the specific case of IPV is not exempt from them. Perhaps most notable is that, at this time, we cannot conclusively demonstrate that criminal justice approaches are effective interventions for reducing IPV. The state of our scientific knowledge is poor, although it is growing and improving year-on-year. The evidence we do possess is often based on official data (with its inherent biases) and is heavily focused on criminal justice as it is practiced in the US. It is a small relief that most research suggests that there is no effect, rather than a harmful effect, from contemporary criminal justice policies and practices. Given this state of affairs, the importance of developing, testing, and funding other types of interventions that have different outcome measures (e.g., reducing harm rather than crime reduction, increasing health and well-being, rather than increasing arrest rates) cannot be overstated. We need to correct the imbalance while continuing to refine and improve criminal justice approaches to IPV.

Note

1 Also see Salomon (this volume) for a discussion on victim lawyers in Norway.

References

Beccaria, C. (1764) 'On crimes and punishments' from *On Crimes and Punishments*, New York: Bobbs-Merrill, 8–19; 55–9; 62–4; 93–9; reprinted in E. McLaughlin and J. Muncie (eds.), *Criminological Perspectives: Essential Readings*, London: Sage, 5–15.

Bell, M.E., Perez, S., Goodman, L.A. and Dutton, M.A. (2011) 'Battered women's perceptions of civil and criminal court helpfulness: the role of court outcome and process', *Violence Against Women*, 17: 71–88.

Bourlet, A. (1990) *Police Intervention in Marital Violence*, Milton Keynes: Open University Press.

Britton, A. (2012) 'Intimate violence', in K. Smith (ed.), *Homicides, Firearm Offences, and Intimate Violence*, London: Home Office, Suppl. Vol. 2, 83–115.

Buzawa, E.S., Buzawa, C.G. and Stark, E. (2012) *Responding to Domestic Violence: The Integration of Criminal Justice and Human Services*, 4th edn., Los Angeles, CA: Sage.

CAADA, Co-ordinated Action Against Domestic Abuse (2012) *Insights into domestic violence prosecutions*. Online. Available at www.caada.org.uk/policy/IDVA_Insights_Into_domestic_violence_prosecutions_final_executive_summary.pdf (accessed 25 May 2014).

Cattaneo, L.B. and Goodman, L.A. (2010) 'Through the lens of therapeutic jurisprudence: the relationship between empowerment in the court system and well-being for intimate partner violence victims', *Journal of Interpersonal Violence*, 25: 481–502.

Cissner, A.B., Labriorla, M. and Rempel, M. (2013) *Testing the Effects of New York's Domestic Violence Courts: A Statewide Impact Evaluation*, New York: Center for Court Innovation.

Cook, D., Burton, M., Robinson, A.L. and Vallely, C. (2004) *Evaluation of Specialist Domestic Violence Courts/Fast Track Systems*, London: Crown Prosecution Service and Department of Constitutional Affairs.

Dobash, R.E. (2003) 'Domestic violence: arrest, prosecution and reducing violence', *Criminology & Public Policy*, 2: 313–18.

Ford, D.A. (1991) 'Prosecution as a victim power resource: a note on empowering women in violent conjugal relationships', *Law and Society Review*, 25: 313–34.

Garland, D. (2001) *The Culture of Control: Crime and Social Order in Contemporary Society*. London: Oxford University Press.

Garner, J.H., Fagan, J. and Maxwell, C.D. (1995) 'Published findings from the spouse assault replication program: a critical review', *Journal of Quantitative Criminology*, 11: 3–28.

Hester, M. (2009) 'The contradictory legal worlds faced by domestic violence victims', in E. Stark and E.S. Buzawa (eds.), *Violence Against Women in Families and Relationships* (vol. 2), Santa Barbara, CA: Praeger, 127–46.

Holder, R. (2006) 'The emperor's new clothes: justice and court initiatives on family violence', *Australian Journal of Judicial Administration*, 16: 30–47.

Kingsnorth, R. (2006) 'Intimate partner violence: predictors of recidivism in a sample of arrestees', *Violence against Women*, 12: 917–35.

Lewis, R. (2004) 'Making justice work: effective legal interventions for domestic violence', *British Journal of Criminology*, 44: 204–24.

Lewis, R., Dobash, R.P., Dobash, R.E. and Cavanagh, K. (2000) 'Protection, prevention, rehabilitation or justice? Women's use of the law to challenge domestic violence', *International Review of Victimology*, 7: 179–205.

MacDonald, Z. (2002) 'Official crime statistics: their use and interpretation', *The Economic Journal*, 112: 85–106.

Maguire, M. (2012) 'Crime statistics and the construction of crime', in M. Maguire, R. Morgan and R. Reiner (eds.), *The Oxford Handbook of Criminology* (5th edition), Oxford: Clarendon Press, 206–44.

Manning, P.K. (1993) 'The preventive conceit: the black box in market context', *American Behavioral Scientist*, 36: 639–50.

Maxwell, C.D. and Garner, J.H. (2012) 'The crime control effects of criminal sanctions for intimate partner violence', *Partner Abuse*, 3: 469–500.

Maxwell, C.D. and Robinson, A.L. (2013) 'Can interventions reduce recidivism and revictimization following adult intimate partner violence incidents?' in *The Evidence for Violence Prevention Across the Lifespan and Around the World: Workshop Summary*, Washington, DC: National Academies Press, 15–23.

Maxwell, C.D., Garner, J.H. and Fagan, J. (2002) 'The preventive effects of arrest on intimate partner violence: research, policy and theory', *Criminology & Public Policy*, 2: 51–80.

Miller, S. and Meloy, M.L. (2006) 'Women's use of force: voices of women arrested for domestic violence', *Violence Against Women*, 12: 89–115.

Mills, L.G. (2003) *Insult to Injury: Rethinking our Responses to Intimate Abuse*, Princeton, NJ: Princeton University Press.

Nelson, E.L. (2013) 'Police controlled antecedents which significantly elevate prosecution and conviction rates in domestic violence cases', *Criminology & Criminal Jusice*, 13: 526–51.

Peterson, R.R. (2008) 'Reducing intimate partner violence: moving beyond criminal justice interventions', *Criminology & Public Policy*, 7: 537–45.

Quetelet, A. (1842) 'Of the development of the propensity to crime' in *A Treatise on Man*, Edinburgh: Chambers, 82–96, 103–8; reprinted in E. McLaughlin and J. Muncie (eds.) (2013) *Criminological Perspectives: Essential Readings*, London: Sage, 23–39.

Robinson, A.L. (2008) 'Measuring what matters in specialist domestic violence courts', in *Ten Years of Austrian Anti-Violence Legislation*, Vienna: Federal Minister for Women and Civil Service, 227–34.

Robinson A.L. (2005) *The Cardiff Women's Safety Unit: Understanding the Costs and Consequences of Domestic Violence, School of Social Sciences*: Cardiff University.

Robinson, A.L. and Cook, D. (2006) 'Understanding victim retraction in cases of domestic violence: specialist courts, government policy, and victim-centred justice', *Contemporary Justice Review*, 9: 189–213.

Römkens, R. (2006) 'Protecting prosecution: Exploring the powers of law in an intervention program for domestic violence', *Violence Against Women*, 12: 160–86.

Simon, J. (1997) 'Governing through crime', in L. Friedman and G. Fisher (eds.), *The Crime Conundrum*, Boulder, CO: Westview, 171–89.

Skogan, W.G. (1977) 'Dimensions of the dark figure of unreported crime', *Crime & Delinquency*, 23: 41–50.

Sloan, F. A., Platt, A.C., Chepke, L.M. and Blevins, C.E. (2013) 'Deterring domestic violence: do criminal sanctions reduce repeat offenses?' *Journal of Risk and Uncertainty*, 46: 51–80.

Stark, E. (2007) *Coercive Control: How Men Entrap Women in Personal Life*, New York: Oxford University Press.

Visher, C. A., Harrell, A., Newmark, L. and Yahner, J. (2008) 'Reducing intimate partner violence: an evaluation of a comprehensive justice system–community collaboration', *Criminology & Public Policy,* 7: 495–523.

Walklate, S. (2007) *Imagining the Victim of Crime*, Maidenhead: Open University Press.

Young, J. (2004) 'Voodoo criminology and the numbers game', in J. Ferrell, K. Hayward, W. Morrison and M. Presdee (eds.), *Cultural Criminology Unleashed*, London: GlassHouse Press, 13–28.

Chapter 6

Perils of using law

A critique of protection orders to respond to intimate partner violence

Heather Douglas and Heather Nancarrow

Since the 1980s, the predominant legal response to intimate partner violence (IPV) in most Australian states and territories has been a court order under civil "domestic" or "family" violence laws. These laws vary among states and territories, including the terminology used, the definitions of violence (types of behaviors), and the types of relationships covered. Laws in all jurisdictions include intimate partner relationships, and therefore address IPV. Where possible we use the term IPV; however, at times we use the term "domestic violence" or "family violence," such as when referring to specific legislative reforms or reviews.

Regardless of the differences in terminology and definitions, the civil laws in the various states and territories operate in essentially the same way. An application for an order, which we refer to as a "domestic violence order" (DVO), is considered by the court and determined on the civil law standard of proof (the balance of probabilities). A DVO includes a standard condition requiring the perpetrator to refrain from committing domestic violence (DV). It may include other conditions requested by an applicant, such as not being able to enter specified premises, or to have no contact at all with the person for whose protection the order is made. A breach of a civil order is a criminal offense, regardless of the nature of the breach, and the criminal standard of proof (beyond reasonable doubt) is required for a conviction. Penalties for a breach include fines and/or imprisonment.

Civil DV laws were intended, primarily, to protect women from men's violence (Nancarrow forthcoming). In principle, the criminal law had always been available to women physically assaulted, or whose property had been damaged, by their male partners but it had seldom been used in practice. In part, this can be attributed to prevailing attitudes that minimize DV as a private matter (Douglas 2008). However, there are other inter-related barriers to using the criminal law for DV, leaving a gap which the civil laws aimed to fill.

Many women report they want the violence, but not the relationship, to end and they worry about the impact of a criminal charge on their families (ALRC/NSWLRC 2010: 834). Victims may be too scared to pursue criminal charges and, if they do, their testimony may seem weak against that of a coercive, controlling perpetrator (Douglas 2012). There are often no other witnesses to corroborate the victim's account and the nature of the violence inflicted may leave no visible injury. Further, the criminal law is focused on punishing past behavior. To address these barriers, the civil DV laws include exceptional powers for police, removing the burden of pursuing a court order from the victim. Police have the power to (and in some cases, such as Queensland, must) investigate suspected DV and they may apply for a DVO, regardless of the wishes of the victim. Police may also detain a person in custody for several hours, without a charge, to ensure the victim's safety while an application for a DVO is made. Finally, civil DVOs are intended to be used in conjunction with, not instead of, the criminal law where possible.

In this chapter we reflect on Australia's civil law response to IPV and the challenges it has faced in fulfilling its original intention. We pay particular attention to issues facing Indigenous Australian women, who have called for both increased policing and greater attention to alternative forms of justice (Robertson 2000). These apparently conflicting positions reflect Indigenous women's simultaneous experiences of gendered and racialized oppression. They want swift and authoritative intervention to violence perpetrated on them by men; yet they are concerned by the rapidly increasing over-representation of Indigenous men (and women) in the criminal justice system, and the limitations of the colonizing state in representing the interests of Indigenous peoples (Nancarrow 2006, 2010).

Unintended consequences

In this section we consider three of the unintended consequences associated with the introduction and application of DVOs. The first is that the civil DVO system may have trumped the use and relevance of the criminal law as a response to IPV. Second, we consider cross-DVOs where both intimate partners obtain a DVO against each other, and the implications for women's safety and men's accountability for violence in this context. Finally, we consider the implications of police charging the minor offense of a DVO breach rather than assault or criminal damage, for example, when such an offense has occurred and a DVO is in place. We draw on the findings of recent Australian studies to consider some aspects of secondary victimization that continue to arise as a result of this approach.

Civil interventions have trumped criminal prosecution

The introduction of DVOs was not intended to exclude criminal prosecution from the range of legal responses (Egger and Stubbs 1993). Research has suggested, however, that where there is a report made to police about IPV, the standard police response is to support one of the parties to obtain a DVO or to apply for a DVO on behalf of one of the parties. Douglas and Godden (2003) inspected 694 Queensland court files that included applications for DVOs and in only three (0.4 percent) of these files was there prosecution of a criminal matter. This research concluded that civil IPV legislation essentially trumped the operation of the criminal law, leading in effect to the decriminalization of IPV.

DV workers interviewed as part of Douglas and Godden's study (2003) suggested a range of reasons for lack of criminal prosecution and police investigation, including that: Women lack information about the possibility of pursuing a DVO and criminal prosecution concurrently; women feared retribution and further relationship breakdown from pursuing criminal prosecution; and women were uncomfortable about police involvement and court processes and were skeptical about the possibility of appropriate sentencing outcomes.

In a second study, over 50 percent of police officers surveyed in Queensland in 2005 accepted that an important factor influencing their decision not to prosecute was that "a protection order is a better alternative to criminal prosecution" (CMC 2005: 49). Other factors such as lack of serious injury (34 percent of respondents) and lack of involvement of a weapon (20 percent of respondents) were also important in the decision not to prosecute a criminal offense. Police use of civil DVOs as an alternative, rather than in addition to criminal prosecution appears to continue to be a common experience in several Australian jurisdictions, even though this approach is often in conflict with policy guidelines (ALRC/NSWLRC 2010: 354–5).

Advocacy for increased use of criminal justice sanctions represents a dilemma, however, for many Indigenous Australian women. This is due to the history of violence and subjugation perpetrated on Indigenous Australians in the process of colonization, largely effected through agents of the criminal justice system. As a solution to this dilemma, Queensland's Aboriginal and Torres Strait Islander Women's Taskforce on Violence (ATSWTFV 2000), an investigation conducted entirely by Indigenous women, recommended restorative justice as an alternative to the formal criminal justice system. In contrast, a simultaneous mainstream investigation of the criminal law response to violence against women, including IPV, recommended that restorative justice approaches must never be used instead of the formal criminal justice system (OWP 2000).

Considering the results of the two task force investigations, Nancarrow's research (2006, 2010) revealed several interrelated factors in Indigenous women's stated preference for restorative justice as the primary response to IPV. Significantly, Indigenous women understood civil DVOs as part of the criminal justice system because of the central role of police in the application and enforcement of orders. Their justice objectives differed from those of non-Indigenous women, emphasizing rehabilitation and restoration of relationships between the offender and the victim/s, and the offender and the broader community; they also identified that criminal justice system intervention resulted in more, not less, violence (Nancarrow 2006, 2010). Concern about increased violence as a result of criminal justice system intervention included: escalated violence by the perpetrator; assault and/or ostracization by broader family, kinship, and community members; and concern for the perpetrator being victimized by, and within, the criminal justice system. Making IPV a public problem through the mainstream criminal justice system reflects not only "an incomplete analysis of the relationship between battered women and the state" (Coker 2002: 132), but a lack of cultural competence. Indigenous women's struggles for freedom from gender oppression occur within a larger context of freedom from racialized oppression. Indigenous women seek ways of holding Indigenous men accountable for violence that unify rather than split Indigenous communities along gender lines, and for those in Nancarrow's (2006, 2010) research, this could be achieved through community-controlled processes as a more appropriate, and effective, "public" realm.

Cross-domestic violence orders

In the vast majority of cases of IPV, applications for DVOs are lodged by or on behalf of one partner (typically a woman) against the other (typically a man) (Douglas and Fitzgerald 2013: 57). However, in a smaller, but substantial, proportion of cases DVOs are sought by, or for, both partners and may result in cross-DVOs being made by a court. In relation to intimate heterosexual relationships, the occurrence of cross-DVOs in some Australian jurisdictions has risen in recent years. Between 5 and 11 percent of orders in one study in New South Wales were cross-DVOs (Wangmann 2010: 957), and a Queensland study found that 16 percent of all DVOs were cross-DVOs (Douglas and Fitzgerald 2013: 73). While some cross-applications may be genuine, in that each party faces a threat of continued violence and both parties are equally in need of protection from each other, concerns have been raised that this may not be the case in a significant proportion of cases (ALRC/NSWLRC 2010: 877–82).

Research suggests that male respondents to a DVO application might make a counter-application as a form of intimidation (Wangmann 2010: 967), and that cross-applications may be used by men as a tactic or bargaining tool to achieve mutual withdrawal of a DVO application (ALRC/NSWLRC 2010: 877). Support workers in the IPV field have argued that reactive cross-applications may disproportionately affect female IPV victims, whose earlier claims for protection can be trivialized or even silenced in the event of a cross-DVO (Douglas and Fitzgerald 2013).

In the Australian context, the rise in cross-DVOs may be an unintended consequence of the introduction of a presumption of "equal shared parental responsibility" in the Family Law Act 1975 (Cth) (FLA). It is notable that this presumption does not apply where a parent has engaged in family violence (Rhodes 2008). Thus there may be a perceived benefit for a perpetrator to apply for a cross-DVO as a way of neutralizing a claim of IPV (ALRC/NSWLRC 2010: 828, 878). Alongside the "equal shared parental responsibility" presumption, the FLA directs a judge who is making a decision regarding a child's best interests to consider any DVO that involves the child or a member of the child's family, including whether the DVO is final and whether it was contested (Chisholm 2011). Research both in the United States and Australia has identified the manipulative use of DVOs as "strategic ploys" to gain advantage in the family court (Chisholm 2011: 84; Muller *et al.* 2009: 627). Parkinson, Cashmore, and Webster (2010: 313) interviewed family lawyers and found that interviewees generally believed that, in some situations, DVOs were used for tactical advantage in family court proceedings and immigration issues.

A breach of a condition of a cross-DVO can be difficult to enforce because it may be more challenging for police to identify the party in need of protection. Indeed, the existence of a cross-DVO may provide a disincentive to the vulnerable party to alert police of any breach, further diminishing their protectiveness (Wangmann 2010: 967). Alternatively, both parties are put at risk of prosecution of a breach charge (ALRC/NSWLRC 2010: 371). Based on her analysis of a sample of 185 people charged with breaches of DVOs and dealt with at either one of two north Queensland courts between 2000 and 2012, Nancarrow (forthcoming) identified that Indigenous women are particularly vulnerable to this risk. Her analysis reveals that 80 percent of the Indigenous women were subject to cross-DVOs, compared to 62 percent of the non-Indigenous women and less than half of the Indigenous and non-Indigenous men (42 percent and 43 percent, respectively).

Breaches of domestic violence orders

Throughout Australia, breach of a DVO is a criminal offense, although it is a "summary offense," a classification reserved for the least serious offenses such as offensive language and urinating in public. Breach charges are targeted to the breach of conditions of the DVO and a standard condition requires the respondent to be of good behavior; therefore, any criminal offending may be understood as a breach of the DVO. Maximum penalties for breach of a DVO vary widely among Australian jurisdictions but all provide the option of imprisonment. In many cases where a breach charge is pursued the offending behavior may be quite serious (ALRC/NSWLRC 2010).

In a Queensland study involving 350 breach charges, police identified the offending behavior as assault in 55 percent of cases, but only charged assault alongside the breach in 5 percent of cases. Police identified criminal damage in 33 percent of cases, but only charged criminal damage alongside breach in 3 percent of cases, and they identified stalking in 17 percent of cases but did not charge stalking in any of the cases (Douglas 2008: 450). While in some cases there may be reasons to explain the prosecution of a breach charge in preference to a more serious criminal offense (such as charge negotiation and sufficiency of evidence), there are practical and ideological ramifications for preferring a breach charge rather than a more serious criminal offense. Practical ramifications include: generally lower penalties; criminal histories showing a "breach" rather than the criminal behavior complained of (such as assault, damage, or stalking); and, because breach is a summary matter, criminal injuries compensation will be unavailable to the victim (Douglas 2008: 449). Properly naming women's harms is a well-recognized feminist strategy (Howe 1994). Thus, on an ideological level there is a risk that the choice of the lower-level breach charge in preference to a more serious criminal charge will be interpreted as trivializing or minimizing the harm.

Nancarrow (forthcoming) finds that compared to their non-Indigenous counterparts Indigenous men and women are significantly more likely to have a conviction recorded and are significantly less likely to be penalized with a fine for a first breach offense. However, in general, fines are the most common sentencing response to breach charges and in a significant proportion of cases no conviction is recorded (ALRC/NSWLRC 2010: 544). Fines are an inappropriate response for offenses related to IPV. They often fail to have an impact on the offender because, in a controlling relationship, the victim may ultimately pay the fine or otherwise suffer the impact of it being paid (ALRC/NSWLRC 2010: 478). Other concerns include offenders redirecting income toward paying a fine that may have been previously assigned for child support payments or threatening or using further violence to pressure the victim to pay the fine (Douglas 2008: 465). Victims usually want to see a penalty imposed that reflects the seriousness of the offense but also provides support for behavior change (Douglas and Godden 2003). Ultimately the imposition of fines and the decision not to record a conviction may reflect magistrates' lack of understanding of the context of IPV and may contribute to a perception that a breach of a DVO is a trivial offense, even where the behavior complained of is an assault or stalking. In essence, such responses from police in relation to the decision to charge, and from magistrates in the choice of sentence, may operate as a form of secondary victimization.

Current innovations and future directions

Legislative reforms to better define intimate partner violence

Definitions of and approaches to "domestic" or "family" violence, which include IPV, vary across different areas of law, even within Australian states and territories. In response to the blueprint for Australia's National Plan to Reduce Violence against Women and their Children 2010–2022 (NCRVAWC 2009), the Australian Government commissioned an extensive review aimed at harmonizing relevant state, territory, and federal laws to ensure the safety of women and children was not compromised in the interaction of DV, child protection, and family law processes. The review, conducted by the Australian and New South Wales Law Reform Commissions (2010), recommended that state and territory legislation include: guiding principles that expressly locate DV within a human rights framework; provisions that explain the gendered nature and dynamics of DV, particularly vulnerable groups; and a common definition that contextualizes and lists, but does not limit, the range of physical and non-physical behaviors that may constitute DV.

Specifically, the commissions recommended that definitions contextualize DV as "violent or threatening behaviour, or any other form of behaviour that coerces or controls a family member or causes that family member to be fearful" (ALRC/NSWLRC 2010: 246). In 2012, the federal Family Law Act 1975 adopted this definition. The commissions argued that contextualizing DV in this way includes behavior that might otherwise seem harmless and excludes behavior that may be committed in other contexts that does not constitute coercive control, or engenders fear, such as incident-based conflicts and resistance to coercive control (ALRC/NSWLRC 2010: 235). Such a definition in state DV laws, guided by the principles and provisions recommended by the commissions, has the potential to significantly reduce the incidence of cross-DVOs.

Victoria and Queensland have subsequently changed their definitions of violence but have taken a different approach to that recommended by the two commissions. In those jurisdictions, coercion, control, and engendering fear are relegated to particular forms of abuse, rather than the overarching context for any behavior that would constitute DV where coercive control is also present. Discrete or defensive acts by either party could, therefore, be construed as DV, so the problem of cross-DVOs is not directly addressed. However, the definition in both states' legislation is to be read in conjunction with guiding principles, consistent with those recommended by the commissions. Both also make provision for the court to consider DVO applications together. In addition, Queensland's guiding principles include identifying the person "most in need of protection" in cases of competing claims.

Responding directly to concerns that the civil DVO system has rendered the criminal law irrelevant to IPV, Queensland's guiding principles also include that "a civil response under this Act should operate in conjunction with, not instead of, the criminal law." Further research is required to assess the effects of these innovations, responding to unintended consequences of the civil DVO system.

Major policy changes

Gendered harm—emergence of typology literature

Claims of gender symmetry in IPV have been the subject of debate for decades. Some (e.g., Dutton 2006; Straus 2010) argue that men and women almost equally perpetrate acts of physical violence to resolve conflict in intimate relationships, while others (e.g., Dobash and Dobash 2004; Dragiewicz and DeKeseredy 2012) argue that when context is considered, it is nearly always men abusing their female partners. The competing claims could be summarized as concern with incident-based violence where the motivation is conflict resolution, versus concern with an ongoing pattern of coercive controlling behaviors where the context is gender inequality, and control over the life of the other party is the motivation. Proponents of both sides of the argument recognize that women are more often harmed, and suffer greater harm, regardless of the context and motivation.

Efforts to reconcile the gender symmetry debate include the creation of an IPV typology by Michael Johnson and colleagues (e.g., Johnson 1995; Kelly & Johnson 2008) based on the presence or absence of coercive control as the motivation for the violence. The typology is contested on the basis it oversimplifies a complex issue; is open to misinterpretation with serious risks for safety; and that the research on which the typology is based cannot illuminate the context or motivation for violence (e.g., Dragiewicz and DeKeseredy 2012; Wangmann 2010). It appears, however, to have gained traction in Australia. While advocating that definitions of "family violence" incorporate the concept of coercive control, as discussed above, the Australian and New South Wales Law Reform Commissions concluded that "it is inappropriate for such typologies to be translated into legislative frameworks" (2010: 284), although in some cases it may be appropriate to receive expert evidence about typologies of violence to assist with the exercise of judicial discretion. Nevertheless, as highlighted by Rathus (2013), the Family Law Court promotes differentiation of IPV by type as best practice and it seems inevitable that the new definition of "family violence" in the FLA is likely to be conflated with the typologies. DVOs are frequently used in the Family Law Court to support claims of IPV and, as noted above, there is a perception among family law practitioners that DVOs are used for tactical purposes (Parkinson *et al.* 2010: 313). It is therefore likely that police and courts dealing with IPV under state and territory laws will increasingly attempt to discern the type of violence they are dealing with. If this approach is used in the context of DVOs there is a risk that many IPV incidents will be understood as a form of conflict resolution rather than as coercive controlling violence. Prematurely adopting a typology approach to IPV, as well as accepting a proposition of gender symmetry, risks compromising safety and wasting resources through misguided policy and legislative reforms.

Civil vs. criminal responses

The need for an effective criminal response to IPV to operate alongside DVOs has been re-emphasized in current Australian debates. Recent feminist scholarship has questioned the relevance of criminal justice responses to IPV, particularly the development of "no-drop policies" and presumptive or mandatory arrest policies (Goodmark 2012). Indeed critical discussion has emerged from the perceptions of those working in the IPV field that some forms of criminal justice response may result in a loss of autonomy for victims of IPV and other unintended consequences such as increased arrest of women (Bailey 2010: 1255). A recent Australian report focused attention on improving the culture of those institutions where decisions are made about prosecution. It recommended improved police decision making and prosecutorial practice, through education and training, and emphasized the importance of integrated responses (ALRC/NSWLRC 2010: 77–8). In some states there have been efforts to address the concern that DVOs appear to be considered as an alternative option, rather than an addition, to criminal interventions. For example, some jurisdictions have experimented with the development of police and prosecutorial policies applicable to IPV to encourage, without mandating, higher levels of prosecution. In Victoria a new police code of practice introduced in 2004 states that police must pursue both criminal charges and DVOs where appropriate. It states that one of the four main functions police have in response to IPV is to investigate and identify criminal offenses (Victoria Police 2004: 2–3). This code of practice resulted in a significant increase in IPV assaults being prosecuted with no decrease in DVOs (Victoria Police 2011: 28). Tasmania family violence legislation emphasizes the criminal nature of IPV through the creation of additional offenses of "economic abuse" and "emotional abuse or intimidation" and provides for a presumption against bail (Family Violence Act 2004 (Tas) ss 8–9, 12). In the Northern Territory a prosecutorial guideline has been specifically developed for IPV cases. The guideline sets out the particular context of DV and confirms that "suitable prosecutions may proceed without the evidence of an unwilling victim" (NTDPP 2013: guideline 21.3).

Conclusion

Safety remains the core concern for legal responses to IPV, and DVOs are a central part of these responses. Recent policy and law reform efforts in Australia have continued to focus on civil protection orders as the key legal response to IPV. However, some unintended consequences have flowed from this approach and continue to cause concerns. First, at least in a practical sense, IPV has been largely decriminalized in Australian states, and further, cross-DVOs have continued to proliferate in some states. While an improved criminal justice response is considered to be important, Australian jurisdictions have generally been reluctant to introduce forms of mandatory criminal responses, preferring instead to try to change cultural attitudes and ultimately behaviors within institutions and the community. Developments in police policies and prosecution guidelines may help to ensure that criminal prosecution is properly considered in the IPV context. Changes to protection order legislation in Queensland that aim to ensure that those who are in need of protection are able to obtain DVOs may help to reduce the number of inappropriate cross-orders.

References

ALRC/NSWLRC, Australian Law Reform Commission and New South Wales Law Reform Commission (2010) *Family Violence—A National Legal Response: Final Report*, Canberra: Australian Law Reform Commission.

Australian Government (2009) *The National Plan to Reduce Violence Against Women: Immediate Government Actions*, Barton, ACT: Commonwealth of Australia.

Bailey, K. (2010) 'Lost in translation: domestic violence, "the personal is political" and the criminal justice system', *Journal of Criminal Law and Criminology*, 100: 1255–300.

Chisholm, R. (2011) 'The Family Law Violence Amendment of 2011: a progress report, featuring the debate about Family Violence Orders', *Australian Journal of Family Law*, 12: 79–95.

CMC, Crime and Misconduct Commission (2005) *Policing Domestic Violence in Queensland: Meeting the Challenges*, Brisbane: Crime and Misconduct Commission.

Coker, D. (2002) 'Transformative justice: anti-subordination practices in cases of domestic violence', in H. Strang and J. Braithwaite (eds.), *Restorative Justice and Family Violence*, Melbourne: Cambridge University Press, 128–52.

Dobash, R.E. and Dobash, R.P. (2004) 'Women's violence to men in intimate relationships: working on a puzzle', *British Journal of Criminology*, 44: 324–49.

Douglas, H. (2012) 'Battered women's experiences of the criminal justice system: decentring the law', *Feminist Legal Studies*, 20: 121–134.

Douglas, H. (2008) 'The criminal law's response to domestic violence: what's going on?', *Sydney Law Review*, 30: 439–69.

Douglas, H. and Fitzgerald, R. (2013) 'Legal processes and gendered violence: cross-applications for domestic violence protection orders', *UNSW Law Journal*, 36: 56–97.

Douglas, H. and Godden, L. (2003) 'The decriminalisation of domestic violence: examining the interaction between the criminal law and domestic violence', *Criminal Law Journal*, 27: 32–43.

Dragiewicz, M. and DeKeseredy, W.S. (2012) 'Claims about women's use of non-fatal force in intimate relationships: a contextual review of Canadian research', *Violence Against Women*, 18: 1008–26.

Dutton, D. G. (2006) *Rethinking Domestic Violence*, Vancouver: University of British Columbia Press.

Egger, S. and Stubbs, J. (1993) *The Effectiveness of Protection Orders in Australian Jurisdictions*, Canberra: Commonwealth of Australia.

Goodmark, L. (2012) *A Troubled Marriage: Domestic Violence and the Legal System*, New York: University Press.

Howe, A. (1994) 'The problem of privatised injuries: feminist strategies for litigation', in M. Fineman (ed.), *At the Boundaries of Law: Feminism and Legal Theory*, New York: Routledge, 148–67.

Johnson, M.P. (1995) 'Patriarchal terrorism and common couple violence: two forms of violence against women', *Journal of Marriage and Family*, 57: 283–94.

Kelly, J.B. and Johnson, M.P. (2008) 'Differentiation among types of intimate partner violence: research update and implications for interventions', *Family Court Review*, 46: 476–99.

Muller, H., Desmaris, S. and Hamel, J. (2009) 'Do judicial responses to restraining order requests discriminate against male victims of domestic violence?', *Journal of Family Violence*, 24: 625–37.

Nancarrow, H. (forthcoming) *Legal Responses to Initmate Partner Violence: Gendered Aspirations and Racialised Realities*, Brisbane: Griffith University.

Nancarrow, H. (2010) 'Restorative justice for domestic family violence: hopes and fears of Indigenous and non-Indigenous Australian women', in J. Ptacek (ed.), *Restorative Justice and Violence Against Women*, New York: Oxford University Press.

Nancarrow, H. (2006) 'In search of justice for domestic and family violence: Indigenous and non-Indigenous Australian women's perspectives', *Theoretical Criminology*, 10: 87–106.

NCRVAWC, National Council to Reduce Violence against Women and Their Children. (2009) *Time for Action: The National Council's Plan for Australia to Reduce Violence Against Women and Their Children*, Canberra: Commonwealth of Australia.

NTDPP, Northern Territory Office of the Director of Public Prosecutions (2013) *Guidelines*. Online. Available at www.nt.gov.au/justice/dpp/html/guidelines/domestic_violence.shtml (accessed 25 May 2014).

Office of the Status of Women (1995) *Community Attitudes to Violence Against Women: Detailed Report*, Canberra: Department of Prime Minister and Cabinet.

OWP, Office of Women's Policy (2000) *Report of the Taskforce on Women and the Criminal Code*, Brisbane: Queensland Government.

Parkinson, P., Cashmore, J. and Webster, A. (2010) 'The views of family lawyers on apprehended violence orders after parental separation', *Australian Journal of Family Law*, 24: 313–36.

Rathus, Z. (2013) 'Shifting language and meaning between social science and the law', *UNSW Law Journal*, 36: 358–89.

Rhodes, H. (2008) 'The Dangers of shared care legislation: why Australia needs (yet more) family law reform', *Federal Law Review*, 36: 279–99.

Robertson, B. (2000) *The Aboriginal and Torres Strait Islander Women's Task Force on Violence Report*, Brisbane: Queensland Government.

Sentencing Advisory Council (2008) *Sentencing Practices for Breach of Family Violence Intervention Orders: Final Report*, Melbourne: Sentencing Advisory Council.

Straus, M.A. (2010) 'Thirty years of denying the evidence on gender symmetry in partner violence: implications for prevention and treatment', *Partner Abuse*, 1: 332–61.

Victoria Police (2011) *Crime Statistics 2010–2011*. Online. Available at www.police.vic.gov.au/content.asp?Document_ID=40111 (accessed 25 May 2014).

Victoria Police (2004) *Code of Practice for the Investigation of Family Violence: Supporting an Integrated Response to Family Violence in Victoria*. Online. Available at: www.police.vic.gov.au/files/documents/464_FV_COP.pdf (accessed 25 May 2014).

Wangmann, J. (2010) 'Gender and intimate partner violence: a case study from NSW', *University of New South Wales Law Journal*, 33: 945–69.

Section II: Justice system responses to intimate partner violence

Questions for critical thought

1. How could victims' preferences be better incorporated into decisions made by police and prosecutors?
2. Do you think psychological abuse should be included in a criminal code definition of intimate partner violence? Explain your rationale.
3. Investigate how the criminal and civil legal systems respond to intimate partner violence in your locale. What are the strengths and limitations of using these two branches of law? How could they work together to improve women's safety? Provide examples of your ideas.
4. Should there be intimate partner violence responses tailored to specific populations, such as Indigenous people? If so, describe the features these responses should contain.

Further reading

Buzawa, E.S., Buzawa, C.G., and Stark, E. (2012) *Responding to Domestic Violence: The Integration of Criminal Justice and Human Services*, 4th edn., Thousand Oaks, CA: Sage.

Institute of Medicine and National Research Council (2014) *The Evidence for Violence Prevention Across the Lifespan and Around the World: Workshop Summary*, Washington, DC: The National Academies Press.

Mills, L.G. (2003) *Insult to Injury: Rethinking our Responses to Intimate Abuse*, Princeton, NJ: Princeton University Press.

Miller, S.L. and Iovanni, L. (2013) 'Using restorative justice for gendered violence: Success with a postconviction model', *Feminist Criminology*, 8: 247–68.

Ptacek, J. and Frederick, L. (2009, January). *Restorative Justice and Intimate Partner Violence*, Harrisburg, PA: VAWnet, a project of the National Resource Center on Domestic Violence. Online. Available at: www.vawnet.org (accessed 25 May 2014).

Walklate, S. (2007) *Imagining the Victim of Crime*, Maidenhead: Open University Press.

Websites

Australian Government, The National Plan to Reduce Violence against Women and Their Children: A framework of action over several years to bring attitudinal and behavioral change at the cultural, institutional, and individual levels, with a particular focus on young people.

www.dss.gov.au/our-responsibilities/women/programs-services/reducing-violence/the-national-plan-to-reduce-violence-against-women and their-children

Australia's National Research Organisation for Women's Safety Ltd (ANROWS): An independent, not-for-profit company established as an initiative under Australia's National Plan to Reduce Violence against Women and their Children 2010-2022.
http://anrows.org.au

Canadian Domestic Homicide Prevention Initiative: A domestic violence death review brings together community agencies, service providers, and government representatives with expertise in domestic violence to investigate and review deaths that occur in the context of domestic violence. The purpose is to create recommendations aimed at preventing deaths in similar circumstances and reducing domestic violence in general.
www.learningtoendabuse.ca/cdhpi

Centre for the Study of Legal and Social Responses to Violence: Various projects that seek to build knowledge and contribute to society's understanding about violence and efforts to reduce and prevent violence, with emphasis on the study of various forms of violence against women for which there is growing recognition that collaborative, multi-sector responses are required if prevention initiatives are to be effective.
www.violenceresearch.ca

SECTION III

Justice system responses to sexual violence

Learning objectives

In reading this section, you will be able to:

1. Explain why few sexually assaulted women report to police, and discuss the legal and non-legal factors that lead police and prosecutors to dismiss large numbers of cases.
2. Understand how and why validation of their experiences can be beneficial for victims' healing and empowerment, regardless of the outcome of criminal proceedings in sexual assault cases.
3. Recognize why, in the absence of widespread social and economic changes, legal responses are an ineffective means to reduce sexual violence or deter perpetrators.
4. Explain how legal representation and advocacy throughout the criminal justice process provides women with better information on which to make decisions.
5. Identify barriers that limit the effectiveness of recent police changes and court reform measures.
6. Define the concept of victim empowerment and understand its application to sexual assault.

Chapter 7

Policing and prosecuting sexual assault

Assessing the pathways to justice

Cassia Spohn, Katharine Tellis, and Eryn Nicole O'Neal

In June 2010, the *Baltimore Sun* reported that the Baltimore Police Department led the country in the percentage of rape cases that were deemed to be false or baseless and thus were unfounded. According to the report, from 2004 through 2009 about a third of the rapes reported to the police department were unfounded, a rate three times the national average. Also in June 2010, the *New York Times* reported that New York Police Commissioner Raymond W. Kelly had appointed a task force to look into the handling of rape complaints and to recommend new training protocols for dealing with victims of sexual assault. The review was prompted by complaints from rape victims, who said that their allegations of sexual assault were unfounded or downgraded to misdemeanors. These news stories—along with others regarding the mishandling of rape cases in Milwaukee, Cleveland, New Orleans, and Philadelphia—culminated in a 2010 United States Senate Hearing convened by Senator Arlen Specter to examine the systematic failure to investigate and prosecute rape on the part of police departments and prosecutors' offices nationwide.

More than three decades after the inception of the rape laws reform movement in many countries around the world—which saw significant changes to the definition of rape, the elimination of resistance and corroboration requirements, and the enactment of rape shield laws—the response of the criminal justice system to the crime of sexual assault remains problematic. Victims are reluctant to report the crime to the police and, when they do, they are often met with skepticism and suspicion on the part of police and prosecutors. This results in a substantial number of cases classified as unfounded, a low arrest rate, and shockingly low rates of prosecution and conviction. In this chapter, we provide an overview of the response of the criminal justice system to the crime of sexual assault. We focus on decision making by police and prosecutors, who serve as the "gatekeepers" (Kerstetter 1990) of the system and whose decisions determine whether the case will proceed through the criminal justice process.

Sexual assault reporting and case attrition

There is compelling evidence that sexual assault is a seriously underreported crime worldwide. The National Violence Against Women Survey in the US found that only 19 percent of women who were raped since their 18th birthday reported the crime; a similar survey in Canada found that only 6 percent of sexual assaults were reported to the police (Du Mont *et al.* 2003; Tjaden and Thoennes 2006). The International Violence Against Women Survey, a project created to facilitate international comparisons, found that, in all countries, victimized women often kept violence to themselves, only seeking formal help when the incident was considered serious or life-threatening (Johnson *et al.* 2008). Reasons that victims give for not reporting included: fear of retaliation from the rapist; feelings of shame and embarrassment; a belief that the rape was a minor incident and not a police matter; and a concern that police and prosecutors would question their veracity and credibility (Lievore 2003).

In incidents where victims *do* report, arrest and prosecution are unlikely. Despite decades of legal reforms designed to enhance the likelihood of arrest and prosecution in sexual assault cases, research consistently finds that attrition in these types of cases remains a problem in the criminal justice system. Studies have found that between 23 and 35 percent of sexual assault cases reported to law enforcement in the US result in an arrest (Alderden and Ullman 2012a, 2012b; Bachman 1998). Of those cases presented to a prosecutor, only 39 percent will result in felony charges (Alderden and Ulman 2012a). Although the arrest rates vary depending on the jurisdiction where the study took place and whether the suspect is a stranger or someone previously known to the victim, most research shows that less than one-third of suspects in cases reported to the police are arrested and an even smaller percentage are successfully prosecuted.

Criminal justice decision making

Sexual assault case outcomes continue to be affected by both legal and extralegal factors. Legal factors—particularly the seriousness of the crime and the strength of evidence—play an important role in sexual assault case processing decisions; extralegal factors—such as personal characteristics of the victim and offender—also influence these decisions. International research in Israel (Ajzenstadt and Steinberg 2001), Europe (Kelly 2010), Australia (Dylan *et al.* 2008), and Hong Kong (Cheung *et al.* 1990) uncovers similar findings.

The decision to arrest

Studies examining the police decision to make an arrest highlight the importance of both evidentiary factors and victim characteristics (Alderden and Ullman 2012a, 2012b; Bachman 1998; Bouffard 2000; Spohn and Tellis 2013). Legal factors that have been found to increase the likelihood of arrest in sexual assault cases include the presence of a witness, the suspect's use of a weapon, and the victim's willingness to cooperate (Alderden and Ullman 2012b; Bouffard 2000; Kerstetter 1990; Spohn and Tellis 2013).

Victim attributes and interpersonal contextual factors also influence the decision to arrest. Research in the US finds that police are more likely to make an arrest if the victim and suspect were known to each other or had a prior relationship, if the victim agreed to undergo a forensic exam, if the officer was male, and if the credibility of the victim was not in question and the crime was more serious (Alderden and Ullman 2012b; Bouffard 2000; Spohn and Tellis 2013). In a study where police officers evaluated vignettes, whereas officers' perceptions of the suspect's level of intoxication had no effect on their evaluation of the suspect's credibility, blame, or guilt, perceptions of the victim's intoxication did affect their assessment of the case (Schuller and Stewart 2000).

Innovative research into the neurobiology of trauma offers important insights into the behavior of sexual assault victims following an attack, behavior which commonly leads police and others to disbelieve their stories. This research finds that the part of the brain responsible for decision making and memory can be temporarily impaired when encoding or conjuring up details of a traumatic event, so that memories become fragmented and victims have difficulty providing a linear account, a situation that is exacerbated with alcohol use (Campbell 2012). Fragmented memories become interpreted as untruthful as victims struggle to put together a coherent story. This new knowledge has been incorporated into training for police and other agencies who respond to sexual assault victims in the US, to improve their investigative strategies.

Police unfounding decisions

The decision by police to "unfound" a case, known in some countries as "de-criming," is one of the most important, and highly criticized, decisions made in the criminal justice system. If the police officer investigating the crime believes the victim's account of what happened and determines that the incident constitutes a crime, the case becomes one of the "crimes known to the police" that will be included the jurisdiction's crime statistics. If, on the other hand, the officer does not believe the victim's complaint and therefore concludes that a crime did not occur, the case is coded as unfounded and excluded from the official tally. Technically, cases can be unfounded only if the police determine that a crime did not occur. In reality, police may use the unfounding decision to clear cases in which they disbelieve the victim's account or are convinced that a crime occurred but believe that the likelihood of arrest and prosecution is low. Police often unfound sexual assault reports inappropriately, basing their actions on cultural stereotypes about "real rape" and factoring into the decision extralegal considerations such as complainants' risky behavior at the time of the incident, complainants' character and reputation, mental health issues, presence of injury or threats with weapons, uncertainty about details of the attack, unwillingness to cooperate in the prosecution of the suspect, and delayed reporting (Kelly *et al.* 2005; Lonsway *et al.* 2009; Spohn and Tellis 2013). Since police departments are evaluated in terms of clearance rates, this "encourages officers to unfound ambiguous or difficult cases, including those where a victim is reluctant, emotional, uncooperative, or compromised in some way (e.g., had smoked marijuana, was a prostitute, had a former sexual relationship with the rapist)" (Martin 2005: 53).

Allegations that women lie about sexual assault are not new. In fact, Sir Matthew Hale, an English judge, opined in the seventeenth century that rape "is an accusation easily to be made and hard to be proved, and harder to be defended by the party accused, tho never so innocent" (Hale 1678, reprinted 1972). Estimates of the number of false reports vary. The two most rigorous reviews of false report research, which included studies from the US, Australia, New Zealand, and the United Kingdom, found that unfounding rates ranged from 1.5 percent to 90 percent (Lisak *et al.*, 2010). These variations reflect differences in the way false reports are defined and measured, as well as differences in the reliability and validity of the research designs used to evaluate false reports. Methodologically rigorous studies estimate that reports of sexual assault that are actually false are within the range of 2–8 percent (Lonsway *et al.* 2009).

Despite social advancements in the past several decades regarding rape awareness, negative attitudes and belief in "rape myths" are still pervasive. Rape myths are widely held beliefs about rape (e.g., causes, consequences, perpetrators, victims) that are used to justify and excuse sexual violence against women (Gerger *et al.* 2007). Some rape myths include: that women fantasize about being raped; that women routinely lie about rape; that men cannot rape their intimate partners; that rape is simply unwanted sex and not a violent crime; and that victims are usually attacked by strangers. These myths are widely held and influence how criminal justice personnel proceed with rape allegations (Gerger *et al.* 2007). In fact, researchers have shown that police officers are inherently distrustful of sexual assault victims' claims (Jordan 2004) and believe in some of the more common rape myths (Page 2008). This research demonstrates that legal decision making is vulnerable to the same biases that characterize general information processing, such as the propensity to concentrate on information that is consistent with pre-existing beliefs (McEwan 2003).

The decision to prosecute

All decision makers in the criminal justice system have significant discretionary power, but the prosecutor stands apart from the others. Although the roles and responsibilities of prosecutors vary among (and sometimes within) countries, in those with adversarial (as opposed to inquisitorial) justice systems, the prosecutor is the person who ultimately decides whether a case will be prosecuted, the charges that will be filed, and whether a plea bargain will be offered. The prosecutor also may recommend sentence. However, none of the discretionary decisions made by the prosecutor is more critical than the initial decision to prosecute, which has been characterized as "the gateway to justice" (Kerstetter 1990: 182). Prosecutors have wide discretion at this stage in the process; in most jurisdictions there are no legislative or judicial guidelines on charging, and a decision not to file charges ordinarily is immune from review. The UK is an interesting exception: Police and the prosecution service have signed a joint national protocol, which includes specialist rape prosecutors in each prosecutorial district, who receive compulsory training. Importantly, cases cannot be dropped without a second opinion from another specialist prosecutor, thus ensuring oversight of this critical decision (Government Equalities Office, 2010).

Research on prosecutors' charging decisions in sexual assault cases reveals that these decisions are strongly influenced by legally relevant factors such as the seriousness of the crime, the offender's prior criminal record, and the strength of the evidence in the case (Alderden and Ullman 2012b; Kingsnorth *et al.* 1999; Spohn and Tellis 2013), as well as by extralegal factors such as the victim's behavior at the time of the attack (whether she was hitchhiking, drinking, or using drugs), the character or reputation of the victim, and the background characteristics of the defendant and victim (Campbell 1998; Frohmann 1991; Lievore 2003; Spohn and Tellis 2013; Spohn *et al.* 2001; Tellis and Spohn 2008). Research also shows that different predictors may affect prosecutors' decisions in stranger and acquaintance cases (Kingsnorth *et al.* 1999). Because all members of society are exposed to the same messages and stereotypes about rape, prosecutors know that juries are not likely to convict in cases that stray too much from the "real rape" scenario and may therefore refuse to file charges based in part on these extralegal factors (Lonsway *et al.* 2009).

Strengthening the evidence in sexual assault cases has meant improving comprehensive forensic evidence collection, which is a primary objective of the widely implemented Sexual Assault Nurse Examiner (SANE) community intervention programs (Alderden and Ullman 2012b; Kingsnorth *et al.* 1999; Spohn and Tellis 2013). SANE programs use highly trained forensic nurses to provide inclusive medical care, crisis counseling, and forensic evidence collection (Campbell *et al.* 2005). According to the International Association of Forensic Nurses (IAFN),[1] an organization of nurses working to develop, promote, and disseminate information internationally about forensic nursing science, there are currently more than 700 SANE programs operating in the US, Australia, and Canada. These programs are operated by nurses who have completed specialized training in areas of evidence collection, use of job-specific equipment, detection of injury, sexual assault-specific medical treatment (e.g., sexually transmitted disease treatment), court room procedures (e.g., expert testimony), and crisis response (Ledray 1997).

SANE programs have the ability to enhance the likelihood of successful prosecution in sexual assault cases through improved collaboration with law enforcement, higher victim reporting rates, and improved forensic evidence collection (Ledray 2001). The recent work by Campbell and colleagues (2005, 2009) in the US confirms the importance of SANE programs. For example, a comprehensive review of empirical international literature found that SANE programs are effective in: (1) assisting in the psychological recovery of victims; (2) providing consistent and inclusive post-assault medical care; (3) accurately recording forensic evidence; (4) enhancing prosecution by providing comprehensive expert testimony and improved forensic evidence collection and documentation; and (5) improving relationships among service providers by bringing agencies together in efforts to provide inclusive services to victims (Campbell *et al.* 2005). Additionally, forensic evidence collected by SANEs accounts for significant variation in case outcomes when controlling for victim and assault case characteristics, although the causal mechanisms are unclear and future research is necessary to uncover why SANE cases progress through the system differently that other cases (Campbell *et al.* 2009).

Victim empowerment

Victims of sexual assault who report the crime to the police and cooperate with police and prosecutors as the case moves forward often confront criminal justice officials who are skeptical of their allegations and who question their credibility (Jordan 2004). In the context of a complicated relationship between victims and legal personnel, victim empowerment becomes increasingly important. Variously defined and broadly used, the concept of empowerment has two central components: a psychological sense of power and a real ability to effect change in important outcomes. "In the context of the court system, an empowering experience would be one where the victim felt she had been able to express her wishes and saw those wishes reflected in decisions or responses at various points in the court system" (Bennett Cattaneo and Goodman 2010: 484).

Empowering women victims of violence has been a goal of advocacy organizations since their inception, but it is less commonly addressed among traditional criminal justice organizations. In many aspects, sexual assault victims' needs are considered to be secondary to the criminal justice system's concerns. A central characteristic of empowerment is control. As illustrated by Frohman's (1991) ethnographic study of sexual assault prosecution, prosecutors often manage complainants by constraining their power. Because victims of a sexual violation have been deprived of control and personal power during the assault, regaining some control during the criminal justice process is essential to facilitate their empowerment and recovery (Ullman and Townsend 2008).

The uniqueness of an "empowerment"—or sometimes feminist—approach lies in the creation of an environment in which victims feel safe and empowered by being involved in decisions that affect them and being informed about the progression of their case. This client-centered approach is very different from a model where the service provider, the medical professional, or the legal counselor is considered the expert who will direct the process and make decisions. Empowering sexual assault victims starts with giving them a voice in decision making throughout the criminal justice process

Numerous studies have documented negative experiences of victims' contacts with the police and the criminal justice system (Campbell 2006). But other studies have shown that perceptions of procedural justice—fair treatment by police and other agents of the criminal justice system, regardless of the outcome—can help reduce the trauma associated with the experience and help victims recover from the negative psychological sequelae of their victimization. One Australian study found that the validation of victims' experiences by the police was beneficial as it gave victims a sense of closure and empowerment and feelings of safety (Elliott *et al.* in press). When the police acknowledge that what happened was wrong and not to be tolerated, victims can feel validated but also valued as individuals and members of the community. The importance of "being seen as a person by the police" (Jordan 2008: 712) has been identified as a critical step on the way to victims' empowerment and healing.

Although high rates of attrition in sexual assault cases should be an urgent concern, victims' sense of empowerment is not solely determined by the outcome of the criminal justice process; it is affected by many aspects of what happens during this process. Further, empowering victims is not the sole responsibility of individuals within the system. Research has shown how organizations—but also community and societal contexts—can constrain or facilitate victims' empowerment. The meaning and ultimate goal of empowerment at these various levels is likely to differ, just as there are various ways in which not only the criminal justice system but other informal and formal sources of support can contribute to disempowerment (e.g., coercing the victim for her own good to testify, intrusive evidence collection) (McDermott and Garofalo 2004). While the term "empowerment" has been widely used, further research is needed to clarify how it is experienced by victims, how it translates into practice, and what specific aspects of victims' experience are empowering and disempowering.

Future inquiry

Further investigation is necessary in numerous areas of sexual assault case processing, including SANE program effectiveness, unfounding and false allegations of sexual assault, and attitudes of police and prosecutors toward sexual assaults and sexual assault victims. Identifying and discussing the extensive research and gaps in this body of literature is beyond the scope of this chapter. Therefore, we identify two important areas of inquiry and suggest steps for future examination: reducing barriers to victim participation in sexual assault case processing and addressing wider issues of attrition, and improving the response to intimate partner sexual assault (IPSA).

Due to the salience of victim cooperation, which is a practical constraint on the prosecutor's decision to file charges or proceed with the case, it is important to examine the circumstances that surround barriers to victim participation in the justice system. This effort may help to inform and guide law enforcement and prosecutors to develop protocols to improve their response to and support for victims at all stages of case processing. Further research from the victim perspective is needed to more fully understand the concrete ways that police, prosecutors, and grassroots supports for victims can empower victims and support their decisions, which may have the collateral benefit of reducing attrition. Integrating qualitative and quantitative methodologies, such as victim interviews, may prove useful as these approaches allow individuals to assign meaning to their experiences (Gerbert *et al.* 1999). Broadening the base of research to include marginalized groups of women and those most reluctant to engage with the justice system would provide an opportunity to hear the voices of historically silenced groups (Davis *et al.* 2001).

Few studies address decision making in IPSA cases, including date rape, a topic that is arguably a challenge and an under-developed area in sexual assault case-processing literature. Additionally, the role played by rape myths may be particularly salient for IPSA, which is surrounded by various legal and cultural myths (Berman, 2004). In fact, some criminal justice professionals continue to adopt this viewpoint by considering intimate partner violence a victimless crime involving a minor conflict (Buzawa and Buzawa, 1996). Future research on IPSA should examine the ways in which legal and extralegal factors influence case processing and should attempt to determine why these factors play a role.

Conclusion

Understanding and evaluating the response of the criminal justice system to sexual violence is critically important, as is identifying system-generated barriers that affect whether victims will report and cooperate with police and prosecutors. While summary assessments of reporting, arresting, and prosecution rates are valuable, an equally—if not more—important area of inquiry is the exercise of discretion, which affects whether police take a report, make an arrest, or present a case to prosecutors and whether prosecutors take the case forward. Although legal factors such as case seriousness and the strength of evidence are salient predictors of these decisions, perceptions of victim "righteousness" (Spohn and Tellis 2013) continue to affect the extent to which a criminal justice response is activated when a victim reports a sexual assault, particularly if it is not reported immediately and the suspect is a nonstranger.

Note

1 See the Database of the International Association of Forensic Nurses. Online. Available at https://m360.iafn.org/frontend/search.aspx?cs=1932 (accessed 25 May 2014).

References

Ajzenstadt, M. and Steinberg, O. (2001) 'Never mind the law: legal discourse and rape reform in Israel', *Affilia*, 16: 337–59.

Alderden, M.A. and Ullman, S.E. (2012a) 'Creating a more complete and current picture: examining police and prosecutor decision-making when processing sexual assault cases', *Violence Against Women*, 18: 525–51.

Alderden, M.A. and Ullman, S.E. (2012b) 'Gender difference or indifference? Detective decision making in sexual assault cases', *Journal of Interpersonal Violence*, 27: 3–22.

Bachman, R. (1998) 'Factors related to rape reporting and arrest: new evidence from the NCVS', *Criminal Justice and Behavior*, 25: 8–29.

Bennett Cattaneo, L. and Goodman, L.A. (2010) 'Through the lens of therapeutic jurisprudence: the relationship between empowerment in the court system and well-being for intimate partner violence victims', *Journal of Interpersonal Violence*, 25: 481–502.

Berman, J. (2004), 'Domestic sexual assault: a new opportunity for court response', *Juvenile and Family Court Journal*, 55: 23–3.

Bouffard, J.A. (2000) 'Predicting type of sexual assault case closure from victim, suspect, and case characteristics', *Journal of Criminal Justice*, 28: 527–42.

Buzawa, E.S. and Buzawa, C.G. (1996) *Domestic Violence: The Criminal Justice System Responses*, Thousand Oaks, CA: Sage.

Campbell, R. (2012) *The Neurobiology of Sexual Assault: NIJ Research for the Real World*. Online. Available at www.nij.gov/events/Pages/research-real-world.aspx (accessed 25 May 2014).

Campbell, R. (2006) 'Rape survivors' experiences with the legal and medical systems: do rape victim advocates make a difference?', *Violence Against Women*, 12: 30–45.

Campbell, R. (1998) 'The community response to rape: victims' experiences with the legal, medical, and mental health', *American Journal of Community Psychology*, 25: 355–79.

Campbell, R., Patterson, D., Bybee, D. and Dworking, E.R. (2009) 'Predicting sexual assault prosecution outcomes: the role of medical forensic evidence collection by sexual assault nurse examiners', *Criminal Justice and Behavior*, 36: 712–27.

Campbell, R., Patterson, D. and Lichty, L.F. (2005) 'The effectiveness of sexual assault nurse examiner (SANE) program: a review of psychological, medical, legal, and community outcomes', *Trauma, Violence, & Abuse*, 6: 313–29.

Cheung, F.M., Andry, R.G. and Tam, R.C. (1990) *Research on Rape and Sexual Crime in Hong Kong*, Shatin: Centre for Hong Kong Studies, Chinese University of Hong Kong.

Davis, K., Taylor, B. and Furniss, D. (2001) 'Narrative accounts of tracking the rural domestic violence survivors' journey: a feminist approach', *Health Care for Women International*, 22: 333–47.

Davis, R.C., Kunreuther, F. and Connick, E. (1984) 'Expanding the victim's role in the criminal court disposition process: the results of an experiment', *The Journal of Criminal Law and Criminology*, 75: 491–505.

Du Mont, J., Miller, K. and Myhr, T. (2003) 'The role of "real rape" and "real victim" stereotypes in the police reporting practices of sexually assaulted women', *Violence Against Women*, 9: 466–86.

Dylan, A., Regehr, C. and Alaggia, R. (2008) 'And justice for all? Aboriginal victims of sexual violence', *Violence Against Women*, 14: 678–96.

Elliott, I., Thomas, S. and Ogloff, J. (in press) 'Procedural justice in victim–police interactions and victims' recovery from victimisation experiences', *Policing and Society*.

Frohmann, L. (1991) 'Discrediting victims' allegations of sexual assault: prosecutorial accounts of case rejections', *Social Problems*, 38: 213–26.

Gerbert B., Caspers, N., Bronstone, A., Moe, J. and Abercrombie, P. (1999) 'A qualitative analysis of how physicians with expertise in domestic violence approach the identification of victims', *Annals of Internal Medicine*, 131: 578–84.

Gerger, H., Kley, H., Bohner, G. and Siebler, F. (2007) 'The acceptance of modern myths about sexual aggression (AMMSA) scale: development and validation in German and English', *Aggressive Behavior*, 33: 422–40.

Government Equalities Office (2010) *The Stern Review: A Report by Baroness Vivien Stern CBE of an Independent Review into How Rape Complaints are Handled by Public Authorities in England and Wales*, London: Home Office.

Hale, M. (1678) *Pleas of the Crown: A Methodical Summary*, London: Professional Books. Reprinted in 1972.

Johnson, H., Ollus, N. and Nevala, S. (2008) *Violence Against Women: An International Perspective*, New York: Springer.

Jordan, J. (2008) 'Perfect victims, perfect policing? Improving rape complainants' experiences of police investigations', *Public Administration*, 86: 699–719.

Jordan, J. (2004) 'Beyond belief? Police, rape and women's credibility', *Criminal Justice*, 4: 29–59.

Kelly, L. (2010) 'The (in)credible words of women: false allegations in European rape research', *Violence Against Women*, 16: 1345–55.

Kelly, L., Lovett, J. and Regan, L. (2005) *Gap or a Chasm? Attrition in Reported Rape Cases*, London: Home Office.

Kerstetter, W.A. (1990) 'Gateway to justice: police and prosecutorial response to sexual assaults against women', *Journal of Criminal Law and Criminology*, 81: 267–313.

Kingsnorth, R., MacIntosh, R. and Wentworth, J. (1999) 'Sexual assault: The role of prior relationship and victim characteristics in case processing', *Justice Quarterly*, 16: 275–302.

Ledray, L. (2001) *Evidence Collection and Care of Sexual Assault Survivor: The SANE-SART Response.* Online. Available at www.mincava.umn.edu/documents/commissioned/2forensicevidence/2forensicevidence.html (accessed 25 May 2014).

Ledray, L. (1997) 'SANE program staff: Selection, training, and salaries', *Journal of Emergency Nursing*, 23: 491–5.

Lievore, D. (2003) *Non-reporting and Hidden Recording of Sexual Assault: An International Literature Review*, Canberra: Office of the Status of Women.

Lisak, D., Gardinier, L., Nicksa, S.C. and Cote, A.M. (2010) 'False allegations of sexual assault: an analysis of ten years of reported cases', *Violence Against Women*, 16: 1318–34.

Lonsway, K.A., Archambault, J. and Lisak, D. (2009) 'False reports: moving beyond the issue to successfully investigate and prosecute non-stranger sexual assault', *The Voice*, 3: 1–12.

Martin, P.Y. (2005) *Rape Work: Victims, Gender and Emotions in Organization and Community Context*, New York: Routledge.

McDermott, M.J. and Garofalo, J. (2004) 'When advocacy for domestic violence victims backfires: types and sources of victim disempowerment', *Violence Against Women*, 10: 1245–66.

McEwan, J. (2003) *The Verdict of the Court: Passing Judgment in Law and Psychology*, Oxford: Hart.

Page, A.D. (2008) 'Gateway to reform? Policy implications of police officers' attitudes toward rape', *American Journal of Criminal Justice*, 33: 44–58.

Schuller, R.A. and Stewart, A. (2000) 'Police responses to sexual assault complaints: the role of perpetrator/complainant intoxication', *Law and Human Behavior*, 24: 535–51.

Spohn, C. and Tellis, K.M. (2013) *Policing and Prosecuting Sexual Assault: Inside the Criminal Justice System*, Boulder, CO: Lynne Rienner Publishers.

Spohn, C., Beichner, D. and Davis-Frenzel, E. (2001) 'Prosecutorial explanations for sexual assault case rejection: guarding the gateway to justice', *Social Problems*, 48: 206–35.

Tellis, K.M. and Spohn, C. (2008) 'The sexual stratification hypothesis revisited: testing assumptions about simple versus aggravated rape', *Journal of Criminal Justice*, 36: 252–61.

Tjaden, P. and Thoennes, N. (2006) *Extent, Nature, and Consequences of Rape Victimization: Findings from the National Violence Against Women Survey*, Atlanta, GA: Centers for Disease Control and Prevention.

Ullman, S.E. and Townsend, S.M. (2008) 'What is an empowerment approach to working with sexual assault survivors?', *Journal of Community Psychology*, *36*: 299–312.

Chapter 8

The long and winding road

Improving police responses to women's rape allegations

Jan Jordan

In recent years there have been criticisms made of the ways in which the police interact with women reporting rape and sexual violence (SV) attacks. Internationally pressure has been placed on the police by non-governmental organizations (NGOs), feminist academics, and professionals seeking to improve the rape reporting experience. There is no doubt that some important changes have been made. These include providing more comfortable physical environments within which to conduct both forensic medical examinations and police interviews; extending and improving police training in relation to SV, in some areas through the deployment of specialist sexual assault invesigators; and developing more integrated and collaborative models of service delivery for victim/survivors (Darwinkel *et al.* 2013; Lovett *et al.* 2004). However, Spohn and colleagues (this volume) provide a clear overview documenting how, despite more than three decades of action by rape reformers, criminal justice system agency responses to allegations of SV remain "problematic."

While attention has been given to women's experiences in court, and in particular the high attrition rates that show how difficult it is to secure a conviction within the current trial system (Kelly *et al.* 2005; Lonsway and Archambault 2012), what remains evident is that the majority of rapes are never reported (Du Mont *et al.* 2003; Temkin and Krahé 2008) or, if they are, may proceed no further than the initial police investigation stage (Brown 2011; Stanko and Williams 2009). Developments in New Zealand suggest at least a stated commitment by senior management to improve police service delivery in this area. The impetus to do so has seen feminist and NGO sector efforts strengthened by scandalous cases attracting media exposure and public ire. One of these involved a woman believed to have falsely complained about rape in 1988 by a man subsequently convicted as one of the country's worst serial rapists (Jordan 2008). A second involved a young woman making historical allegations of group rape against three police officers, who was instead blamed for her actions and saw her attackers acquitted by a jury (Nicholas 2007; Rowe 2009). It took years for these two cases to reach court, and both have recently attracted renewed attention and debate.

The fact that these cases initially occurred in the 1980s may provide grounds for optimism. Since then there have been changes in police rape investigations, and it is widely believed that such scandalous cases are now historical relics. Repeated verbalizations of what could be called the police mantra state precisely that: "Everything's changed, and it couldn't happen now." This chapter asks: Or could it?

In attempting to answer this question, I examine two key beliefs that have dominated societal and police responses when women make rape allegations: that women cry rape falsely, and that if a woman is raped, then the blame rests with her. Two New Zealand cases illuminate both police responses at the time and the factors prompting greater public discussion more recently. To critically respond to the allegation that "everything's changed," recent research findings are explored and a third case study from 2013 considered.

Historical context

In societies with a patriarchal history, a legacy remains from centuries of questioning the credibility and worth of women. From Eve in the Garden of Eden onwards, women were perceived as natural born liars, beings to be neither trusted nor entrusted with responsibility and power (Taslitz 1999).

Within this context the crime of rape was initially viewed as a property offense committed by one man against another (Brownmiller 1975)—women were objects of possession, their subjective experience irrelevant. Centuries later, while women's legal status has significantly improved in many countries, considerable scepticism and denial of sexual victimization remains. How the police respond to a woman alleging she has been raped is critically important. They are positioned as the gatekeepers to the criminal justice system, controlling the extent to which a case proceeds or not (Jordan 2004). The credibility threshold victims must reach in police eyes is a key contributor to the high rape attrition rates evident globally (Daly and Bouhours 2010). Many of the factors now widely recognized as increasing victim vulnerability, such as drug and alcohol issues, a history of mental illness, and experiences of childhood sexual abuse, are the same ones that police often interpret as signifying questionable credibility (Jordan 2004, 2012). This can then translate into scenarios where real victims are doubted and rapists exonerated, as the first case study demonstrates.

Case Study 1 presents a clear example of a raped woman being wrongfully disbelieved by police. Although eventually she was believed, she survived eight years without recognition and validation, eight years that saw many other women violated by the same man. The principal reason she was eventually believed resulted from the offender becoming the centre of a highly publicized hunt for a serial stranger rapist. As international research has repeatedly shown, stranger rapes are relatively rare, yet still perceived as consistent with the "real rape" stereotype and likely to attract fuller and less querulous police attention (Brown and Horvath 2009; Kelly *et al.* 2005).

CASE STUDY 1

In 2013 the media in New Zealand "discovered" a rape allegation written off as false by the police many years previously (Quilliam 2013). It involved a rape allegedly committed on 31 December 1987 by an offender who was shortly afterwards identified and named by the complainant. The police investigation was brief—the alleged offender, Rewa, said he had an alibi for that evening, and the complainant led to believe that this was confirmed by police at the time. The investigation did not proceed. Factors likely to have undermined her credibility in the eyes of the police included her being a young, Māori woman with a history of using drugs who was also known to associate with gangs (Jordan, 2008). The history of the man she named counted for less, despite it including previous convictions on a rape charge.

The alleged offender was left in the community to continue raping women, which he did for the next eight years before finally being apprehended in 1996 and charged as one of the most prolific serial rapists ever known to the New Zealand Police. During the investigation, the detectives realized that the man named in the 1987 attack was the serial rapist. They worked hard to repair their severed connection with the complainant, ensuring that this time round she had a very different experience of the police and would agree to testify in court. Finally she had the satisfaction not only of seeing the man who raped her convicted, but of knowing the police believed her (Jordan 2008).

The case resurfaced in 2012–13 when it was publicly alleged that, had the police believed the 1987 complainant, Rewa would have been prevented from committing the subsequent rapes, as well as one woman's murder. Perceptions of police culpability increased when it was revealed that the man Rewa said could give him an alibi then, and whom the victim was told had done so, was never located by police. In accepting the offender's word, the police disbelieved her, and multiple other women were left vulnerable to rape and, in one case, murder. The case is currently under review by the Independent Police Conduct Authority (Quilliam 2013).

From the 1970s onwards, studies have identified high levels of police scepticism regarding the veracity of rape complaints (Kelly *et al.* 2005; O'Keeffe *et al.* 2009). The observation is often made about rape that in the reporting of no other crime does the complainant experience such immediate and intense police suspicion. Over time there is evidence of both improvement in victims' satisfaction levels with how police respond, as well as indicators of continuing scepticism (Lonsway, 2010). It is estimated that between half and two-thirds of SV cases reported are either "no-crimed" or result in no further police action, which gives an inflated impression of the level of "false" complaints (Kelly 2010;

O'Keeffe *et al.* 2009). Thus, despite moves instructing detectives to commence their investigation of SV complaints assuming them to be true, the scepticism vein continues to permeate and influence police responses. This prompted American researcher Kim Lonsway (2010: 1367) to recently conclude:

> The underlying skepticism that sexual assault survivors face when they disclose may be the single most damaging factor in our societal response. It may also be the most powerful tool in the arsenal of rapists because it allows them to commit their crimes with impunity.

Being believed is one of the most important ways by which human identity and experience is validated. Consequently, not to be believed impacts at a core level that can potentially undermine an individual's sense of themselves and their worth in the world. Given that the most likely offenders are men known to the victims and with whom they may be in a relationship (Du Mont *et al.* 2003), combined with confusion around the nature of consent (Gavey 2005), the first belief-hurdle victims need to jump is internal—do *I* believe I have been raped? It is little wonder that many doubt whether others, and especially the police, will believe them, and unsurprising that it is still the case that most rape victims choose not to report it to the police (Wolitzky-Taylor *et al.* 2011), or even tell anyone of their experience (Ahrens 2006). This leads to the second key factor explored in this chapter—the extent to which victims of rape are judged and blamed for "getting themselves raped."

The societal reluctance to hold men accountable for sexually coercive behavior is a deeply embedded vein within our culture. "Boys will be boys," "they can't stop themselves," "it's just instinct," "the alcohol made him do it"—the excuses tumble over each other in society's efforts to absolve men from blame. The statements we typically hear about the woman, however, are not so forgiving—"she was asking for it," "she'd drunk way too much," "she could have said no," "what was she thinking accepting a ride from him?" In a strangely ironic twist, the active male is transformed into a helpless testosterone-led creature, while the supposedly passive woman champions her own fate.

Despite the strenuous efforts of many feminists and advocates to challenge adherence to traditional rape myths, these sit doggedly in place. When a woman is raped, typically the first questions concern what she was wearing, how she was behaving, and how much she had been drinking. A 2005 study of public attitudes in the United Kingdom revealed a strongly judgmental stance towards victims if they were wearing sexy clothing or were drunk at the time of the rape (Amnesty International 2005; Walklate 2008). A more recent study in London found nearly two-thirds of the sample believed victims should accept responsibility if they had been drinking to excess or had blacked out before the rape (The Havens 2010, cited in Horvath *et al.* 2011). Evidence from participants in mock juror trials also shows many people willing to forgive the rapist while blaming the victim (Munro and Kelly 2009).

CASE STUDY 2

In recent years one case prompting significant public debate and governmental review in New Zealand has been the police treatment of Louise Nicholas. As a teenager living in a provincial town, she experienced multiple instances of rape perpetrated by groups of policemen who would arrive at her flat, often in uniform, armed with quantities of alcohol. Her later attempts to report these officers sparked a long history of police denials and cover-ups until a journalist approached her in 2004 suggesting she tell her story (Nicholas 2007). This was prompted in part by one of the men involved in the earlier group rapes now being a prominent, high-ranked officer who was being considered as a future Commissioner of Police. Despite her trepidation, Louise agreed to speak out, at which point the floodgates opened as other women came forward to describe rape experiences similar to hers. Question marks were raised more generally regarding how the police investigated sexual assaults, with then Prime Minister, Helen Clark, ordering a Commission of Inquiry into Police Conduct in 2004. This resulted in 60 recommendations that the police are now endeavouring to implement (Bazley 2007).

The case involving the officers who had violated Louise finally went to trial in 2006, and the defense worked hard to blame her for what had transpired. She spent three nightmarish days on the stand being grilled and blamed. The now high-ranking officer involved, although on suspension, disobeyed orders by arriving in court dressed in full police regalia, an obvious attempt to impress those present and intimidate the complainant (Dewes 2006). He and the two other accused former police officers produced witnesses testifying to their good character while Louise was called "a police slut" (Taylor 2007) and "a maggot-lying bitch" (Cook 2007). The jury decided she was lying and culpable and all three accused were acquitted. Only later was it revealed that two of these men were secretly transported to court each day from a nearby prison where they were serving sentences for raping a young woman about the same time and in very similar circumstances to Louise. This statement of fact was withheld from the court as it could be prejudicial to the interests of the accused, yet no such ban existed on inferences prejudicial to the interests of the complainant. Louise commented later about her trial experience: "Defence lawyers get extremely personal. There is nastiness, there is name-calling. There's no fairness in the courtroom. My life was dissected basically—screwed up and thrown back in my face" (Fitzsimons 2007).

Being so blatantly confronted with how the system worked to protect these men's reputations while damning hers, public outrage was provoked (*Dominion Post* 2007). The resulting Commission of Inquiry was followed by the government establishing a Taskforce for Action on Sexual Violence, funding a series of major research projects into SV, and undertaking an extensive review of alternative models to the adversarial justice system,[1] all of which generated useful information as well as a sense of optimism for the future.

Case Studies 1 and 2 both involved rape offenses committed in the 1980s and 1990s. The fact that they have recently resurfaced to become the focus of media attention and public debate may provide some reassurance that changed perceptions in the intervening years have enabled such a revisiting to occur. While there may be some truth to this observation, a third and very

CASE STUDY 3

At the time of writing, New Zealand Police are under scrutiny again following revelations regarding what appears to be their mis-handling of rape allegations made against a group of young males in Auckland. The boys, aged 17–18 and calling themselves the Roast Busters, allegedly plied teenage girls, some as young as 13, with alcohol then bragged online about sexually violating them (Maas 2013).

When the story initially broke in the media in November 2013, a police spokesperson said they had been aware for two years of this group's existence and activities but unable to intervene because none of the victims had laid a formal complaint (Dudding 2013). This statement was quickly contested when a teenage girl appeared on national television advising that, two years previous when she was 13 years old, she had in fact made a formal complaint to the police and been video interviewed. She said she felt some of the questions put to her by detectives were inappropriate, including reference to the clothes she was wearing that night, and the case did not proceed (Field and Maas 2013).

It also emerged that three other teenage girls had gone to the police, and been identified as victims, although none wanted to make a formal complaint. Other revelations included that police had known for some time that one of the boys involved was a police officer's son and another the son of a prominent entertainer. The response from the public was swift, and diverse. Many commentators were outraged that the police had known about these men's actions for two years yet appeared to have done nothing to stop their behavior, warn the public, or take down the Facebook pages where the offensive material was posted (MacLennan, 2013). On the other hand, some commentators defended the police and asked questions about the girls' appearance and behavior. Only a few called for attention to be focused on such issues as how and why young men felt entitled to rape drunk teenage girls, and on the wider social and cultural issues surrounding *their* actions and behavior (Dudding 2013).

The young men involved, born just a few years before the dawn of the twenty-first century, displayed attitudes chillingly familiar from generations ago. Before the Facebook page was taken down, comments included one boy recounting how his first "roast" of an unconscious girl made him feel like "the man." He boasted that his response, if later challenged by a girl, was to sneer, "Go ahead. Call the cops. They can't unrape you."

recent case cautions us from becoming too euphoric about the death and burial of rape myths.

So where does this leave us? On one level, it was encouraging to see news of this case spark wide-ranging public debate, and various actions ensue that could be interpreted as providing some reassurance that many sectors of society were outraged over what occurred. On another level, it was sobering to hear such condemnation and blaming of the girls involved. Police perceptions of victim responsibility were reflected in their insistence that the girls involved needed to come forward, with scant awareness demonstrated of the reasons why they might not. Two of the critical questions prompted by this case are the need to explain and understand police responses and the tenacity of victim-blaming myths, factors that, as the next section shows, are inextricably linked.

Barriers to change

Reliance on legal means to remedy societal wrongs will always be inherently limited. The law can be a mechanism for justice only as much as the social context within which it operates enables it. While the police play a critical role influencing the potential for rape victims to access justice, their ability to do so is constrained in part by their own occupational culture. The history of policing has produced hierarchical and conservative organizations focused as much on protecting state interests as on proteching the public they profess to serve. This was an institution developed initially to protect male property interests, and still one of those most tenaciously resisting pressures to gender equality. The police are not born in uniform nor raised in a social vacuum. Their formative years, just like those of victims and offenders, are spent internalizing dominant mores and societal attitudes about men, women, sex, and rape.

Once within the police, this masculinist organizational culture reinforces gendered assumptions (Brown and Heidensohn 2000). This means much more than simply the proportion of officers who are female or promoting women into top management positions, although both these factors may be influential. Being recognized by one's peers as a good police officer necessitates adopting enough of the dominant male attitudes and attributes to gain acceptance within the organization. In reflecting the wider social context, police culture is likely to display its more conservative and status-quo-preserving features.

A further defining feature within police culture has been identified as the suspiciousness and cynicism central to the work (Chan 1997; Reiner 2000). Equipping officers for the historical role of crime fighter necessitated training them to be sceptical, to look for fabrications and cover-ups, notice inconsistencies, and detect nervous or jumpy demeanors. The latter behaviors often correspond to how trauma victims are likely to present, struggling for precise recall and battling their own internalized rape myths. While police departments around the world may be working to develop ways of interviewing rape victims that are less interrogatory than those of the past, achieving fundamental changes in officers' unspoken attitudes and demeanors, when these are reinforced by the organizational culture, is more difficult than altering interview styles and approaches. Although early results suggest a more narrative approach is considerably less traumatizing for those being interviewed and likely to yield fuller disclosures and information (Darwinkel *et al.* 2013), we need to guard against assumptions that changes in policies and methods will translate automatically into changed mindsets and improved experiences for victims.

In addition to these barriers to improving police responses to SV are restraints inherent within the broader culture. In recent years, assumptions have often been made that we now live in egalitarian societies enjoying an enlightened age of post-feminism. Scratch the liberal surface, however, and the stench of patriarchy wafts through. It is evident in the many ways in which rape victims are still regarded suspiciously, the assumption often being that their allegation stems from regretful or revengeful sex. It is apparent in our promptness at raising questions about the victim's behavior, her alcohol or drug consumption, her mode of dress, how flirtatious her behavior might have been. The alleged offender, on the other hand, is still more likely to have his intoxication used to excuse the behavior of an otherwise decent kind of chap, with previous sexual encounters viewed simply as proof that he is a red-blooded "normal" young man.

Also pervasive in our gendered world is the continuing objectification of women's bodies. In the 1970s, faced with shock revelations regarding how prevalent women's experiences of sexual and physical violence were, feminists tackled directly issues such as pornography and sexist advertising. It was widely recognized that reducing any person to the status of an object, rather than a living, feeling human being, could contribute to the use of violence against them. Academic and rape survivor Susan Brison (2002: 55) later described: "the difficulty of regaining one's voice, one's subjectivity, after one has been reduced to silence, to the status of an object, or, worse, made into someone else's speech, an instrument of another's agency."

Today the objectification of women continues, obscured beneath a rhetoric of women's choice and liberation, in the form of girls' and women's bodies becoming more explicitly sexualized and objectified through Brazilian waxing, child beauty pageants, eating disorders, cosmetic surgery, bikinis for preschoolers, misogynist music videos, and pornographic billboards. One cannot help but notice how the supposedly liberating acceptance of sexual explicitness and freedom fits so conveniently with patriarchal presentations of objectified females and sexually entitled males.

This is the social environment within which we seek to teach our children to make respectful decisions around ethical sex. It is also within this environment that our future police officers are raised, alongside both the future victims and perpetrators of SV. Given such a misogynist backdrop, one might be tempted to ask how we could ever realistically hope to reduce the rates of SV and significantly improve police responses to its occurrence?

The road continues

The answer need not be all doom and gloom. Social change is possible; and it is happening—it just takes a long time. Take for example laws surrounding rape in marriage. It is comparatively very recent in our social history that laws were changed to recognize that married women had the right to say no to sex with their husbands and have that no respected. Yet, the number of prosecutions brought by wives is negligible (Bennice and Resick 2003), and notions of male sexual entitlement remain (Bouffard 2010). It would be naïve in the extreme to imagine that the passing of a law would be accompanied by an immediate reversal of the attitudes prompting its initial passing.

Nor can reforms in police policies or training be expected to achieve the fundamental changes required. Despite such reforms, women's experiences overall appear to have changed very little. Rape reporting remains low, police scepticism remains high, and rape attrition rates reassure most offenders that the odds of their being convicted are still remote (Kelly *et al.* 2005).

The old "us vs. them" split between police and public has not been eradicated by moves towards community policing and increased victim-centredness. This is evidenced in part by the ways the police typically respond to external criticism. When scandals erupt, two responses are often alleged: "It wouldn't happen now—we've moved on," and "It's just because there's a few bad apples in the barrel."

Stating that "it wouldn't happen now" suggests a knee-jerk response born more of defensiveness than of a studied examination of the facts. There are factors associated with former notorious cases that might not occur again, but in part this could also be due to the police becoming increasingly aware of the dangers of leaving paper trails of incriminating evidence.[2]

The mantra asserting "everything's changed" can also be dangerous through obscuring recognition of the many areas where change is still needed. It is easy for a complacency to develop that SV has been addressed by so many reviews and inquiries that it can be signed off as resolved. There are many indicators to suggest such a stance is not only erroneous but at risk of reducing the impetus for real change. It is little surprise that we can see a global pattern emerging in the form of a review-go-round, each review prompted by a scandal and leading to recommendations that are then reiterated following subsequent scandals and reviews (Brown 2011; Cook 2011; Jordan 2011).

The "rotten apple in the barrel" analogy is an interesting one, implying that the fundamental container around the police is solid and secure, with a handful of miscreants damaging the organization in the eyes of the public. Such a perspective enables the police to be seen to be taking action against wrongdoing within their ranks by disciplining or removing the bad apples. The apple barrel analogy is misleading, inferring as it does that the bad apples bob around on their own within the policing barrel, contradicting the dominant organizational framework of the police as an hierarchical command structure operating within a particular cultural framework.

A major danger associated with this refrain arises from its power to keep systemic faults and issues obscured while locating blame within individuals. A more apt and appropriate picture may be one that instead views all police as situated along a socio-cultural continuum. While individuals may differ as to which values and perspectives they internalize the most, miscreant officers become those whose views place them at extreme points on this continuum. In ways similar to how men who are violent have been portrayed as over-socialized rather than under-socialized, officers with extreme views enable us to see and identify the strands of belief woven more generally throughout the organization's ethos.

The barrel's solidity is reflected, I would argue, in the ways in which the various initiatives and reviews have yet to yield substantive changes. Despite review recommendations suggesting that alternative models of justice should be examined, the New Zealand Law Commission's major project investigating this area has recently been shelved by the Minister of Justice. It is difficult not to become cynical that much of the government's response is little more than token window dressing to appease critics until things can quietly slip back to how they were before. As Taslitz, an American academic warned (1999: 42):

> Legal change is, accordingly, generally incremental. It is just enough reform to look good to large segments of the public, to preserve the system from collapse, and to make everyone feel proud, but not enough reform as to wreak radical change . . . Patriarchal rape tales will not give up the ghost easily.

Conclusion

In reviewing police responses to rape victims, I have endeavored to move from a consideration of the on-going influence of rape myths to a preliminary analysis of significant barriers to change. The three case studies presented, although from New Zealand, will likely resonate with readers in other jurisdictions, given the ubiquity of the legacy of patriarchy. The very concept of patriarchy, however, is in danger of being undermined by popular rhetoric asserting both growing gender equality and gender symmetry. Attempts to relegate its relevance to museum display cases are potentially dangerous for their propensity to obscure recognition of on-going gender inequalities and especially violence against women. The legacy of patriarchy remains evident in a multitude of ways, including rape prevalence statistics and continuing high attrition rates, notions of male sexual entitlement, and victim-blaming attitudes. It oozes from many forms of pornography, song lyrics, movie scripts, romance novels, and advertising billboards, along with popular magazines and newspapers—in other words, much of the socio-cultural context that serves as wallpaper to our daily lives.

While feminists continue to advocate for change and reforms, progress seems both manifestly evident and interminably slow. Once it may have been believed that merely showing the realities and impacts of discrimination would automatically galvanize everybody from governments to individuals to change; now we keep being reminded of how efforts to change the gender status quo are resisted, if not blatantly then covertly. It would be naïve to expect those who have benefited from traditional practices to eagerly surrender them in favor of a system intended to hold them more accountable. While we may have journeyed some distance along the road, there are many winding bends, and switchbacks, still to negotiate. While driving with caution is recommended, drive on we must!

Notes

1 For a review, see www.lawcom.govt.nz/project/alternative-models-prosecuting-and-trying-criminal-cases (accessed 25 May 2014).

2 For example, detectives on a specialist sexual assault investigation course I was addressing recently were adamant that a search of police files now would yield nothing incriminating or judgmental about their attitudes toward complainants. When asked why, they said they had learned not to write down any examples of prejudicial thinking.

References

Ahrens, C.E. (2006) 'Being silenced: the impact of negative social reactions on the disclosure of rape', *American Journal of Community Psychology*, 38: 263–74.

Amnesty International (2005) Sexual Assault Research: Summary Report, London: Amnesty International UK.

Bazley, M.C. (2007) *Report of the Commission of Inquiry into Police Conduct, vol. I*, Wellington, New Zealand: Commission of Inquiry into Police Conduct.

Bennice, J.A. and Resick, P.A. (2003) 'Marital rape: history, research, and practice', *Trauma, Violence, & Abuse*, 4: 228–46.

Bouffard, L.A. (2010) 'Exploring the utility of entitlement in understanding sexual aggression', *Journal of Criminal Justice*, 38: 870–9.

Brison, S. (2002) *Aftermath: Violence and the Remaking of the Self*, Princeton, NJ: Princeton University Press.

Brown, J. (2011) 'We mind and we care but have things changed? Assessment of progress in the reporting, investigating and prosecution of alleged rape offences', *Journal of Sexual Aggression*, 17: 263–72.

Brown, J. and Heidensohn, F. (2000) *Gender and Policing*, London: Palgrave MacMillan.

Brown, J. and Horvath, M. (2009) 'Do you believe her and is it real rape?' in M. Horvath and J. Brown (eds.), *Rape: Challenging Contemporary Thinking*, Cullompton, UK: Willan, 325–42.

Brownmiller, S. (1975) *Against Our Will: Men, Women and Rape*, Harmondsworth, UK: Penguin.

Chan, J. (1997) *Changing Police Culture: Policing in a Multicultural Society*, Cambridge, UK: Cambridge University Press.

Cook, K. (2011) 'Rape investigation and prosecution: stuck in the mud?', *Journal of Sexual Aggression*, 17: 250–62.

Cook, S. (2007) 'Police sex case: "Why would I lie about this, why would I make this up?"', *New Zealand Herald*, 4 March: 18, 20.

Daly, K. and Bouhours, B. (2010) 'Rape and attrition in the legal process: a comparative analysis of five countries', *Crime and Justice*, 39: 565–650.

Darwinkel, E., Powell, M. and Tidmarsh, P. (2013) 'Improving police officers' perceptions of sexual offending through intensive training', *Criminal Justice and Behavior*, 40: 895–908.

Dewes, H. (2006) 'From teen tearaway to top cop', *The Dominion Post*, 1 April: 14.

Dominion Post (2007) 'All acquitted but two are already in jail for rape', *Dominion Post*, 2 March: 1.

Dudding, A. (2013) 'Dark underbelly of society raises potent ghosts', *Sunday Star Times*, 10 Nov.: 10.

Du Mont, J., Miller, K. and Myhr, T.L. (2003) 'The role of "real rape" and "real victim" stereotypes in the police reporting practices of sexually assaulted women', *Violence Against Women*, 9: 466–86.

Field, M. and Maas, A. (2013) 'Rape complaint against Roast Busters in 2011', *Dominion Post*, 7 Nov.: 4.

Fitzsimons, T. (2007) 'Steps toward new culture', *Dominion Post*, 10 August: 5.

Gavey, N. (2005) *Just Sex? The Cultural Scaffolding of Rape*, Hove, UK: Routledge.

Horvath, M. A. H., Tong, S. and Williams, E. (2011) 'Critical issues in rape investigation: an overview of reform in England and Wales', *The Journal of Criminal Justice Research*, 1: 1–18.

Jordan, J. (2011) 'Here we go round the review-go-round: rape investigation and prosecution—are things getting worse not better?', *Journal of Sexual Aggression*, 17: 234–49.

Jordan, J. (2008) *Serial Survivors: Women's Narratives of Surviving Rape*, Sydney: The Federation Press.

Jordan, J. (2004) *The Word of a Woman: Police, Rape and Belief*, Houndmills, UK: Palgrave MacMillan.

Jordan, J. (2012) 'Silencing rape, silencing women' in J. Brown and S. Walklate (eds.), *Handbook on Sexual Violence*, Abingdon, UK: Routledge, 253–86.

Kelly, L. (2010) 'The incredible words of women: false allegations in European rape research', *Violence Against Women*, 16: 1345–55.

Kelly, L., Lovett, J. and Regan, L. (2005) *A Gap or a Chasm? Attrition in Reported Rape Cases*, London: Home Office.

Lonsway, K. (2010) 'Trying to move the elephant in the living room: responding to the challenge of false rape reports', *Violence Against Women*, 16: 1356–71.

Lonsway, K.A. and Archambault, J. (2012) 'The "justice gap" for sexual assault cases: future directions for research and reform', *Violence Against Women*, 18: 145–68.

Lovett, J., Regan, L. and Kelly, L. (2004) *Sexual Assault Referral Centres: Developing Good Practice and Maximising Potentials*, London: Home Office.

Maas, A. (2013), 'We didn't target drunk young girls', *Sunday Star Times*, 10 Nov.: 1.

MacLennan, C. (2013) 'Police force fails NZ's women . . . again', *New Zealand Herald*, 8 Nov.: A031.

Munro, V. E. and Kelly, L. (2009) 'A vicious cycle? Attrition and conviction patterns in contemporary rape cases in England and Wales', in M. Horvath and J. Brown (eds.), *Rape: Challenging Contemporary Thinking*, Cullompton, UK: Willan, 281–300.

Nicholas, L. (2007) *Louise Nicholas: My Story*, Auckland: Random House.

O'Keeffe, S., Brown, J. and Lyons, E. (2009) 'Seeking proof or truth: naturalistic decision-making by police officers when considering rape allegations', in M. Horvath and J. Brown (eds.), *Rape: Challenging Contemporary Thinking*, Cullompton, UK: Willan, 229–53.

Quilliam, R. (2013) 'Police watchdog: why we're doing a u-turn on Rewa rape inquiry', *New Zealand Herald,* 24 August: A005.

Reiner, R. (2000) *The Politics of the Police*, 3rd edn., Oxford: Oxford University Press.

Rowe, M. (2009) 'Notes on a scandal: the official enquiry into deviance and corruption in the New Zealand Police', *Australian and New Zealand Journal of Criminology*, 42: 123–58.

Stanko, B. and Williams, E. (2009) 'Reviewing rape and rape allegations in London: what are the vulnerabilities of the victims who report to the police?', in M. Horvath and J. Brown (eds.), *Rape: Challenging Contemporary Thinking*. Cullompton, UK: Willan, 207–28.

Taskforce for Action on Sexual Violence (2009) *Report of the Taskforce for Action on Sexual Violence*, Wellington, New Zealand: Ministry of Justice.

Taslitz, A. E. (1999) *Rape and the Culture of the Courtroom*, New York: New York University.

Taylor, P. (2007) 'The Louise Nicholas Saga—Out Of The Shadows', *New Zealand Herald*, 11 August: B1–3.

Temkin, J. and Krahé, B. (2008) *Sexual Assault and the Justice Gap: A Question of Attitude*, Oxford: Hart.

Walklate, S. (2008) 'What is to be done about violence against women? Gender, violence, cosmopolitanism and the law', *British Journal of Criminology*, 48: 39–54.

Wolitzky-Taylor, K.B., Resnick, H.S., McCauley, J.L., Amstadter, A.B., Kilpatrick, D.G. and Ruggiero, K.J. (2011) 'Is reporting of rape on the rise? A comparison of women with reported versus unreported rape experiences in the National Women's Study-Replication', *Journal of Interpersonal Violence*, 26: 807–32.

Chapter 9

Victim lawyers in Norway

Hege Salomon

The expression "victim lawyer"[1] as used in this chapter refers to a Norwegian legal provision where victims of certain crimes, such as rape, incest, and domestic violence (DV) are entitled to legal counsel at the state's expense in order to protect their interests. Victims who are represented by a victim lawyer are granted certain rights in criminal proceedings. The victim lawyer is appointed by the District Court or the Court of Appeal at no cost, regardless of the victim's financial situation.

Recent history of the victim lawyer in Norway

The system of victim lawyers in Norway was established by the 1981 Norwegian Criminal Procedure Act.[2] A comparable system exists in all Nordic countries (Norway, Sweden, Denmark, Finland, and Iceland), but this chapter will focus specifically on the victim lawyer's role in Norway.

In medieval times, criminal cases were initiated by the victim, but the state gradually took over this role in the eighteenth century. The current Norwegian Criminal Code dates back to 1902.[3] Knut Storberget, Minister of Justice from 2005 to 2011, used to comment that the Norwegian criminal legislation was written "by men and for men. I believe that we would have had a different criminal justice system if the victims were men" (2009: 8). After the system of victim lawyers was established, however, much advocacy work has been undertaken to improve the rights of crime victims, especially those of women and children.

Over the years, the government has appointed several public commissions, the work of which has contributed to the gradual improvement of the rights of crime victims. Specifically, the report *Contradiction and Dignity* concluded that the victim's role in criminal proceedings still needed to be strengthened, and proposed ways to give victims more influence in the investigation, prosecution, and trial of their case (Robberstad 2002).

In the 2003 report *The Right to a Life without Violence* (NOU, Norges offentlige utredninger[4] 2003), the Committee on Violence against Women

(Kvinnevoldsutvalget) highlighted some of the challenges regarding the absence of protection for victims of DV. The report also made recommendations on how to enhance the rights of these victims. Robberstad's efforts led to the appointment by the government of another committee, the Victim's Committee *(Fornærmedeutvalget)*. The Victim's Committee proposed several changes in the report *Victims in the Criminal Procedure—New Perspectives, New Possibilities* (NOU 2006). The report led to revisions of large sections of the Criminal Procedure Act in 2008, thus providing substantial improvement to the victim's status in criminal proceedings. The victim was no longer considered only a witness, but a participant in the case. The term "participant"—and not "legal party"—is to be used because the victim's rights are limited and not equal to the defendant's rights, for example when it comes to the right to appeal.

The United Nations Committee of the Convention on the Elimination of Discrimination Against Women (CEDAW) criticized Norway in its 2003 report, stating its concern that "an extremely low percentage of reported rapes results in convictions and that the police and public prosecutors dismiss an increasing number of such cases."[5] Specifically, these findings indicate that 90 percent of all rape cases are never reported to the police, and that approximately 10 percent of the reported cases lead to conviction (NOU 2008). As a result, a public committee on rape *(Voldtektsutvalget)* was appointed by the Norwegian government. In the report *From Words to Action*, the committee came up with a number of suggestions to protect rape victims, including establishing a separate unit within the police, working only on sexual crimes, thus improving the quality of the police work and increasing the number of convictions (NOU 2008).

The figures indicated by these reports have been confirmed by a national survey published in late February 2014. This study concluded that 9.4 percent of women and 1.1 percent of men in Norway have been raped; 10.5 percent of the women who experienced rape reported the case themselves to the police. In total, 17.5 percent of the cases were known to the police (Thoresen and Hjemdal 2014).

Who is entitled to be represented by a victim lawyer?

Originally all victims of rape, incest, and other serious sexual offenses[6] were entitled to have a victim lawyer.[7] Through the 2008 revisions of the Norwegian Criminal Procedure Act, the application of the victim lawyer provision was extended to other crimes. Victims of trafficking, DV,[8] female genital mutilation, and forced marriage now automatically have the right to a victim lawyer. The provision also applies to any case where the perpetrator has breached a restraining order. In cases where a person under 18 years old has died as a result of a criminal act, the person with parental responsibility for the victim also is entitled to a victim lawyer.

However, there are also crimes that depend on the judge's discretion as to whether a victim lawyer is to be granted. The court may appoint a victim lawyer if there are reasons to believe that the victim has incurred considerable harm to their body or health as a result of the crime, and therefore is deemed in need of a counsel.

The role of the victim lawyer

According to Section 107c of the Criminal Procedure Act, the victim lawyer shall protect the victim's interest in connection with the investigation and the main hearing of the case. The victim lawyer is a link between the police and the victim. The victim lawyer shall also give the aggrieved party such additional assistance and support as is reasonable in connection with the case. In other words, the victim lawyer provides more than legal counsel. Additional assistance and support imply, for example, answering questions from the media, helping victims to connect to medical and psychological professionals, and showing victims the courtroom before the trial. The rules pertaining to the defense lawyer apply to the victim lawyer, unless the legislation states otherwise.

The role of the victim lawyer before reporting to the police

Victims of rape and other serious crimes such as DV are entitled to up to three hours of free counseling with a victim lawyer in order to obtain information and advice about the legal consequences of reporting the crime to the police. Many victims are hesitant to report and might have conflicting thoughts about going through a criminal procedure. As shown by a Swedish study, many rape victims do not define their victimization as against the law (Justitiedepartementet 2004). A Norwegian study also found that there were instances where women victims of rape did not label their experience as rape, particularly when there was alcohol and drugs involved, and when they had a previous relationship with the man (Stefansen and Smette 2006). Both studies suggested victims' reactions were reflecting their feelings of shame or guilt. The Swedish study also mentioned lack of knowledge of the justice system as reason for not reporting.

In my experience as a victim lawyer for the last 14 years, many victims of sexual offenses and DV fear that there is not enough evidence for conviction and that the police, prosecutors and judges will not believe their testimony. They do not always trust the police investigating the case and may fear cross examinations by defense lawyers in court. The victim lawyer can detail the pros and cons of reporting a crime to the police, and may also explain legal concepts, such as the burden of proof, the reporting process, what to expect during an investigation, and eventually how the trial might proceed. The opportunity for free legal counsel at this early stage provides victims with better grounds upon which to make decisions. In my experience, the right to a victim lawyer was an important improvement because it encourages victims to report to the police, in particular for sexual and DV offenses. However, the figures regarding the number of reported crimes against women are inconclusive, as there is no clear increase in the number of crimes reported by women.

The role of the victim lawyer during investigation

The police are required to inform victims of their rights to be represented by a victim lawyer when they are interviewed. During the interview the victim lawyer may ask supplementary questions to the victim and request a victim impact statement be drafted. The victim lawyer's role at this stage also includes asking the police about their progress in the investigation.

The victim lawyer represents a link between the victim and the police, receiving and giving information from both parties. The victim lawyer may suggest investigative actions to the police.[9] The lawyer may even propose that the court appoint an expert witness during the investigation to examine the effects of the crime on the victim.[10] The expert witness, usually a psychologist or psychiatrist, will be paid by the court. The victim lawyer has the right to be present during all investigative actions that involve the victim, such as reconstructions or crime scene inspections. If there are preliminary hearings (e.g., remand on custody hearing), the victim and the victim lawyer have the right to be notified beforehand and also to attend the hearings. In addition, victims in Norway may present civil claims for compensation for injuries incurred in conjunction with the criminal case, and assisting victims in this process is an important part of the victim lawyer's work. Even if the case is dropped by the prosecutor, the victim lawyer may still apply for compensation on behalf of the victim through the Norwegian Criminal Injuries Compensation Authority.

If the prosecutor decides to drop the charges, the victim has a right to appeal the decision. My experience is that an appeal from the victim lawyer may lead to further investigation of the case, which may lead to the suspect being charged and possibly convicted. In some cases, the victim lawyer may present new evidence or argue that the evidence is sufficient for charges to be filed. The victim lawyer has a greater knowledge of the case and personal knowledge of the victim. The prosecutor, on the other hand, relies on documents and often deals with a heavy workload; therefore the victim lawyer may influence the prosecutor to press charges. For example, in one of my cases, the prosecutor had initially dropped the charges because the victim did not run away from the crime scene immediately after being raped, but stayed with the perpetrator until she met a friend she had telephoned. Although this behavior may be regarded as surprising by some, it is understandable when interpreted in the context of the victim's fear. The appeal was accepted by the Director of Public Prosecutions and the perpetrator was found guilty in the Lower Court and, later, by a jury in the Court of Appeal. He was sentenced to four years in prison, but sadly, right after he was released from jail he raped another young woman in the center of Oslo.[11] This time there was DNA evidence linking him to the rape and he was sentenced to jail again.

The role of the victim lawyer during trial preparation

If a case is brought to trial, the victim lawyer will get a closing date from the court for filing claims and entering supplementary evidence (e.g., documents and witnesses, for instance a psychologist who can document the consequences of the crime). Both the victim lawyer and the victim will be informed of the trial date.

The victim has the right to meet the prosecutor before the trial starts. The meeting with the prosecutor may take place with or without the victim lawyer present. When this right was introduced some prosecutors were reluctant to speak to the victim because of their obligation of objectivity. However, most prosecutors now seem to realize the advantage of knowing the victim's personality as well as receiving updates regarding their situation (e.g., the victim may have dropped out of school due to the trauma of victimization). The prosecutor may explain to victims their role as an objective party in the case, and that facts weakening the victim's testimony will also be followed up in the prosecutor's questioning during the trial. In this way all parties will be better prepared for the court case. For most victims, meeting with the prosecutor will make the trial appear more predictable, having a face and a person to relate to, not only a title. Such a meeting may relieve some victims of the discomfort they may feel before the trial.

The role of the victim lawyer during the trial

The 2008 revisions in the Criminal Procedure Act brought an important change to the organization of court trials. Whereas previously the defendant would testify first, followed by the victim, whose sole status was that of a witness, a victim represented by lawyer now has the status of a participant and is entitled to follow the entire trial, and usually testifies in advance of the defendant. As explained above, victims are not granted the status of "legal parties" in criminal proceedings because they cannot appeal the conviction or the sentence, but can only appeal the decision on civil claims (i.e., compensation). The victim lawyer may directly influence criminal proceedings, for example by requesting that the defendant leave the courtroom while the victim testifies, or that the courtroom be closed to the public. In addition, the victim lawyer will also act as an attorney and might ask questions to the victim, the defendant, and the witnesses. Usually the victim lawyer will ask questions to clarify the victim's claims, and the prosecutor will often decide to let the victim lawyer ask the victim about the consequences of the crime and their current situation. The Norwegian system also allows the victim lawyer to call on witnesses and file documents as evidence, such as reports from doctors or psychologists. If compensation is requested, the victim lawyer will present closing arguments. However, the victim lawyer is not allowed to present closing arguments concerning the guilt of the defendant. The victim lawyer does not comment on the length, type, or terms of the sentencing in their closing arguments.

Moral dilemmas may arise sometimes. For example, in an incest case the victim may have changed her mind after reporting the crime, and neither wants the perpetrator to be punished nor to file civil claims. In this case the lawyer will present the victim's opinion, but it will be up to the prosecutor to argue the question of guilt and the sentence. Another example is that if the victim lawyer knows that their client is lying about a fact, they might have to consider withdrawing themselves, as they must never contribute to the conviction of an innocent person.

The role of the victim lawyer after the trial

When a conviction has been reached in a criminal case, it is the prosecuting authority who decides whether an appeal will be made concerning the question of guilt and penalty imposed. However, if the victim was awarded compensation, they may appeal the decision on the civil claims, even if the case itself is not appealed. The victim also may submit new claims to the Court of Appeal, even if no claims were filed in the lower court. The only condition is that there is a causal link between the harms sustained by the victim and the crime. Sometimes the case is not fully examined by the lower court, for example, and the victim provides new evidence only after the first trial, for instance medical expenses or a loss of income. In that case, such claims can be filed with the Court of Appeal.

Compensation

Victims or bereaved parties may be entitled to monetary compensation from the perpetrator of a criminal act. If the case is brought to trial, the compensation claim can normally be filed alongside the criminal proceedings. There are many advantages to this arrangement. First, the victim does not have to testify both in the criminal and the civil hearings. Second, most of the evidence connected to the civil claim for compensation will be presented as evidence in the criminal proceedings. In addition, this provision will contribute to lower judicial costs for both the court system and society.

If a victim lawyer has been appointed by the court, the lawyer will file the claim on behalf of the victim. If not, the prosecuting authority will file the claim. However, the prosecuting authority does not have the time to closely monitor victims' claims and is likely to be less familiar with compensation laws. Thus a victim lawyer is likely to be more successful than a prosecutor at securing compensation for victims.

The Norwegian criminal injuries compensation authority

If a victim is granted compensation in criminal proceedings, the victim lawyer may send an application to the Norwegian Criminal Injuries Compensation Authority[12] *(Kontoret for voldsoffererstatning)*. The compensation authority will normally process the claim and compensate the victim as established by the court decision. This means that the victim does not depend on the perpetrator's ability or willingness to settle and does not have to interact with the perpetrator. The compensation authority will later attempt to be paid back by the perpetrator.

Compensation may be awarded provided that there is a preponderance of clear and convincing evidence that a crime has been committed. This indicates that the burden of proof is not the same concerning compensation claims as it is concerning the question of guilt. A perpetrator may be acquitted, but at the same time ordered to compensate the victim. Further, one may obtain compensation from the Criminal Injuries Compensation Authority even if criminal charges have been dropped or if the perpetrator remains unknown. If the victim of a violent crime dies as a consequence of the crime, their family may likewise be entitled to compensation. Of note, children who have witnessed or experienced violence to a person close to them may also be entitled to compensation, if this experience was detrimental to their trust or sense of security and this can be documented, for instance by a statement from a public nurse.

The challenges of the victim lawyer

In 2000, when I first began working as a victim lawyer, this position was considered of low status compared to the other parties in the criminal case. For example, the courts would set a date for the trial without conferring with the victim lawyer and often the victim lawyer was not even informed about the date of the trial. The victim lawyer did not have a defined role in court and was not very visible. Much of the victim lawyer's work was not recognized because it was typically happening before trial, when preparing and supporting the victim as well as providing or suggesting evidence or actions during the investigation. But it is true that many victim lawyers were not very invested in their cases either, providing minimal effort when it came to presenting evidence in court or filing compensation claims.

Victims' rights have been in place for a few years now, and victim lawyers have become more active and are generally better skilled at fulfilling their responsibilities. The role of victim lawyers is more clearly defined and their work has become more visible in the media as a result of the coverage of some prominent criminal cases in recent years.

Regular public victim lawyers at the court

Any lawyer who passed the bar exam can practice as a victim lawyer in Norway; no specific personal or legal condition is imposed. For this reason, victim lawyers' qualifications may vary. Each district court has recently established a system of "regular public victim lawyers" that are available for victims who have not asked to be represented by a specific lawyer. In Oslo District Court, for example, 15 victim lawyers are appointed by the court on a general basis for a specified period of time.

The July 2011 terrorist attacks in Norway

On July 22, 2011 a tragedy occurred in Norway that was beyond everyone's belief and that affected our entire nation. The far right terrorist Anders Behring Breivik bombed central Oslo and opened fire at a youth camp on the island Utøya. He killed 77 people, most of them teenagers, and injured more than 240 individuals. More than 900 people were directly affected by the attacks. Challenges arose as to how to provide the victims sufficient legal advice and support. At the same time, the Court of Oslo wanted to ensure an efficient and dignified trial. It was an important goal not to shower the perpetrator with a lot of attention for his ideas or criminal actions.

The court proceedings around this tragedy illustrate some of the challenges of implementing the victim lawyer policy in multi-victim cases. Because the Norwegian legislation allows victims to choose the lawyer they want to represent them, the situation was challenging for the court. There were 170 victim lawyers appointed in connection to this case. Oslo District Court managed the challenge by appointing three of the victim lawyers to coordinate the others. They had meetings with the judges, the prosecutors, and the defense lawyers. They also established mailing lists of all victim lawyers to discuss evidence, claims, and any other questions that arose. During the trial the coordinating victim lawyers provided the other victim lawyers with daily summaries of the proceedings, since not all of them could be present in court. They were also allowed to connect electronically with the other lawyers during the trial, and through this channel they were able to receive questions and additional information. A new courtroom was built in Oslo courthouse with limited space. The idea was to send video links to the other rooms of the courthouse and to several district courts throughout Norway. The teenagers who had attended the youth camp were political representatives from all over Norway, and many of the victims and their families had hometowns far away from the capital city. In this case, the Oslo Court broadcasted the case to district courts, allowing the victim lawyers to "virtually attend" the trial with their clients.

As a result of the 2011 attacks, the Criminal Procedure Act was modified, allowing the courts to appoint coordinating victim lawyers in criminal cases involving a large number of victims. This legal provision has the advantage of easing the work of the court and the prosecutor, while still granting victims the right to a lawyer of their choice and for cases to be handled individually. Coordinating lawyers must have a clearly defined role. One issue that requires further discussion is whether or not, in addition to a coordinating role, they also should have clients of their own, which may lead to conflicts of interest.

Other cases with multiple victim lawyers

Obviously cases with a large number of victims only pertain to certain offenses (e.g., homicide, human trafficking); no Norwegian DV case has ever required the appointment of dozens of victim lawyers as in the case described above. However, in 2008 a child molester was apprehended and charged for having sexually assaulted 66 boys.[13] Fourteen victim lawyers were involved in the case, with two appointed as coordinating lawyers. The victim lawyers were not present during the entire trial. Before the trial some of the victims were instructed by the court to change lawyers to reduce the number of lawyers. Some victims found it difficult to change lawyers after trust had been established.

Other examples of cases involving multiple victim lawyers were cases of sexual assault and rape, but the number of victims in these cases has usually been less than ten. Sometimes the court wants all victims to be represented by one single lawyer, but when the victims have already chosen their lawyer, imposing on them the requirement to change their decision would be contrary to the right to free choice of legal representation. In some cases of DV both the mother and the children might be victims. In these cases the question arises whether they should have the same or different victim lawyers, as there may be a conflict of interest between the mother and the children if the DV perpetrator is the children's father. The mother might be seeking custody against the father and this may be influenced by the outcome of the criminal case. Also in some cases the mother might reconcile with the father, which will make it difficult for a victim lawyer to represent simultaneously the mother's and the children's best interests if these happen to diverge.

Do victim lawyers represent a threat to defendants' rights?

Some defense lawyers, public prosecutors, and judges critically claim that victim lawyers now have too much power and influence in criminal proceedings. In cases with multiple victims, there might be several victim lawyers but only one public prosecutor and one defense lawyer. Some think that a victim lawyer acts as an extra prosecutor and that there is no longer a balance between victims' and defendants' rights.

In my opinion, after having worked in this field for several years, those accusations are unwarranted. In many cases, the presence of a victim lawyer may in fact lead to a more thorough review of the evidence and thus strengthen the case. Sometimes their presence may improve the probabilities of conviction, but as long as these convictions are the result of more thorough investigation and prosecution processes, no innocent person should be found guilty and this outcome would be in the best interest of society.

Further, the victim lawyer does not address the question of guilt as such. It is always the responsibility of the prosecutor to decide whether charges should be filed and to argue for conviction. But it might be true that the victim lawyer may facilitate the court's decision, by asking for or presenting evidence during the investigation process or the trial. Victim lawyers must follow legislation, such as the Criminal Procedure Act, norms and professional standards concerning the conduct for lawyers in general, and the guidelines for victim lawyers in particular. So long as victim lawyers are aware of these rules and the Attorney's Oath stating that lawyers are to "promote justice and hinder injustice," it is difficult to see how anyone can claim that victim lawyers threaten defendants' rights.

Evaluation of the system of victim lawyers

There has been no large-scale evaluation of the system of victim lawyers as such. However, a group of judges at the District Court of Oslo has evaluated the costs of victim lawyers in their jurisdiction.[14] They pointed out that the cost of the system was NOK 28.7 million in 2005, but had risen to NOK 119.4 million in 2012.[15] They also pointed out that the appointment of multiple victim lawyers called for larger courtrooms, and longer—thus more expensive—proceedings. Their conclusion was that the number of appointments should be reduced to lower costs, especially in large cases with several victim lawyers. They also suggested that the Criminal Procedure Act should be modified when applied to cases with multiple victims. Main suggestions included limiting victims' right to select the victim lawyer of their choice and allowing authorities to deny the victim lawyers' right to be present during the entire trial. That said, it is important to consider the above figures in connection with the rising number of repeated sexual offenses, as well as an all-time-high number of reports of severe DV in 2012.[16]

A large-scale evaluation of the system would be valuable for all parties involved. In addition to cost, it is vital to understand how victims experience the proceedings with or without a lawyer by their side. Some aspects, such as the victim lawyer's ability to clarify issues related to the case by presenting vital evidence in court, are difficult to measure and quantify.

If a societal goal is to protect victims of violent crimes, the victim lawyer would obviously play an important role. My conclusion therefore is that victim lawyers work in the best interest of the victim, in the best interest of society, and sometimes even the best interest of the defendant, inasmuch as more questions will be answered and the court will come closer to the truth of the matter.

Notes

1 In some instances, the Norwegian *"bistandsadvokat"* has also been translated by the expression "counsel for the aggrieved party." The expression "victim lawyer" will be used throughout this chapter.

2 Criminal Procedure Act of 22 May 1981 no. 25, with subsequent amendments, most recently by Act of 24 June 2011, no. 32.

3 A revision of the Criminal Code was approved by the National Assembly in 2005, but at the time of writing, the date the legislation will go into effect had not been set.

4 *"Norges offentlige utredninger"* stands for Public Reports of Norway.

5 Sixth periodic reports of Norway under article 18 of the CEDAW, CEDAW/C/NOR/6 supplement A/58/38, §419.

6 For example, misuse of a position, or a relationship of dependence or trust, exploiting mental illness or retardation, sexual activity with a child under the age of 16, incest (The General Civil Penal Code, sect. 192–7, 199, and 200 subsect. 2–33).

7 Criminal Procedure Act, sect. 107a.

8 The law requires severe or repeated domestic violence. Establishing the severity of domestic violence is a matter of judicial discretion; factors such as pain, extent of injury, and living under a reign of terror are considered relevant. The Supreme Court stated that three or more incidents of domestic violence make up repeated domestic violence.

9 The police do not have an obligation to follow up, but in my experience they usually do.
10 Criminal Procedure Act, §237, subsect. 2.
11 Borgarting Lagmannsrett, case 06-144933AST-BORG/03 of 8 December 2006.
12 The term "injuries" suggests physical injuries, but compensation can be granted for any consequences of the crime (e.g., psychological trauma, loss of earnings).
13 See NRK, Norwegian Broadcasting Corporation Online. www.nrk.no/norge/1.7166652.
14 See Norwegian Broadcasting Corporation. Online. www.nrk.no/norge/1.11426553.
15 Exchange rate, 1$ for NOK 6 (February 2014).
16 For latest available data, see Statistics Norway, Offences Reported to the Police 2012. Online. Available at www.ssb.no/lovbrudda.

References

Justitiedepartementet (2004) *Anmälan och utredning av sexualbrott*, no. 2004:1 (Notification and Investigation of Sexual Offenses), Stockholm: Justitiedepartementet.

NOU, Norges offentlige utredninger (2008), *Fra Ord til Handling*, no. 2008:4 (From Words to Action), Oslo: Justis-og politidepartementet.

NOU, Norges offentlige utredninger (2006), *Ofre i Straffeprosessen, Nye Perspektiver, Nye Muligheter*, no. 2006:10 (Victims in the Criminal Procedure: New Perspectives, New Possibilities), Oslo: Justis-og politidepartementet.

NOU, Norges offentlige utredninger (2003), *Retten til et Liv Uten Vold*, no. 2003:31 (The Right to a Life without Violence), Oslo: Justis-og politidepartementet.

Robberstad, A. (2010) *Mellom tvekamp og inkvisisjon: Straffeprosessens grunnstruktur belyst ved fornærmedes stilling* (Between Duel and Inquisition: The Basic Structure of Criminal Procedure in Light of the role of the Victim), Oslo: Universitetsforlaget.

Robberstad, A. (2002) *Kontradiksjon og verdighet* (Contradiction and Dignity), Oslo: Universitetsforlaget.

Robberstad, A. (1994) *Bistandsadvokaten, Ofrenes stilling i straffesaker* (The Victim Lawyer, Victims' Position in Criminal Cases), Oslo: Universitetsforlaget.

Salomon, H. (2013) *'Bistandsadvokatens rolle'* (The Role of the Victim Lawyer), *Kritisk Juss*, 1: 34–39.

Stefansen, K. and Smette, I. (2006) *'Det var ikke en voldtekt, mer et overgrep. Kvinners fortolkning av seksuelle overgrepserfaringer'* (It was not rape, it was abuse. Women's interpretation of experiences with sexual abuse), *Tidsskrift for Samfunnsforskning*, 1: 33–53.

Storberget, K. (2009) *Bjørnen sover: Om vold i familien* (Sleeping Bear: About Domestic Violence), Oslo: Aschehoug.

Thoresen, S. and Hjemdal, O.K. (eds.) (2014) *Vold og voldtekt i Norge: En nasjonal forekomststudie av vold i et livsløpsperspektiv* (Violence and Rape in Norway: A National Prevalence Study of Violence in a Lifetime), Oslo: Norwegian Centre for Violence and Traumatic Stress Studies. Online. Available at www.nkvts.no/biblioteket/Publikasjoner/Vold_og_voldtekt_i_Norge.pdf (accessed 25 May 2014).

Section III: Justice system responses to sexual violence

Questions for critical thought

1. Document evidence of rape myths in your day-to-day life expressed in casual conversation, social media, music videos, television programs and movies, advertising, and other media. Were any of these comments or behaviors met with a negative reaction? A positive reaction? If so, by whom?
2. What are your ideas for changing your peers' attitudes that blame victims and excuse the behavior of perpetrators of sexual violence? For family members? For institutions such as police and other state agencies?
3. Interview police officers in your local area about cases of sexual violence. Is there a "culture of skepticism"? How might this affect their investigations?
4. Three decades after the rape crisis movement began, case attrition remains high. Suggest changes to policy and practices inside and outside the criminal justice system that might reduce case attrition and enhance victim empowerment.

Further reading

Brown, J.M. and Walklate, S.L. (eds.) (2012) *Handbook on Sexual Violence*, Oxon, UK: Routledge.

Gavey, N. (2005) *Just Sex? The Cultural Scaffolding of Rape*, New York: Routledge.

Spohn, C. and Tellis, K. (2014) *Policing and Prosecuting Sexual Assault: Inside the Criminal Justice System*, Boulder, CO: Lynne Rienner.

Temkin, J. and Krahé, B. (2008) *Sexual Assault and the Justice Gap: A Question of Attitude*, Oxford: Hart Publishing.

UN Women (2011) *2011–2012 Progress of the World's Women: In Pursuit of Justice*. Online. Available at http://progress.unwomen.org/pdfs/EN-Report-Progress.pdf (accessed 25 May 2014).

Websites

hollaback!: A movement to end street harassment, powered by a network of local activists around the world aiming for a better understanding of street harassment, igniting public conversations, and developing innovative strategies to ensure equal access to public spaces.
www.ihollaback.org/

National Sexual Violence Resource Center: Collection of information, resources, and tools to build programs and policies to end sexual violence.
www.nsvrc.org/resources

Sexual Violence Research Initiative: Global research initiative that aims to promote high-quality sexual violence research, particularly in developing countries, with the help of a coordinated network of researchers, policy makers, activists, and donors to ensure that sexual violence is addressed from the perspective of different disciplines and cultures.
www.svri.org

SECTION IV

Victim crisis and advocacy

Learning objectives

In reading this section, you will be able to:

1. Identify the challenges involved and factors that promote multi-agency communication and collaboration.
2. Appreciate the multiple oppressions minority ethnic women and women with disabilities face and understand how these affect their experiences of intimate partner violence and reactions to it so as to develop appropriate responses.
3. Explain how and why violence is often attributed to minority cultures rather than gendered power relations.
4. Discuss pre-migration experiences that can contribute to intimate partner violence but that are often overlooked when devising responses to support victims and perpetrators.
5. Realize that intimate partner violence services must be culturally responsive if they are to respond effectively to the needs of immigrant women and men.

Chapter 10

Breaking down barriers

New developments in multi-agency responses to domestic violence

Nicky Stanley

Increasing awareness of the widespread nature of domestic violence (DV) around the world (WHO 2013) has led to the recognition that the response to DV cannot be confined to one sector. Not only is DV an extensive problem, it is also a complex one which affects all aspects of women's lives. Women themselves apprehend impacts of DV across many spheres of activity and experiences and do not compartmentalize their needs in line with professional or service responsibilities. While specialist agencies whose work has been informed by feminist understandings of power and violence have led the way both in bringing DV to public attention and in developing services for women, DV is a problem that demands a multi-agency response. It affects the health, safety, employment, education, and welfare of women and their families, and responses therefore need to engage a wide range of agencies. Increasing recognition of the extent to which different forms of harm and abuse overlap (Hamby and Grych 2013) provides a further argument for the involvement of health, mental health and substance misuse services, criminal justice services, children's social services, housing, welfare and immigration services alongside specialized DV services which are usually delivered by the voluntary sector. In this chapter, DV is conceptualized as intimate partner violence, but discussion of multi-agency work inevitably includes consideration of its impact on children.

Over the last few decades in the United States and the United Kingdom, multi-agency coordinating councils or DV forums at the local level have emerged as a key mechanism for engaging a range of organizations in the task of tackling DV (Allen 2006; Hague *et al.* 1996). At the same time, national and state legislation and policy have promoted interagency collaboration and have given the police and other services, such as housing and welfare, powers to intervene to protect and support women and their children who experience DV. Relationships between state and voluntary organizations are now likely to be shaped by contractual arrangements, and the current recession has had a substantial impact on such arrangements in the US and the UK, with specialized DV organizations increasingly forced to compete for limited funding. While competition for scarce resources can contribute to fragmentation, restrictions in public spending have also accelerated a move toward joint commissioning and increased the pressure for services to collaborate to avoid duplication and reduce costs.

Ideological and theoretical differences also have had an impact on relationships between agencies in this field. Although work with DV perpetrators is now commonly conceptualized as a means of reducing victimization and protecting women, doubts about the effectiveness of such interventions persist and may resurface in contexts where organizations are competing for limited funding. The gulf between child protection and specialized DV services derives from their very different conceptions of the primary client or victim, and in the past child protection services' lack of focus on the perpetrator has resulted in perceptions from both mothers and DV organizations that child protection services "blame" mothers and hold them responsible for protecting their children from abusive men (Shlonsky *et al.* 2007). The increased visibility of male victims of DV represents a challenge to feminist constructions of DV, although there is evidence that women's experience of DV is more severe and prolonged than that of men and has greater impact (Ansara and Hindin 2010; Walby and Allen 2004). Awareness of male victims has led to debates about opening up to men services that were formerly women only, and some local authorities in the UK have interpreted equality duties as a requirement for specialized DV services to make provision for male victims.

The chapter draws on a range of research studies; while many of those selected reflect the author's UK base, initiatives and studies from North America and Australia also are considered. Although the breadth and quality of research in this field is developing rapidly, evidence of recent developments is mostly provided by local studies; these often include qualitative process accounts which can be particularly helpful in illuminating the development of multi-agency interventions. Different levels of intervention provide the structure for this chapter, which begins by considering collaboration at the level of prevention and moves on to address identification and frontline responses, information exchange and interventions for survivors and their families. Whole-system approaches are then examined and the chapter ends by drawing together key themes that identify what makes for effective multi-agency responses to DV.

Collaboration in prevention

Education is the setting where DV prevention programs are most likely to be delivered. These preventive interventions are usually described as "healthy relationships" or "dating violence" programs and a range of models and approaches have been rolled out in the US, Canada, Australia, and the UK. One of the debates in this field concerns the question of whether such programs should be delivered by teachers or by specialists from the DV sector (Fox *et al.* 2014). Most of the school-based programs in North America are delivered by education professionals who receive support and training from education specialists. In the UK, where programs are delivered on a more local basis and are not yet mainstreamed, preventive interventions are more likely to be developed and delivered in partnership between schools and specialized DV practitioners, and this approach can assist in ensuring that a program's original theoretical underpinning continues to inform its delivery. A third model entails using specialized DV staff to train and support teachers who deliver these programs in schools.

Maintaining a link between school-based programs and specialized DV services offers a means of providing an informed service response to those children and young people who disclose experience of abuse in their own or their parents' relationships in response to a healthy-relationships/dating-violence lesson. Whilst some qualitative research studies supply accounts of individual teachers providing supportive responses to children and families experiencing DV, the capacity of education professionals to respond to individual children and young people who disclose experience of DV is circumscribed by such factors as the skills and knowledge of individual teachers, the demands of the curriculum and attainment targets, and the availability of school support staff and school nurses. In England and Wales, the government definition of DV has been amended to include 16- and 17-year-olds who experience violence in their own relationships (Home Office 2013). However, there is an identified lack of appropriate support services for both young victims and perpetrators who disclose these experiences (Barter *et al.* 2009).

Engaging health services in the frontline response to domestic violence

Initial disclosures of DV often take place in the setting of generalist services such as health, education, housing, and the police. Ensuring that practitioners are sufficiently skilled and prepared to receive disclosures and provide an initial response that is safe and supportive is the first step in constructing an effective multi-agency response. The frontline response to disclosures of DV may require an approach and skill set that differ from those generally adopted in generalist services where practitioners may only engage with service users for short periods. Feder and colleagues' (2006) review of qualitative research on women's expectations when disclosing DV to health professionals found that women wanted a confidential approach that was non-judgmental and compassionate, that avoided medicalizing the problem, and that acknowledged its long-term nature and the difficulty of a quick resolution. These women valued a dialogue that was not rushed and that progressed at their pace and they wanted a shared approach to decision making. They did not want health professionals to pressure them to disclose, leave the relationship, or bring criminal charges. Some of these expectations represent a major challenge for health practitioners who are trained to see problems as symptoms and whose large caseloads require them to move swiftly from one patient to the next.

Moreover, an appropriate and sympathetic hearing is frequently not sufficient on its own, nor is it likely that generalist practitioners will be able to offer this if they themselves lack knowledge and confidence about local services for women experiencing DV. A fear of being overwhelmed by what they might discover can render professionals in generalist services unwilling to venture into sensitive areas with service users. Hester's (2006) study of the capacity of health visitors and social workers to raise the issue of DV with mothers found that their confidence and ability to do so increased when they were provided with appropriate training, tools, and a safety planning booklet to offer their clients.

The Identification and Referral to Improve Safety (IRIS) program currently being rolled out in primary healthcare settings across England and Wales has built on some of these findings. The program includes training sessions for health practitioners, inserting a prompt to ask about abuse in medical records, and a referral pathway to a named DV advocate who also delivers training and further consultancy. A randomized control trial (Feder *et al.* 2011) found that the intervention substantially increased both disclosures and referrals to specialized DV agencies. The authors note that partnership with the specialized DV sector was a key feature of the intervention, with specialized DV workers both delivering training to primary care staff and providing the point of contact to which practitioners could refer their patients. In this model, practitioners in generalist services are supported by the knowledge that they do not have to manage the consequences of DV disclosures alone but can look to the specialized DV sector to provide services. The success of the IRIS project conveys two key messages for those planning services at the local level. First, there is a need for partnership between specialized and generalist services in which partners are known to one another. Second, identification of DV needs to be backed up and followed through by specialized services that are easily accessible.

Exchanging information

One of the key arguments for collaboration between agencies is that assessment and management of risk will be more accurate and appropriate when informed by a wide range of information (Stanley and Humphreys in press). However, information exchange and sharing is rarely straightforward in the field of DV. Agencies differ in their working definitions of DV, in their primary client focus, in their approaches to collecting and recording information, and in their confidentiality requirements and expectations. While new technology has opened up new means of sharing information, the easy accessibility of material transmitted online has made for difficulties in keeping information secure and ensuring women's safety.

Some of these problems were exemplified in a UK study of police notifications of DV incidents to child protection social workers (Stanley *et al.* 2010). This study found that information supplied by the police was insufficiently child focused for social workers' purposes. Police and social workers had differing expectations of when and whether victims would be asked to give consent to professionals sharing information, or even whether they should be told that information was being shared. Interviews with frontline police officers revealed a lack of understanding as to how the information they passed to social workers was used, and most were unaware how little of the information they recorded was conveyed to social workers. Both social workers and police officers acknowledged that they had limited understanding of one another's roles and suggested that joint training and opportunities to "shadow" one another might assist in this respect.

A positive example of information sharing is provided by the Multi-Agency Risk Assessment Conferences (MARACs) in England and Wales. Led by the police, these multi-agency forums meet to share information, and assess and manage risks for high-risk victims of DV. Evaluations of the MARACs (Robinson 2004 and chapter 5, this volume; Steel *et al.* 2011) found that they succeeded in improving information sharing and trust between agencies. They also have had some success in reducing revictimization in the short term: Robinson (2004) reported that six in ten women experienced no further threats or violence in the six months following the MARAC. However, the MARACs also demonstrate the way in which interagency collaboration can act to "squeeze out" women's perspectives. Victims themselves are not invited to attend the MARAC, but are represented by an advocate. Women are often the best source of information about risks and needs, and when they are excluded from communication between professionals there is a danger that assessment and planning for their safety will become something that is done *to* them rather than *with* them.

Multi-agency interventions for survivors and families

New approaches are emerging for engaging agencies that have traditionally been resistant to incorporating a DV agenda into their work. The extent to which mental health services engage with DV varies across the world, but recognition of the relationship between DV and mental health needs has generally been low in mental health services in Europe and Australia. Howard and colleagues' (2009) review of the research on DV and severe psychiatric disorder found that adult mental health services only occasionally screen for or routinely enquire about DV, and that information about experience of DV in childhood and adulthood rarely informed intervention.

Laing and Humphreys (2013) describe the Towards Better Practice study in New South Wales, Australia, which used a series of linked research studies to bring DV and mental health workers together to explore barriers and facilitators to collaboration; an action research framework was used to plan and develop collaborative strategies. Outcomes included a joint mental health and DV assessment process and the creation of a specialized DV/mental health worker who took referrals from the mental health service and promoted ongoing collaboration and training. The researchers found that collaboration was facilitated by a shared sense of purpose that developed trust, relationship building, "institutional empathy," and neutral leadership. Women's perspectives were integrated into the process from the outset.

Family-focused multi-agency services which deliver support to both mothers and children are emerging. For instance, the Cedar Project in Scotland used co-facilitators who were seconded from a wide range of state and voluntary organizations to work alongside project staff to deliver concurrent group programs to children and their mothers who had experienced DV. An evaluation of this project by Sharp and Jones (2011) found that by working jointly co-facilitators of groups contributed to improved communication and knowledge sharing between agencies as well as increased awareness of relevant resources. The researchers argue that, despite tensions between staff around sharing information and differing child protection thresholds, the process of "learning together in practice" (Sharp and Jones 2011: 114) achieved a positive effect on wider agency understandings and practice. However, they note that individuals need support from workplace managers to fully realize these benefits.

Some projects aim to deliver services for perpetrators alongside those for mothers and children. An example of this approach is provided by two DV projects in Northern England evaluated by Donovan *et al.* (2010). Both projects had three arms which provided early intervention services for mothers and children and perpetrator programs. The projects were located within multi-agency partnerships and received referrals directly from the police, following incidents of DV. The evaluation reported success in reducing reported incidents and repeat referrals; the majority of victims were assessed as being at reduced risk following engagement with the projects. However, the organizations were less successful in their work with perpetrators: Recruitment to these programs was low and the researchers found that frontline practitioners in other organizations did not generally consider it their role to motivate abusive men to attend such programs. There were other challenges encountered with respect to multi-agency engagement which fell away over time, leaving a small core of committed agencies. This was particularly evident when there had been a lack of early planning around agency roles and co-ordination mechanisms. The projects struggled to establish credibility with other agencies and to attract sufficient engagement from senior managers.

These difficulties are particularly relevant in contexts where child protection services refer abusive men to non-mandatory perpetrator programs (see Stanley 2011) since these programs are highly dependent on a commitment from other organizations to prepare and motivate men to use them. Rather than simply handing abusive men over to the independent DV sector for "treatment," child protection services need to be prepared to engage in frontline work with abusive fathers, assess their suitability for perpetrator programs, and build their motivation. In this respect, child protection staff require opportunities to draw on the skills and experience of those involved in delivering perpetrator programs to develop their own skills and confidence in working with abusive men (Stanley *et al.* 2012), an area where more partnerships could usefully be forged.

Whole-system approaches

Whole-system approaches draw attention to the role of the wider community and the environment in sustaining and ending DV. Such approaches are difficult to plan and implement but, where they have been embedded, they have been highly influential. The most celebrated of these approaches is the Domestic Abuse Prevention Project in Duluth, Minnesota (Shepard and Pence 1999), which includes support services for women and perpetrator programs and coordinates policies and protocols across a range of agencies to produce a comprehensive and consistent approach to tackling DV. Also in the US, the Green Book initiative, which was implemented in five states between 2000 and 2005, aimed to improve collaboration and coordination between DV agencies, child protection, and the courts. The initiative involved a range of measures that included the establishment of multi-agency teams, groups, and referral routes or pathways; co-location of staff, interagency training, agreed protocols for identification and assessment, and the representation of all levels of staff and survivors at interagency meetings. An evaluation (Banks *et al.* 2008) highlighted the value of co-location, multi-agency meetings, and a whole-community approach in facilitating collaboration. The researchers also emphasized the importance of training in developing "institutional empathy," which was defined as an understanding of the context shaping how other agencies operate. Interestingly, the courts play a key role in both these initiatives: Neutral and effective leadership was identified as an essential ingredient in the success of the Green Book intervention.

The One Stop Shop or Family Justice Center model originated in San Diego, California, and has been replicated in the US, Canada, and the UK. These centers aim to address service fragmentation by providing a range of services for women experiencing DV, in one central location. Multi-agency teams provide a wide range of services which may vary from one center to another. However, the full range of services offered can include support through the criminal justice system; legal and housing services; advice on finances, benefits, employment, and immigration issues; advocacy, counseling, and safety planning; interventions for mothers and children; medical examinations; adult education; substance misuse services, and (in one center in East London) a forced marriage unit. An evaluation of eight Family Justice Centers in California (EMT Associates 2013) found that women came with multiple needs and the vast majority used more than one type of service offered at the centers, receiving between 1.3 and 4.4 different services. The two services most commonly used were legal assistance and advocacy/support. These findings argue for the value of co-located services.

Moreover, consultations with service users and providers in Wales undertaken as part of a review of DV services (Berry *et al.* 2014) suggested that one-stop centers may be particularly appropriate for women in rural areas, who can access a range of services in one journey, and that they also can offer an opportunity to provide responsive attitudes and sensitivity to the language and cultural needs of minority ethnic women who may have a range of complex needs. Women using the Californian Family Justice Centers, for example, described receiving immigration services that assisted them in becoming legal residents as one of the most important benefits they experienced (EMT Associates 2013).

What factors promote collaboration?

This chapter concludes by drawing out key themes from the previous discussion. A policy framework that promotes and incentivizes multi-agency collaboration clearly contributes to positive outcomes. The Australian Towards Better Practice (TBP) study described above was implemented in a context where New South Wales Health had recently made routine screening for DV mandatory in mental health services. There are debates about the appropriateness of routine screening for all health and social care settings, and implementing screening in the absence of services to support victims of DV is ill advised, but this requirement appears to have sent out a message that DV was "everybody's business." Where the policy framework is weak or absent, commitment to a multi-agency response may be located in individuals rather than the organization, and agency engagement may prove transitory or inconsistent.

Neutral leadership is important but the participation of staff from all relevant services across a variety of organizational levels in developing new policies and structures also appears to be key. Involving women who have experienced DV and made use of services in multi-agency planning and forums is likely to ensure that services remain relevant to the needs of those who use them. However, thought and planning needs to be given to how this is achieved so that women's participation in such structures is real and meaningful rather than tokenistic.

Some of the multi-agency initiatives described in this chapter have experienced a lack of buy-in from other organizations. This may be explained by differences in definitions of role, need, or agency thresholds. Addressing these issues explicitly and early in the process of planning a new initiative appears to be helpful. Generalist services need to avoid the temptation to simply pass the problem of DV on to specialized DV services. While many victims will need the services of the specialized DV sector, preventive work and a frontline response to DV can and should be delivered by other agencies, either on their own or in partnership with DV services. Staff in these services need the awareness, confidence, and skills that derive from training, and a knowledge of relevant resources and clear referral procedures, which include safety and confidentiality protocols. Use of referral pathways can be promoted and reinforced by having a named point of referral and receiving feedback from agencies to which clients are referred.

Another key theme to emerge from the work discussed above is the value of practitioners from different services "doing it together." Joint work with a practitioner from another discipline provides a means of acquiring new skills and knowledge as well as learning that encompasses the perspective and procedures of another organization. Co-location is one means of ensuring that staff from different organizations and professions work together, but staff can also be seconded or "lent," as in the case of the co-facilitators from other agencies who contributed to the Cedar Project in Scotland. Research was used as a medium for active learning in the Australian TBP study and this approach has the potential to be used as a means of building other multi-agency partnerships.

Interagency training is commonly conceptualized as the glue which will stick agencies together, but such training has to do more than simply impart awareness, knowledge, and skills pertaining to DV. It should equip practitioners to recognize the differences in aims, practice, and procedure between their organizations, with the aim of embedding what has been described as "institutional empathy." Those planning and delivering such training need to ensure that acknowledgement of difference is woven into the training format and content so that staff are not expected to attend training that is at an inappropriate length or level for them. Moreover, such training needs to be reinforced by supervision and organizational support that allows practitioners to reflect on and explore the implications of what they have learned. Managers should take account of the fact that among those working in this field, there will be practitioners for whom the work evokes personal experience of DV, and structures and resources should be available to respond to this issue.

Whole-system and integrated approaches require resources and extensive planning but they offer myriad opportunities for staff from a wide range of agencies to work alongside one another and exchange knowledge and skills. They are popular with clients in that fluidity of movement between services reflects the way needs overlap in women's lives. Integrated one-stop-shop centers may be particularly helpful in facilitating access to the full spectrum of services for women who experience barriers of language, culture, or distance when contacting services.

Conclusion

This brief "whistle-stop" tour of recent multi-agency initiatives has been inevitably partial in coverage and examples employed. However, it has provided considerable evidence of innovation and positive development in an area of work that came into existence just over 40 years ago. We are moving into a period where DV is a recognized part of the remit for generalist services, rather than being consigned to specialized "women's services." A key challenge now is to ensure that the expertise and knowledge accrued in the specialized DV sector continue to inform the changing landscape of multi-agency relationships and collaborative work.

References

Allen, N.E. (2006) 'An examination of the effectiveness of domestic violence coordinating councils', *Violence Against Women*, 12: 46–67.

Ansara, D.L. and Hindin, M.J. (2010) 'Exploring gender differences in the pattern of intimate partner violence in Canada: a latent class approach', *Journal of Epidemiology and Community Health*, 64: 849–54.

Banks, D., Dutch, N. and Wang, K. (2008) 'Collaborative efforts to improve system response to families who are experiencing child maltreatment and domestic violence', *Journal of Interpersonal Violence*, 23: 876–902.

Barter, C., McCarry, M., Berridge, D. and Evans, K. (2009) *Partner Exploitation and Violence in Teenage Intimate Relationships*, London: NSPCC.

Berry, V., Stanley, N. Radford, L., McCarry, M. and Larkins, C. (2014) *Building Effective Responses: An Independent Review of Violence against Women, Domestic Abuse and Sexual Violence Services in Wales*, Cardiff: Welsh Government. Online. Available at http://wales.gov.uk/statistics-and-research/building-effective-responses-independent-review-violence-against-women (accessed 25 May 2014).

Bullock, K., Sarre, S., Tarling, R. and Wilkinson, M. (2010) *The Delivery of Domestic Abuse Programmes: An Implementation Study of Domestic Abuse Programmes in Probation Areas and Her Majesty's Prison Service*, London: Ministry of Justice.

Donovan, C., Griffiths, S., Groves, N., Johnson, H. and Douglass, J. (2010) *Evaluation of Early Intervention Models for Change in Domestic Violence: Northern Rock Foundation Domestic Abuse Intervention Project, 2004–2009*, Newcastle-upon-Tyne: Northern Rock Foundation.

EMT Associates (2013) *Final Evaluation Results: Phase II California Family Justice Initiative Statewide Evaluation*, Burbank, CA: EMT.

Feder, G., Davies, R.A., Baird, K., Dunne, D., Eldridge, S., Griffiths, C., Gregory, A., Howell, A., Johnson, M., Ramsay, J., Rutterford, C. and Sharp, D. (2011) 'Identification and referral to improve safety (IRIS) of women experiencing domestic violence with a primary care training and support programme: a cluster randomised controlled trial', *Lancet*, 378: 1788–95.

Feder, G., Hutson, M., Ramsay, J. and Taket, A.R. (2006) 'Women exposed to intimate partner violence: expectations and experiences when they encounter health care professionals: a meta-analysis of qualitative studies', *Annals of Internal Medicine*, 166: 22–37.

Fox, C.L., Hale, R. and Gadd, D. (2014) 'Domestic abuse prevention education: listening to the views of young people', *Sex Education: Sexuality, Society and Learning*, 14: 28–41.

Hague, G., Malos, E. and Dear, W. (1996) *Multi-Agency Work and Domestic Violence*, Bristol, UK: Policy Press.

Hamby, S. and Grych, J. (2013) *The Web of Violence: Exploring Connections Among Different Forms of Interpersonal Violence and Abuse,* New York: Springer.

Hester, M. (2006) 'Asking about domestic violence: implications for practice', in C. Humphreys and N. Stanley (eds.), *Domestic Violence and Child Protection: Directions for Good Practice*, London: Jessica Kingsley Publishers, 97–109.

Hester, M. and Westmarland, N. (2005) *Tackling Domestic Violence: Effective Interventions and Approaches*, London: Home Office.

Home Office (2013) *New Government Domestic Violence and Abuse Definition*, London: Home Office.

Howard, L.M., Trevillion, K., Khalifeh, H., Woodall, A., Agnew-Davies, R. and Feder, G. (2009) 'Domestic violence and severe psychiatric disorders: prevalence and interventions', *Psychological Medicine*, 40: 881–93.

Laing, L. and Humphreys, C. with Cavanagh, K. (2013) *Social Work and Domestic Violence*, London: Sage.

McCauley, J., Yurk, R.A., Jenckes, M.W. and Ford D.E. (1998) 'Inside "Pandora's box": abused women's experiences with clinicians and health services', *Journal of General Internal Medicine*, 13: 549–55.

Peckover, S. (2003) '"I could have just done with a little more help": an analysis of women's help seeking from health visitors in the context of domestic violence', *Health and Social Care in the Community*, 11: 275–82.

Robinson, A. (2004) *Domestic Violence Multi-Agency Risk Assessment Conferences for Very High-Risk Victims in Cardiff, Wales: A Process and Outcome Evaluation*, Cardiff: Cardiff University.

Sharp, C., Jones, J. with Netto, G. and Humphreys, C. (2011) 'We Thought They Didn't See', *Cedar in Scotland: Children and Mothers Experiencing Domestic Abuse Recovery, Evaluation Report*, Edinburgh: Scottish Women's Aid and Research for Real.

Shepard, M.F. and Pence E.L. (eds.) (1999) *Coordinating Community Responses to Domestic Violence: Lessons from Duluth and Beyond*, Thousand Oaks, CA: Sage.

Shlonsky, A., Friend, C. and Lambert, L. (2007) 'From culture clash to new possibilities: a harm reduction approach to family violence and child protection services', *Brief Treatment and Crisis Intervention*, 7: 345–63.

Stanley, N. (2011) *Children Experiencing Domestic Violence: A Research Review*, Dartington: research in practice.

Stanley, N. and Humphreys, C. (in press) 'Multi-agency risk assessment and management for children and families experiencing domestic violence', *Child and Youth Services Review*.

Stanley, N., Graham-Kevan, N. and Borthwick, R. (2012) 'Fathers and domestic violence: building motivation for change through perpetrator programmes', *Child Abuse Review*, 21: 264–74.

Stanley, N., Miller, P., Richardson Foster, H. and Thomson, G. (2010) *Children and Families Experiencing Domestic Violence: Police and Children's Social Services' Responses*, London: NSPCC.

Steel, N., Blakeborough, L. and Nicholas, S. (2011) *Supporting High-Risk Victims of Domestic Violence: A Review of Multi-Agency Risk Assessment Conferences (MARACs)*, London: Home Office.

Walby, S. and Allen, J. (2004) *Domestic Violence, Sexual Assault and Stalking: Findings from the British Crime Survey*, London: Home Office Research, Development and Statistics Directorate.

WHO, World Health Organization (2013) *Global and Regional Estimates of Violence against Women: Prevalence and Health Effects of Intimate Partner Violence and Nonpartner Sexual Violence*, Geneva: WHO.

Chapter 11

Providing services to minority women and women with disabilities

Ravi K. Thiara

The historical development of responses to violence against black and minority ethnic (BME) women in the United Kingdom, as elsewhere, can be attributed to the determined political activism of such feminists. In this, they contested the claims of second wave feminism about a "sisterhood," assertions of the sanctity of communities that paid little attention to gendered power relations, and state policies of multiculturalism, which emphasized non-interference in communities. By so doing, BME feminists created a space for the recognition of specific experiences of violence against women (VAW) as rooted in multiple oppression and intersectional discrimination, which required particular responses. This call for specificity over the last four decades created a raft of service responses which, recently, have undergone transformation as a result of the shift toward mainstreaming responses to VAW. Similarly, issues about women with disabilities (WWD) and domestic violence (DV) have been foregrounded by feminists within the disability rights movement. Thus politics (resistance and recognition) and provision (specialist services and mainstreaming) are intimately bound when considering the development of responses to BME women and WWD. This complex and contradictory history, too rich to elaborate fully in this chapter, however, acts as a crucial starting point for our discussion.

This chapter begins with a focus on social location through the lens of intersectionality and argues that this is crucial to framing any examination of violence against BME women and WWD and in understanding their experiences and responses to them. To elaborate this specificity, issues are presented separately for BME women and WWD.

Importance of social location

The utility of singular categories—gender, "race"/ethnicity, disability, sexuality, age, class—has long been shown to be limited, and an examination of their intersection (which re/create positions of privilege and subordination) in explaining and re/producing the discursive and social location of diverse groups favored instead. This intersection transforms single categories so that "race changes gender and gender changes race" (Kelly 2013: 2), resulting in women's experiences that are unique, relational, and contextual. Intersectionality, as used in theorizations of social location rather than individual identities (Chio *et al.* 2013), suggests that forms of oppression/discrimination intersect to produce unique experiences of privilege and marginality, so that social groups can be simultaneously located as dominant and subordinate, an insight which allows for a nuanced analysis.

These insights have been utilized to explain the experiences of VAW among BME women and WWD in the UK, North America, and elsewhere (Nixon 2009; Sokoloff and Dupont 2005). Intersectional analysis, advocated since the late 1970s, has become increasingly influential in discourses of VAW. For BME women and WWD, these intersections shape experiences of violence, access to justice and protection, and to personal empowerment and autonomy. In the UK, the complex web of immigration regulation, racialization of communities, and policies aimed at living with the "other" have shaped policy and practice responses to violence against BME women, just as constructions of disability (as individual vulnerability) have underpinned responses to WWD.

An analytic understanding of the complexity created by the "situatedness" of BME women and WWD along intersecting axes of power and disadvantage is crucial for responding effectively to women's experiences of violence. This complexity is often considered in problematic ways within current policy and practice responses. While intersectional analysis in the VAW field is used to show how intersections shape individual experiences of violence, the responses of others and the outcomes for those experiencing violence, it has rarely, if ever, been used to interrogate processes of differentiation *within* minority communities. Instead BME women are similarly constructed as victims through discursive processes of "collective victimhood."

Black and minority ethnic women

The migration and settlement of those from former colonial states,[1] or the global South, has transformed the make-up of many locales across Europe, North America, and Australia. In the UK, although this migration has been reflected in the demographic landscape since the Second World War, newer waves of migration have led to the term "super diversity" being used to characterize contemporary British society. While shaped by local contexts of migration, discourses about immigration and the "immigrant other," underpinned by "racialization"/"minoritization" processes, have shaped policy and welfare responses to communities. Earlier phases of assimilation and integration gave way to a policy of multiculturalism, which, as a result of the increased focus on the "war on terror," has shifted to an emphasis on community cohesion and multi-faithism (Patel and Siddiqui 2010). Despite these shifts, "race"/ethnicity continue to (re)produce racialized power relations. Both multiculturalism and multi-faithism are critiqued for making invisible issues of gender within communities, which create contradiction for addressing the issue of VAW within BME communities.

There is patchy evidence about the prevalence of violence in BME women's lives, though we now have prevalence data on different countries of the global South. While research suggests that it cuts across all social categories, some European studies suggest that minority women experience higher rates of violence and male control (Condon *et al.* 2011). Some also suggest that minority women take longer to seek help and consequently experience chronic abuse over longer periods (Thiara 2010). Women's uncertain immigration status and lack of knowledge about their rights and options are often used to exert greater control and coercion over women who typically remain entrapped for many years (Anitha 2011).

Although forms of VAW are similar, the contexts in which it occurs and how women are able to respond often vary. Much of the literature on violence against BME women highlights these contexts and how options and constraints for disclosure shape women's responses (Gill 2004; Thiara 2011), so that cultural contexts and social dis/location shape "what it is possible to say, when and to whom. Not to mention how, if at all, their words will be heard, believed and responded to" (Kelly 2013: 3). The ways in which violence reduces women's "space for action" (Kelly 2013) has particular implications for BME women who may find themselves in uniquely vulnerable situations (e.g., women with uncertain immigration status) where they are subjected to a web of coercive control by perpetrators and their family networks in the abusive context and later in the post-separation period (Thiara 2013). This "space for action" is further restricted when professionals/agencies struggle to understand, or fail to address, women's complex positioning within their communities and in society. Despite some positive developments, the failure of agencies to develop positive responses to women's complex situations has been ongoing since the 1990s, when "cultural privacy" and "race anxiety" were highlighted as marking dominant responses (Burman *et al.* 2004). The absence of a complex analysis of BME women's intersectional location in practice responses, which tend to be focused on the unique forms of violence against BME women, is widely accepted. Shifting this focus enables greater scrutiny of those "contexts which are not only conducive to VAW, but also make it harder to name and reduce the likelihood of being believed/taken seriously, leaving women without protection and support" (Kelly 2013: 3). Thus, research on BME women highlights the delayed help-seeking because of, among others, fear of racist responses from mainstream agencies, lack of knowledge about support services, and a reluctance to criminalize their menfolk (Kanyeredizi 2013; Thiara and Gill 2012). Even while increased attention is given to issues of forced marriage and "honor"-based violence, what is often missed in this "hyper gaze" is the failure of agencies to respond appropriately to women seeking help.

Complexity of culture and gender

The complexity and contradiction created for BME women by intersecting social locations can be seen in the operation of cultural and gender processes. How agencies respond to this is illustrated by the policy discourses and responses to forms of violence seen to affect BME women uniquely, responses which privilege culture over gender (for how this operates in the arena of family law see Thiara and Gill 2012). The changing contour of VAW discourse since the 1990s, especially the mainstreaming of VAW with its emphasis on multi-agency responses, has seen an unprecedented focus across much of Europe on issues of forced marriage, "honor" based violence, and female genital mutilation. Policy and public discourse has foregrounded explanations of such violence as rooted in culture rather than gendered power relations. Immigration control is offered as a solution to this violence while there exists a "systematic failure to protect women from the more routine cases of domestic violence" (Patel and Siddiqui 2010: 264). The re-casting of DV and sexual violence as forced marriage or "honor"-based violence has led to a reported increase in such cases, by practitioners who struggle to understand "cultural issues." In this way, gender disappears as an explanation in discourses that view VAW within minority communities as a matter of culture, in which they are reluctant to intervene. Such culturalization of communities, which views them as more patriarchal and thus inherently more violent, in the quest to proffer explanations for violence against BME women, is concerning in a context where services with expertise and understanding of complex issues are being cut. In this way, different explanations are given for the same forms of violence within BME and majority communities (Chantler and Gangoli 2011). This is in contrast to BME feminists who view culture as an important consideration in understanding and responding to women, but reject it as the sole explanation for VAW.

In addition, culture is invoked by powerful elements within minority communities to argue against interference, which is uncritically accepted by professionals who fear being viewed as racist. Notwithstanding problems of essentializing culture and communities across time and space, such responses lead to the construction of minority women as victims who need to be saved, an approach that conflicts with BME feminists who emphasize processes of cultural re/creation. That BME feminists have been at the forefront of the VAW movement, and women in the same communities "experience high levels of surveillance, have restricted social networks and are subjected to local and transnational regimes of control" (Kelly 2013: 6), precisely illustrates the fluidity and contestation that simultaneously exist in BME communities.

Within a context of essentialist constructions of culture, BME women's experiences of VAW in common with all women remain invisible. Such developments also have created contradictions within BME women's organizations, with some uncritically reinforcing such constructions while others foreground the diversity of BME women's experiences and social contexts within an explicit gendered analysis to argue that violence against BME women cannot be a parallel discourse but has to be located within wider VAW phenomenon/debates. To view forced marriage, "honor"-based violence, and female genital mutilation as aspects of VAW, it has been argued, results in the problematization of such practices and has the potential for transformation, whereas to cast them as "cultural" issues re-inscribes VAW and represents culture as solely negative and existing only within minoritized communities. Siddiqui (2013), in the UK, for instance, has helpfully argued for "honor"-based violence not to be seen as a form of violence itself but as the motive underpinning forms of violence such as forced marriage, DV, and sexual violence.

Despite this hyper-visibility of forms of violence against BME women and the creation of a parallel discourse, and aside from the increasingly dwindling refuge-based specialist BME provision, such women are increasingly accorded little specialist intervention in mainstream services. Current multi-agency responses betray a lack of knowledge and expertise about BME women. Given the reluctance of BME women to access statutory services, emphasis on community cohesion and the closure of specialist BME services has created consternation among activists and service providers who have built up expertise over the last four decades about these issues.

Interventions for black and minority ethnic women

> For many BME survivors of gender based violence, an effective service is one in which the response to their experiences of violence is framed not only within an analysis of gender but also of "race," culture and ethnicity.
>
> (Larasi 2013: 268)

The specialist BME VAW sector developed and led by and for BME women in the UK is unique (Larasi 2013) and has been underpinned by an intersectional analysis from its inception. Black feminists in the UK, as elsewhere, finding neither voice nor expression for their concerns in the White feminist movement or the anti-racist movement, carved out a pioneering path. The formation of specialist BME VAW services from the late 1970s occurred because of the invisibility of BME women within the refuge movement and the racism encountered in safe houses for women. Focused around the provision of crisis accommodation, these groups provided holistic services underpinned by an empowerment approach and provided a political home for Black feminists. These groups created the space to "recognize nuance, shared journeys and cultural contexts" (Larasi 2013: 271). Most notably, these organizations challenged gender oppression within communities and societal racism while demanding women be afforded protection and support through the state, thus creating a "third way" which continues to be valued by BME women.

BME VAW organizations have undergone considerable transformation, and despite developing valued services over four decades, they face the biggest threat to their existence as a result of mainstreaming and cuts to services. As the landscape of VAW provision changes, BME services are being fundamentally eroded through policies of competitive commissioning, localism, and community cohesion. Research in the UK has shown how such processes disadvantage smaller autonomous (feminist) groups in favor of larger generic service providers, which often lack expertise about BME women and a wider equalities ethos (Wilson and Roy 2011). This is concerning since BME women are seemingly more willing than before to venture outside for help, creating the real possibility that the reduction of specialist services will result in greater reliance by women on community mechanisms to deal with violence against them. Feminists have long fought for the rights of women to protection and justice, and in the absence of BME specialist services they are less likely to find the requisite responses from generic multi-agency professionals. As the "faith agenda" has gained currency in the UK, provision for BME women also has become more contradictory, with faith groups increasingly providing VAW services or offering parallel processes for dispute resolution and arbitration (Bano 2010). These developments are considered to erode the "secular spaces" long valued by women from minority communities (Patel and Siddiqui 2010). Under contradictory policies of community cohesion and multi-faithism, findings which show that BME women "actively seek and appreciate the spaces and options provided by secular community based women's organizations" (Kelly 2013: 9) are increasingly likely to be disregarded and protection for women reduced.

Moreover, while the mainstreaming of VAW has seen greater engagement of statutory services, in relation to BME women, it is evident that even where specificity is recognized, this is narrowly conceptualized as cultural differences, and where the "needs" of BME women are considered, these are reduced to language, religious, and culinary practices, resulting in a reductionist approach which excludes those women considered not to have such cultural requirements. This has often resulted in a focus on the visibly "unintegrated other," where such "needs" are addressed through the provision of interpreters and/or cultural awareness training (Thiara 2014). Insights about the constraints, options, and possibilities afforded by their social locations are often not even on the agenda of many practitioners. The criminalization of forced marriage, after a contested debate about this in the UK, highlights how the lack of attention to women's social dis/location can create contradictions. Although the criminalization of forced marriage is a way for the state to ensure this is challenged and those guilty punished, women's reluctance to prosecute their families where their communities are already victimized suggests these things are thorny and that at times protection may be more appropriate than prosecution.

Women with disabilities

> Unravelling the complex relationship between patriarchy, a disabling society, and other forms of discrimination and marginalization such as homophobia and racism is essential to understanding the solutions to violence against disabled women.
>
> (Bashall and Ellis 2012: 106)

Although increased attention has been given to issues of disability, a focus on WWD's experiences of DV remains scant, despite struggles by these women to place the issue on national and international agendas. Much of this has argued for violence against WWD to be contextualized within wider violence against people with disabilities and for any analysis to be underpinned by the social model and a human rights approach. Dominant protectionist approaches, which construct WWD as "vulnerable adults," have also been challenged (Bashall and Ellis 2012). Despite some gains made from these efforts, however, violence against WWD continues to be marginalized and reflected in the absence of coordinated local and national strategies. Similar to BME feminists, WWD also challenged the patriarchal attitudes of the people with disabilities movement and the disablism of the women's movement through the formation of autonomous groups, such as Sisters against Disablement in the UK, DisAbled Women's Network in Canada, and Women with Disabilities in Australia.

The living conditions of WWD, marked as they are by social isolation, lack of personal, social, and economic independence, create vulnerable situations for women and increase their risk of being targeted for violence (Brownridge 2009). Research from the 1980s in Canada revealed high rates of violence against WWD, showing that 40 percent of respondents had been raped, abused, or assaulted, over half of women disabled from birth or early childhood had experienced abuse, and women with multiple disabilities had experienced multiple forms of abuse. Only around a tenth of women who had been abused sought help, but only half of these received assistance (Ellis and Bashall 2012: 94). Research in the UK, Australia, and North America shows that rates of violence experienced by WWD are higher than they are for women without disabilities and that they experience violence from a range of intimates, including paid caregivers, family members, and intimate partners who use women's disabilities in the perpetration of abuse. This research consistently shows that women's access to services remains extremely limited, leading to the assertion that WWD "lose out on both counts" (Hague *et al.* 2008; Nosek *et al.* 2001).

The importance of recognizing WWD's intersectional locations has been urged since the 1980s, but contemporary policy and practice persists in separating these women out as "vulnerable adults," whereby "violence against disabled women is often still not dealt with in a way that recognizes that disabled women are women" (Ellis and Bashall 2012: 94). As Morris (1996: 7–8) noted, recognition of this intersection disrupts the ways in which VAW is defined while underlining the commonalities between WWD and non-disabled women. National research on women with physical and sensory impairments and DV in the UK (Hague *et al.* 2008), alongside concerted campaigning by feminists with disabilities, has placed this issue on the agenda and, to some extent, created a shift in practice. Despite these initial moves to address disability, however, more is required to ensure that VAW strategies are fully inclusive of WWD and that refuges and support services are fully accessible.

In the UK, as elsewhere, disability legislation over the last two decades has created some shifts in the ways in which disability is viewed, from "special needs" to a more equality/rights-based issue. In the main, legislation has begun to address the "minimum" requirements of physical access and information. Requirements to conduct disability impact assessments have created space for agencies such as the London Metropolitan Police to scrutinize issues of disproportionality in relation to responses to DV against WWD (Bashall and Ellis 2012). However, measures to address the specific attitudinal, practical, or resource barriers faced by WWD remain lacking. Moreover, public campaigns around DV lack accessible information and resources. The cuts to public sector services and changes to welfare benefits for people with disabilities, resulting in their increased dependency, alongside the absence of good-practice guidance on DV and disability, means that WWD will remain at the mercy of a postcode lottery (Coy *et al.* 2007). It has been argued that in any attempt to address barriers encountered by WWD and to develop effective responses, understanding this political and social context of the lives of WWD is crucial.

Much of the research has highlighted a number of critical issues that need to be addressed in relation to violence against WWD. The ways in which DV is defined has long been critiqued for assuming that perpetrators are "family" members, and calls been made for definitions to be extended to take account of violence against WWD, such as abuse by paid/voluntary caregivers in private homes and in residential or semi-residential settings that are "home" to women (Bashall and Ellis 2012). The dominant approach of "safeguarding vulnerable adults," with its emphasis on individual vulnerability (protectionist model) in responses to violence against WWD, also has been problematized, with calls to reframe this within a social model that emphasizes justice and redress and situational vulnerability (rights-based model) to replace the individualized medical model (EHRC 2009: 73). Without this shift, it is likely that WWD's reluctance to disclose abuse will continue for fear of being institutionalized or returned to the "care" of the family. Despite developments in multi-agency responses, for WWD it is likely that the narrow definition of DV and the separation of DV and safeguarding procedures will continue to restrict the solutions and options offered to them (Thiara *et al.* 2012).

Research and activists' struggles highlight the need for a "sea change" in current practice. They have developed some key principles for good practice in responding to WWD, including: a social model approach that seeks to remove barriers for WWD; an inclusive approach to all forms of VAW; and partnerships with WWD at all levels, encapsulated in the slogan "nothing about us without us" (Bashall and Ellis 2012). The UK national study *Making the Links: Disabled Women and Domestic Violence* (Hague *et al.* 2008) identified the need for more comprehensive services for WWD experiencing DV across all sectors, and the need for more training and awareness-raising for professionals in all relevant sectors as key to improving responses. Particular components identified for effective responses, which all require attention to challenging stereotypes of WWD, not reinforcing their dependence, and adopting an inclusive approach to VAW, include: information provision for women; raising professional and community awareness; safe and appropriate options for refuge that meet a range of needs; tailored and appropriate holistic support; justice through appropriate CJS support and effective prosecution; short- and long-term recovery; learning and training; and revision of risk assessment procedures to include the unique risks faced by WWD.

The UK study made the following suggestions for good practice by agencies (Hague *et al.* 2008):

- Be informed about WWD's needs.
- Take advice from, and consult with, WWD.
- Develop accessible services.
- Provide accessible well-publicized DV services (including refuge accommodation) that WWD know about.
- Do not threaten WWD with institutionalization if no refuge space is available.
- Develop good accessible alternative accommodation, both temporary and permanent, plus support to use it.
- Develop disability equality schemes and reviews, with input from WWD.
- Take WWD seriously and avoid being patronizing.

Conclusion

There are many commonalities in women's experiences of violence and its consequences, and it is important to hold on to the threads that tie women together in the ways in which violence and coercive control regulate and constrict their options and autonomy. The differences wrought between women by their intersectional locations also have to be considered in any effective responses, as the discussion in this chapter highlights. It has been argued that this is ever more important since the issues that BME women and WWD encounter continue today as before: negative social constructions of their experiences and communities; threat of and actual racism/ablism from helping professionals; silencing in the community; barriers of language and immigration status; negation of their subjectivity and agency; and a negation of their rights to positive protective responses and justice. This chapter is written at a time when, despite greater focus on VAW at policy and political levels, resources are shrinking fast. Despite the development of innovative interventions by BME women's organizations, and some promising practice on meeting the needs of WWD, it would appear that they are the earliest victims of the reduction in services. While arguably healthy, contestation about the best ways to support BME survivors is creating a considerable challenge for the BME VAW movement and it is likely that constricted services and shifting policy imperatives will result in reduced access to protection and justice for the very women who require it most. In the face of such challenges, it is imperative that the voices of survivors, increasingly disappearing in the multi-agency terrain, are reclaimed and used to create critical conversations and actions in policy and practice arenas.

Note

1 Migration from South Asia, Africa, and the Caribbean was common in the post-war period, and these groups and their descendants still comprise the largest sections of the BME population. Unless indicated otherwise, the term BME includes these and other visible minorities.

References

Anitha, S. (2011) 'Legislating gender inequalities: the nature and patterns of domestic violence experienced by South Asian women with insecure immigration status in the United Kingdom', *Violence Against Women*, 17: 1260–85.

Bano, S. (2010) 'Shariah councils and the resolution of matrimonial disputes: gender and justice in the "shadow" of the law', in R.K. Thiara and A.K. Gill (eds.), *Violence Against Women in South Asian Communities: Issues for Policy and Practice*, London: Jessica Kingsley, 182–210.

Bashall, R. and Ellis, B. (2012) 'Nothing about us without us: policy and practice', in R.K. Thiara, G. Hague, R. Bashall, B. Ellis and A. Mullender, *Disabled Women and Domestic Violence: Responding to the Experiences of Survivors*, London: Jessica Kingsley, 106–36.

Brownridge, D. (2009) 'Situating research on safety promoting behaviours among disabled and deaf victims of interpersonal violence', *Violence Against Women*, 15: 1075–9.

Burman, E., Smailes, S. and Chantler, K. (2004) 'Culture as a barrier to service provision and delivery: domestic violence services for minoritized women', *Critical Social Policy*, 24: 332–57.

Chantler, K. and Gangoli, G. (2011) 'Violence against women in minoritised communities: cultural norm or cultural anomaly?' in R.K. Thiara, S. Condon, and M. Schröttle (eds.), *Violence Against Women and Ethnicity: Commonalities and Differences Across Europe*, Opladen: Barbara Budrich, 353–66.

Chio, S., Crenshaw, K.W. and McCall, L. (2013) 'Toward a field of intersectionality studies: theory, applications, and praxis', *Signs*, 38: 785–810.

Condon, S., Lesne, M. and Schröttle, M. (2011) 'What do we know about gendered violence and ethnicity across Europe from surveys?' in R.K. Thiara, S. Condon and M. Schröttle (eds.), *Violence Against Women and Ethnicity: Commonalities and Differences Across Europe*, Opladen: Barbara Budrich, 59–76.

Coy, M., Kelly, L. and Foord, J. (2007) *Map of Gaps: The Postcode Lottery of Violence Against Women Support Services in the UK*, London: End Violence Against Women Coalition.

EHRC, Equality and Human Rights Commission (2009) *Disabled People's Experiences of Targeted Violence and Hostility*, London: Office for Public Management.

Ellis, B. and Bashall, R. (2012) 'Understanding our history: the personal is political', in R.K. Thiara, G. Hague, R. Bashall, B. Ellis and A. Mullender, *Disabled Women and Domestic Violence: Responding to the Experiences of Survivors*, London: Jessica Kingsley, 82–105.

Gill, A. (2004) 'Voicing the silent fear: South Asian women's experiences of domestic violence', *Howard Journal of Criminal Justice*, 43: 465–83.

Hague, G., Thiara, R.K., Magowan, P. and Mullender, A. (2008) *Making the Links: Disabled Women and Domestic Violence*, Bristol, UK: Women's Aid.

Kanyeredzi, A (2013) 'Finding a voice: African and Caribbean heritage women help seeking', in Y. Rehman, L. Kelly and H. Siddiqui (eds.), *Moving in the Shadows: Violence in the Lives of Minority Women and Children*, Farnham, UK: Ashgate, 205–24.

Kelly, L. (2013) 'Moving in the shadows: introduction', in Y. Rehman, L. Kelly and H. Siddiqui (eds.), *Moving in the Shadows: Violence in the Lives of Minority Women and Children*, Farnham, UK: Ashgate, 1–10.

Larasi, M. (2013) 'A fuss about nothing? Delivering services to black and minority ethnic survivors of gender violence—the role of the specialist black and minority ethnic women's sector', in Y. Rehman, L. Kelly and H. Siddiqui (eds.), *Moving in the Shadows: Violence in the Lives of Minority Women and Children*, Farnham, UK: Ashgate, 267–82.

Morris, J. (1996) *Encounters with Strangers*, London: The Women's Press.

Nixon, J. (2009) 'Domestic violence and women with disabilities: locating the issue on the periphery of social movements' *Disability and Society*, 24: 77–89.

Nosek, M., Howland, C. and Hughes, R. (2001) 'The investigation of abuse and women with disabilities: going beyond assumptions', *Violence Against Women*, 7: 477–99.

Patel, P. and H. Siddiqui (2010) 'Shrinking secular spaces: Asian women at the intersect of race, religion and gender', in R.K. Thiara and A.K. Gill (eds.), *Violence Against Women in South Asian Communities in the UK: Issues for Policy and Practice*, London: Jessica Kingsley, 102–27.

Siddiqui, H. (2013) '"True honour": domestic violence, forced marriage and honour crimes in the UK', in Y. Rehman, L. Kelly and H. Siddiqui (eds.), *Moving in the Shadows: Violence in the Lives of Minority Women and Children*, Farnham, UK: Ashgate, 169–84.

Sokoloff, N.J. and Dupont, I. (2005) 'Domestic violence at the intersections of race, class and gender', *Violence Against Women*, 11: 38–64.

Thiara, R.K. (2014) *Evaluation of Domestic Violence, Maternity and Health Project*, London: Standing Together.

Thiara, R.K. (2013) 'Post-separation violence in the lives of Asian and African-Caribbean women', in Y. Rehman, L. Kelly and H. Siddiqui (eds.), *Moving in the Shadows: Violence in the Lives of Minority Women and Children*, Farnham, UK: Ashgate, 113–26.

Thiara, R.K. (2011) '"Hard feisty women—coping on your own": African-Caribbean women and domestic violence', in R.K. Thiara, S. Condon and M. Schröttle (eds.), *Violence Against Women and Ethnicity: Commonalities and Differences Across Europe*, Opladen: Barbara Budrich, 226–40.

Thiara, R.K. (2010) 'Continuing control: child contact and post-separation violence', in R.K. Thiara and A.K. Gill (eds.), *Violence Against Women in South Asian Communities: Issues for Policy and Practice*, London: Jessica Kingsley, 156–81.

Thiara, R.K. and Gill, A.K. (2012) *Domestic Violence, Child Contact, Post-Separation Violence: Issues for South Asian and African-Caribbean Women and Children*, London: NSPCC.

Thiara, R.K., Hague, G., Bashall, R., Ellis, B. and Mullender, A. (2012) *Disabled Women and Domestic Violence: Responding to the Experiences of Survivors*, London: Jessica Kingsley.

Wilson, A. and Roy, S. (2011) 'In the name of "rights": BAMER women, terrorism and violence against women', in R.K. Thiara, S. Condon and M. Schröttle (eds.), *Violence Against Women and Ethnicity: Commonalities and Differences Across Europe*, Opladen: Barbara Budrich, 291–305.

Chapter 12

A culturally integrative model of domestic violence response for immigrant and newcomer families of collectivist backgrounds

Mohammed Baobaid, Nicole Kovacs, Laura MacDiarmid, and Eugene Tremblay

The last 30 years has witnessed an expansion of formal services to address domestic violence (DV). More recently, attention has been placed on a desire to coordinate multi-agency approaches. Although not a new concept, a multi-agency approach to DV has been the topic of recent discussions in the research literature (Barran and Feder 2010).

In the context of DV, multi-agency approaches work to engage a range of stakeholders to support women and children experiencing abuse, enhance collaboration, and reduce competition for resources (see Stanley this volume). Addressing DV from a multi-agency approach allows multiple organizations, such as police, child protection services, and housing supports, to collaboratively address the needs of women and children while, at the same time, working toward the reduction of a one-size-fits-all approach.

As will be argued in this chapter, however, responses to DV, including multi-agency approaches, are not always culturally responsive. More specifically, when addressing the contextual factors of many immigrant and newcomer families, a need to understand and work within a collectivist approach is required. There are many precipitating factors, for example pre- and post-migration challenges, which may lead to violence in immigrant and newcomer families, that are currently not being addressed in the existing design of services. In this chapter, we explore the difference between individualist and collectivist communities as it relates to DV and introduce an innovative multi-agency approach, one that incorporates a culturally integrative framework in working with immigrant and newcomer families of collectivist backgrounds.

More than cultural sensitivity

Growing interest and concern has been placed on providing culturally sensitive services to victims of DV who may not be part of the mainstream culture, often referred to as making use of "multicultural approaches" (Sokoloff 2008: 244).

Many organizations are beginning to make use of interpretation services, including bilingual workers, providing education for practitioners on cultural differences, and conducting outreach to cultural communities. However, interventions developed and implemented in an individualistic, Western society may not be easily adaptable to women from collectivist societies (Haj-Yahia 2011).

There are many types of collectivism; however, the most prevalent are those in which individuals emphasize their extended family, tribe, cultural/ethnic community, and nationality over the individual. As such, collectivist communities tend to sacrifice personal needs, aspirations, goals, and expectations for the benefit of the collective (Haj-Yahia 2011). Individualist cultures, on the other hand, tend to be more accepting of individual choice, more often emphasizing personal pleasure, achievement, and autonomy (Yoshioka and Choi 2005).

The differences between collectivist and individualist communities are important. Addressing options for women affected by DV may be deeply influenced by the priority placed on her own needs and goals over those of her family and/or community. More specifically, a woman who lives within a collectivist community may not have the same level of access to services as a woman from an individualist culture, especially if those services emphasize divorce, independent living, or single parenthood as among possible solutions (Yoshioka and Choi 2005). It is important to account for differences between individualist and collectivist societies, as they may not be well understood by mainstream service providers (Baobaid and Hamed 2011).

DV is often a new and uniquely Canadian concept for many newcomer and immigrant families in Canada (Baobaid and Hamed 2011). As we will discuss, alternative ways of addressing DV within collectivist communities should be considered, ways that include a holistic approach incorporating community leaders, informal and formal supports, as well as the abuser and the abused (Midlarsky *et al.* 2006).

Before presenting our model to address DV from a cultural perspective, we briefly explore some challenges, including pre-migration challenges, facing newcomer and immigrant families.

Challenges facing immigrant and newcomer families

Although social services are beginning to take account of cultural differences, challenges remain facing immigrant and newcomer families who experience DV. A small body of research documents these challenges faced by women of collectivist backgrounds (Merchant 2000). Examples can include financial dependence on the husband, unfamiliarity of laws, and language barriers, isolation, fear of discriminatory treatment, fear of racism, loss of social supports, and being cut off from extended family and cultural community (Alaggia *et al.* 2009; Merchant 2000).

Research has determined women often enlist help from their family of origin, their husband's family of origin, close friends, or other informal agents in their environment when experiencing DV before seeking support from formal services (Haj-Yahia 2011). This is also true of women in collectivist communities; it may also take several years before a woman seeks support from formal services. This usually occurs at a point when she feels disappointment with the level or type of support received from the collective, fear of being seriously harmed, or fear for her children (Haj-Yahia 2000, 2011).

One area where there is a lack of research is the intersection of pre-migration trauma and violence against women and children in the host country. Pre-migratory experiences of violence that were disruptive to family and community relations are important factors in how well families and individuals will adapt in the host country. Immigrants may face adjustment challenges that prevent them from integrating into the host society, while others may live with post-traumatic stress disorder (PTSD). Many also feel ashamed to seek help or do not know who to trust to receive help (Baobaid 2010).

Building trust is a challenge as many immigrants are hesitant to trust someone who does not speak their language or understand their culture. Conversely, sometimes people from tight-knit communities do not trust a service provider from within their community for fear of exposure. As a result, mainstream service providers may encounter challenges in their attempts to effectively address DV in immigrant and newcomer communities within a collectivist context, without an understanding of the socio-cultural differences these communities possess.

These challenges are not presented to justify or deny violence against women or condone victim blaming. Rather, the objective is to place emphasis on the collectivist orientation to DV that differs from the dominant cultural attitudes and beliefs in Canada (Baobaid and Hamed 2011).

A shift in response

The Muslim Resource Centre for Social Support and Integration (MRCSSI) in London, Canada, developed a Culturally Integrative Family Safety Response (CIFSR) model. Informed by both practice and research, the model seeks to account for these differences to ease the way for abused women of collectivist backgrounds and their families to find help and support to end the violence they are experiencing. More specifically, the model is based on experience and research with Muslim immigrant and newcomer families from a collectivist community. Using our CIFSR model in the context of child protection, the MRCSSI has reduced Muslim children entering care by 75 percent, and within the last three consecutive years, there has not been any Muslim child taken into care in London.

The Culturally Integrative Family Safety Response model

The CIFSR model establishes and promotes dialogue between the cultural community and mainstream anti-violence agencies. This facilitates an environment of mutual understanding and trust, which supports the collaborative development of prevention and intervention materials, resources and services that meet the needs of immigrant women and empower women to articulate their needs and social realities. The engagement of service providers outside their mandates allows more flexibility in response. To illustrate, engaging a police officer or child protection worker during escalating conflict and imminent risk allows the family to receive vital information that may divert a violent event. A violent event is defined, for the purpose of this chapter, as an event where mandated services (e.g., police, child protection authorities) have engaged with a family in an investigation response to a reported threat or an act of violence toward a family member. This process allows the mandated service provider access to family-based information that may shape future interventions that would engage the collaboration of cultural community members.

Guiding principles

Previous research conducted by MRCSSI determined that, to meet the needs of newcomer and immigrant women and families affected by DV, it is important to meaningfully engage a diversity of voices from their respective communities and the local service-provider community in the process (Baobaid 2010).

MRCSSI has made a conscious effort to include a multiplicity of stakeholders from the Muslim community, including the various Islamic cultural and religious groups, religious leadership, local women's organizations/groups, and youth, as well as a broad representation of local service-provider agencies. Likewise, participatory project activities are conducted, such as engagement with mandated service providers (child welfare agencies, police, probation and parole) in which protocols of understanding are developed between MRCSSI and these service providers. This allows MRCSSI the opportunity to provide training on collaboration with partner agencies and opportunities for dialogue, exchange of knowledge, perspectives, concerns, and ideas, and developing customized responses. Working with the bottom line of keeping family members safe from violence has allowed MRCSSI to inform mandated service providers of cultural factors and has helped craft responses that are culturally integrative. These activities also helped to build a mutual understanding and common ground for collaborative work on anti-violence strategies that reflect the specific experiences of DV in collectivist communities and that integrate the expertise of both service providers and immigrant and newcomer communities.

Building common ground for members of the Muslim community to work in collaboration with local service providers is a key ingredient to meeting the needs of Muslim women and children victimized by violence and male perpetrators of violence. Without the expertise and guidance of stakeholders, creating an environment that is safe and responsive to Muslim women and families affected by DV would be very difficult. Project partners, such as child welfare agencies, police, and the legal system have played a significant role in shaping the process as they helped define objectives and determined how best to achieve them. The contributing voices of the Muslim community in particular played an important role in integrating some religious elements that emphasized the Islamic religion's rejection of DV. For example, early on in the process, the Imam played a crucial role in championing the message that Islam does not condone DV.

In addition, the strong involvement of members of the Muslim community and the service-provider community translated into greater capacity building in both communities. The participation and contributions of a diversity of stakeholders generated valuable knowledge by improving understanding of the socio-cultural dynamics of DV in the Muslim community and by supporting meaningful strategies for change.

This collaboratively enabled members of the Muslim community to learn from one another, allowing them to develop a greater understanding of the expertise of the local service-provider community, and make it possible for these service providers to gain a deeper awareness of the experiences, knowledge, needs, and values of the Muslim community. Through this process, a framework was developed to focus on connection and exchange, and supported the development of an environment in which services were modified to be more appropriate for Muslim women and families affected by DV. As a result, service-provider agencies were able to engage in more effective outreach and service relationships with abused women in the Muslim community, due to an improved contextualized understanding of their challenges, concerns, and needs.

To overcome barriers leading to cross-cultural disconnection in service relationships, it is important to appreciate and acknowledge the experiences and perspectives of Muslim women who are abused. The development of culturally appropriate community responses to address DV refers to the establishment of service relationships with members of the Muslim community, and public education materials that integrate religious/cultural knowledge, values, and perspectives. The integration of the understandings, values, and concerns of members of the Muslim community on the issue of woman abuse enables the project to respond in a manner that is meaningful and engaging. Members of the Muslim community need to be able to relate to any process that seeks to support Muslim women and families affected by DV; otherwise our experiences in this community have shown that strategies for change and support will not have the intended impact. The inclusion of Islamic perspectives and teachings provides a familiar context to public education on DV for members of the Muslim community.

To support the development of a safe environment for Muslim women where they can speak out about DV and seek help, men and women of the Muslim community need to be involved. While the main strategy lies in empowering women through raising awareness and providing support services, a significant part of the strategy for change lies in the inclusion of Muslim men. Service providers or religious leaders may refer a man for services to our agency. Usually, the motivation to engage in services results from the involvement of mandated service providers who become engaged following a violent event in the family. Our work with the man is to engage him in services within the context of the family, for example, by providing supervised access to children, engaging support networks, and providing resource information and counseling.

The Culturally Integrative Family Safety Response model in action

Before we move forward with a description of the CIFSR model, it is important to note that all programs offering direct service at MRCSSI function by engaging mainstream organizations surrounding a family and that we attempt to build a coordinated response at all times. Engagement, when there is a critical incident, is dependent on the mandated service provider's conditions of engagement in regards to the safety of the victim, and this is often dictated by law and court procedures. Nevertheless, mandated service providers are engaged in a team approach and work in collaboration providing tools that allow for culturally informed pathways of engagement that ensure better outcomes. Knowledge of our community allows MRCSSI to engage religious and cultural community leaders within the team when needed to support the mandated service provider. By engaging community leaders, their capacity and awareness to support at-risk families is enhanced.

To respond to the complex needs of immigrant and newcomer families, the MRCSSI designed a CIFSR. One example is the Safe Integration Program (SIP). The main goal of SIP is to develop a coordinated response to address risk factors of DV before the violence begins, before a pattern of violence is established, or when violence imminent. The SIP process develops a collaborative collectivist structure that engages all organizations surrounding the family to support the family and respond to its needs. Community agencies, such as settlement services, medical doctors, and school social workers, are included in the process of conferring with the family and reviewing and focusing attention on risk factors for DV identified by the Safety and Risk Assessment.

The model of a Coordinated Organization Response Team (CORT) defines the boundaries of the mandates of service providers, identifies the gaps in service delivery to meet the needs of the family and, through collaborative engagement, identifies and supports stretching the boundaries of agency mandates to meet the needs of the family in regards to risk factors for DV. Engaging newly arrived immigrants from conflict zones who have experienced trauma and violence prior to their journey of immigration allows MRCSSI to intervene during the early stages of the post-migration period. This would be akin to recognizing that certain population groups would be at risk of diabetes and developing strategies to inform the target population and offer early screening in the hopes of identifying and reducing the progression of the disease. It is assumed that those who have lived through prolonged periods of trauma or have experienced cumulative trauma over extended periods may be prone to episodes of maladjustments during the post-migration period which may result in an increased risk for DV. The screening and engagement of these newly arrived immigrants coupled with intensive engagement of Canadian service providers in coordinated service delivery focused on addressing the risk factors of DV has shown positive outcomes. The family's needs are met in a coordinated service-delivery model and service providers are supported at understanding the culture and values of the family and recognizing and helping these families address their complex needs. Because the potential for a critical incident is present but has not occurred, mandated service providers such as child welfare and police services would not otherwise be engaged to respond as per a mandate defined in law. A secondary goal is to provide intensive support during the post-migration period to alleviate stressors and further traumatization.

Clients are referred principally from the Cross Cultural Learner Centre, a settlement agency in London. MRCSSI's Safe Integration Counsellor attends orientation sessions of newly arrived refugee families at the Cross Cultural Learner Centre, and presents the concept of PTSD and the impact of trauma and post-migration stressors on newly arrived individuals and families. The individuals are made aware of the availability of support services and about SIP. An offer is made to screen families and individuals for intensive support services. These individuals and families are thus able to become aware of the symptoms and impact of trauma and the supports that are available.

The following diagram depicts the Safe Integration Process. Each section of the diagram is further discussed below.

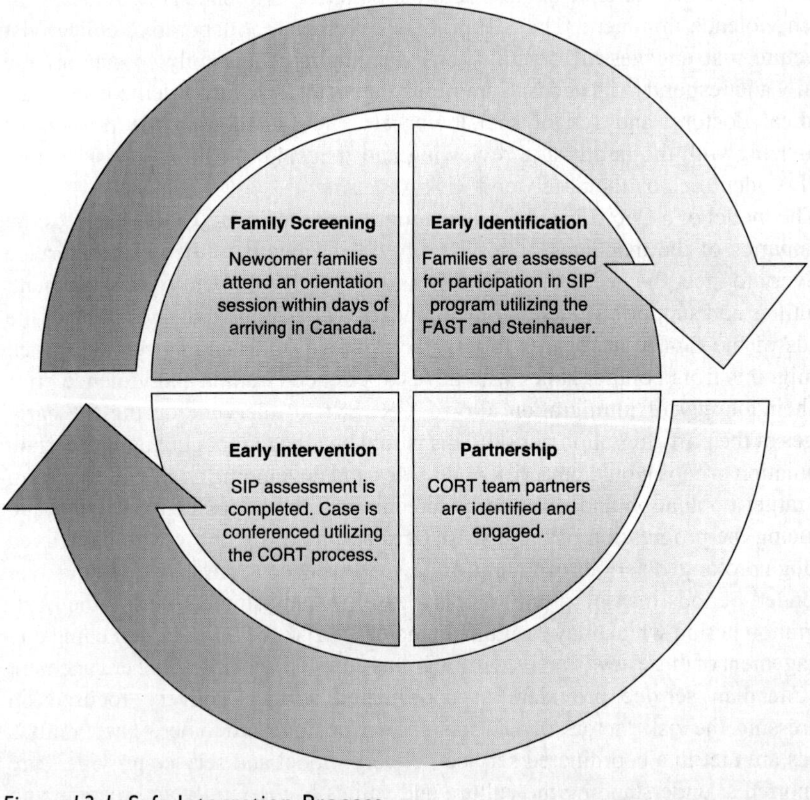

Figure 12.1 Safe Integration Process.

Family screening

Research suggests that, when left untreated, trauma may result in DV (Baobaid 2010). This violence often surfaces during the post-settlement period and can carry over across generations if left untreated. This period of time can also be marked by further risk factors for violence and family conflict through the high potential for post-migration stressors or repeated trauma. Hence, newly arrived immigrants from conflict zones have a higher likelihood of having suffered trauma. It is the experience of our settlement partner agency, the Cross Cultural Learner Center, that immigrants arriving from conflict zones bear a much higher likelihood of being impacted in their everyday functioning due to their exposure to trauma.

Early identification

After the orientation session, a family member may request to be screened to participate in the SIP or to drop in to ask further questions without necessarily committing to the program. If the individual or family is eligible for participation in the program, an intensive process of evaluation occurs over a four-week period utilizing the Four Aspects Screening Tool (FAST) developed by Baobaid (2010).

Weekly sessions are scheduled which may consist of half-day sessions in the family home gathering information on the family's journey, identifying patterns of communication between family members, identifying key family members residing outside the household, determining key organizations involved with the family, and obtaining the required authorizations to contact service organizations. Organizations are contacted, introduced to the concept of the Safe Integration Program and encouraged to participate as part of the CORT team.

The FAST model allows a quick assessment to determine the characteristics and realities of the family, including potential risk factors for DV. It recognizes where the family is situated in regards to normal life cycle stages, and allows for an exploration of the importance of the ethno-cultural, religious, and migration experience aspects as stressors. This process is further enhanced through the use of guideline 1.1a from the Steinhauer Parental Capacity Assessment tool (Steinhauer 1992). The Steinhauer guideline assists in the early identification and contributes to the overall risk assessment. This allows for the unveiling of a narrative of the family's journey. A genogram is completed that often includes extended family and traces cross-generational patterns; an eco-map surrounding the genogram is also developed which includes all service organizations and helps in the recruitment of potential CORT members for case coordination purposes. The following diagram depicts the Four Aspects Screening Tool.

The FAST model was developed as a screening tool to identify sources of risk of DV specifically within collectivist communities. The four aspects of the FAST model include: ethno-cultural aspects, migration experience aspects, religious

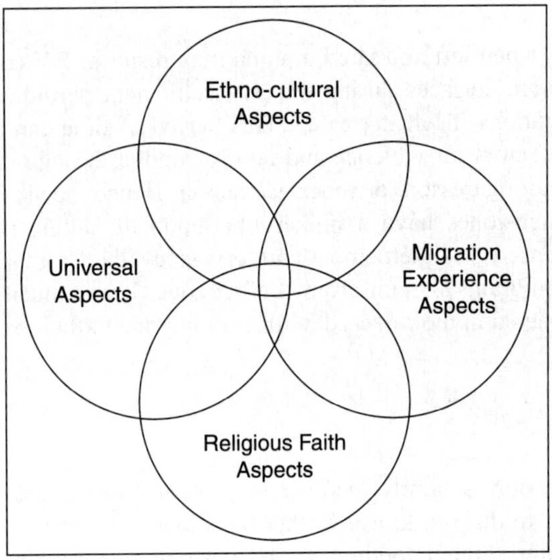

Figure 12.2 Four Aspects Screening Tool (FAST).

faith aspects, and universal aspects. Each aspect is accompanied by a list of suggested questions to gauge risk level.

The assessment will determine whether the family has significant factors that could impact their current functioning or lead to a critical situation when coupled with post-migration stressors. This 30-day intensive assessment process and screening culminates in the completion of the SIP family assessment. There are six risk factors that are considered in the Safe Integration Assessment. These are:

1. *Pre-migration:* Hearing the journey of the client and the past experience of the family members is one of the key factors that assist in better understanding the family, and provides information that will inform future interventions. It allows MRCSSI to help service providers better understand the family's realities and struggles.
2. *Family relations:* This includes cross-generational coalitions, conflict between the parents, or parent–child conflict. The existence of a relative or a parental figure outside the family who may have a strong influence can be a support or a stressor. A parent or other family member may be missing or suspected killed or abducted. The parent may be unavailable due to serious mental illness or isolation and an older child may have taken on parental responsibility. An opportunistic predator also may be present in the family home and present a risk. Within the 18-month period in which SIP was implemented we have identified in some families the existence of a male predator who offers his expertise in interpreting the laws and customs of

Canada, and at the same time, has access to young adult females in the family whom he has opportunities to sexually exploit.

3. *Social isolation:* This represents family connections to the cultural or religious community. Some immigrant refugees arrive in Canada and wish to distance themselves from their cultural and religious community and fully integrate into Canadian culture. They may choose to move to an area that will not put them in contact with their community and they will not attend community events, choices that may be in conflict with other family members. Social isolation also can occur when the individual engages in behaviors that result in their being rejected by both the mainstream and their community of origin. As one example, a youth may attempt to maintain contact back home by spending long hours on the Internet in social networks, thereby rejecting opportunities for socialization in their new host culture.
4. *Post-migration:* Many newcomers experience loss of economic status or social position, lack of recognition of professional qualifications, and narrowing of opportunities. Both males and females may be confused about how they are expected to socialize with the other sex. Men may be affected by their change of status as providers or by a lack recognition of their qualifications. Cultural norms and expectations may become confused when in contact with mainstream society.
5. *Family expectation:* The family's or individual's expectations may contradict those of their new host culture. The family may have expectations of accessing services immediately, due to their social status. Some parents may have unrealistic expectations in regards to the education of their children in Canadian schools. Choice of living arrangements and belief of entitlements may further complicate the situation. Some parents may call police to intervene in their family to mediate a conflict with their child and are horrified when the child is arrested and a restraining order imposed. Individual rights of children in Canada may run counter to their belief that the child belongs to them.
6. *Mental health:* Individuals may have been significantly traumatized or have a mental health condition which precedes but is complicated by the trauma. Mental health is not often recognized within collectivist cultures and rejected as having any significance. More intensive case coordination is required to inform the service providers of these beliefs and help monitor change, in particular when children are involved. When this is the case, CORT team members will often come together to advocate for the involvement of a mental health professional in the team.

The above factors are considered within the assessment that is completed by the SIP counselor using the knowledge of the client's journey in consultation with the MRCSSI supervisor. The level of concern in each risk category is determined by combining this information.

The CORT Process

MRCSSI prepares and codes the level of severity and transfers this information to a "signs of safety" worksheet that identifies both risk and strengths. This forms the basis of the first CORT meeting that occurs six weeks after initial early identification. A genogram and an eco-map are prepared for the CORT meeting and all participants are provided a copy, along with the signs of safety.

Together, within the CORT process, the coding is validated and new information is added to the assessment. The CORT partners develop a determination of responsibility in regards to addressing the risk factors of DV and as well identify gaps of service delivery. The next step is to review in partnership with the CORT members how and who will address these gaps. At times this will require outside consultation within the service providers' organization to allow for stretching mandates to meet the needs.

Conclusion

DV is a multi-faceted issue which is further complicated when recent immigrants of diverse cultures are involved (Midlarsky *et al.* 2006). Diverse cultural community leaders have started to publicly address this issue; however, there is still a lack of capacity in many immigrant and newcomer communities to recognize warning signs of DV or provide victims and perpetrators with the culturally sensitive and appropriate supports they may require. Multi-agency responses should be inclusive to cultural communities in the development of solutions and supports to respond to DV.

This chapter has proposed a CIFSR model for working with newcomer and immigrant families in the context of DV. This model of responses may not be transferable, however. The model is based on MRCSSI work and has been implemented as a pilot project within the Muslim community in a particular context. It is still in an early stage of development to consider transferability to other collectivist communities living in the West. The validity of the tools used within this model and the consistency of outcomes is not yet confirmed and contain the limitations associated with qualitative methods and clinical data. As a result, more research is required to determine the impact this model is having for immigrant and newcomer families.

Based on our experience so far, it is recommended that interventions involving immigrant and newcomer families of collectivist communities consider the inclusion of the community of origin in the process. In addition, it is recommended the provincial child protection associations conduct evaluations of this model to determine the extent to which it could or should be transferred to other communities. This approach offers the potential for communities to build the capacity to recognize and identify early warning signs and provide support for those who have experienced DV and migration-related trauma. It is our hope that through our model and response, we can begin to build bridges that allow for the exchange of ideas, support, and ongoing learning with the ultimate goal of discovering new ways of working together that will help the immigrant and newcomer communities from collectivist backgrounds reduce DV (Baobaid and Hamed 2011).

References

Alaggia, R., Regehr, C. and Rishchynski, G. (2009) 'Intimate partner violence and immigration laws in Canada: how far have we come?', *International Journal of Law and Psychiatry*, 23: 335–41.

Baobaid, M. (2010) *Guidelines for Service Providers: Outreach Strategies for Family Violence Intervention with Immigrant and Minority Communities: Lessons Learned from the Muslim Family Safety Project*, London, ON: Changing Ways.

Baobaid, M. and Hamed, G. (2011) *Addressing Domestic Violence in Canadian Muslim Communities: A Training Manual for Muslim Communities and Ontario Service Providers*, London, ON: Muslim Resource Centre for Social Support and Integration.

Barran, D. and Feder, G. (2010) 'Interventions to support victims of domestic violence: Health service responses and a multi-agency model', *Injury Prevention*, 16: 276–89.

Haj-Yahia, M.M. (2011) 'Contextualizing interventions with battered women in collectivist societies: issues and controversies', *Aggression and Violent Behavior*, 16: 331–9.

Haj-Yahia, M.M. (2000) 'Patterns of violence against engaged Arab women from Israel and some of their psychological implications', *Psychology of Women Quarterly*, 24: 209–19.

Merchant, M. (2000) 'A comparative study of agencies assisting domestic violence victims: Does the South Asian community have special needs?', *Journal of Social Distress and the Homeless*, 9: 249–59.

Midlarsky, E., Venkataramani-Kothari, A. and Plante, M. (2006) 'Domestic violence in the Chinese and South Asian immigrant communities', *Annals of the New York Academy of Sciences*, 1087: 279–300.

Sokoloff, N.J. (2008) 'Expanding the intersectional paradigm to better understand domestic violence in immigrant communities', *Critical Criminology*, 16: 229–55.

Steinhauer, P. (1992) *The Least Detrimental Alternative: A systematic guide to case planning and decision making for children in care*, Toronto: University of Toronto Press.

Yoshioka, M.R. and Choi, D.Y. (2005) 'Culture and interpersonal violence research: paradigm shift to create a full continuum of domestic violence services', *Journal of Interpersonal Violence*, 20: 513–19.

Section IV: Victim crisis and advocacy

Questions for critical thought

1. What are the challenges for interagency communication and collaboration between providing generalist and specialized "women's services"?
2. What are the strengths and limitations of the one-stop-shop model to responding to violence against women?
3. Do you think the culturally integrative model of domestic violence can be implemented successfully in cultural communities in your locale? What are some challenges that you would anticipate? How would you overcome these challenges?
4. Can you suggest agencies or organizations in your local community that should be invited to collaborate with collectivist communities and mainstream service providers to develop and implement culturally inclusive practices?

Further reading

Humphreys, C. and Stanley, N. (eds.) (2006) *Domestic Violence and Child Protection: Directions for Good Practice*, London: Jessica Kingsley.

Morgan, M. and Coombes, L. (2013) 'Empowerment and advocacy for domestic violence victims', *Social and Personality Psychology Compass*, 7: 526–36.

Nichols, A.J. (2013) 'Meaning-making and domestic violence victim advocacy: an examination of feminist identities, ideologies, and practices', *Feminist Criminology*, 8: 177–201.

Oxfam International (2012) *Ending Violence Against Women: An Oxfam Guide*, Oxford: Oxfam International. Online. Available at www.oxfam.org/sites/www.oxfam.org/files/ending-violence-against-women-oxfam-guide-nov2012.pdf (accessed 25 May 2014).

Stanley, N., Miller, P., Richardson-Foster, H., and Thomson, G. (2011) 'Children's experiences of domestic violence: developing an integrated response from police and child protection services', *Journal of Interpersonal Violence*, 26: 2372–91.

Websites

Connect Centre for International Research on New Approaches to Prevent Violence and Harm: The center at the University of Central Lancashire is developing a program of strategically focused international research activity on preventing violence and harm across the life course and making connections across disciplines about violence and abuse and its impacts.

www.uclan.ac.uk/research/environment/groups/connect_centre_int_research_new_approaches_prevent_violence_harm.php

Stop Violence Against Women, A Project of the Advocates for Human Rights: A forum for information, advocacy, and change in the promotion of women's human rights around the world. It compiles information about domestic violence, trafficking in women, sexual harassment, sexual assault, and gender violence worldwide.
www.stopvaw.org/Stop_Violence_Against_Women

WAVE, Women Against Violence Europe: Informal network of European women's NGOs working in the field of combating violence against women and children (women's refuges, counseling centers, SOS hotlines/helplines, organizations focusing on prevention and training, among others). Sets out to promote and strengthen the human rights of women and children and to prevent violence against women and children.
www.wave-network.org

SECTION V

Behavior change programs for abusers

Learning objectives

In reading this section, you will be able to:

1. Identify the purpose of behavior change programs for abusers and how different theoretical explanations of intimate partner violence influence the assumptions, organization, and content of these programs.
2. Understand the limitations of behavior change programs for abusers in preventing future violence against women and children.
3. Question the outcomes of behavior change programs and how "success" ought to be determined.
4. Critically question the appropriateness of treating intimate partner violence perpetrators as a homogeneous group.

Chapter 13

Behavior change programs for intimate partner violence abusers

A means to promote the safety of women and children?

Donna Chung

Initial responses to intimate partner violence (IPV) focused on making women and their children safe from male partner abusers by providing emergency refuge accommodation and support services, and enhancing legal protections and law enforcement. However, the continuing problem of IPV led to intervention programs being developed for abusers in the late 1970s and early 1980s. The logic was that unless there was an attempt to stop men's abusive behavior toward their female partners, IPV would not be curtailed. Consequently, patriarchal societal values condoning IPV would continue to be reinforced, women would be abused for longer periods as abusive behavior went unimpeded, and, even if women managed to escape, abusers would re-partner and go on to abuse subsequent women. In hindsight, the outcomes expected from such programs were ambitious.

Programs targeting male abusers aimed at changing attitudes and behavior using a group-based intervention. Some programs operated as a component of a criminal justice system or community-wide coordinated response whereas others were stand-alone community-based programs where men participated without the coercion of the justice system. In recent times there has been a shift away from stand-alone, voluntary programs toward increased emphasis on incorporating programs into a coordinated criminal justice response. Therefore, abusive men are unlikely to benefit unless their partners report the violence to the police.

During their four-decade history, IPV programs for male abusers have been controversial for a number of reasons. These include, but are not limited to, doubt about their effectiveness in increasing women's safety and stopping men's violence, and concern that the funding of such programs would occur at the expense of providing services for women and children affected by IPV. This chapter presents the development of abuser programs by discussing the underpinning theoretical and practice approaches. Debates about program success and effectiveness are addressed with reference to the evaluation research, and elements of program organization, practice, and reach are critically reviewed in light of the current state of abuser programs.

The development of IPV programs for abusers

IPV programs for abusers[1] began running in a small number of agencies in North America in the late 1970s. Since then they have expanded across other countries (e.g., the United Kingdom, Australia, New Zealand, Spain, France, Finland, and Germany) and developed in approach and practice. Early programs were influenced by feminist theory and social learning theory that were then key IPV explanations. The major theoretical or explanatory influences on the development of programs for abusers can be broadly categorized as: Feminist Approaches, Social Learning Theory, and Multi-level Explanatory Frameworks.

Feminist approaches: an early and continuing influence

The global women's movement that began in the 1960s had as its primary goal the elimination of sexism and the achievement of gender equality. Raising awareness about ending male violence against women (VAW) was a major area of feminist activism as this was deemed a leading cause of women's oppression and inequality. From these feminist activist beginnings emerged explanations of IPV and programs to address it. A decade later, when programs for abusers were beginning, feminist analyses were a growing influence highlighting the gendered dynamics of IPV, particularly patriarchal attitudes and beliefs about male entitlement, ownership, and control over female partners.

Men's use of violence and abuse was understood as a powerful means of maintaining (and furthering) gender inequality and forcing the woman to remain in the relationship through coercive and intimidating tactics. Feminists advocated for the criminalization of IPV as important for raising awareness of the seriousness of the problem and pressing for law enforcement and criminal justice responses to stop IPV and promote the protection of victims.

Feminist analyses have influenced programs for IPV abusers since their beginnings in the 1980s and continue to do so in some of the following ways:

- Emphasizing sexist and stereotyped views toward women and beliefs about the rights of men in relationships to justify the use of violence (Flood and Pease 2009). Therefore, much of the early work challenged individual men's values, beliefs, and behaviors that condoned, minimized, and excused VAW. Most group work interventions were initially psycho-educational in approach, aimed at challenging and changing abusers' values, attitudes, and behaviors.
- Men are considered solely responsible and accountable for their abusive actions. Female partners are not responsible for triggering the violence, nor can it be excused.
- Accountability for violent behavior involves contact with female partners to understand how safe they are and how the violence has them.
- Program practices based on feminist understandings include male and female co-facilitators modeling respectful and equal gender relations.

Social learning theory: understanding men's continuing use of IPV

In the 1970s and early 1980s social learning theory was also used to understand IPV and family violence more generally (e.g., Straus *et al.* 1980). The underlying premise of Bandura's (1977) social learning theory is that behavior is learned through observation of influential others, whom individuals may then copy or imitate. Social learning theory has been applied to explain the behavior of adults and adolescents using IPV. In short, the use of violence is learned through observation in early and current environments (e.g., peer groups, occupational groups, family and friends) and maintained through rewards and reinforcements (Pipes and LeBov-Keeler 1997). When there are no direct negative consequences for the abuse, there is little motivation for change. Social learning theory as an explanatory framework for IPV lacks an analysis of power at the individual and structural levels.

Social learning theory provided a means for men to understand the patterns and purpose of their abusive behaviors in relationships, and programs offered alternative strategies or techniques, which participants could practice during the group intervention and at home. The use of new skills and techniques was critical, as social learning theory assumed men would be able to experience the positive changes in their surrounding environment (e.g., partner's and family members' reactions) when behaving non-violently.

Moving toward multi-level explanatory frameworks

IPV explanations are an area of considerable debate, with feminists taking a largely socio-political analysis, and social learning theorists and other more psychologically oriented practitioners strongly focusing on the impact of the local environment on the individual. This resulted in a diversity of abuser programs, many of which combined feminist analysis with individually focused social learning interventions (e.g., the use of skill practice and homework) (Gondolf 2011). This reflects the proliferation of programs in the last 30 years and how individual practitioners have managed the tension of responding to individual men while understanding IPV as a structural problem. Watts (2001: 172) notes the importance of levels of explanatory theory when dealing with complex social problems that have social structural roots but are enacted by individuals with varying levels of personal agency.

The issue is not about which theory or level of description is likely to be "correct," but rather which framework is likely to lead to the development of the most effective interventions. In this respect the differing theoretical explanations are not necessarily dichotomous. Indeed, a sole focus on either individual or structural factors is likely to be inadequate.

There is therefore a need to continue to develop multi-level explanations of IPV at three levels: Individual, community, and socio-political levels

(Dobash *et al.* 2000). In this respect behavior change programs for abusers represent part of the change at the individual level while also signaling to the community the unacceptable and illegal nature of IPV. At a community level, this approach is operationalized by the Duluth Abuse Intervention Program (DAIP), a coordinated community response program, under the visionary leadership of the late Ellen Pence. DAIP focuses on the protection, safety, and rights of victims to live violence free, while holding men accountable for their use of violence against female partners. Within this approach, IPV programs for abusers are one component of a coordinated response to end IPV.

Programs: organization, content, and intervention

Since inception, programs for IPV abusers have continued to develop in organization and content. Programs involve group-delivered interventions for abusers that are psycho-educational or cognitive behavioral in approach, with different models employed across various organizations (Day *et al.* 2009a).

It is important to distinguish IPV abusers' programs from general violence programs, such as anger management programs. The latter have an emphasis on intra-psychic behavior change, specifically anger management, impulse control and self-regulation, and are not specific to IPV. They may use some similar techniques, for example, teaching men skills to recognize when they are becoming angry and how to exit the situation without using violence. Some of the key differences between anger management programs and those for IPV abusers are that the former are stand-alone behavioral programs concentrated on anger and developing appropriate responses, whereas IPV programs examine how abusive tactics are used as a form of power and control in relationships, have a victim accountability component, and are typically part of a coordinated community response to promote women's and children's safety.

Program organization

Internationally, programs vary in how they have been established; however, because this is a relatively new and small field of practice, research undertaken in one country is often utilized in other countries, so there are some similarities across programs. Programs for IPV abusers are organized in two main ways: Programs contained within the criminal justice system (CJS) and those external to the CJS.

Programs within the CJS are part of the wider CJS response to IPV. They were a consequence of feminist activists' calls for the criminalization of IPV, which translated into police pro-arrest policies and a strengthened law enforcement and court response (Buzawa and Buzawa 1996). There was also a demand for more appropriate sentencing options (as opposed to fines and incarceration) such as behavioral change programs. The organization of these programs is not uniform across jurisdictions: They can be part of a sentence, a bail condition, or a diversionary option to encourage abusers to take responsibility for change. For example, where program attendance is part of a sentence, the perpetrator has been found guilty and as part of his sentence is required to attend the program. Where programs are diversionary, a criminal record could be avoided if a perpetrator successfully completes the program. The assumption is that early intervention may be more likely to bring about change.

IPV programs outside the CJS are run and/or funded by government departments such as health and social services and non-government agencies. Men attending group programs could have been referred from various pathways and are not court-ordered to attend. Program referral pathways include self-referral, referral from other non-statutory agencies, and from statutory services such as child protection. These programs often evolved from connections with women's IPV services that identified men seeking help for their violence. Since this time, programs have expanded, often becoming part of a coordinated community response.

The majority of programs are run in community-based settings, offered on a weekly or more frequent basis over a set number of weeks. For men court ordered to attend programs, non-compliance is reported by program providers. This is the main difference for men attending programs outside the CJS, where practitioners are not required to report to the court on individuals' attendance or progress and there are no legal consequences to dropping out. A small number of programs are delivered within prison settings. Men attending may be incarcerated for IPV or it may have been identified as an existing concern along with other crimes.

Program content

As many IPV abuser programs are located within the CJS, they have been influenced by other criminal justice approaches such as cognitive behavioral therapy (CBT), motivational interviewing, and solution focused and narrative therapies. These rational talking therapies have been used to respond to a range of issues including substance misuse and depression. CBT is based on working with individuals to identify thoughts, beliefs, and feelings contributing to current problems and relearning new responses and thoughts which will lead to changes in behavior. CBT is one of the most popular and widely evaluated psycho-social interventions, shown to be successful in improving depression and other mental health concerns (Sheldon 2011). While not evaluated on a large scale with IPV abusers, its success in other areas has provided impetus for its use in IPV programs. Solution focused and narrative therapies have been more recently incorporated with the aims of also reorienting thoughts and beliefs in order to lead to behavior change. Motivational interviewing is underpinned by an understanding of a person's motivation and readiness for change.

While approaches differ, the format of IPV abuser programs are still group-work-based interventions, with participants engaging in examining their beliefs and behaviors, and alternatives provided to current ways of thinking and behaving.

Throughout the programs, participants' risk of further and escalating violence is assessed with protocols, such as checklists and checks on women and children to assess their safety in high-risk situations.

To maximize women's and children's safety, standards of practice have been developed in North America, the UK, and Australia. Some of these have been developed by organizations or coalitions representing agencies that either run programs for abusers or are more generally involved in ending VAW and against children. Examples include Respect in the UK and No to Violence in Australia, and the Virginia Standards for Batterer Intervention Programs in the United States. In other instances, governments have prepared standards of practice to ensure programs delivered or contracted out meet standards of good practice. Each set of standards varies although they are similar and cover key components of program delivery and evaluation such as: Referral pathways into programs; assessment for program suitability; risk assessment of the participant on entering and during the program; risk management strategies for participants identified as high risk and for group-work interventions with abusers; safety contact and accountability processes for female (ex-)partners; interagency working arrangements; and monitoring and evaluation.

IPV abuser programs differ from most other criminal justice interventions because they include contact with the victim—the female (ex-)partners—throughout the program. This reflects the unique aspects of IPV—that there has been an intimate relationship and there may be continuing contact between the abuser and the victim. Partner safety contact is a means of assessing risk or escalation of violence, supporting victims, and promoting their safety.

An ethical concern about victim/partner safety contact is that women may not wish to participate for understandable reasons such as: They have ended the relationship and wish to move on (they may find the contact intrusive, and for it to be unhelpful to be speaking about the abuser); or, they feel he is responsible for his use of violence and it is not their responsibility to participate in stopping his violence. Good practice indicates that women's decisions not to participate are respected; however, it is hoped that non-participation will not place the woman at further risk of IPV and without support. To this end, programs often include the potential to contact women should risk of violence be suspected. Another ethical concern is that abusers tend to minimize and underreport violence (Day *et al.* 2009a). Therefore, relying solely on participants' self-reports is unreliable for determining risk of IPV, which can leave women and children unsafe. These dilemmas are part of a broader discussion about the overarching goals of IPV abuser programs and the related question of what constitutes success for these programs.

What is the primary purpose of programs for IPV abusers and are they working?

The introduction of programs for IPV abusers was controversial; consequently, ensuing debate as to the value of the programs resulted in calls for their evaluation

(Babcock *et al.* 2004). For example, practitioners and researchers often express concerns about high attrition and few or no consequences for offenders who do not complete programs. Retention is an ongoing challenge; however, efforts to address this through CJS changes have begun to see improvements in some areas (Gondolf 2007). Other debates focus on methodology, including the commonly argued positivist position that there is a lack of large random control trials necessary to demonstrate effectiveness. Other issues concern variation in what is defined as a program for IPV abusers and how this makes evaluative comparisons difficult.

The question of whether programs are effective does not have a simple answer. With respect to the primary purpose of IPV abuser programs, is it to promote women's and children's safety or change participants' violent and abusive behavior? There is now much agreement that it is the former (see Gondolf 2007; Westmarland and Kelly 2012) and men's behavior change is a secondary goal. What denotes success or effectiveness goes to the core of what evaluation methodologies would constitute "evidence" of success. There is also the practicality of what can be evaluated within a limited time frame and budget to show impact, as these are publicly funded programs and their continuation relies on this form of accountability. Recidivism is a commonly used effectiveness measure for CJS programs although it is well known that a majority of IPV incidents are unreported to authorities (Australian Bureau of Statistics 2006), and others are not acts for which a criminal justice response would be invoked, e.g., psychological abuse. Further, increased police reporting and higher conviction rates may indicate women are more confident that reporting to police will help them, and/or that enhanced CJS's processes may be resulting in increased convictions (Klein and Crowe 2008).

To address the complexity of IPV and the impact of abuser programs a multi-method research design is necessary. The large-scale multi-site evaluation of CJS programs conducted by Gondolf (2002) used a multi-method approach, as does a current UK study of programs based outside the CJS (Westmarland and Kelly 2012). Gondolf's research indicates IPV abuser programs have an impact on reducing re-assaults following program completion: 30 months after program completion, less than 20 percent of men had re-assaulted partners and 85 percent of women reported feeling very safe. However, one-quarter of men had assaulted their partners more than once during and after program completion. The only variable distinguishing men who did not desist was their higher use of alcohol. While evaluation research is cautious about program success (Babcock *et al.* 2004), multi-method evaluation research across North America (Gondolf 2002), the UK (Westmarland and Kelly 2012), and Australia (Day *et al.* 2009b) indicates the following common findings:

- Men undertaking IPV abuser programs show increasing problem awareness of their behavior and its impact on others.

- Partners generally saw it as positive for abusers to enter programs, but it was important partners had realistic expectations of the likelihood and type of progress to be expected.
- Incidents of physical violence decreased while attending the program.
- (Ex-)partners and children were linked to support services and had their own needs met due to the (ex-)partner contact process referring them.
- Partners felt safer but did not trust the abuser's violent behaviors were completely absent.
- Attrition rates and poor program attendance continued to be high.
- Safety and protection of women and children was influenced by the quality of programs' accompanying coordinated responses.

The difficulty in knowing whether programs for IPV abusers "work" is partly attributable to the complex dynamics of IPV and the number of people affected by just one abuser. Day and colleagues (2009a: 205) describe this:

> Domestic violence perpetrator programs are nested within a related set of responses (addressing the safety of women and children) making the evaluation of their effectiveness influenced by what is occurring in other areas, unlike other offender programs which are unrelated to their victims' lives. They also draw attention to problems in the consistency with which the Duluth model is adapted by organizations that claim its use. Of course this may be, in practice, because such programs are by nature of their design difficult to implement, rather than any indictment of the study or the agency.

Despite these difficulties, programs offer a means to hold men accountable for their actions. Risk assessment and management and the opportunity to link women and children with support are possible when programs are a component of a coordinated community response. The programs are a "work in progress" requiring continuing evaluation to identify their possibilities for promoting women's and children's safety.

Challenges and future considerations for more inclusive programs

The intervention mode for IPV abuser programs is rational talking therapy. This raises challenges for programs taking on a diversity of men; for example, how well can the program respond to participants with learning disabilities? With the exception of a small number of programs running for specific cultural and language groups, how effectively can men who are not proficient in the dominant language participate?

There is continuing interest in abuser typologies which assumes that interventions could be better tailored to different groups of men to improve effectiveness. Edleson's (2012) recent research review concluded there is not persuasive evidence to warrant programs based on the abuser "personality" or typological category. This supports Gondolf's (2002) contention that "one size fits most." Wangmann (2011) is cautious about the application of typologies, particularly where "categories" of abusers are linked to levels or types of risk, as they can minimize a woman's risk at best and have dire consequences for their safety at worst. Wangmann is not advocating a universal approach but warning against a prescriptive predictive approach to categorizing IPV abusers.

A challenge facing IPV abuser program providers is that a high proportion of men referred are identified as having complex and multiple problems in addition to IPV (Mignone *et al.* 2009). These primarily concern drug and alcohol dependency and mental health diagnoses. Until the last decade there was some reluctance to address the co-occurrence of IPV and particularly alcohol misuse among abusers, on the presumption that it would translate into reducing accountability (Braaf 2012, Galvani 2010). Braaf (2012) argues that given the implications for women's safety and the extent of alcohol involvement in IPV, it is imperative for IPV abuser programs to have specialized approaches to address this co-occurrence. This is pressing given that alcohol misuse can be the basis for exclusion from some abuser programs and that re-assaults are associated with alcohol use more than any other variable (Gondolf 2002). In some areas, specialized programs have been trialed, such as the Dade County Domestic Violence Court, which ran an integrated IPV and substance abuse program because up to 50 percent of the men attending court were substance dependent. Some fundamental differences existed between the two programs, and integrating them proved challenging, particularly deciding whether IPV or substance use should be the priority and what should be the content and order of treatment delivered. Nevertheless, evaluation findings showed men attending the integrated program re-assaulted partners at a lower rate than those in the control group (6 percent compared with 14 percent; Goldkamp 1996).

Similarly, a number of men also display mental health problems such as depression, anxiety, and borderline personality disorder. Mental health screening during program assessment is critical yet differs across programs. Again, there has been a reluctance to focus on mental health problems due to concerns they would be understood to cause and excuse IPV. For example, there has been a recent increase in literature arguing that men's use of violence and abuse against their partners is not the result of gendered dynamics or social learning but instead the result of attachment disorders requiring psychodynamic treatments rather than the programs described above (Gondolf 2011). Attachment theory has had resurgence in child abuse and family violence areas in the past few years. It is suggested that men with attachment disorders will display overly aggressive behaviors, jealousy, and increased violence as the result of fear of abandonment or separation. Gondolf (2011) argues the evidence for attachment disorders in IPV abusers is weak, as is evidence that the "deeper treatment" that this requires is beneficial.

The common co-occurrence of IPV and other problems poses a particular challenge, as many social and health services are designed around single issues or policy domains, so that programs cannot accommodate this complexity. It is also challenging for practitioners expected to have wide-ranging knowledge and skills in how to assess and intervene with interrelated problems. It is critical to develop approaches that can deal with abusers' multiple issues, as these require a sophisticated response that has women's and children's safety as the primary goal.

A further challenge in extending the reach and effectiveness of IPV abuser programs is that they are often only viable to run in urban and regional areas, so the possibility of providing interventions in more isolated locations requires consideration about the intervention mode and partner-safety contact processes. These challenges for the development of IPV abuser programs are not easily resolved, as most programs run with limited resources and staff time often already stretched. However, a commitment to the safety of all women and children and to uphold their rights to safety means innovative developments are timely.

Conclusions

Programs for IPV abusers have grown, particularly as they have become a part of CJS responses. Evidence of effectiveness is equivocal and we are still finding out who these programs have an impact on and why. Evidence suggests they can promote women's and children's safety and provide them support and advocacy services. Their impact on safety is likely to be greater as part of a coordinated community response. It is important that the indicators of "success" continue to be expanded to better reflect the complex array of dynamics associated with IPV, moving beyond a reduction in the reporting of violence. Abuser programs are confronting some of the same challenges as those working with women and children, namely, how to respond to people who have a number of intersecting problems alongside IPV. The demand for evaluation research will continue, so it is important that complexities are increasingly well understood to inform future evaluation designs and practice.

Note

1 Different terms have been used to describe IPV programs for abusers, including domestic violence perpetrator programs, batterer intervention programs and men's behavior change programs.

References

Australian Bureau of Statistics (2006) *Personal Safety Survey 2005*, Canberra: Australian Bureau of Statistics.

Australian Institute of Criminology (2007) *Guilty Outcomes in Reported Sexual Assault and Related Offence Incidents*, Canberra, Australian Institute of Criminology.

Babcock, J., Green, C. and Robie, C. (2004) 'Does batterers' treatment work? A meta-analytic review of domestic violence treatment', *Clinical Psychology Review*, 23: 1023–53.

Bandura, A. (1977) *Social Learning Theory*, Englewood Cliffs, NJ: Prentice Hall.

Braaf, R. (2012) *Elephant in the Room: Responding to Alcohol Misuse and Domestic Violence*, Sydney: University of New South Wales, Australian Domestic and Family Violence Clearinghouse.

Buzawa, E. and Buzawa, C. (1996) 'The increased policy preference for arrest', in E. Buzawa and C. Buzawa (eds.), *Domestic Violence: The Criminal Justice Response*, Thousand Oaks, CA: Sage, 125–42.

Day, A., O'Leary, P., Chung, D. and Justo D. (2009a) *Domestic Violence—Working with Men: Research, Practice Experiences and Integrated Response*, Annandale, NSW: Federation Press.

Day, A., Chung, D., O'Leary, P. and Carson, E. (2009b) 'Programs for men who perpetrate domestic violence: an examination of the issues underlying the effectiveness of intervention programs', *Journal of Family Violence*, 24: 203–12.

Dobash, R.E., Dobash, R.P., Lewis, R. and Cavanagh, K. (2000) *Changing Violent Men*, London: Sage.

Edleson, J.L. (2012) Groupwork with Men who Batter: What the Research Literature Indicates, Harrisburg, PA: VAWnet, a project of the National Resource Center on Domestic Violence. Online. Available at www.vawnet.org (accessed 25 May 2014).

Flood, M. and Pease, B. (2009) 'Factors influencing attitudes toward violence against women', *Trauma, Violence, & Abuse*, 10: 125–42.

Galvani, S. (2010) *The Role of Alcohol in Violence Against Women*, Saarbrucken, Germany: Lambert Academic.

Goldkamp, J.S. (1996) *Role of Drug and Alcohol Abuse in Domestic Violence and its Treatment: Dade County's Domestic Violence Court Experiment, Final Report*, Washington, DC: National Institute of Justice.

Gondolf, E. (2011) 'The weak evidence for batterer program alternatives', *Aggression and Violent Behavior*, 16: 347–53.

Gondolf, E. (2007) 'Theoretical and research support for the Duluth Model: a reply to Dutton and Corvo', *Aggression and Violent Behavior*, 12: 644–57.

Gondolf, E. (2002) *Batterer Intervention Systems: Issues, Outcomes and Recommendations*, Thousand Oaks, CA: Sage.

Klein, A.R. and Crowe, A. (2008) 'Findings from an outcome examination of Rhode Island's specialized domestic violence probation supervision program', *Violence Against Women*, 14: 226–46.

Mignone, T., Klostermann, K. and Chen, R (2009) 'The relationship between relapse to alcohol and relapse to violence', *Journal of Family Violence*, 24: 497–505.

Pipes, R. and LeBov-Keeler, K. (1997) 'Psychological abuse among college women in exclusive heterosexual dating relationships', *Sex Roles*, 36: 585–603.

Sheldon, B. (2011) *Cognitive-Behavioural Therapy: Research and Practice in Health and Social Care*, London: Taylor and Francis.

Straus, M.A., Gelles R.J. and Steinmetz, S.K. (1980) *Behind Closed Doors: Violence in the American Family*, Garden City, NY: Doubleday.

Walker, K., Bowen, E. and Brown, S. (2013) 'Desistance from intimate partner violence: a critical review', *Aggression and Violent Behavior*, 18: 271–80.

Wangmann, J. (2011) *Different Types of Intimate Partner Violence: An Exploration of the Literature*, Sydney: University of New South Wales, Australian Domestic and Family Violence Clearinghouse.

Watts, A.G. (2001). 'Career guidance and social exclusion: a cautionary tale', *British Journal of Guidance & Counselling*, 29: 156–76.

Westmarland, N. and Kelly, L. (2012) 'Why extending measurements of "success" in domestic violence perpetrator programmes matters for social work', *British Journal of Social Work*, 42: 1–19.

Chapter 14

New approaches to assessing effectiveness and outcomes of domestic violence perpetrator programs

Liz Kelly and Nicole Westmarland

> I'm just not convinced, my instinct tells me perpetrator programs don't work.
> (Chief executive)
>
> Well, I think they're bollocks. That's what I came here to say.
> (Victim-survivor)

To say that domestic violence perpetrator programs (DVPPs) are still controversial is perhaps to understate the strength of feelings held by some, including those quoted above, who attended a recent workshop about DVPPs. As Chung (this volume) notes, despite a four-decade history of such programs, doubts about their effectiveness persist. However, given that many offenders continue abuse after separation, or abuse new partners, and that most who are fathers will be awarded child contact, there is surely a necessity, rather than an option, to do "something" with men about their violence.

We are in the process of conducting a British evaluation of DVPPs, comparing (amongst other things) women whose partners have been on a program with women whose partners have not been on a program. We do not yet know the changes that such programs make. However, we do know that DVPPs have been held to a narrow and, we argue, unhelpful, definition of what "success" means, while being held to a standard higher and more rigid than most other social and even medical interventions. In this chapter, we describe what we mean by this, outline the indicators we have developed to extend measures of success, and give examples from our ongoing research that investigates what (non-criminal justice) DVPPs "add" to coordinated community responses to domestic violence (DV) using Project Mirabal as an example.[1]

British domestic violence perpetrator programs

Despite advances in research, policy, and practice, DV shows only minimal signs of abating. It continues to blight the lives of (predominantly) women and children as victims and survivors and men as perpetrators. The focus of much work to date has been on interventions to improve the safety of women and children: for example, women's refuges and advocacy. It has become clear that to reduce and prevent DV, the spotlight must be placed on men and their behavior, alongside, rather than replacing, interventions for women and children.

One response to DV perpetrators is to refer them to a DVPP. In England and Wales (but not Scotland) these have traditionally been divided into "criminal justice" and "community" programs. However, as "community" programs, which historically took many voluntary referrals, are increasingly being filled with child protection and child contact referrals (from social work and family courts), a more accurate description probably is "non-criminal justice." Most services that run British DVPPs are members of the organization Respect, which, amongst other things, runs the Respect phoneline, the UK helpline for domestic violence perpetrators, and manages the accreditation of programs.[2] The Respect Accreditation Standard sets out the requirements for organizations to manage DVPPs and integrated support services (ISS) for current and former partners. It is important, for contextual reasons, to understand that having ISS for (ex-)partners is an essential and "normalized" part of running a DVPP in Britain and the rest of the United Kingdom. They are not an "optional extra," for the reasons described by Respect (2012: 2):

> Organisations running a DVPP without an ISS cannot be considered for accreditation as they are unsafe and cannot achieve the standard. An ISS is an essential feature of a Respect accredited Domestic Violence Prevention Service, for many reasons. An ISS helps to ensure that women's expectations of the DVPP are based on realistic expectations and that they and others do not rely solely on the service to bring about an immediate cessation of violence and abuse. It helps to ensure that women's safety can be monitored and kept the highest priority. It also helps to ensure that work with the men attending the program is informed by current understanding of the women's experiences. It is now widely accepted that working with perpetrators of DV can only be undertaken safely if there is an ISS that contacts partners and ex-partners and provides them with a support service.

British programs vary and are constantly developing, but often take an approach which combines techniques from cognitive behavioral and other therapeutic interventions with awareness raising and educational activities, usually using an understanding of DV which is pro-feminist and based on research evidence about the nature of DV. Most consist of weekly group-work sessions which aim to educate men about how to eliminate their use of violent, abusive, and controlling behaviors and promote the value of gender-equal relationships. Such programs are now widespread within the criminal justice field (through probation for men mandated by the criminal courts) but community-based/non-criminal justice programs (for men mandated by family courts, child protection, or self- or partner-mandated) remain sparse. All of the British non-criminal justice programs that we are aware of are for male heterosexual perpetrators, with no group work available for gay men, lesbian or heterosexual women, or transsexual men and women. As far as we know, only London has specifically developed group-work programs for ethnic-minority men (Rehman *et al.* 2013).

This shortage of programs is linked to a lack of clarity about whether perpetrator programs "work." In the UK there have been two published evaluations of community-based programs (Dobash *et al.* 2000; Burton *et al.* 1998). While both showed program effects, they were largely based on criminal court-mandated men (who previously attended community programs before the expansion of criminal-justice-led programs) and the evaluations had methodological limitations.

In the United States, two contradictory sets of findings are put forward. The first claims to have found a program effect (largely through the work of Gondolf, see for example, 2004) and the second claims there is no program effect (largely through the work of Dutton, see for example, 2006). None of these studies has been accepted universally in the UK as providing evidence as to whether perpetrator programs "work" or not. In addition, most of the studies conducted in the US have also relied on court-mandated research participants and had other methodological limitations. The findings cannot be easily translated to the UK because of the different community contexts. Finally, the UK community-based programs are required to have associated women's support projects that make proactive contact with all partners and ex-partners of program men, and their work has expanded into undertaking risk and case management as part of multi-agency responses. Neither was generally the case in the projects taking part in the research done in the US. It is this expansion of the work of DVPPs which led us to place them more centrally within coordinated community responses in our research, asking what they contribute to overall responses to DV.

Beyond "no more violence" or "completion"

As part of the Project Mirabal pilot study, we sought to understand how funders/commissioners, project staff (group-work facilitators, women's support workers and managers), victim-survivors, and perpetrators who were on or had been on programs understood success. We conducted a total of 73 semi-structured interviews from five DVPPs across England and Scotland in 2009–10. Perhaps not surprisingly, given that the stated aim of many programs was to increase the safety of women and children, "no more violence" emerged strongly as a score outcome for funders, commissioners, some program staff, and wider community partners.

For the women we interviewed, though, "success" meant far more than just "ending the violence." They knew physical violence might stop, but unhealthy atmospheres laden with tension and threat could remain.

Project staff felt that success was seen by funders and commissioners predominantly as program completion, which they saw as an unhelpful oversimplification of their intervention.

> I think funders view success as how many bums on seats there are. How many people get through a program, you know, how many sort of completed. How fast you can churn people through a sausage machine really.
>
> (Program worker)

Others described the broad net of change that could happen if even one man changed his behavior.

> I'm aware of one family, just one guy changes radically here, it's not just him and his partner and his kids, there's all the people who have connections with them, that's a wide circumference of people that are affected. So, although we don't . . . you know, we've only run two groups and we get maybe eight, nine, ten guys through in a 12-month period, because the program's longer than 12 months, that's how many men we get. I mean there's a lot of people involved there, there's a lot of people, that's not just eight or nine, you're talking . . . when you've added the partners, ex-partners, children, stepchildren, larger family when they're involved, it's about 70 or 80 people very likely.
>
> (Program worker)

As part of Project Mirabal we conducted lengthy, in-depth interviews with men who were enrolled in the programs at the beginning of their participation, at the point they drop out (if relevant), and at the end point of the program. We also conducted interviews with the (ex-)partners of enrolled men at the start and end points. At the time of writing we are still analyzing these interviews; however, it is clear that some men who attended all sessions and "successfully completed" the program have failed to make significant changes in their behavior, whereas some men who failed to complete the program have been able to make at least marginal changes. Two examples are given in the boxes below.

In the first example, Steve reports changes and insights which likely led to fairly significant improvements for his ex-partner and their child, despite not completing the program. In contrast, Tony would be able to tick both the "completed" and the "no more violence" boxes, while using the program learning in problematic ways and continuing to micro-manage Sandra's everyday activities in a way that creates a tense, fearful, and controlling atmosphere. There will undoubtedly be examples that show the opposite to be the case—where completers make more changes than those who leave the program. But we use these two examples above to illustrate the problematic nature of equating either "completion" or "no more violence" with "success."

The place of domestic violence perpetrator programs

Throughout our evaluation, we have heard broad statements such as those that open this chapter. This was evident in our pilot study where program staff were very aware that their service was often not seen as a "popular one."

BOX 1. EXAMPLE OF NON-COMPLETER

Steve (pseudonym) is a white man in his 40s based in Northern England with a history of DV and police involvement. He was involved with Sarah (pseudonym) for 1.5 years and they had a son together. Following a violent confrontation in public in front of their son, a restraining order was put in place and child contact was stopped. When contact proceedings re-started it was recommended that Steve attend a DVPP. He completed half the program and was not permitted to continue, due to conflict with one of the facilitators, alongside financial problems which he reported made it difficult to travel to the group. Steve gave an example of where he would have used control to get his own way before attending the program, but following the program the couple had their first Christmas without a fight or argument.

> *Yeah at times let's say when it's been around Christmas times, I've badgered her to bring him round and she hasn't and it's ended up in violence [. . .] [This Christmas] . . . I didn't . . . expect her to bring him round because obviously she's got the family going round there and all that kind of thing, so what's the point in me saying "Right I want you to bring him round on Christmas Day or Boxing Day" when I know really it is a totally unreasonable request. [. . .] Before I was expecting Sarah to drop everything to bring Harry to me or whatever . . . and I didn't even care whether it was an unreasonable thing to do, I didn't care about how she felt or what she thought . . . but like now, I say, Christmas I didn't even ask, the only thing I did ask was "Look can you make sure Harry after he's opened his presents, make sure he rings me on Christmas day?" and she went "Yeah not a problem" [. . .] that probably would have been, apart from when Harry was probably 1 years old, that's one of the first Christmases where me and Sarah didn't have a fight or an argument.*

> I think there are still significant numbers of people out there working in social care who as far as perpetrators are concerned it's all "prosecute, bang them up, and throw away the key."
>
> (DVVP Service worker)

This inclination is perplexing, since many of these individuals would be critical of right-wing penal policies in general. As Lewis and colleagues (2001) highlighted, the idea that the law is a deterrent to DV offenders is one that is often supported with insufficient questioning or consideration of other modes of intervention. They argue that feminists on the left are generally very mindful of offenders' civil liberties, except when considering men who commit offenses against women and children.

BOX 2. EXAMPLE OF A COMPLETER

Sandra (pseudonym) is a white woman in her 40s living in the South of England with her husband Tony (pseudonym) and her two teenage children from a previous relationship. Two years into their relationship a neighbor overheard a dispute and rang the police. They went to Relate For Couples counseling, where staff advised that Tony should attend the DVPP. Although Tony went on to complete the program, Sandra gave examples of his ongoing control and micro-management of her household work:

> *Probably there has been an improvement there, but he'll still make his opinions known, but he'll add at the end of it now, "But I'm not allowed to say that, or think that." [. . .] Erm, he lost it Tuesday morning [. . .] I'd swept the kitchen floor. Now I sweep that kitchen floor about five times a day, and I'm not sure if I was on my own I'd do it that frequently to be honest, but I'm always paranoid that I don't want him to walk in there and see any crumbs on the floor. So I'd swept the kitchen floor, my daughters had got up that morning, had some cereal and as usual, as teenagers do, you know, tipped it into a bowl and some cereal had obviously gone over the top and some had spread on the floor, and yes it is careless and yes it's not great, but heigh-ho, that's life. Erm, and so he'd walked in, and he'd gone, "There's crumbs on the floor again. Can't you lot—don't you lot—don't—" and he starts, again in earshot of the children . . . and then I said, "Look I only swept it before we went to bed last night, you know, I'm in a rush to get to the train, but I'll—I'll sweep it before I go and, you know, I—or if I don't get to do it then I—I'll, you know, do it when I get back or whatever." And he—he was make—I think it was tuna sandwiches, and he—he'd like put his tuna into a bowl, erm, and he got this bowl of tuna and he threw it on the floor, and he went, "There!" he said, "I might as well do the same as your children. Just throw all the food on the floor." And then he just—then he throws the cup of tea, and then he walks out."*

One strand of Project Mirabal involves interviewing staff employed at other organizations that comprise the Coordinated Community Response that DVPPs are situated within. In one of the areas in particular, this strong belief that the law and not perpetrator programs was the way forward was stated very strongly by two police officers.

> I'm simply not convinced of its cost-effectiveness and I'm not convinced that on the majority of perpetrators that it works.
>
> (Police officer)

The officers said they were very unlikely to refer men to the DV perpetrator program, stating: "We refer people to jail, that's where they should be!" While this is a statement many, and arguably most, feminists would also make, it is, nonetheless, rhetoric rather than reality. The "tough on DV perpetrators" message has been voiced by many politicians, for example one minister who, when asked at a public meeting whether hostels should be opened for DV perpetrators to be ejected to (instead of women and children needing to leave their homes to go into shelters) and where they could take part in behavioral change work either individually or in groups, replied with just one sentence: "We already have hostels for violent men: They are called prisons."

Sending more men to prison for DV probably would send a powerful message out both individually and collectively to DV perpetrators. However, the problem with this argument is that: (a) It is not a solution, since many DV victim-survivors do not make a police report, and many of the behaviors that comprise the coercive control which is so destructive for women and children do not currently constitute crimes; (b) of those men who are arrested, a small proportion are prosecuted and hardly any receive custodial sentences (Hester 2006; Hester and Westmarland 2006); and, (c) sending someone to prison is an expensive option that does not necessarily change men's behavior, nor stop the violence. The reality is that prison, even for a short time, is an unlikely outcome for the vast majority of DV offenders.

Expanding our understandings of "success"

Through our pilot study interviews, we asked what the various stakeholders in DVPPs wanted to get out of programs. Some men were still participating in a program and were talking about their hopes, and others had already completed their program. Some of the female (ex-)partners had separated, others were still living with their partners.

From the thematic analysis of the 73 interviews we developed six measures of success, which we explain below. These measures have provided the framework for the indicators of success that we have used to develop our survey and interview instruments within our full research study.[3] In light of the previous discussion, it is crucial to note that the first two measures were more important to the victim-survivors we interviewed than ending violence.

1. *An improved relationship between men on programs and their (ex-)partners which is underpinned by respect and effective communication.*
   Improved and respectful relationships encompassed changes in relation to (ex-)partners and children whether or not they continued living together as a family; indeed being able to accept separation and make the best of it was seen as being as "successful" as remaking relationships within the family. This was particularly the case where communication of one form or another was going to be ongoing for many years because of child contact. Having "honest" communication was mentioned regularly by the men, as was being

able to rebuild and sustain it in a context of broken trust. Many recognized that holding onto previous patterns was not an option if their hope of not losing their partner was to be an outcome of the program. One man, for example, explained that he had previously attended a number of anger management courses but that these had simply taught him to remove himself from the situation rather than to be able to openly and honestly communicate.

2. *For (ex-)partners to have an expanded "space for action" which empowers through restoring their voice and ability to make choices, while improving their wellbeing.*
For the female (ex-)partners, this meant no longer living with the shadow of fear, which in turn created space in which it was possible to think, act, and express themselves without being scared of what might happen. One woman put this succinctly as having the option of disagreeing about something that was important.

> Basically the fact that if we argue, it doesn't end up with physical violence and that it can be a normal argument and I don't have to worry about my safety.
>
> ((Ex-)partner of DVPP participant)

Qualitative DV researchers have long documented the debilitating impacts it has on women's sense of self (see, for example, Hoff 1990; Kirkwood 1993), narrowing what Nordic researcher Eva Lundgren (2004) has termed their "life space," and Liz Kelly (2007) refers to as "space for action." Women talked about being able to enter the house without being scared, stay out late without feeling they would have to "walk on egg-shells" the next day, choose to spend time with family and friends without being challenged; all are examples of what we term "expanded space for action," and which chime with the limits on freedom that Evan Stark (2007) makes such a core component of the harms of coercive control.

3. *Safety and freedom from violence and abuse for women and children.*
Following Stark (2007), we refer here not just to safety but "freedom" from violence, in recognition that the reduction or cessation of violence and abuse overlapped with the previous two measures of success. The reduction or cessation of violence and abuse was discussed more often and more explicitly by men on programs than by the women (ex-)partners, undoubtedly in part because program content focuses on this. Many maintained they had already made this change. This was the measure of success most frequently mentioned by funders and commissioners, and it included the ability both to engage men who were not in contact with the criminal justice system and to enable safe child contact to take place. Safety/freedom from violence was also the most prominent for practitioners. This was generally linked to the stated goals of programs, and included both being and feeling safer for women and children. Most emphasized ending violence and abuse, with some offering a more

qualified reduction in violence or risk and others ending physical violence and reducing emotional abuse. The latter two possibly reflect a desire not to over-claim what programs could achieve. "Feeling safer" was sometimes expanded upon through phrases like "no longer living in fear." While the majority of practitioners were aiming for a total cessation of violence, a minority argued that less ambitious changes were more realistic:

> At best, you know, no longer abusive, at worst that their abuse has significantly reduced.
>
> (Practitioner)

Here we see a perspective where a range of changes in the same direction is considered by practitioners as positive.

4. *Safe, positive, and shared parenting.*
For the women (ex-)partners, positive parenting refers not only to the fact that children benefited from the changes noted above, but also that parenting the children together was enhanced, with family activities more frequent, men being more attentive to the needs of the children and/or access no longer something to be dreaded. For both current and ex-partners, being able to trust the man with the children played a significant part in this. More accurate multi-agency assessments, which included a report on the man's dangerousness and potential for change rather than relying solely on professional judgments about the woman's capacity to protect, were seen as important to some funders/commissioners.
The contribution programs could make to multi-agency risk management plans was emphasized. For example, a full assessment, which revealed the extent and length of abuse, can be fed into Multi-Agency Risk Assessment Conferences or similar forums, family court proceedings, and shift the attitudes and interventions of partner agencies. In particular, detailed information on perpetrators had the potential to widen the focus from the victim and increase the emphasis on addressing the risks posed by the perpetrator.

5. *Enhanced awareness of self and others for men on programs, including an understanding of the impact that DV has had on their partners and children.*
Here we refer to an expanded understanding of what intimate partner violence consists of and its impact. For both women and men, recognition of what constitutes violence—or not—emerged as a consequence of being asked about its presence within relationships, in both risk assessment and safety planning processes. Some reflected on how the services had enabled them to reflect on previous misconceptions.

> Well, before I went on the course if they'd have asked us that question [about DV being present in any other relationships], I would have said it didn't happen but . . . [I learned a] lot from the course that I went to . . .

> It's little things that you don't realize at the time, [like] the shouting, the slamming doors, the banging things down, all that's in a way DV . . . but at the time I didn't realize it . . . I would say that [there have been other relationships where there has been DV].
>
> (Program participant)

Awareness of self and others was a commonly cited desired outcome for men by practitioners, presumably reflecting that they believe this to be the foundation of not only choosing to change, but more importantly being able to maintain this after completing the program. The outcomes they were seeking here included: empathy; the ability to reflect on behavior and feelings; ability to "be in" relationships with others; taking responsibility for their actions and their impacts on others; willingness to seek help; ability to identify what they had changed and why it made a difference; and, capacity to name and discuss problematic behavior.

6. *For children, safer, healthier childhoods in which they feel heard and cared about.*
   While to some extent this overlaps with indicator 4, here the focus is on the children themselves, rather than parenting. This was raised primarily by practitioners and funders/commissioners rather than by the women and men. For practitioners working in perpetrator programs, children's safety has become a more specific focus, both while living with the perpetrator and where child contact is an issue. This is in large part due to increased referrals from social work and Children and Family Court Advisory and Support Service (CAFCASS),[4] and being commissioned to do risk assessments with respect to contact hearings. Again the notion of safety encompassed more than physical safety and encompassed: physical and emotional health and wellbeing; happiness; freedom from fear; and/or having to protect their mother or siblings. Some workers took the risks to children very seriously, making reference to decisions to remove perpetrators from the household if children "were terrified," and the importance of appropriate child contact decisions being made by the courts and other professionals.

   Children's future relationships were a very strong theme for funders/commissioners, often linked to the ubiquitous, though strongly contested, cycle-of-abuse theory (that children who live with domestic abuse are more likely to be abusive/abused in their own future relationships). Some responses were more immediate and connected to the realities of the everyday lives of children and young people, referring to: knowing violence is wrong; improved and more stable peer relationships; for teenage boys, positive interactions with girlfriends; and, for teenage girls, seeking more equal relationships.

Our research tools that we are currently using in Project Mirabal—a qualitative interview schedule and a quantitative telephone survey—allow us to explore changes on all six indicators, thus offering more nuanced measurements and assessments of DVPPs' success.

Reflections

In this chapter we have argued that measuring the success of DVPPs solely in terms of the notions of "completion" and "no more violence" are flawed in terms of what we know about the patterns and harm of DV, the work that DVPPs do, and the hopes and aspirations of victim-survivors. Having described two cases where "completion" and "lack of" did not equate with "no more violence" and "violence" respectively, we then critiqued the "law and order" approach put forward by some community partners and experienced by ourselves as academics while undertaking our current evaluation of British DVPPs through Project Mirabal. Instead, we suggest six more nuanced holistic indicators of success which reflect more accurately both the work of programs and what would make a difference in the lives of women and children.

Notes

1 For updates on Project Mirabal, see www.dur.ac.uk/criva/projectmirabal.
2 For more information, see Respect website, www.respect.uk.net.
3 For more information about these measures and an analysis of what this means for social work, see Westmarland and Kelly (2013).
4 CAFCASS combines family court welfare service, guardian *ad litem*, and other key functions where children come within the purview of the family court.

References

Burton S., Regan L. and Kelly L. (1988) *Supporting Women and Challenging Men: Lessons from the Domestic Violence Intervention Project*, Bristol, UK: Policy Press.

Dobash R.E., Dobash R.P., Cavanagh K. and Lewis R. (eds.) (2000) *Changing Violent Men*, Thousand Oaks, CA: Sage.

Dutton, D.G. (2006) *Rethinking Domestic Violence*, Vancouver: University of British Columbia Press.

Gondolf, E. (2004) 'Evaluating batterer counseling programs: a difficult task showing some effects and implications', *Aggression and Violent Behavior*, 9: 605–31.

Hester, M. (2006) 'Making it through the criminal justice system: attrition and domestic violence', *Social Policy and Society*, 5: 79–90.

Hester, M. and Westmarland, N. (2006) 'Domestic violence perpetrators', *Criminal Justice Matters*, 66: 34–9.

Hoff, L. (1990) *Battered Women as Survivors*, London: Routledge.

Kelly L. (2007) 'A conducive context: trafficking of persons in Central Asia', in M. Lee (ed.), *Human Trafficking*, Cullompton: Willan, 73–91.

Kirkwood, C. (1993) *Leaving Abusive Partners: From the Scars of Survival to the Wisdom for Change*, Newbury Park, CA: Sage.

Lewis, R., Dobash, R.E., Dobash, R.P. and Cavanagh, K. (2001) 'Law's progressive potential: the value of engagement with the law for domestic violence', *Social & Legal Studies*, 10: 104–30.

Lundgren, E. (2004) *The Process of Normalising Violence,* Stockholm: ROKS.

Rehman, Y., Kelly, L. and Siddiqui, H. (eds.) (2013) *Moving In The Shadows: Violence in the Lives of Minority Women and Children*, Farnham, UK: Ashgate.

Respect (2012) *The Respect Accreditation Standard.* Online. Available at http://respect.uk.net/wp-content/themes/respect/assets/files/accreditation-standard.pdf (accessed 25 May 2014).

Stark, E. (2007) *Coercive Control: How Men Entrap Women in Personal Life*, New York: Oxford University Press.

Westmarland, N. and Kelly, L. (2013) 'Why expanding measures of success matters for social work', *British Journal of Social Work*, 43: 1092–110.

Chapter 15

What do we mean by domestic violence? Mandatory prosecution and the impact on partner assault response programs

Mark Holmes

In 1980, The Canadian Advisory Council on the Status of Women published *Wife Battering in Canada: The Vicious Cycle*. It advocated that "The law must be used to convey the message that assault is a crime whether it occurs within or outside the home" (MacLeod 1980: 64). Two years later the Solicitor General of Canada wrote to the Canadian Association of Chiefs of Police, strongly encouraging them to support the position that charges should be laid in wife assault cases, and since then all provincial/territorial governments have directed police, and in most cases Crown Attorneys, to rigorously investigate and prosecute cases of wife battering (MacLeod 1987: 82).

Also in 1982, having entered the second year of a Master of Social Work program, I was one of several men invited to a meeting with women employees of a shelter for abused women. Men had been telephoning the shelter, sometimes angry and in search of their partners; other times seemingly remorseful and searching help. The shelter staff believed that it was men's responsibility to work with abusive men, and challenged us to undertake this project. Some did begin programs for "batterers," as they were referred to at the time.[1] In 1984, the New Directions Program was founded in Ottawa and I remain its coordinator 30 years later.

The evolving criminal justice response: the impact on programs for men who abuse

Contrary to what might have been expected, given directives to police, the courts were not initially a primary source of referrals for New Directions. Only seven of the first 200 men who registered for New Directions between January 1985 and August 1987 were court-referred. For the most part, men were being referred by their partners, family counseling centers, and other community agencies.

However, the criminal justice response to domestic violence[2] (DV) evolved. In Ottawa, I believe this was strongly influenced by the creation in the late 1980s of the Regional Coordinating Committee to End Violence Against Women. For the first time, battered women's advocates and other community organizations met regularly with representatives of the police, probation and parole services and the Crown Attorney's office. Gaps in the criminal justice response to DV were identified and remedies sought. In 1987, funding to support New Directions was obtained from the Ministry of Correctional Services. In 1988, 30 probationers were referred, but they represented less than 20 percent of all clients.

Referral patterns changed during the following years. Between 1993 and 1995, 160 of the 401 men referred to New Directions were on probation. Whereas previously just 200 referrals were generated in two and a half years, this number was now being seen in one year. The percentage of referrals on probation similarly increased from 21 percent in 1988 to 40 percent in 1995.

Then, in March 1996, the *Toronto Star*, a widely read newspaper in Canada's largest city, published a series of eight articles called "Spousal Abuse: Hitting Home." During a one-week period, *Toronto Star* reporters had attended every bail court in Toronto, identifying 133 spousal abuse cases. Each case had been tracked through the criminal justice system. By the time the articles were published eight months later, 100 of the cases had been completed in Court:

- Thirty-seven percent of victims recanted on the witness stand or failed to attend court.
- Almost half of all accused violated terms of release by contacting or harassing the victim/complainant.
- In none of the cases was evidence other than the testimony of the victim/complainant presented (i.e., no forensic report, crime scene photographs, 911 recordings, or witnesses' or police officers' testimonies).
- There were frequent adjournments. By the date the first article was published, the 133 cases had generated 730 court appearances. The prosecution was represented by different Crown Attorneys, meaning there was little consistency for the victim/complainant.

To its credit, the Government of Ontario responded to these findings.[3] In 1997, the Domestic Violence Court (DVC) program was launched with two pilot projects in Toronto. In one site a "Coordinated Prosecution" model was implemented and in the other an "Early Intervention Program" offered a different approach.

The Coordinated Prosecution model addressed the findings of the *Toronto Star* investigation. Police were expected to take photographs at the scene and interview witnesses. Complainants were invited to provide a sworn videotaped statement which, under certain circumstances, could be used at trial. 911 tapes were obtained and played in court, to support the woman's testimony. There was also an attempt to minimize inconsistency in the prosecution process by assigning a single Crown Attorney to each case. The Victim/Witness Assistance Program was expanded to provide support to the victim.

The Early Intervention model focused on cases that were a first offense, caused no significant emotional or physical harm to the victim, and where no weapons were used. The accused was required to accept responsibility by entering an early guilty plea. Sentencing was adjourned until completion of an intervention program. If the program was completed satisfactorily, the Crown would recommend a conditional discharge and a period of probation.

The project's evaluation was promising (Moyer *et al.* 2000); in 1998 the DVC program was expanded to six additional sites, including Ottawa. By 2004, every criminal court jurisdiction in Ontario had a DVC program that was able to process both Coordinated Prosecution and Early Intervention cases (see Ministry of the Attorney General of Ontario 2000). An essential component of every DVC program is a Partner Assault Response (PAR) program. These programs are similar to those known as batterer intervention programs in the United States. Funded by the Ministry of the Attorney General and located in community-based social service agencies, PAR programs are governed by Provincial Standards and currently provide 12 weeks (previously 16 weeks up to April 1, 2014) of education and counseling to court-ordered individuals who have committed a DV offense. Outreach and support services are also offered to the victim.

The Ottawa DVC, in its first year of operation, did more to effectuate mandatory charging and prosecution of DV cases than had been accomplished in the 16 years since the letter to the Chiefs of Police. New Directions intake interviews jumped from 266 in 1997 to 485 in 1999 at end of the first year of the DVC. Between 1984 and 1998, New Directions conducted 1,976 intake interviews, i.e., an average of 141 per year. In the 14-year period following the DVC implementation, intake interviews averaged 530 annually.

Equally noteworthy is the change in the ratio of court-ordered vs. voluntary clients. During the first 14 years of New Directions, fewer than 40 percent of referrals originated with the criminal justice system. That percentage increased to an average of 87 percent during the next 14 years, peaking at 91 percent in 2012. Since it is not reasonable to believe that the rate of DV almost doubled between 1997 and 1999, I believe that the DVC, with a reinforced focus on mandatory charging and prosecution, must be seen as the catalyst for these dramatic increases. In 2001, the first female offender was referred to New Directions. In 2012, 13 percent of referrals were women, almost all charged with an offense against a male partner.

The quantitative impact of mandatory charging and prosecution on New Directions is obvious. But as will be later discussed, the increased case volume wasn't the only important transformation.

Power and control: the influence of Duluth

In 1987, I attended a conference in Baltimore, sponsored by The House of Ruth, a women's shelter. My recollection is that the conference provided a backdrop for a debate between two competing paradigms. On the one hand were those who favored a therapeutic approach to changing the behavior of violent men. Attention was focused on the intra-psychic lives of men. As described by Adams (1988: 3), it was believed the etiology of DV "includes poor impulse control, low frustration tolerance, fear of intimacy, fear of abandonment, dependency, underlying depression and impaired ego functioning due to developmental trauma." Positioned against this paradigm was one articulated most clearly by Ellen Pence, Michael Paymar, and Barbara Hart,[4] arguing that violence against women, including DV, was "individually willed yet socially constructed" (Schechter 1982: 238). Although it was an individual man who punched, swore at, yelled at, or sexually assaulted his partner, his actions could only be understood by situating them within the social context of that man's life. In 1987, this social context was one of sexism, income, social and political inequality, and a socialization process that privileged men over women. In the words of Pence and Paymar (1986: 18):

> A man's violence against his partner is inextricably linked to his perception of the world and her place in it. Without a change in his world view, the violent man will continue to find "legitimate" reasons to impose his will physically on his partner.

Intervention with abusive men should therefore focus on re-education, not therapy. Violence and abuse were seen as purposeful and intentional actions used by a man to establish and maintain power over his partner. The role of facilitators was to help men identify individual beliefs that supported the use of controlling behaviors and show how these are linked to the patriarchal values of society. New beliefs, based on equality and respect, were identified. Adherence to these can lead to non-abusive behavior.

The consensus at the conference was that our work needed to be informed by the latter paradigm. I returned to Ottawa energized. Within a few months, I had traveled to Minnesota to participate in training delivered by Ellen Pence and Michael Paymar. Upon my return, New Directions began to use the so-called Duluth Model.[5] In 1995, with funding from Health Canada and the Ontario Women's Directorate, an evaluation of New Directions was conducted (Davies *et al.* 1995). The results were encouraging, and we felt we were generally on the right track.

Beyond our understanding of Duluth: the challenges of typologies

In 1999, within a year of the DVC opening, experienced New Directions facilitators were reporting that something different was happening in the groups. Men were expressing more anger and resentment, and group dynamics were less collaborative. Initially, we speculated that this was the result of a change in our groups' composition. Groups now comprised almost exclusively court-ordered men, whereas previously more than half had no involvement with the criminal justice system and volunteered for the program. Perhaps we were experiencing more of the minimization, denial, and blaming knowingly associated with court-ordered perpetrators. But it seemed there was more. Men were not engaging with the Duluth approach as they had in the past. Before, most men had been able to identify the beliefs that supported their controlling tactics and generally able to articulate the intent of their behavior (i.e., controlling their partners). Now, many were disavowing the existence of such beliefs. They would often admit using specific abusive behaviors but were claiming that there was no pattern to such actions and that they had no desire to impose power and control over their partners.

Over the next several years, we became somewhat more open to the possibility that New Directions clients were not a homogeneous group. In the past, my assumption was that group participants were "batterers" who regularly used the tactics described on the Power and Control Wheel (Pence and Paymar 1986: 3) with the intention of dominating and controlling their partners. While I had always believed in the importance of working with these men in a respectful way, it was also true that I viewed them through this "Power and Control" lens. Was I in need of a new prescription? Some years later, I came across the following observation, written around the time I and many colleagues were struggling with these issues. Pence and Shepard (1999: 28–9) captured our feelings exactly:

> He does it for the power, he does it for control, he does it because he can—these were the jingles that, in our opinion, said all there was to say . . . By determining that the need or desire for power was the motivating force behind battering, we created a conceptual framework that, in fact, did not fit with the lived experience of many of the men and women we were working with . . . I found that many of the men I interviewed did not seem to articulate a desire for power over a partner. Although I relentlessly took every opportunity to point out to the men in groups that they were so motivated and merely in denial, the fact that few men ever articulated such a desire went unnoticed by me and many of my co-workers. Eventually, we realized that we were finding what we had pre-determined to find.

Gradually and, as I have come to learn, belatedly, we began to question the one-size-fits-all approach of our program, and by extension, the DVC program. Belatedly, because as early as 1995, Michael Johnson (1995: 283) was arguing persuasively that "a large number of families suffer from occasional outbursts of violence from either husbands or wives or both, while a significant number of other families are terrorized by systematic male violence enacted in the service of patriarchal control." This was a revelation. Johnson was saying that we needed to distinguish among different types of DV perpetrators. Perhaps we also needed to tailor our interventions to suit the specific needs of these perpetrators. According to Stark (2007: 104):

> A key implication of Johnson's terminology is that situational violence and intimate terrorism have different dynamics and qualitatively different

> outcomes and so should be judged by different moral yardsticks. *They also require a different response.* Abuse should no more be considered a simple extension of using force than a heart attack should be treated as an extreme instance of heartburn.
>
> [emphasis added]

We were beginning to understand that similar behaviors could be used for very different reasons and in very different contexts. A push might be "violence that is not connected to a general pattern of control . . . involving specific arguments that escalate to violence but showing no relationship-wide evidence of an attempt to exert general control over one's partner" (Johnson and Leone 2005: 323). Johnson refers to this type of DV as *situational couple violence*. But the exact same push, appearing insignificant when de-contextualized, might have occurred in a relationship defined by coercion, intimidation, isolation, and fear, "violence that is embedded in a general pattern of controlling behaviors, indicating that the perpetrator is attempting to exert general control over his partner" (Johnson and Leone 2005: 322). Johnson calls this type of DV *intimate terrorism*. Both pushes constitute an assault and their perpetrators can be arrested and charged. They can both end up sitting together in New Directions, but it is clear that the intent of these two pushes is very different. Could this mean that the appropriate intervention for each perpetrator had to be different?

We knew what to do with the intimate terrorists (although that was not the language in use at the time) because intervention programs had been designed to work with these men. In the 1980s and 1990s, when one referred to DV perpetrators, it was the intimate terrorists one had in mind: the men using the tactics of the Power and Control Wheel. They were the ones who came to the attention of the police, as their violence was often too serious to ignore, and they were the men referred to intervention programs. However, as the practice of mandatory charging and prosecution was enhanced, men and women who had not previously come to our attention were being caught up in the criminal justice net. Our programs were not well prepared to effectively work with individuals using what I now believe was situational couple violence.

Consider a few of the incidents that have recently resulted in referrals to New Directions. All information comes from police reports.

1. A woman is driving with her partner. An argument develops about financial problems. The man stops the car, and as the argument continues, she kicks him in the shin. A passing motorist calls the police. She is arrested and released on conditions that prohibit her from returning home to her partner and child. She pleads guilty to assault. There is no history of DV.
2. A man drunkenly grabs the phone out of his wife's hand, believing she has been talking too long. She swears at him and walks away. He pushes her. He becomes upset at her behavior and threatens to kill himself. When police arrive, she explains what has transpired and he is arrested for assault. She

tells police that he has never previously assaulted or threatened her. She had called the police, not because she was afraid or wanted him arrested but because of his threat of suicide.

3. A man is referred to New Directions for the second time in two years, following his third DV conviction. All assaults are serious and have resulted in injuries. He also uses significant controlling behaviors. There have been two different victims. There are ongoing controlling behaviors, including stalking, frequent and unwanted texting, and forcible confinement.
4. A 39 year-old male had been married for 13 years, but is now separated. One month before being charged, he was apprehended under the Mental Health Act and transported to hospital after threatening suicide. He is released after one day. Two weeks later, he is discovered after a suicide attempt and is hospitalized for ten days. One week later, upon learning of his wife's new partner, he calls and threatens her. He pleads guilty to uttering threats.
5. A man is referred to New Directions following convictions for criminal harassment and assault. He has a lengthy criminal record for DV against different women, as well as for other violent offenses, including manslaughter. His violence has been indiscriminate.

It is clear to me that these are different types of DV. Example 3 shows a pattern of abusive and controlling behaviors, occurring with more than one woman, and likely fits the category Johnson (2008: 32) refers to as dependent intimate terrorism.

> Dependent intimate terrorists rank high on measures of emotional dependency and jealousy. These are men who are obsessed with their partners, desperate to hold them, and therefore jealous and controlling. They are not particularly violent outside the family. It is their emotional obsession with their partners that drives their need to control.

The man described in example 5 fits the antisocial type described by Pence and Das Gupta (2006: 13):

> [This violence is] not restricted to a particular partner or gender. A person may have certain antecedents such as childhood abuse and lack of moral maturity that have led to the development of anti-social personality. As a result, s/he may be abusive in a number of social settings: bars, work, home, sports field, etc. Such an individual may have little understanding of the consequences of his/her behavior and no feeling of shame or remorse regarding his/her violence. The anti-social individual is generally not amenable to change through self-reflection or therapy.

Examples 1 and 2 are probably situational couple violence, where "the violence is not driven by a general motive to control, but arises out of the dynamics of particular situations" (Johnson, 2008: 61). And example 4 could be referred to as pathological violence. "At the root of pathological violence are physical conditions related to mental illness or altered mental states due to neurological damage and/or drug or alcohol abuse. In such situations, generally, when the cause is removed, the resultant violence also ends" (Pence and Das Gupta, 2006: 13).

What these examples have in common is the commission of a criminal offense, but not much else. The criminal justice system is incident focused, in that it responds to a particular behavior that is alleged to be contrary to the criminal code. It is the individual action that is investigated, prosecuted, and sanctioned. The context in which that action occurred is not usually considered. The system tends not to ask whether a slap is part of an ongoing pattern of coercion or is an isolated incident related to situational factors.

In practice, this failure to consider the context means that cases tend to be dealt with similarly. Following arrest, the accused, if released, is on conditions that usually include non-communication with the victim. This condition, with few exceptions, remains in place until the case is concluded. Prosecutors are instructed not to withdraw the charge or divert the case. A referral to a PAR program is almost always a condition of sentence or bail.

This one-size-fits-all approach has taken intervention programs away from their historical focus. When New Directions started 30 years ago, we intended to work with men who employed "an ongoing patterned use of intimidation, coercion, and violence as well as other tactics of control to establish and maintain a relationship of dominance over an intimate partner" (Pence and Das Gupta, 2006: 5). I believe these men are Johnson's (2008) intimate terrorists and Stark's (2007) coercive controllers. These are the men who cause women to flee to shelters.

In addition to these men, we are now expected to work with men whose violence is situational or associated with alcohol abuse or mental health issues. Women are being referred to us as offenders, although in my experience their violence is almost always used to either resist their partner's abuse or is situationally motivated. It is my belief that zero tolerance, and in particular mandatory prosecution, has resulted in individuals being caught up in the criminal justice system who were not the intended targets when police were encouraged to arrest wife assault perpetrators back in 1982.

This is not to say that individuals who use situational couple violence or whose violence is linked to addictions or mental illness should not be held accountable for their actions. They also need support, counseling, and resources. Abusive behavior is never acceptable and should never be condoned. But should the criminal justice system intervene in the same way with a woman who kicks her partner out of frustration as it does with a man whose slap or punch is part of an ongoing pattern of abuse and coercion? This line of thinking delineates critical issues that require further exploration.

- Is it time to reconsider mandatory prosecution of DV, or at least systematically study its unintended consequences?
- Should the criminal justice system distinguish offenses perpetrated by an intimate terrorist and those situationally motivated?
- If so, what protocols must be developed to ensure accurate assessments? How do we minimize the risk that intimate terrorists are mistakenly identified as perpetrators of situational couple violence?
- Should PAR programs work with women? If so, should this work be guided by different principles than the work with men?
- Are there assessment tools that can accurately distinguish among various types of DV perpetrators? If not, who will develop them?
- Should PAR programs consider a differential response, whereby different lengths, intensities, and curricula are employed, depending on the type of client?
- Are some women deterred from calling police as a result of the current mandatory arrest and prosecution practice?
- Might mandatory charging still be defensible, since most situationally violent offenders do not seek help and may need the "encouragement" of the criminal justice system? But should prosecution practices be more flexible, to allow consideration of diversion or restorative justice approaches?

Conclusion

Over 15 years ago, the Government of Ontario decided to enhance the criminal justice response to DV through the creation of specialized DV courts, with a renewed commitment to mandatory charging and prosecution. A consequence of an approach that focuses primarily on discrete incidents of violence has been the arrest and prosecution of individuals who would not have fit the definition of "abuser" proposed by the 1970s activists of the battered women's movement.

For PAR programs, this has meant moving away from our historical focus on coercive and controlling violence. We now work with many men and women who do not fit the definition of intimate terrorists or batterers. This has had a significant impact on the nature of our work. All men and women who use violence or other abusive behaviors in their intimate relationships could benefit from support and assistance. These behaviors, even if rare, are inconsistent with values of respect and equality. But I would argue that not all of these individuals require the full force of a traditional criminal prosecution, with the personal, social, and financial consequences this intrusion often brings. At the same time, caution must be exercised, so that women are not put at increased risk by inaccurate assessment.

As a society, and in our communities, we must try to find a way to provide the appropriate assistance to individuals, couples, and families who are using or experiencing violence. In some instances, the seriousness of the situation requires state intervention through criminal sanctions. I believe that 40 years after the second wave of feminism brought "wife battering" into our collective consciousness, it is time to think more critically and have a more nuanced understanding of the different types of violence that sometimes occur in relationships. All intervention programs will then be better positioned to offer the most appropriate assistance, which can only benefit the women, children, and men impacted by DV, in all its manifestations.

Notes

1 In 1984, it was common to refer to violence in a relationship as *wife battering* and to perpetrators as *batterers*. This continues in some jurisdictions, with American programs often referred to as batterer intervention programs. When referring to individuals who use violence in their relationships, I prefer to label the behavior, not the person.

2 There has been criticism of using the term "domestic violence," as feminists argue it obscures its gendered nature. I am sympathetic to this analysis but have chosen to use this term because it is the language used by the Government of Ontario, and much of this chapter describes the state response through the criminal justice system.

3 The *Toronto Star* alone was not responsible for the DVC program. The day before the first article, Arlene May was murdered by her estranged common-law partner, Randy Iles. The coroner's recommendations included that "The Attorney General should ensure that there are dedicated domestic violence courts, which incorporate both the early intervention approach as employed in the North York model and the vigorous prosecution approach utilized in the Toronto K-Court model, where the volume of cases warrant such courts."

4 Ellen Pence and Michael Paymar were community activists from Duluth, Minnesota, who were instrumental in the development of the Duluth Model, a coordinated community response to domestic violence. Barbara Hart is an attorney who at the time worked with the Pennsylvania Coalition Against Domestic Violence.

5 Although the Duluth Model is sometimes simplistically used to describe a curriculum for use in groups for men who are abusive, it actually refers to a coordinated community response to end domestic violence, of which groups for men form only one part.

References

Adams, D. (1988) 'Counseling men who batter: a profeminist analysis of five treatment models', in M. Bograd and K. Yllo (eds.), *Feminist Perspectives on Wife Assault*, Beverly Hills, CA: Sage, 176–99.

Davies, L., Holmes, M., Lundy, C. and Urquhart, L. (1995) *Re-Education for Abusive Men: The Effect on the Lives of Women Partners*, Ottawa: Health Canada.

Gondolf, E. (2002) *Batterer Intervention Systems: Issues, Outcomes and Recommendations*, Thousand Oaks, CA: Sage.

Johnson, M. (2008) *A Typology of Domestic Violence: Intimate Terrorism, Violent Resistance, and Situational Couple Violence*, Lebanon, NH: Northeastern University Press.

Johnson, M. (1995) 'Patriarchal terrorism and common couple violence', *Journal of Marriage and the Family*, 57: 283–94.

Johnson, M. and Leone, J. (2005) 'The differential effects of intimate terrorism and situational couple violence: findings from the National Violence Against Women Survey', *Journal of Family Issues*, 26: 322–40.

MacLeod, L. (1987) *Battered But Not Beaten: Preventing Wife Battering in Canada*, Ottawa: The Canadian Advisory Council on the Status of Women.

MacLeod, L. (1980) *Wife Battering in Canada: The Vicious Circle*, Ottawa: The Canadian Advisory Council on the Status of Women.

Ministry of the Attorney General of Ontario (2000) *Implementing the Domestic Violence Court Program*, Toronto: Author.

Moyer, S., Rettinger, J. and Hotton, T. (2000) *The Evaluation of the Domestic Violence Courts: Their Functioning and Effects in the First Eighteen Months of Operation, 1998–1999*, Toronto: Ministry of the Attorney General of Ontario.

Pence, E. (1999) 'Components of community intervention projects', in E. Pence and M. Shepard (eds.), *Coordinating Community Responses to Domestic Violence: Lessons from the Duluth Model*, Thousand Oaks, CA: Sage, 28–9.

Pence, E. and Das Gupta, S. (2006) *Re-Examining 'Battering': Are All Acts of Violence Against Intimate Partners the Same?* Online. Available at www.praxisinternational.org/files/praxis/files/ReexaminingBattering.pdf (accessed 25 May 2014).

Pence, E. and Paymar, M. (1986) *Power and Control: Tactics of Men who Batter*, Duluth, MN: Minnesota Program Development Inc.

Schechter, S. (1982) *Women and Male Violence*, Boston, MA: South End Press.

Stark, E. (2007) *Coercive Control. How Men Entrap Women in Personal Life*, New York: Oxford University Press.

Section V: Behavior change programs for abusers

Questions for critical thought

1. What are the most appropriate indicators of "success" for behavior change programs? How would these indicators be defined and measured? Would these indicators differ for different "types" of intimate partner violence? If so, describe how.
2. How important is it to provide support to women whose partners are involved in behavior change programs? What should that support entail and who/what should provide it?
3. What are the benefits and limitations of the courts ordering men to attend a behavior change program for abusers?
4. Describe some of the unintended consequences of a mandatory arrest and prosecution strategy for domestic violence cases.
5. Discuss how the word "batterer" (used in most US-based intervention programs) can obscure the fact that not all aggression used in intimate partner relationships is the same?

Further reading

Edleson, J.L. (2012, February) *Groupwork with Men who Batter: What the Research Literature Indicates*, Harrisburg, PA: VAWnet, a project of the National Resource Center on Domestic Violence. Online. Available at www.vawnet.org (accessed 25 May 2014).

Gondolf, E. (2012) *The Future of Batterer Programs: Reassessing Evidence-Based Practice*, Boston, MA: Northeastern University Press.

Guzik, K. (2009) *Arresting Abuse: Mandatory Legal Interventions, Power and Intimate Abusers*, DeKalb, IL: Northern Illinois University Press.

Stark, E. (2007) *Coercive Control: How Men Entrap Women in Personal Life*, New York: Oxford University Press.

Websites

Men and Gender Equality Project (MGEPP): The MGEPP seeks to build the evidence base on how to change public institutions and policies to better foster gender equality and to raise awareness of the need to involve men in health, development, and gender equality issues.
www.promundo.org.br/en/activities/activities-posts/projetos-especiais

No to Violence, Male Family Violence Prevention Organisation: Information about programs for men using violence against their female partners.
http://ntv.org.au

Respect UK: Membership organization for work with domestic violence perpetrators, male victims, and young people.
www.respect.uk.net

VAWnet, National Online Resource Center on Violence Against Women: Resource library of materials on violence against women and related issues, with particular attention to its intersections with various forms of oppression. Includes resources on domestic violence, sexual violence, funding, research, and international issues. Its peer-reviewed Applied Research Papers are extremely useful. VAWnet supports local, state, and national prevention and intervention strategies.
www.vawnet.org

SECTION VI

Preventing male violence against women

Learning objectives

In reading this section, you will be able to:

1. Identify the range of strategies used to prevent intimate partner and sexual violence and factors that contribute to their effectiveness.
2. Recognize the importance of engaging men in preventing violence against women.
3. Define bystander intervention and describe its objectives.
4. Explain how bystander intervention programs have been tailored to specific populations to reduce violence against women.
5. Realize the importance of coalitions of women's organizations independent of government, or "epistemic communities," for influencing government policy on violence against women.

Chapter 16

Current practices to preventing sexual and intimate partner violence

Michael Flood

Intimate partner violence (IPV) and sexual violence are the outcome of a complex interplay of individual, relationship, community, institutional, and societal factors. Given this, violence prevention too must work at these multiple levels. This is recognized in common models of violence prevention, including the "ecological" model popularized by the World Health Organization (WHO), and other frameworks such as the "spectrum of prevention" (Davis *et al.* 2006; WHO 2002).

This chapter describes and assesses a range of strategies of primary prevention—strategies to prevent initial perpetration or victimization. These strategies are intended to strengthen individual knowledge and skills, build healthy relationships and families, involve and develop communities, promote community norms of nonviolence, improve organizational practices and workplace and institutional cultures, lessen gender inequalities, and address the larger cultural, social, and economic factors that contribute to violence. The chapter takes as given that much intimate partner and sexual violence concerns men's violence against women (VAW). It uses the term "violence against women" for a range of forms of VAW experiences, including physical and sexual assaults and other behaviors which result in physical, sexual, or psychological harm or suffering to women. At the same time, the chapter draws on scholarship regarding prevention of a range of forms of interpersonal violence, including those perpetrated by females and against males.

Evaluating prevention

What are the most effective strategies with which to prevent IPV and sexual violence and sexual violence? While there is an increasingly robust body of experience and scholarship with which to answer this question, there are also significant challenges. Few primary prevention interventions have been evaluated. In addition, many existing evaluations do not have an adequate design to allow assessment of their efficacy (Tolan *et al.* 2006). A number of weaknesses are typical in existing evaluations (Flood 2011: 361–2):

> To the extent that impact evaluations have been undertaken, often they are poorly designed, limited to retrospective reports of participants' satisfaction,

> or only assess proxy variables associated with VAW rather than this violence itself . . . In most cases, post-intervention assessments are made only immediately after the program or only weeks later and there is no longer-term follow-up. Evaluations often assess only attitudes, not behaviours or social and sexual relations, and do not address the intervention's impact on perpetration or victimisation. Evaluations rarely examine the mediators of changes in attitudes, behaviours or other factors, that is, of the causal processes through which the program achieves change.

For example, in a review of interventions for the primary prevention of IPV, the authors could find only 11 programs which had been rigorously evaluated (with a pre- and post-test design or a comparison group), and *all* of these addressed adolescent dating violence (Whitaker *et al.* 2006). In a more recent view of published studies over 2000–11 of programs addressing adolescent dating violence, only two of the nine programs used a comparative design with a control group (Leen *et al.* 2013: 169). Nevertheless, there is certainly a wide range of strategies of primary prevention which are promising or worthy of consideration, and there is some evidence with which to assess their effectiveness.

The following discussion arranges prevention interventions by broad type of strategy, but also arranges these loosely by the level or domain of the social order to which they correspond. It moves from micro to macro, from interventions focused on individuals and relationships to those focused on communities or entire societies (Davis *et al.* 2006). Where possible, the discussion describes existing strategies and interventions in terms of the level of evidence of their effectiveness, including:

- *Effective* strategies and interventions: with evidence of implementation, evidence of effectiveness, and a theoretical rationale.
- *Promising* strategies and interventions: with evidence of implementation and a theoretical rationale.
- Other *potentially promising* strategies and interventions: with a theoretical rationale only.

All the strategies identified have at the very least a theoretical rationale, making them "potentially promising." Of these, some have been implemented, making them "promising." And of these, some have been evaluated, making them "effective" (if the results of their evaluations demonstrate some level of effectiveness; Flood 2011: 362).

Forms of intervention

Community education (face-to-face education)

Intervention efforts based on direct participation in face-to-face education programs represent one of the most widely used strategies for violence prevention, and partially as the result of this, they also have the most extensive body of evidence of effectiveness.

Violence prevention education programs can have positive effects on participants' attitudes toward and participation in intimate partner and sexual violence. A series of evaluations demonstrate for example that school and university students who have attended rape education sessions show less adherence to rape myths, express less rape-supportive attitudes, and/or report greater victim empathy than those in control groups. In a review by Whitaker and colleagues (2006), for example, nine of eleven violence prevention programs in high schools reported at least one positive effect (in knowledge, attitudes, or behavior), with five of the nine programs measuring attitudes reporting positive changes. In a systematic, evidence-based review of sexual assault prevention programs, based on English-language evaluation publications between 1990 and 2003 regarding programs among university, high-school and middle-school populations, 14 percent of the 59 studies showed exclusively positive effects on knowledge and attitudes, although none used behavioral outcomes regarding perpetration or victimization. Three-quarters (80 percent) reported mixed effects, and 6 percent reported only null or negative effects (Morrison *et al.* 2004). A review of 69 education programs for university students on sexual assault found evidence that these programs increased participants' factual knowledge about rape and improved their rape-related attitudes, although they were not effective in increasing levels of rape empathy or in preventing assaults (Anderson *et al.* 2005).

Particular violence prevention education programs in North American schools have been well evaluated, with positive results. For example, four years after the Safe Dates program, adolescents who had received the program continued to report less physical and sexual dating violence perpetration (and victimization) than those who had not. Two other school-based programs for preventing dating violence, originating in Canada, show positive impacts in reducing boys' self-reported perpetration and children's incidents of physical and emotional abuse (World Health Organization and London School of Hygiene and Tropical Medicine [WHO and LSHTM] 2010: 44–5). At least one training program among adult men and women, implemented in low- and middle-income countries, also has shown positive impacts in rigorous evaluations. In South Africa, men's perpetration of physical or sexual IPV was reduced compared to controls, while in Gambia, couples' quarreling and men's acceptance of wives' refusals to have sex were reduced (WHO and LSHTM 2010: 49).

At this time, there are significant weaknesses in efforts in violence prevention using face-to-face education. Existing evaluations show that not all educational interventions are effective, the magnitude of change often is small, changes in attitudes often "rebound" to pre-intervention levels one or two months after the intervention, and some even become worse. Most evaluations address only attitudes and not only behaviors, whereas there is mixed evidence regarding where improvements in attitudes lead to reductions in perpetration. Some strategies appear to be ineffective: They provide "factual" information alone in addressing rape, educate women about self-defense without teaching actual skills, and use confrontational styles in addressing participants (WHO and LSHTM 2010: 46–7). Far too few education-based interventions have been evaluated, and existing evaluations often are limited in methodological and conceptual terms (Cornelius and Resseguie 2007; Murray and Graybeal 2007; Whitaker *et al.* 2006: 160–1).

More information is required regarding the effectiveness of various aspects of the delivery of violence prevention programs in schools, such as their timing, locale, and content (Wolfe and Jaffe 2003). Given that multi-component programs in schools—combining teacher training, parenting education, community involvement, and other strategies—have been shown to be more effective in reducing other forms of violence; they are likely also to be more effective in relation to IPV and sexual violence (WHO and LSHTM 2010: 45–6).

There are other promising strategies of primary prevention among children and adolescents that take place outside school settings, although there is less evidence of their effectiveness. As Vezina and Herbert (2007) and Rosewater (2003) argue, prevention programs should not only address adolescents in schools, but those who have dropped out of school, and should address adolescents through other means and contexts associated with increased risks of victimization. These include homeless youth, children living in poverty or in families receiving welfare, teenage mothers, and children and young people under the care of children's services after abuse. Such programs, at least those which have been evaluated, are relatively rare, and most prevention programs are in school settings and universally targeted (Leen *et al.* 2013: 169; Whitaker *et al.* 2006).

There is a case for programs aimed at specific at-risk populations and environments, and for targeting the internalizing and externalizing problems among youth which are associated with IPV (Vezina and Herbert 2007). It is possible that early identification and treatment of conduct and emotional disorders in children will lead to reductions in violence in later adolescence and adulthood (WHO and LSHTM 2010: 42). Psychological interventions for children and adolescents subjected to maltreatment or exposed to IPV are valuable, with some evidence that they enhance the prevention of IPV. More generally, cognitive-behavioral skills training and social development programs that teach social and emotional skills and pro-social behavior may have the potential to prevent subsequent IPV and sexual violence. Given that bullying programs have been shown to be effective in reducing both bullying and being bullied, they may have some influence on other forms of violence, although evidence is lacking (WHO and LSHTM 2010: 42–4).

There is some evidence too that education programs focused on primary prevention among college women can reduce women's risk of sexual violence victimization (Yeater and O'Donohue 1999). Such programs typically address the behaviors in which women can engage, which will either decrease their risk of being sexually assaulted or increase their chances of escaping from a sexual assault. Hanson and Broom's (2005) cumulative meta-analysis finds that such programs have a small beneficial effect, with some demonstrated to reduce college women's risks of subsequent victimization. Self-defense programs may help to increase women's resistance particularly to sexual assault by strangers, but their efficacy is only poorly documented (Yeater and O'Donohue 1999). Less evidence is available concerning the effectiveness of violence prevention education among other populations such as professional athletes, coaches, and teachers.

Prevention efforts among youth can address the associations between IPV and poverty, low work attachment, and low educational attainment, and other social factors. For young children, promising strategies include the provision of quality child care, home visiting programs, intensive clinical work with battered mothers and their young children, and encouraging parental involvement in children's early education and school. Among adolescents and young adults, relevant measures include mentoring programs, premarital relationship education, and welfare-to-work strategies, and interventions among adults to encourage better parenting practices (Vezina and Herbert 2007). Home visitation and parent education programs have been shown to be promising in reducing child maltreatment, and it is possible therefore that they may lessen IPV and sexual violence among the grown-up children of parents involved in such programs (WHO and LSHTM 2010: 41).

Some responsible-fatherhood programs support positive parenting and encourage shared power and decision making, and these may have promise in reducing the violence associated with asymmetries of power in relationships and families. Premarital relationship education and couples counseling programs try to increase the skills and orientations which are protective against IPV, for example by teaching communication and conflict resolution skills. Few evaluations of such programs have been conducted, but there is some evidence that they reduce the likelihood of IPV (Hamby 1998).

Communication and social marketing

Communication and social marketing campaigns are a second widely used strategy for the primary prevention of IPV and sexual violence. A review by Donovan and Vlais (2005) documents a wide variety of international campaigns, aimed at diverse groups and including government-funded and grassroots efforts. There is evidence that social marketing campaigns can produce positive change in the attitudes associated with IPV. Soul City, a multimedia project in South Africa combining prime-time radio and television dramas with other educational activities, produced positive change in knowledge and attitudes (WHO 2002). Another well-known example is Men Can Stop Rape's "My strength is not for hurting" campaign. This used media materials, in tandem with school-based Men of Strength (MOST) Clubs for young men and other strategies, to build norms of sexual consent, respect, and non-violence, with a United States evaluation showing positive impacts on attitudes (Kim and White 2008). It is less clear if such campaigns are effective in changing behavior.

Three further approaches are promising ones for the primary prevention of IPV. Using a "social norms" approach, campaigns gather and publicize data on men's attitudes and behavior to undermine men's conformity to sexist peer norms and increase their willingness to intervene in violent behavior. After a social norms initiative on a US university campus, college males reduced their overestimation of other males' sexist beliefs and comfort with sexism. "Bystander intervention" approaches involve individuals as bystanders to violence and violence-supportive behaviors or situations, encouraging and teaching skills in pro-social intervention. Experimental evaluations among US undergraduates show that approaching men and women as potential bystanders or witnesses to behaviors related to sexual violence can improve knowledge of sexual violence, acceptance of rape myths, bystander self-efficacy, and self-reported bystander behaviors (Flood 2011). Finally, in a "media advocacy" approach, journalists and news media have been encouraged to portray IPV in appropriate ways, for example as social problems requiring public intervention.

Community engagement and development

Given the evidence that social norms, gender roles, and power relations underpin IPV, strategies that address these will be critical to successful prevention efforts. Strategies of community engagement and community mobilization are seen by some as central to violence prevention (Family Violence Prevention Fund 2004). The bulk of primary prevention efforts thus far have addressed individuals and their intimate relationships, while community and societal strategies have been under-utilized. Violence prevention should build local communities' capacity to respond effectively to violence, encourage their ownership of the issue, and address the social contexts in which IPV occurs (Rosewater 2003).

Community development and community mobilization are promising strategies—they have been tried and they have a strong theoretical rationale. Effective community engagement requires developing community relationships (with groups, organizations, formal and informal leaders), identifying community needs, connecting members to services and informal supports, and above all, changing the social and community conditions which lead to violence (Davis *et al.* 2006; Family Violence Prevention Fund 2004; Stith *et al.* 2006). Other community-based strategies which may be promising in reducing intimate partner and sexual violence address moderating or contributing factors such as alcohol use, thereby reducing alcohol availability, regulating alcohol prices, and treating alcohol-use disorders (WHO and LSHTM 2010: 51–2).

Advocacy

Advocacy refers to strategies of primary prevention which go beyond community engagement toward collective mobilization, fostering and sustaining groups, networks, and social movements dedicated to the prevention of IPV. Collective advocacy by the women's movements and feminism formed the foundations of contemporary service and policy responses to IPV. Advocacy remains a key strategy of primary prevention. In various countries, women's groups and networks, campaigns, and events such as Take Back the Night, V-Day, and Slutwalk play a critical role in raising community awareness of intimate partner and sexual violence, undermining violence-supportive social norms, and fostering cultures of respect, consent, and gender equality.

An important development is the emergence of campaigns organized by men. The most widespread example is the White Ribbon Campaign, in which men are encouraged to show their opposition to men's VAW by purchasing and wearing a white ribbon. Another well-developed example is EngenderHealth's Men As Partners program, which uses community education, grassroots organizing, and advocacy. These campaigns, like a host of other campus-based or grassroots men's groups and networks, work to engage men in personal and collective efforts at violence prevention.

Community mobilization strategies can catalyze broader social change by shifting social norms and power relations (Flood 2011). Still, they have been evaluated only rarely. For example, there are only a handful of studies globally of men's involvements in community-based violence prevention. Nearly all are from North America, few are longitudinal, most rely on self-reports, and none assesses the impact of men's involvement using pre- and post-involvement measures of impact. Nevertheless, these studies provide some support for the claim that men who participate in men's anti-violence activism undergo positive change (Flood, in press).

More widely, efforts to empower and mobilize communities, and in particular to increase women's economic and social power, have potential to reduce IPV and other violence (WHO and LSHTM 2010: 49). For example, initiatives which combine women's economic empowerment with other strategies fostering gender equality—such as the Intervention with Microfinance for AIDS and Gender Equity (IMAGE) and Stepping Stones programs—have been effective in reducing IPV.

Organizational and workforce development

There is a strong rationale for prevention efforts which change the practices of organizations and workforces, both to "scale up" these efforts and to transform violence-supportive cultures (Flood 2011: 370–1). Thus far, primary prevention strategies addressing organizations are under-developed. Education programs in workforces have been shown to improve attitudes toward sexual harassment, and this approach may have promise in changing attitudes toward other forms of violence and abuse. Workplace education is one component of a broader effort to change the practices and cultures of community organizations and institutions, and this can have a significant impact on community norms (Davis *et al.* 2006).

There is very little evidence of the effectiveness of such strategies. Nevertheless, there are some examples of organizations' systematic adoption of prevention programming. In Australia, for instance, after a series of sexual assault scandals, a national sporting body—the Australian Football League (AFL)—developed a program including model anti-sexual harassment and anti-sexual discrimination procedures across the sport, organizational policies and procedures to ensure a safe and inclusive environment for women, changes to AFL rules relating to problematic or violent conduct, the education of players and other officials, dissemination of policies and procedures at community club level, and a public education program. Another key form of violence prevention relevant to this area of action is increasing workforce and organizational capacity to prevent violence.

Legislative and policy reform

Law and policy are crucial tools of primary prevention. At the broadest levels, national and state-based plans of action for eliminating violence are necessary elements in any systematic prevention effort. Violence prevention requires a whole-of-government approach, with a national funding base, involving integrated prevention plans at national and state levels. Law and policy are promising tools too in supporting particular strategies of primary prevention, whether these concern school curricula, alcohol availability, media content, or gun use.

Challenges

There are two broad sets of challenges that confront the violence prevention field. The first concerns challenges of definition, measurement, and conceptualization, and the second concerns challenges of programming and policy.

Challenges of definition, measurement, and conceptualization

First, there are increasingly intense debates over how to define, measure, and explain the very phenomena with which this field is concerned. For a start, there is debate over whether to define violence in relationships and families in narrow or broad terms. In the "narrow" camp, definitions of IPV and sexual violence focus on physically aggressive acts and on sexual assaults involving forced penetration, using instruments such as the Conflict Tactics Scales to measure these. In the "broad" camp, definitions include a greater range of physical and sexual behaviors which cause harm, as well as non-physical behaviors such as psychological and verbal abuse, and a variety of controlling and coercive strategies, and use instruments which gather data also on the intensity, impact, history, and meaning of violent behaviors.

Overlapping with this debate is an even more heated debate regarding the patterns and prevalence of interpersonal violence. There is fundamental disagreement in the scholarship regarding IPV and gender. One body of scholarship, focused on "conflict" in families, typically finds gender symmetries at least in the use of violence. On the other hand, feminist studies, crime victimization studies, and other scholarship find marked gender asymmetries, arguing that men's VAW is far greater in frequency, severity, and impact than women's violence against men (Allen 2011). Overlapping with this is increasing discussion of diverse patterns of IPV, from "coercive controlling violence" to "situational couple violence." These debates have powerful implications for how to prevent violence, including the populations and risk factors to address.

Challenges in prevention programming and policy

There are also significant challenges in *how* to conduct violence prevention. This chapter focuses on four. First, the most effective interventions in IPV and sexual violence are "comprehensive"—they use multiple strategies to address multiple behaviors, in multiple settings, and at multiple levels (Casey and Lindhorst 2009: 98; Nation *et al.* 2003). For example, interventions may incorporate strategies addressing individuals, peer groups, and communities and have multiple strategies addressing the same outcome. Because both the strategies and the factors they address are interrelated, such interventions are more effective than less comprehensive efforts. Overlapping with this, there is a need for integrated programs and systems for prevention. In schools, for example, violence prevention programming and policy should be integrated (a) across developmental stages (across age spans and years); (b) across levels of prevention and treatment, from universal, classroom programs to "indicated" or "secondary" prevention efforts to targeted groups and individuals; and (c) across the institutional structures of schools and community agencies (Greenberg 2004). Similar approaches are needed in other institutions or settings such as the military, sports, and workplaces. However, comprehensive and integrated interventions are rare in the violence prevention field, and political and funding support for them typically is absent.

A second key challenge concerns the transferability of violence prevention initiatives and strategies across contexts, communities, and cultures. Most efforts to prevent intimate partner and sexual violence have taken place in high-income countries, including those for which there is evidence of effectiveness. It is not clear to what extent and in what ways such efforts can be transferred to and adopted in other contexts. Access to the resources and infrastructure associated with effectiveness in high-income contexts may not be available in low- and middle-income settings, and the factors and dynamics associated with intimate partner and sexual violence themselves may be different in such contexts. In any country or context, there are challenges in dealing with the intersections of multiple forms of social difference and inequality. While the demand that violence prevention efforts be "culturally appropriate" has been made most often in relation to efforts with non-White and non-English-speaking participants and communities, an attention to social and cultural specificity is necessary in work with *any* group in *any* cultural context (Flood 2005/2006).

The third challenge is in identifying and implementing the most effective forms of programming and pedagogy. Focusing on face-to-face education in schools, for example, there is a growing consensus that particular features of pedagogy are more likely to generate substantial and sustained change: the use of quality teaching materials; interactive and participatory classroom processes; attention to cognitive, affective, and behavioral domains; skills development; and sufficient duration and intensity. In addition, more effective programs adopt a whole-of-school approach, have a program framework and logic or theory of change, and are based on content which addresses the factors known to be antecedents to violent behavior (Flood *et al.* 2009). However, evidence regarding effectiveness for other dimensions of pedagogy is absent, mixed, or dependent on the purpose or character of the prevention effort. Should single-sex or mixed-sex classes be used? Should education be provided by teachers, community educators, or peer educators? Does the sex of the educator matter? More research is needed regarding these issues, which raises the fourth challenge.

The final challenge concerns evaluation. Minimum standards for evaluation of violence prevention interventions include the assessment of the intervention's impact on violence-related variables (such as attitudes and behaviors), the use of standardized measures, a pre-test/post-test design, and a dissemination process that includes both academics and service providers. Ideally, evaluations will include assessment of impact on behaviors in particular, the use of both quantitative and qualitative measures, longitudinal assessment, measures of contexts and settings, program implementation and fidelity, and experimental or quasi-experimental designs incorporating control or comparison groups or settings.

The gold standard of evaluation in much health promotion research is the experimental design, ideally through a randomized controlled trial. However, this design often is inappropriate for evaluation of the community-based projects and programs typical in violence prevention. Community organizations often do not have the capacity to conduct evaluations of this nature, the programs they implement typically have features which rule out an experimental design, and experimental designs may be politically and practically inappropriate. In response to the evaluation challenge, in the violence prevention field there has been an increasing emphasis on building local evaluation capacity—on nurturing evaluation knowledge, attitudes, and skills to build sustainable evaluation practice among individuals and in organizations.

Conclusion

The violence prevention field is an increasingly mature one. It shows growing diversity and sophistication in the methods it uses to prevent initial perpetration of or victimization in IPV and sexual violence. The field steadily is accumulating a substantial body of scholarship attesting to the effectiveness of particular strategies and the potential value of others, and it is adopting increasingly rigorous assessments of these. At the same time, the field faces significant challenges. There are widespread debates regarding the very phenomena which define the field. There is much which is not known about effective strategies for preventing and reducing violence. Above all, there is the challenge of shifting the entrenched social and structural inequalities which are at the root of IPV and sexual violence.

References

Allen, M. (2011) 'Is there gender symmetry in intimate partner violence?', *Child and Family Social Work*, 16: 245–54.

Anderson, L.A. and Whiston, S.C. (2005) 'Sexual assault education programs: a meta-analytic examination of their effectiveness', *Psychology of Women Quarterly*, 29: 374–88.

Casey, E.A. and Lindhorst, T.P. (2009) 'Toward a multi-level, ecological approach to the primary prevention of sexual assault: prevention in peer and community contexts', *Trauma, Violence, & Abuse*, 10: 91–114.

Cornelius, T.L. and Resseguie, N. (2007) 'Primary and secondary prevention programs for dating violence: a review of the literature', *Aggression and Violent Behavior*, 12: 364–75.

Davis, R., Parks, L.F. and Cohen, L. (2006) *Sexual Violence and the Spectrum of Prevention: Towards a Community Solution*, Enola, PA: National Sexual Violence Resource Center.

Donovan, R.J. and Vlais, R. (2005) *VicHealth Review of Communication Components of Social Marketing/Public Education Campaigns Focused on Violence Against Women*, Melbourne: Victorian Health Promotion Foundation.

Family Violence Prevention Fund (2004) *Preventing Family Violence: Lessons from the Community Engagement Initiative*, San Francisco, CA: Family Violence Prevention Fund.

Flood, M. (in press) 'Men's anti-violence activism and the construction of gender-equitable masculinities', in A. Carabí and J. Armengol (eds.), *Moving Ahead: Alternative Masculinities for a Changing World*, London: Palgrave.

Flood, M. (2011) 'Involving men in efforts to end violence against women', *Men and Masculinities*, 14: 358–77.

Flood, M. (2005/2006) 'Changing men: best practice in sexual violence education', *Women Against Violence*, 18: 26–36.

Flood, M., Fergus, L. and Heenan, M. (2009) *Respectful Relationships Education: Violence Prevention and Respectful Relationships Education in Victorian Secondary Schools*, Melbourne: Department of Education and Early Childhood Development, State of Victoria.

Greenberg, M.T. (2004) 'Current and future challenges in school-based prevention: the researcher perspective', *Prevention Science*, 5: 5–13.

Hamby, S.L. (1998) 'Partner violence: prevention and intervention', in J.L. Jasinski and L.M. Williams (eds.), *Partner Violence: A Comprehensive Review of 20 Years of Research*, Thousand Oaks, CA: Sage, 210–58.

Hanson, R.K. and Broom, I. (2005) 'The utility of cumulative meta-analysis: application to programs for reducing sexual violence', *Sexual Abuse: A Journal of Research and Treatment*, 17: 357–73.

Kim, A.N. and White, M.L. (2008) *Evaluation of California's MyStrength Campaign and MOST Clubs*, Sacramento, CA: California Department of Public Health, Epidemiology and Prevention for Injury Control Branch.

Leen, E., Sorbring, E., Mawer, M., Holdsworth, E., Helsing, B. and Bowen, E. (2013) 'Prevalence, dynamic risk factors and the efficacy of primary interventions for adolescent dating violence: an international review', *Aggression and Violent Behavior*, 18: 159–74.

Morrison, S., Hardison, J., Mathew, A. and O'Neil, J. (2004) *An Evidence-Based Review of Sexual Assault Preventive Intervention Programs*, Washington, DC: National Institute of Justice, US Department of Justice.

Murray, C.E. and Graybeal, J. (2007) 'Methodological review of intimate partner violence prevention research', *Journal of Interpersonal Violence*, 22: 1250–69.

Nation, M., Crusto, C., Wandersman, A., Kumpfer, K., Seybolt, D., Morrissey-Kane, E. and Davino, K. (2003) 'What works in prevention: principles of effective prevention programs, *American Psychologist*, 58: 449–56.

Rosewater, A. (2003) *Promoting Prevention, Targeting Teens: An Emerging Agenda to Reduce Domestic Violence*, San Francisco, CA: Family Violence Prevention Fund.

Stith, S., Pruitt, I., Dees, J.E., Fronce, M., Green, N., Som, A. and Linkh, D. (2006) 'Implementing community-based prevention programming: a review of the literature', *The Journal of Primary Prevention*, 27: 599–617.

Tolan, P., Gorman-Smith, D. and Henry, D. (2006) 'Family violence', *Annual Review of Psychology* 57: 557–83.

Vezina, J. and Herbert, M. (2007) 'Risk factors for victimization in romantic relationships of young women: a review of empirical studies and implications for prevention', *Trauma Violence & Abuse*, 8: 33–66.

Whitaker, D., Morrison, S., Lindquist, C., Hawkins, S.R., O'Neil, J.A., Nesius, A.M., Mathew, A. and Reese, L. (2006) 'A critical review of interventions for the primary prevention of perpetration of partner violence', *Aggression and Violent Behavior*, 11: 151–66.

Wolfe, D.A. and Jaffe, P.G. (2003) Prevention of Domestic Violence and Sexual Assault, Harrisburg, PA: VAWnet, a project of the National Resource Center on Domestic Violence. Online. Available at www.vawnet.org (accessed 25 May 2014).

WHO (2002) *World Report on Violence and Health*, Geneva: World Health Organization.

WHO & LSHTM (2010) *Preventing Intimate Partner and Sexual Violence Against Women: Taking action and generating evidence*, Geneva: World Health Organization.

Yeater, E.A. and O'Donohue, W. (1999) 'Sexual assault prevention programs: current issues, future directions, and the potential efficacy of interventions with women', *Clinical Psychology Review*, 19: 739–71.

Chapter 17

New approaches to violence prevention through bystander intervention

Ann L. Coker and Emily R. Clear

There are now many bystander intervention programs being implemented in the United States and internationally. This chapter describes bystander programs that have been applied to student populations to reduce violence against women and have reached a level of evidence that characterizes them as promising or effective strategies and interventions for reducing such violence. We review the evidence for bystander interventions' efficacy and describe the challenges and opportunities faced by researchers and practitioners in the ultimate quest to prevent violence against women. Bystander programs specifically targeting men will not be discussed, as other authors address these programs (Katz, this volume)

Defining bystander interventions

Past research has sought to understand why some individuals intervene when they witness (either seeing or hearing) a potentially risky, dangerous, or emergency situation, and why others do not. These witnesses, referred to as "bystanders," are those who see or hear an act of violence, discrimination, or other unacceptable or offensive behavior. Within crime prevention and social psychology research, the terms "active" and/or "pro-social" bystander are commonly used to refer to the individual who takes action to intervene in response to the actual incident, or who observed or overheard an incident (VicHealth 2011).

The objective of applying bystander interventions universally is to involve all members of a community to change a culture that may silently support the use of violence. For bystander intervention programming, "community" has been defined primarily as a college campus, a middle or high school, a sports team, or a fraternity or sorority. Community also could be defined based on residence, such as a residential community. The primary aspect of a community is that members are engaged with each other and thus are committed to the goals of the intervention. Because bystander interventions approach participants not as potential victims or perpetrators but as potential allies, defensiveness particularly among men is reduced, as are victim-blaming attitudes (Banyard *et al.*, 2004; Berkowitz 2002). Active bystander intervention approaches acknowledge the positive role of men in women's lives and the fact that most men are not violent toward women. This shift invites men to become more personally engaged in violence prevention. Bystander training commits both men and women to positive and proactive behaviors or actions to end violence.

The majority of bystander programs have been directed at reducing sexual violence (SV) against college women (Banyard 2014). Bystander violence prevention programs share a common philosophy that all members of the community have a role in shifting social norms to prevent violence. The ultimate goal is to educate the community to recognize situations that promote violence and to safely and effectively intervene (Moynihan and Banyard 2008).

Banyard and colleagues (2004) were the first to propose the use of bystander violence prevention interventions (from here forward referred to as bystander interventions) as a community-based strategy to reduce SV. McMahon and Banyard (2012) provide a conceptual model describing a continuum of opportunities for individuals and groups to engage in behaviors most appropriate for the situation and the individual bystander. Others have explored the role of bystander intervention in relation to violence prevention and have focused on the effectiveness of the approach, specifically for men (Berkowitz 2002; Foubert 2000; Katz 1994, this volume).

Bystander intervention programs in college settings

Mentors in Violence Prevention (MVP) is one of the earliest bystander programs targeting student-athletes and leaders. MVP initially focused on men to encourage leadership on issues of gender violence, bullying, and school violence (Katz 1994, this volume). Banyard and colleagues (2007) provided the first empirical evidence from students attending a rural, Northeastern US, public college campus. Participation in a bystander intervention focusing on SV changed students' attitudes around rape myths and increased their bystander efficacy, attitudes, and decisional balance in both the one- and three-session intervention groups relative to the control group when comparing pre- and post-intervention measures. Additionally, at two- and four-month post-intervention, self-reports of bystander behaviors were greater for those in either intervention groups relative to the control group. However, no differences in bystander behaviors between students in the intervention groups compared with students in the control group were evident at the 12-month follow-up. Banyard and colleagues (2009) also explored the efficacy of a bystander approach directed at student leaders, namely 123 resident advisors and 73 students who worked as staff at the student center. Engaging the entire community in bystander prevention interventions is recommended by program developers, yet, to date, few researchers have provided data to determine the efficacy of interventions based on roles within a community. When comparing pre- and post-intervention evaluation of the 90-minute Bringing in the Bystander training, the authors noted a reduction in rape-myth acceptance scores over time and an increase in bystander confidence and willingness to intervene among students completing the training. Other evaluations of the Bringing in the Bystander curriculum are underway.

Bystander programs typically use didactic training combined with interactive role-playing to help students learn to (a) identify situations which may require action, and (b) take safe and effective action that they are competent to perform. The inclusion of theatrical components to bystander training can therefore be a compelling means to model both how to identify "risky" settings and how to safely and effectively intervene. Based on Boal's *Theater of the Oppressed*,[1] *interACT* is an example of such a program (Ahrens *et al.* 2011). In an evaluation of the effectiveness of *interACT* to engage participants in effective bystander behaviors, Ahrens and colleagues (2011) recruited 509 students in two undergraduate communication studies classes (70 percent female) for pre- and post-intervention, and a three-month follow-up; 355 students had completed follow-up data. Relative to pre-intervention scores, the proportion of students responding that the theatrical bystander program was helpful was high immediately following participation in *interACT* but showed no difference at the three-month follow-up. Most importantly, the likelihood of bystander interventions increased from pre- to immediately post-intervention and remained higher at the three-month follow-up. The evaluation provides some evidence that different modes of delivering bystander curricula might play a role in program effectiveness; thus it might be important to compare program delivery across studies in relation to differences in participants' developmental age, learning styles, and readiness to adopt the intervention as described by Banyard and colleagues (2010).

One additional study deserves mention as an example of implementing a program designed in one college and testing that program at another. A well-described limitation of the assessment process is when programs are evaluated by members responsible for that program's conception and in the same setting that the program was initially designed, as has been the case in the work noted above. Amar and colleagues (2012) described the implementation and evaluation of *Bringing in the Bystander*, which they adapted for Boston University, a large private university located in Northeastern US. In this pre- and post-evaluation, 202 college students were recruited through letters of invitation sent to student organizations by the investigators. The bystander intervention was delivered in smaller groups of 15–25 participants. A reduction in students' rape-myth acceptance scores was noted when comparing post- to pre-training measures, and an increase in their bystander interventions and ability to take responsibility for their actions also was noted.

A novel program designed by Gidycz and colleagues (2011), The *Men's Project* is part of Ohio University's Community Programming Initiative. The *Men's Project* was based on an integrative model of sexual assault (Berkowitz, 1992) and incorporates a social norms model of change with discussion of intervention techniques for bystanders. Gidycz and colleagues provided promising evidence that combining elements of bystander programming with risk reduction has efficacy to reduce SV. Their program combined a bystander-based sexual assault program for men (based on Berkowitz 1994) with a risk-reduction program for women. First-year residence halls at Ohio University were randomly assigned to the treatment or control groups. College men and women in the treatment groups were invited to participate in either prevention or risk-reduction programs. A total of 635 college students were recruited over two years (56 percent response rate) and surveys were administered before the intervention and at four and seven months after the intervention training. No differences in students' rape-myth acceptance scores or bystander behaviors were observed over time or for either type of intervention. More importantly, however, at four month follow-up, men receiving the bystander-based training reported lower sexually aggressive behaviors over time (1.5 percent) relative to men in the control group (6.7 percent) who did not receive either prevention or risk-reduction programs. At seven months, a reduction in sexual aggression associated with bystander program training was no longer evident, yet statistical power was limited for this comparison (Gidycz *et al.* 2011). To date, this is one of the few evaluations with evidence of a reduction in sexual aggression, one of the ultimate behavioral outcomes for SV prevention programs.

Because college athletes and fraternity members are at high risk of SV perpetration (Boeringer 1999), Moynihan and Banyard (2008) conducted an exploratory study of *Bringing in the Bystander* with members of one fraternity, one sorority, and a men's and a women's intercollegiate athletic team at a Northeastern university in the US. Results indicated that, in general, the intervention was effective in changing students' knowledge, attitudes, and bystander efficacy. This suggests that a bystander violence prevention approach to SV prevention may be an important tool in efforts to address SV in potentially higher-risk settings.

Our team has recently been involved in an evaluation of the *Green Dot* program developed in 2007 at the University of Kentucky, a large institution of higher education with over 25,000 undergraduate and graduate students located in the Southeastern US (Coker *et al.* 2011). The *Green Dot* program was implemented in two phases at the University of Kentucky, beginning in 2008 as follows: The first phase consisted of a 50-minute persuasive speech to college students and primarily targeted first- and second-year undergraduate students. The second phase was an intensive bystander violence prevention training, Students Educating and Empowering to Develop Safety (SEEDS), designed to teach students how to safely and effectively engage their peers in violence prevention. The *Green Dot* bystander interventions significantly increased both observed (e.g., "I saw or heard someone speak up if somebody said that someone deserved to be raped or to be hit by their partner") and actual active bystander behaviors (e.g., "I spoke up if I heard somebody say that someone deserved to be raped or hit by their partner") relative to students receiving no *Green Dot* training. Intensive training significantly increased active bystander behavior frequency relative to those students who received *Green Dot* speeches alone. This two-tier intervention evaluation provides evidence that a short 50-minute generalized training has efficacy to change students' violence acceptance and increase their bystander behaviors, yet the greater effect on bystander behaviors was associated with intensive SEEDS training (Coker *et al.* 2011).

Coker and colleagues (in press) also conducted an evaluation of *Green Dot* efficacy to increase bystander behaviors and reduce violence by comparing violence victimization and perpetration rates reported by students on the *Green Dot* intervention campus (University of Kentucky) with rates in two large public campuses without bystander programs. Undergraduate students were randomly sampled and invited to complete an online survey. The frequency of sexual harassment, unwanted sex, stalking, and dating violence victimization and perpetration at the *Green Dot* intervention campus were compared with frequencies at the two comparison campuses. When comparing the summed frequency of all forms of violence adjusted for demographic differences between the three colleges, both victimization and perpetration rates were significantly lower at the *Green Dot* campus relative to those at the two comparison campuses. Significantly lower rates of violence perpetration at the *Green Dot* campus relative to those at the two comparison campuses were observed among men, yet not among women. Finally, lower overall violence frequency rates were explained by lower rates of sexual harassment and stalking victimization and perpetration in the *Green Dot* campus, and this pattern was more pronounced among men than women. This study provides supportive evidence that the *Green Dot* bystander intervention program is associated with lower rates of violence among college students.

Bystander interventions in younger populations

Miller and colleagues (2012, 2013) recently evaluated the Futures Without Violence program *Coaching Boys Into Men* (CBIM). Using a cluster randomized clinical trial of CBIM in 16 high schools in New York City among 1,513 male athletes age 14–17, Miller and colleagues (2013) found that athletes receiving the intervention, relative to those who did not, self-reported greater intention to intervene, use of more positive bystander behaviors, and most importantly, lower rates of dating violence perpetration at 12-month follow-up. No statistically significant differences in either gender-equitable attitudes or ability to recognize abuse were observed. The same research team evaluated *Parivartan*, an adaptation of CBIM for young men age 10–16 who were members of cricket teams in Mumbai, India (Miller *et al.* 2014). A randomized trial was used in which 309 male cricketers in 46 urban middle schools (27 intervention schools, 19 control schools) were recruited at baseline and followed up for 12 months. The cricket teams' coaches were trained to deliver the program to cricketers. Athletes whose coaches were trained reported a significant increase in gender-equitable attitudes relative to athletes of coaches in the control group. No significant differences were observed between those who did and did not receive *Parivartan* in intentions to intervene, bystander behaviors (whether positive or negative), or abuse perpetration, yet relatively small sample sizes may preclude observing such differences. This evaluation of CBIM in two quite different sites provides evidence of transferability of CBIM across settings as a means to reduce dating violence through bystander approaches combined with changes in awareness and attitudes among a select group of male athletes.

Bystander intervention programs implemented in high school settings

In 2009, the Centers for Disease Control and Prevention (CDC) in the US funded a five-year randomized intervention trial in 26 high schools across Kentucky.[2] Within each of 13 area development districts, two schools were recruited and randomly assigned as either intervention or comparison schools. Intensive training was provided to rape crisis center educators across the state, who delivered the intervention at all 13 high schools assigned to the intervention arm of the trial. The *Green Dot* program was delivered in two phases: (1) a motivational or persuasive speech provided universally to the entire student body, and (2) an intensive bystander training targeting school student leaders (for further details, see Cook-Craig *et al.* in press). *Popular Opinion Leader* literature suggested that, in a well-defined community, if 15 percent of influential members were trained and adopted new behaviors, the result would be a change in social norms in the community.[3]

In our evaluation we plan to measure changes in students' violence acceptance, bystander behaviors, and violence victimization and perpetration pre- and post-intervention over the five-year study. By training a sufficient number of students, we hypothesized that social norms would shift and result in a reduction in victimization and perpetration of SV and other forms of interpersonal violence. When comparing the frequency of self-reported bystander behaviors in the intervention high schools with those in the comparison high schools before and at the first post-intervention survey, active bystander behavior rates were significantly higher in the intervention high schools. The final analyses will be conducted when data collection is complete in the summer of 2014.

Collectively, these early studies provide preliminary evidence of the promise of bystander interventions to change a culture that may silently support the use of violence. However, there are several aspects of current research which need to be addressed to more firmly establish the effectiveness of bystander interventions. In the next section we review the challenges to bystander intervention evaluations (for a comprehensive review of challenges in college settings, see Banyard 2014).

Challenges to bystander intervention evaluation

Violence prevention is the outcome: challenges for study design and power

The ultimate question in violence prevention evaluation is whether the intervention reduces violent victimization and perpetration. Randomized intervention trials are the ideal design to rigorously determine program efficacy measured as a reduction in violence perpetration. Because sexual or physical assaults are relatively rare events, a large number of participants in the intervention and control populations are needed. Thus, collaboration between researchers at a range of sites is important to yield the needed sample size and to determine transferability of a specific program at other sites or select subpopulations (e.g., by gender, sexual orientation, age), particularly when evaluating the efficacy of college-based interventions. Further, to determine the longer-term efficacy of the program, prospective studies with follow-up of at least 3–5 years are required. The recently reported *Coaching Boys Into Men* (Miller *et al.* 2012, 2013) is an example of a randomized design and sufficient follow-up time to begin to see an effect of the program to reduce the ultimate outcome measures, violence perpetration. The above noted CDC-funded project, *Enhancing Bystander Efficacy to Prevent Sexual Violence*, is an example of prospectively following first-year college students to determine the efficacy of a pro-social bystander-based intervention to engage students in actively intervening before, during, and after the occurrence of risky situations, to ultimately reduce sexual and partner violence (Banyard and Moynihan 2011). The *Second Step* evaluation is a good example of a universal application (i.e., delivered to all students) of a program with potential efficacy across a range of violence outcomes for middle-school-aged populations. A recent evaluation which followed middle school students over time indicates efficacy to reduce self-reported physical aggression (Espelage *et al.* 2013).

How much and what format of bystander intervention is enough to change attitudes and behaviors?

Evaluating the dose needed and what format is more effective for intervention efficacy are additional challenges. *InterACT*, based on Boal's *Theater of the Oppressed* and the *Students Challenging Realities and Educating Against Myths* (SCREAM) theater are two examples of bystander-based training delivered in an interactive theatrical format. An evaluation of *interACT* suggests that the performance increased participants' beliefs of bystander intervention effectiveness and increased the students' own likelihood to intervene if presented with the opportunity to do so (Ahrens *et al* 2011). SCREAM is a 75-minute college-based peer education theater model that depicts a sexual assault and includes opportunities before, during, and after the assault for bystanders to become engaged. In a recent evaluation of this program, McMahon and colleagues (2014) found that students who attended SCREAM had significantly lower rape-myth acceptance scores and higher bystander attitudes at post- vs. pre-test surveying. Research is underway to determine the amount or "dose" of SCREAM theater needed for optimal intervention effect.

Measurement challenges for bystander program evaluation: bystander behaviors and violence

A significant challenge for evaluating violence interventions is how violence is measured (see Johnson *et al.* this volume). Violent victimization and perpetration are typically measured by self-report items. Study participants may be the only direct source of information about their experiences particularly with violence in intimate relationships. However, inaccuracies in disclosing both victimization and perpetration are a real possibility. For example, those who perpetrate violence may not disclose their use of violence even when behaviorally specific questions are used; victimization may be similarly under-reported. Police or campus-based reports are known to drastically under-report assaults. To further complicate this measurement issue, bystander interventions may impact disclosure of violence victimization or perpetration at least in the short term. As intervention participants learn more about violence and the means to prevent it, they may become more sensitized to their own recent experiences and recognize these as abusive. Thus in the short term an intervention might increase disclosures of violence. This phenomenon makes longer-term evaluation of program effectiveness imperative.

To comprehensively understand the impact of bystander programs it is important to include a range of violent victimization and perpetration (e.g., sexual harassment, bullying, stalking, unwanted sex, sexual assaults, psychological and physical dating violence). Measuring more socially acceptable forms of violence may be an important approach to identifying the success of bystander interventions in the short term. For example, sexual harassment is often considered a less severe or even harmless form of threatened or forced sexual activity. Similarly, verbal or psychological abuse may be viewed as a less severe form of dating violence than physical violence. Both sets of behaviors can have negative consequences for victims, but only the most severe forms of violence are considered criminal offenses in the US. In terms of prevention, if behaviors are reduced to less severe forms, or if less severe forms are totally prevented, this can be considered a measure of success. Thus, it is important to measure all forms of aggressive behaviors that may cause harm.

Prevention interventions have an important role toward identification of aggressive actions that may be precursors to physical aggression. For example, non-physical forms of violence such as psychological abuse, sexual coercion, controlling behaviors by partners, may escalate to physical or sexual assaults (Kelly and Johnson 2008). Training to identify and effectively intervene to address actions earlier in the continuum of violence may be more effective, as a wider range of potentially harmful behaviors can be addressed. Because bystander interventions teach and empower all community members to be responsible for the collective safety of those in their social network, a social network analysis which tracks how individuals communicate with others to share information, including new bystander training, can be used to measure how the intervention moves or is diffused from those trained to friends, acquaintances, and others affected by those trained. In this way, bystander interventions may benefit the overall population—through diffusion of bystander training, awareness or even changes in social norms—not just those receiving the intervention. Beyond the need to examine peers within a social network, it is also important to evaluate engagement in supporting a bystander intervention by others in the broader community. Parents, siblings, teachers, and business members such as bar owners and tenders, community members and elected officials need to understand and support bystander interventions' efforts. Further, their levels of support need to be evaluated. Such evaluations are methodologically challenging but are needed to help illuminate the multiple levels and degrees of support necessary for bystander interventions to be maximally effective.

Measuring bystander behaviors is also not straightforward. Individuals who are more socially engaged have greater opportunity to identify a situation in need of their own bystander action. Thus measuring the opportunity to intervene is a necessary component to measuring bystander program efficacy. In addition, types of bystander behaviors need to be separately assessed. Bystander interventions have focused primarily on proactive means to prevent violence (e.g., identifying a situation and taking action to reduce the risk of violence occurring); however, intervention may also increase bystanders' ability to empathetically encourage violence disclosure and link individuals to services as needed. The domains or settings in which individuals actively intervene may differ (e.g., actions to address alcohol use, promote individual safety, online vs. in-person behaviors). More research is needed to distinguish types and settings of bystander behaviors and their efficacy to reduce violence. For example, as technology-assisted stalking, harassment, and intimidation become more prevalent, bystander programs should be adapted and evaluated as tools to address these newer forms of aggression.

Personal characteristics of potential bystanders, such as gender, sexual orientation, and prior experiences of violence may differentially influence bystander efficacy and these characteristics may influence the setting or type of behaviors used. A review of the efficacy of 12 mass media advertising campaigns to address physical domestic violence in the US, United Kingdom, Australia, New Zealand, and India suggests promise of these programs to engage bystanders, potentially reach large numbers, and possibly reduce violence (Cismaru *et al.* 2010). Expanding bystander interventions into more community-based settings using a range of modalities including mass media and social networking channels may be an important next step.

Conclusion

In conclusion, or perhaps to start the next important conversation, many bystander intervention programs are being implemented at a range of schools and universities, yet few have been rigorously evaluated. Among those that have been evaluated we do not know which elements of bystander programs (e.g., skills-based training, awareness, and empowerment sessions) and their delivery (e.g., small groups, gender-specific, online, or theater-based training) are most effective, nor in which populations. There are many unanswered questions: Will online bystander training change behavior? By what mechanism do bystander programs change violence (e.g., through changes in social norms, increasing engagement in one's community)? What proportion of a population needs to receive training, to see a reduction in violence? How much does bystander training cost? Many more questions could be posed and many are being answered.

This number of unanswered questions is not uncommon for a nascent field. However, early evidence of bystander interventions is promising and deserves funding to appropriately evaluate program efficacy in diverse settings. Further, given limited study power to detect changes in violence at the population level, pooling data and developing research consortia might be a cost-effective means to begin to provide answers to these and many more questions regarding the development and delivery of bystander intervention curricula, implementation of these interventions, and evaluation of their effectiveness in changing attitudes, behaviors, and ultimately reducing violence.

Notes

1 Theater of the Oppressed, developed by Augusto Boal, is a theatrical form of presenting, an interactive way to connect the audience and performers aiming for social or political change.

2 For details, see Enhancing Bystander Efficacy to Prevent Sexual Violence, grant # 5U01CE001675.

3 For details, see Popular Opinion Leader Guide. Online. Available at www.effectiveinterventions.org/Files/POL_Procedural_Guide_8-09.pdf (accessed 25 May 2014).

References

Ahrens, C.E., Rich, M.D. and Ullman, J.B. (2011) 'Rehearsing for real life: the impact of the InterACT Sexual Assault Prevention Program on self-reported likelihood of engaging in bystander interventions', *Violence Against Women*, 17: 760–76.

Amar, A.F., Sutherland, M. and Kesler, E. (2012) 'Evaluation of a bystander education program', *Issues in Mental Health Nursing*, 33: 851–7.

Banyard, V.L. (2014) 'Improving college campus based prevention of violence against women: a strategic plan for research built on multi-pronged practices and policies', *Trauma, Violence, & Abuse*, 15: 339–51.

Banyard, V.L. and Moynihan, M.M. (2011) 'Variation in bystander behavior related to sexual and intimate partner violence prevention: correlates in a sample of college students', *Psychology of Violence*, 1: 287–301.

Banyard, V.L., Eckstein, R. and Moynihan, M.M. (2010) 'Sexual violence prevention: the role of stage of change', *Journal of Interpersonal Violence*, 25: 111–35.

Banyard, V.L., Moynihan, M.M. and Crossman, M.T. (2009) 'Reducing sexual violence on campus: the role of student leaders as empowered bystanders', *Journal of College Student Development*, 50: 446–57.

Banyard, V.L., Moynihan, M.M. and Plante, E.G. (2007) 'Sexual violence prevention through bystander education: an experimental evaluation', *Journal of Community Psychology*, 35: 463–81.

Banyard, V.L., Plante, E.G. and Moynihan, M.M. (2004) 'Bystander education: bringing a broader community perspective to sexual violence prevention', *Journal of Community Psychology*, 32: 61–79.

Berkowitz, A.D. (2002) 'Fostering men's responsibility for preventing sexual assault', in P.A. Schewe (ed.), *Preventing Violence in Relationships: Interventions Across the Life Span*, Washington, DC: American Psychological Association, 163–95.

Berkowitz, A.D. (1994) 'A model acquaintance rape prevention program for men', in A.D. Berkowitz (ed.), *Men and Rape: Theory, Research and Prevention Programs in Higher Education*, San Francisco, CA: Jossey-Bass, 35–42.

Berkowitz, A.D. (1992) 'College men as perpetrators of acquaintance rape and sexual assault: a review', *Journal of American College Health*, 40: 175–81.

Boeringer, S.B. (1999) 'Associations of rape-supportive attitudes with fraternal and athletic participation', *Violence Against Women*, 5: 81–90.

Cismaru, M., Jensen, G. and Lavack, A.M. (2010) 'If the noise coming from next door were loud music you'd do something about it: using mass media campaigns encouraging bystander intervention to stop partner violence', *Journal of Advertising*, 39: 69–82.

Coker, A.L., Cook-Craig, P.G., Williams, C.M., Fisher, B.S., Clear, E.R., Garcia, L.S. and Hegge, L.M. (2011) 'Evaluation of Green Dot: an active bystander intervention to reduce sexual violence on college campuses, *Violence Against Women*, 17: 777–96.

Coker, A.L., Fisher, B.S., Bush, H.M., Clear, E.R., Williams, C.M., Swan, S.C. and Degue, S. (in press) 'Evaluation of the Green Dot bystander intervention to reduce dating violence and sexual violence on college campuses', *Journal of American College Health.*

Cook-Craig, P.G., Coker, A.L., Clear, E.R., Garcia, L.S., Bush, H.M., Brancato, C.J., Williams, C.M. and Fisher, B.S. (in press) 'Challenge and opportunity in evaluating a diffusion-based active bystanding prevention program: Green Dot in high schools', *Violence Against Women.*

Espelage, D.L., Low, S., Polanin, J.R. and Brown, E.C. (2013) 'The impact of a middle school program to reduce aggression, victimization, and sexual violence', *Journal of Adolescent Health*, 53: 180–6.

Foubert, J.D. (2000) 'The longitudinal effects of a rape-prevention program on fraternity men's attitudes, behavioral intent, and behavior', *Journal of American College Health*, 48: 158–63.

Gidycz, C.A., Orchowski, L.M. and Berkowitz, A.D. (2011) 'Preventing sexual aggression among college men: an evaluation of a social norms and bystander intervention program', *Violence Against Women*, 17: 720–42.

Katz, J. (1994) *Mentors in Violence Prevention (MVP) Trainer's Guide*, Boston, MA: Northeastern University's Center for the Study of Sport in Society.

Kelly, J.B. and Johnson, M.P. (2008) 'Differentiation among types of intimate partner violence: research update and implications for interventions', *Family Court Review*, 46: 476–99.

McMahon S and Banyard V.L. (2012) ‘When can I help? A conceptual framework for the prevention of sexual violence through bystander intervention’, *Trauma, Violence, & Abuse*, 13: 3–14.

McMahon, S., Postmus, J.L., Warrener, C. and Koenick, R.A. (2014) ‘Utilizing peer education theater for the primary prevention of sexual violence on college campuses’, *Journal of College Student Development*, 55: 78–85.

Miller, E., Das, M., Tancredi, D.J., McCauley, H.L., Virata, M.C., Nettiksimmons, J., O’Connor, B., Ghosh, S. and Verma, R. (2014) ‘Evaluation of a gender-based violence prevention program for student athletes in Mumbai, India’, *Journal of Interpersonal Violence*, 29: 758–78.

Miller, E., Tancredi , D.J., McCauley, H.L., Decker, M.R., Virata, M.C., Anderson, H.A., O’Connor, B. and Silverman, J.G. (2013) ‘One-year follow-up of a coach-delivered dating violence prevention program: a cluster randomized controlled trial’, *American Journal of Preventive Medicine*, 45: 108–12.

Miller, E., Tancredi, D.J., McCauley, H.L., Decker, M.R., Virata, M.C., Anderson, H.A., Stetkevich, N., Brown, E.W., Moideen, F. and Silverman, J.G. (2012) ‘Coaching boys into men: a cluster-randomized controlled trial of a dating violence prevention program’, *Journal of Adolescent Health*, 51: 431–8.

Moynihan, M.M. and Banyard, V.L. (2008) ‘Community responsibility for preventing sexual violence: a pilot study with campus Greeks and intercollegiate athletes’, *Journal of Prevention & Intervention in the Community*, 36: 23–38.

VicHealth (2011) Review of Bystander Approaches in Support of Preventing Violence Against Women, Melbourne, Australia: Victorian Health Promotion Foundation.

Chapter 18

Engaging men in prevention of violence against women

Jackson Katz

I have been involved in gender violence prevention for more than three decades, from the first time I wrote an anti-rape editorial for my college student newspaper in the early 1980s to the present, when I develop and implement prevention programs in the education, sports, and military sectors across North America and beyond. Throughout this time, one of the central goals of my scholarship and activism has been engaging men; I and others have been at this since well before the term "engaging men" entered the lexicon.

The idea of bringing ever-greater numbers of men into active participation in the effort to reduce the global pandemic of men's violence against women (VAW) is not merely a passing fad. It will not give way to some as yet unidentified "flavor-of-the-month" approach when this one inevitably runs its course. Rather, engaging men is better understood as the next great step in the long-term feminist project both to increase gender equity and reduce and prevent sexual and domestic violence (DV). Cultural theorists and feminist activists have been making this case for at least the past twenty years. American author and critic bell hooks (2000: 83), comparing the need for men to work against sexism with the need for whites to join in the anti-racist struggle, writes that "men have a primary role to play . . . a tremendous contribution to make to feminist struggle in the area of exposing, confronting, opposing and transforming the sexism of their male peers." Esta Soler, founder of the San Francisco-based organization Futures Without Violence, maintains that activating men is "the next frontier" in the women-led movements against domestic and sexual violence. "In the end," she maintains, "we cannot change society unless we put more men at the table, amplify men's voices in the debate, enlist men to help change social norms on the issue, and convince men to teach their children that VAW is always wrong." (Soler 2000: 2).

The logic behind the premise of engaging men is simple. Not only do men commit the overwhelming majority of VAW; they also continue to hold the majority of economic and political power, and cultural authority worldwide. If there are going to be significant reductions in men's VAW, a critical mass of men will need to join women not only in doing a much better job of holding abusive men accountable for their behavior, but also in helping to transform cultural ideas about manhood in a way that delegitimizes and stigmatizes the misogynist beliefs that often underlie sexist abuse. This is obviously an immense task, and one that must proceed at variable rates of change in different cultural contexts. But building this critical mass of men—in every society in the world—is the urgent task before us.

Just women's issues?

One of the first challenges in this long-term effort is conceptual and linguistic. Gender violence has long been understood as a "women's issue" that only peripherally involves men. To a certain extent, this misperception was inevitable, as women's activism and leadership paved the way and formed the basis of the movements against domestic and sexual violence all over the world. Women put the issue on the legislative and social policy agenda locally and globally. But the idea that *men's* VAW is a *women's* issue is also a variation of classic "blame-the-victim" ideology. It effectively shifts responsibility for violence off of individual men, and male-dominated institutions, and places the onus for preventing violence onto its victims. Thus one of the elements necessary for an expansion of men's work in this area is its reconceptualization as a men's issue, a process that has been underway for the past couple of decades in public talks, professional trainings, scholarly and journalistic books and articles, and in the blogosphere, social media and other new and old media venues (Funk 1993; Katz 2006).

Of course, this conceptual shift comes with its own complications, as contradictions naturally arise when members of dominant groups participate in struggles against systems that provide them with certain privileges. For example, if men's voices, especially white men's voices, are seen as more credible and authoritative than women's, then does using male spokespeople (such as professional athletes) for social media and public service campaigns reinforce sexist ideas about the centrality of men's experience and the validity of men's opinions, even as it seeks to deconstruct the male-dominant system that is the root of the problem in the first place? It is important to note that pro-feminist male activists and theorists, and their feminist allies at the local, national, and international level, have been engaged in critical dialogue for decades about these very sorts of tensions.

Prevention through changing social norms about manhood

A key challenge inherent in the effort to engage men in this work is that violence by individuals is shaped by much broader social norms, cultural practices, and ideologies, that are themselves rooted in larger systems of gendered inequality. Individual change and accountability are necessary. But lasting change is impossible unless the inequitable systems themselves are transformed—social and systemic change that requires substantially more than even the best violence prevention programs and public service campaigns can provide. In recent years the increased popularity of the social-ecological model in the gender violence prevention field (Heise, 1998), and a long-term shift away from the idea of fixing "broken" individuals and toward a more comprehensive public health approach, are evidence that a consensus is growing that preventing men's violence means thinking less individualistically and more systematically. The implication for engaging men is clear: Men who want to substantially reduce VAW need to contribute to broader movements for gender and sexual equality, especially those that address the intersections of race, ethnicity, and socioeconomic class.

Still, the critical question remains: Why would men—outside of a small number of personally motivated or ideologically committed individuals—want to help transform a system that generally privileges them, relative to women? It is one thing for millions of men to take a pledge "never to commit, condone, or remain silent about men's VAW and girls," which is the signature contribution of the White Ribbon Campaign, the best-known and most visible anti-sexist men's initiative in the world, active in 60 countries. Awareness is the first step. But it is another issue altogether to get men not only to question traditional ideas about manhood and power, but to work actively toward changing them. This is a conundrum faced by every social justice movement in which members of the powerful group participate: How does one motivate members of the dominant culture to make substantive changes in the very system that provides them benefits?

One promising approach in the gender equality/gender violence prevention field moves beyond appeals to gender justice or altruism to speak directly to men's self-interest. R.W. Connell (2003: 11) argues that "If large numbers of men are to support and implement gender equality policy . . . it will be necessary for that policy to speak, in concrete and positive ways, to their concerns, interests, and hopes and problems. The political task is to do this without weakening the drive for justice for women and girls that animates current gender equality policy."

One organization that takes this approach in its work with men is the South African NGO Sonke Gender Justice. Part of Sonke's strategy for engaging men relies on making connections between men's VAW and men's fear of violence from other men, as well as their fear of contracting HIV. As Sonke's co-founder Dean Peacock explains, South Africa has the world's largest HIV epidemic, and while young women's rate of infection is far greater, young men face tremendous HIV vulnerabilities: "Lots of pressures to drink, to have sex, and to not reveal any vulnerabilities or confusions about sex. Models of manhood in South Africa and across the world are a recipe for men acting in sexual ways that put themselves and their partners at significant risk" (Dworkin and Peacock 2013: 9). Peacock further clarifies that "it doesn't take much for men to say that they feel tremendous pressure about norms of masculinity and that many of those pressures are quite unbearable and certainly very unrealistic . . . a significant part of our strategy is to get men to recognize the costs (they) pay for contemporary notions of manhood and for living in a patriarchal society . . . of course we want them to reflect on their own experiences of violence at the hands of other men who adhere in particularly rigid ways to those social norms about manhood" (Dworkin and Peacock 2013: 9).

Since the 1990s, some of the best-known organizations in the United States and around the world that do prevention work with men have linked changing cultural ideas and social norms about manhood with reducing men's VAW and children. In the US, the Mentors in Violence Prevention (MVP) program works extensively in schools, post-secondary educational institutions and university and professional athletic organizations, as well as all branches of the US military. MVP features interactive dialogues that focus on the pressures young men feel to remain silent in the face of sexist behaviors by their peers along a broad continuum—from objectifying comments to gang rape—and offers support and strategies for countering those pressures. The Washington, DC-based organization Men Can Stop Rape conducts training events and social media campaigns that help redefine masculine strength. In frequent town-hall-style meetings and conferences, the New York City-based group A Call To Men links violence prevention with the promotion of "a more healthy and respectful" definition of manhood.

The mission of the Rio de Janeiro-based NGO Promundo is the promotion of "caring, non-violent and equitable masculinities and gender relations in Brazil and internationally" through conducting research and developing, evaluating, and scaling up gender transformative interventions and policies. EngenderHealth's Men as Partners program works with men in countries in Africa, Asia, and Latin America to challenge traditional masculine norms that perpetuate gender inequities, in part by addressing the connection between gender-based violence and the spread of HIV and poor reproductive-health outcomes for women.

In recent years, several agencies affiliated with the United Nations (UN) have conducted research that seeks to measure the prevalence and patterns of sexual and intimate partner violence and explore links between ideologies of manhood and gender violence perpetration. One study, the UN Multi-country Study on Men and Violence in Asia and the Pacific, sought to "generate knowledge on how masculinities relate to men's perceptions and perpetration of VAW" (Fulu *et al.* 2013: 1). The study's findings reaffirm that VAW is an expression of women's subordination and inequality in the private and public spheres, and that "factors found to be associated with violence also reflect influential narratives of masculinity that justify and celebrate domination, aggression, strength and a capacity for violence as well as men's heterosexual performance and control over women" (Fulu *et al.* 2013: 6).

But in spite of the proliferation of these sorts of initiatives around the world, and the now widespread acceptance of the idea that in order to be successful, primary prevention initiatives must include a focus on men and masculinities, in actuality a very small number of men have been actively engaged in these sorts of efforts. This is especially striking in light of the enormity of the problem.

To make matters worse, in recent years organized resistance to the idea of critically examining cultural beliefs about masculinity as a central feature of gender violence prevention has increased with the rise of the so-called men's rights movement—a reactionary, anti-feminist movement comprised mostly of white middle-class men from North America, Europe, and Australia. Men's rights activists are openly hostile to feminist claims that men's VAW is based in gendered power imbalances, or even to the very idea that men are privileged in the sex-gender system. Their main activities in the gender violence area include fighting for gender neutrality in the application of DV law, and obfuscating the extent of men's perpetration of sexual violence, through disinformation campaigns that typically make absurd and blatantly false statistical claims (e.g., women's false accusations of rape are as big a problem as men's rape of women). Men's rights proponents are particularly active online, where in comments sections and chat rooms they often attack, in the most caustic, abusive, and sometimes violent language imaginable, well-known feminist advocates and anonymous female (and male) posters who dare to argue that men's violence needs to be understood as a manifestation of the much larger societal problem of gender inequality. Not all of this online abuse is part of an organized effort; men have attacked women who dare to define men's violence, harassment, or degradation as harmful, or simply asserted their rightful place in public spaces (Hess 2014).

To summarize, "engaging men" in gender violence prevention efforts is increasingly regarded as a critical component of the work. The number of men participating in these efforts around the world has expanded. But despite promising initiatives underway in numerous countries, many practical and ideological concerns remain. As Michael Flood (this volume) states, one of these is that not all "work with men" shares a feminist-informed commitment to gender justice.

It is clear that significant conceptual, practical, and political obstacles need to be overcome before the work of engaging men can become truly transformative, not the least of which is the need to increase substantially the number of men and young men who are exposed directly and consistently to in-depth gender violence prevention education and messages. In the remainder of this chapter, I identify three major strategies for accomplishing this.

Design interventions tailored to the needs of specific communities

One of the co-founders of the Institute on Domestic Violence in the African-American community, Oliver Williams, has long maintained there is no "one size fits all" approach to this topic; interventions must be designed to meet the needs of different communities.[1] For example, strategies that emphasize the law enforcement aspects of DV intervention are likely to be met with far less enthusiasm—and hence be less effective—in poor communities and communities of color that often have a more vexed relationship with the police and other agents of state authority than white middle-class communities. In the US, this insight derived largely from the experience of battered women of color and their advocates, who sought an end to the violence but did not want to further stigmatize and criminalize men of color, with predictably devastating results on children and the community as a whole.

A similar principle applies with regard to efforts around the world to engage men in the prevention of gender violence. While it might be possible to apply universal principles (e.g., all men have a role to play in ending men's VAW), the specific form these efforts take must of necessity be sensitive to the cultural, historical and political realities of the societies in which they are undertaken. The reasons for this are pragmatic as well as inspired by ethical or ideological considerations: To be effective, prevention strategies need to speak directly to the needs and aspirations of people in their own communities. The more they grow out of and are seen as being consistent with or building on existing cultural traditions or practices, the more likely they are to generate and sustain the support necessary to have lasting positive effects.

The "no one size fits all" ethos is perhaps most relevant in relation to prevention work with men from marginalized and subordinated populations, including those from communities in both the Global North and the Global South that have been devastated by centuries of racism, colonial violence, and subjugation. It is simply not realistic, nor fair, to enact the same strategies for engaging men in poor and dispossessed communities as it is for engaging more privileged men. Rich and poor men alike share certain patriarchal beliefs and engage in many similar sexist abuses, as do men across the ethnic/racial/religious spectrum. But gender violence in many cultures and sub-cultures in parts of South America, Africa and Asia, as well as indigenous communities in wealthy countries like the US, Canada, Australia, and New Zealand, also can be seen as partly rooted in the severe trauma, material deprivation, political disenfranchisement, and subsequent emasculation of colonized men by white European colonial rulers.

Men from communities devastated by generations of organized exploitation, who have been stripped of other means by which to assert their manhood and gain the respect of their peers, are particularly vulnerable to using violence to establish or maintain their identities as powerful actors in relations with women and other men. But rather than alleviate suffering, this violence often perpetuates it. As Judy Atkinson (2002: 24) writes about violence in Aboriginal Australia, "experiences of violence are traumatic . . . The layered trauma that results from colonization is likely to be expressed in dysfunctional, and sometimes violent, behavior at both individual and large-scale levels of human interaction, and these are retraumatizing." Indigenous Australian women are significantly more likely than other Australian women to be hospitalized for family-violence-related assaults (Al-Yaman *et al.* 2006).

In these sorts of cultural contexts, prevention efforts that engage men need to offer them ways to reclaim respect and dignity not by reproducing patterns of misogyny and sexist abuse but by identifying and reaffirming gender equality values in the local or indigenous culture to whatever extent possible, and by charting a path of powerful and principled non-violence in both interpersonal and political relations. In many communities, but especially those with multi-layered, multi-generational social problems stemming from historical trauma, racism, poverty, and marginalization, one way to incentivize men to increase their involvement in gender violence prevention efforts is to link those efforts to overall community goals. What this means in practice is that honest discussions about gender violence—which includes the violent victimization of boys and men—needs to be part of programs that address street violence, gang violence, teenage pregnancy, alcoholism and drug addiction, all of which a large body of research has shown to be strongly correlated with the experience of violence in families (Leiderman and Almo 2006: 1). Many young men who act out violently have themselves been the victims of child abuse, including child sexual abuse perpetrated by men. While this does not excuse their abusive behavior, it is important to recognize that the same system that produces men who abuse women produces men who abuse other men.

Prevention approaches can and should be customized to match the needs of different communities. But one constant is that men who are committed to working for gender equality and reducing the incidence of gender violence cannot do so by themselves; they must work on projects as partners and allies to women in their communities. More specifically, men who are committed to men's work in prevention need to develop partnerships with women activists and advocates in the domestic and sexual violence fields, in part to get their feedback about what they see as the needs of women and children in their community. An exemplary initiative in this regard is currently underway in Melbourne, Australia, called The Iramoo Zone. Led by Indigenous men, the project nurtures and supports Aboriginal men's leadership in gender violence prevention in partnership with two prominent women's organizations, one Indigenous and the other from the majority culture. The principle of intergender collaboration holds true across the socioeconomic spectrum; it is important that women contribute to the design and implementation of prevention strategies in societies rich and poor. Without their active input it is not clear that men's initiatives would truly advance the egalitarian goals they claim to profess.

Expand the use of the bystander approach as a way to engage men

Bystander intervention is perhaps the most popular gender violence prevention model in use today in North America, and its popularity is growing around the world. It is used in prevention programs in high schools, on university campuses, the US military, and many other institutions, with ethnically and racially diverse populations of women, men, girls, and boys. The goal of bystander training, simply stated, is to help people move beyond a fixation on the perpetrator–victim binary in order to motivate everyone in a given peer culture to get involved in supporting victims and challenging abusive behaviors.

It is important to understand that the bystander approach was introduced to the DV/sexual assault field specifically as a pedagogical strategy designed to engage men and young men in prevention efforts. The process began with the creation in 1993 of the multiracial MVP program at Northeastern University's Center for the Study of Sport in Society in Boston, Massachusetts.

The founding purpose of MVP, which was initially funded by the US Department of Education, was to train popular male student-athletes to use their status in male peer culture to speak out about issues that historically had been considered "women's issues," such as rape, relationship abuse, and sexual harassment. The theory was that if young men with a kind of "manhood credibility" on campus would make it clear to their peers and to younger boys that they would not accept or tolerate sexist or heterosexist beliefs and behaviors, it would open up space for other young men similarly to do so beyond the insular sports culture. MVP was based on the elementary premise in social justice education that members of dominant groups—men, whites, heterosexuals—play an important role in efforts to challenge sexism, racism, and heterosexism. In its second year, MVP evolved into a mixed-gender program; to this day it continues to emphasize the importance of challenging rape and battering-supportive gender norms, but with different, albeit complementary roles in the process for women and men.

In the early days of MVP, my colleagues and I were looking to develop a pedagogical model that could provide critical information and refute common rape myths, but in a way that would, in the words of Esta Soler, "invite, not indict" men, and engage them in critical dialogue (Parks *et al.* 2007: 7). We quickly realized that the "bystander" category offered a way to transcend the limitations of the perpetrator–victim binary, which up until that point had held sway in conventional gender violence prevention theory and practice. In many educational programs developed in the 1970s and 1980s, women were regarded primarily as victims, potential victims, or empowered survivors, and men as perpetrators or potential perpetrators.

Among the many limitations of this narrow approach was that most men did not see themselves this way, and as a result shut down in a way that precluded honest participation or critical dialogue. But when men—and women—are positioned not as potential perpetrators but as friends, family members, teammates, classmates, colleagues, and co-workers of women who are or might one day be abused, or as friends and peers of men who are abusive or perhaps going down that path, then "bystander" represents a virtually universal category that men can't as easily tune out. MVP staff understood that this offered a creative solution to one of the central challenges in gender violence prevention education: How to engage men without approaching them as potential rapists and batterers. While the bystander approach works with many diverse populations in education, the workplace, and communities, it is particularly effective in sports culture, the military, and other settings in which men know each other well and group norms are understood and reinforced.

In recent years, "bystander intervention" programs that emphasize the development of personal skills have proliferated. But at its essence, bystander training is about more than skill-building. People—especially men—need *permission* from each other to act, and reassurance that those who do intervene and interrupt abusive behavior will be respected, not rejected, for actually "stepping up to the plate." Men, as well as women, need the opportunity to talk and ask questions about the dynamics of their relationships with their peers, as well as with those in authority: If I see my friend, teammate, colleague, or co-worker acting disrespectfully to women, what should I do? What are the pros and cons of this course of action, or that one? To whom can I turn for ideas or support? What have others done in similar circumstances?

Because it encourages people to speak out in the face of abusive behavior before, during, or after the fact, the bystander approach contributes to a climate where sexist abuse is seen as uncool and unacceptable, and with men in particular, as a transgression against—rather than an enactment of—the social norms of masculinity. The short and long-term goal is to change the belief systems in male culture that tolerate or encourage sexist and abusive behaviors. In fact, one of the great strengths of the bystander approach is that its core principles transcend most racial, ethnic, religious, and national boundaries. Since the vast majority of world cultures are patriarchies in which male peer systems play a significant role in shaping the misogynist ideologies that sustain rape, sexual exploitation, and men's physical and emotional abuse of women, the opportunities for engaging men as empowered bystanders who can help to transform rape and abuse-supportive norms are virtually limitless.

Make engaging men and boys in the prevention of violence against women an institutional and political priority

Finally, the current scale and scope of efforts to engage men in the prevention of gender violence is woefully inadequate to the level of the problem. Significant reduction in men's VAW worldwide is only possible with an expansion and proliferation of existing efforts, along with bold new thinking about how to transform institutional practices, and the political clout and will to make it happen. As stated in the MenEngage Alliance Call for Action at the UN Commission on the Status of Women 2013, "It is time for approaches that have been shown to lead to changes in men's use of VAW to be taken to scale via large-scale public institutions and with adequate attention to quality, rigor, and protection of women's rights" (MenEngage 2013 1). The Alliance outlined ten concrete steps that the UN and national governments should take immediately to engage men and boys in preventing VAW. Because of the activist spirit of these recommendations, and their direct relevance to the topic of this chapter, I conclude with a condensed version of this list:

1. Create and universally implement school-based gender equality curricula that include discussions of gender-based violence.
2. Scale up national-level awareness and public education efforts to educate men and women about existing laws on VAW and to defuse men's resistance to women's rights by explaining why gender equality is also in men's interest.
3. Scale up bystander intervention approaches that seek to change social norms and create individual and community accountability.
4. Scale up high-quality, evidence-informed mass media and communications strategies that engage men and boys as part of the solution in ending VAW.
5. Test and scale up secondary prevention approaches that offer specific support for men and boys who have witnessed or experienced violence during childhood.
6. Implement VAW prevention together with policies to decrease alcohol consumption.
7. Restrict access to guns.
8. Engage men in VAW prevention in tandem with women's economic empowerment, including micro-credit programs and income support programs.
9. Engage men as fathers and in parent training.
10. Support research and evaluation on integrating programs for men who have used intimate partner violence, as part of comprehensive community support for women survivors of violence.

Do it now.

Note

1 See Williams' academic profile at the University of Minnesota, College of Education and Human Development, at www.cehd.umn.edu/people/profiles/Williams (accessed 25 May 2014).

References

Al-Yaman, F., Van Doeland, M. and Wallis, M. (2006) *Family Violence among Aboriginal and Torres Strait Islander People*, Canberra: Australian Institute of Health and Welfare.

Atkinson, J. (2002) *Trauma Trails, Recreating Song Lines: The Transgenerational Effects of Trauma in Indigenous Australia*, North Melbourne: Spinifex Press.

Connell, R.W. (2003) The Role of Men and Boys in Achieving Gender Equality, Paper presented at the UN Division for the Advancement of Women, Expert Group Meeting, Brasilia, Brazil, October 21–4.

Dworkin, S.L. and Peacock, D. (2013) 'Changing men in South Africa', *Contexts*, 12: 8–11.

Fulu, E., Warner, X., Miedema, S., Jewkes, R., Roselli, T. and Lang, J. (2013) *Why Do Some Men Use Violence Against Women and How Can We Prevent it? Quantitative Findings from the United Nations Multi-country Study on Men and Violence in Asia and the Pacific*, Bangkok: UNDP, UNFPA, UN Women and UNV.

Funk, R.E. (1993) *Stopping Rape: A Challenge for Men*, Philadelphia: New Society Publishers.

Heise, L. (1998) 'Violence Against Women: an integrated, ecological framework', *Violence Against Women*, 4: 262–90.

Hess, A. (2014) 'Why women aren't welcome on the Internet', *Pacific Standard Magazine*, 11. Online. Available at www.psmag.com/navigation/health-and-behavior/women-arent-welcome-internet-72170 (accessed 25 May 2014).

hooks, b. (2000) *Feminist Theory From Margin to Center*, Boston, MA: South End Press.

Katz, J. (2006) *The Macho Paradox: Why Some Men Hurt Women and How All Men Can Help*, Naperville, IL: Sourcebooks.

Leiderman, S. and Almo, C. (2006) *Interpersonal Violence and Adolescent Pregnancy: Prevalence and Implications for Practice and Policy*, Washington, DC: Healthy Teen Network.

MenEngage (2013) *Making Primary Prevention from Gender-based Violence a Global Right*. Online. Available at http://menengage.org/wp-content/uploads/2014/01/MenEngage-10-Point-Call-for-Action.pdf (accessed 25 May 2014).

Parks, L.F., Cohen, L. and Kravitz-Wirtz, N. (2007) *Poised for Prevention: Advancing Promising Approaches to Prevention of Intimate Partner Violence*, Oakland, CA: Prevention Institute.

Soler, E. (2000) 'News from the home front', *Newsletter of the Family Violence Prevention Fund,* Fall/Winter. Online. Available at www.futureswithoutviolence.org (accessed 25 May 2014).

Chapter 19

A feminist "epistemic community" reshaping public policy

A case study of the End Violence Against Women Coalition

Maddy Coy, Liz Kelly, and Holly Dustin

For over a decade, women's organizations lobbied United Kingdom governments to meet international obligations and adopt an integrated strategy on all forms of violence against women and girls (VAWG). Following the development of a VAWG strategy in Scotland, in 2009 the Labour government published the first such approach in Westminster,[1] rooted in a gender equality and human rights framework. The current government has continued this overall direction, with an action plan launched in March 2011 and refreshed annually since. Governments in Wales, London, and some local areas (e.g., Bradford, etc.) have also now taken this approach.

This marked a significant shift in perspective and was largely a result of the work of the End Violence Against Women Coalition (EVAW), an unprecedented UK-wide network of specialized support services, women's organizations, human rights organizations, trade unions, academics and activists[2] whose shared vision was for an integrated VAWG strategy, with prevention at its core. In this chapter we explore EVAW's engagement with policy makers, drawing on how Sylvia Walby (2011) has used Peter Haas' (1992) notion of an "epistemic community" to frame how the creation and use of knowledge by expert networks underpinned arguments used by feminist movements to influence policy and political change.

The End Violence Against Women Coalition

Formed in 2005, EVAW was funded and hosted by Amnesty International as part of its global Stop Violence Against Women campaign. The network itself grew out of the Women's National Commission (WNC), a now abolished quasi-autonomous women's policy agency located within the Westminster government. The WNC convened a VAWG working group, comprising mainly specialized women's support services, which met quarterly for the purpose of sharing developments in the sector and engaging with government officials about policy development and implementation. The success of this forum in influencing policy-making backstage demonstrated that collectively the sector could make persuasive arguments based on member organizations' experience and expertise. However, the group's capacity to criticize government decisions and develop a media profile was limited by both the structural position of WNC, alongside the fact that many members received funding from the state. The need for an independent voice that channeled the expertise of the specialized VAWG sector into both policy and public arenas became clear.

EVAW was launched on November 25, 2005, with four campaign aims: For VAWG to be understood as a cause and consequence of women's inequality; to raise awareness about the nature, extent, and impacts of VAWG in the UK and how it can be prevented; for the UK governments to develop integrated and strategic approaches to ending VAWG; and to share good practice across the UK and learn from the experience in Scotland, where a framework was being developed.

The launch of the coalition was accompanied by the first of a series of reports titled *Making the Grade?*, in the same week that Amnesty UK published a high-profile poll showing that significant proportions of the public endorsed victim-blaming rape myths. The reports were developed by WNC expert members to "audit" and score Westminster (and a year later, Northern Ireland) government departments on their compliance with international obligations to take integrated measures to end VAWG. Overall, scores for government departments consistently hovered around one or two out of ten. While unpopular with politicians, the *Making the Grade?* reports (2005–7) highlighted that approaches to VAWG across government departments were not simply uncoordinated, but unconnected, lacking a gender analysis and conflating VAWG with domestic violence (DV).

From the outset, then, EVAW drew on the knowledge and expertise of its members to evaluate government (in)action on VAWG. Seeking to build momentum about the necessity of adopting an integrated approach, early lobbying linked obligations on VAWG to the then Gender Equality Duty, including a toolkit for local activists to challenge local policy makers. Two influential research reports followed. The first identified violence as cause and consequence of inequality across intersections of discrimination: Age; sexuality; race; religion and belief; disability; and gender (Horvath and Kelly 2007). This report was targeted at the newly established Equality and Human Rights Commission (EHRC) and led to partnership on the second report, which mapped the presence (and thus absence) of specialized VAWG services across all UK regions. Maps were produced that vividly demonstrated "the postcode lottery" of support, particularly for sexual violence services and those for women from minority communities (see Coy *et al.* 2007, 2009). Both projects cemented an enduring relationship between the coalition and feminist academics, and showcased a core function of an epistemic community—that "policy goals must derive from [members'] expert knowledge" (Cross 2013: 142).

The End Violence Against Women Coalition as an epistemic community

An epistemic community has been defined as: "A network of professionals with recognized expertise and competence in a particular domain and an authoritative claim to policy relevant knowledge within that domain or issue area" (Haas 1992: 3). The role of epistemic communities is to provide decision makers with policy-relevant knowledge about issues on which they are uncertain and/or seeking expert input (Dunlop 2009). Walby (2011) argues that feminist advocacy networks which aim to secure policy change on a range of issues can be understood as epistemic communities. Networks and alliances have, for Walby, signaled a shift toward grassroots activists engaging inside and outside the state, particularly around the issue of VAWG. This is a wider conception of an epistemic community, embracing lobbying and campaigning as influencing practices: "Contemporary feminism has increasingly included epistemic communities. These have increasingly made claims to expertise and increasingly argued with key holders of institutional power" (Walby 2011: 64).

Walby (2011: 64) also notes that "feminism is not exclusively an epistemic community; the basis of claims for justice remains varied." This, the creation and use of a knowledge base within EVAW—in Haas' words, the authoritative claim—is an important point to which we will return throughout this chapter. Often narrowly focused on scientists as experts, the value of the epistemic community concept to explain and explore the process of knowledge transfer is underdeveloped (Dunlop 2009; Cross 2013). Tracing the means by which knowledge becomes part of policy formulation is thus an empirical question with relatively scarce answers.

Building on Walby's (2011) innovative application of the concept, we outline how EVAW functions as an epistemic community and offer examples of how some of the coalition's initial policy goals have been achieved through the creation of new knowledge, rooted in the realities EVAW members contend with in their support and advocacy work with survivors of violence. First, we briefly outline some of the processes that have been key to building the coalition and growing a public profile.

Laurel Weldon (2011), in an analysis of government responsiveness to VAWG in 36 countries and 50 American states, concludes that strong autonomous women's movements are critical. Feminist organizations enhance government capabilities to address issues of importance for women's lives. Yet success for women's movements requires "mak[ing] alliances with other movements and interests" (Beckwith 2007: 325). The coalitional structure of EVAW—an aim to enable individuals and organizations to become part of a movement to eliminate VAWG—means that creating an epistemic community was implicitly stitched in from inception. Harnessing a breadth of support and joining up thinking between members is not without complications. In seeking to achieve consensus, tensions had to be explicitly acknowledged and, where possible, resolved through ongoing dialogue and debates. Internal cohesion is fundamental to an effective epistemic community (Cross 2013).

With such varied membership in EVAW—small and large organizations (many focused initially on DV) across the UK—there is little room for complacency about consensus on specific issues or campaign targets. Add to this a funding climate that fosters competition between support organizations that provide similar services, and the potential for discord and division is significant. Long-standing personal relationships undoubtedly helped smooth these edges, but just as important has been the investment in developing shared positions, particularly time spent together creating "a group perspective" grounded in members' experiences (Cross 2013; Weldon 2011). A key principle from the outset was that all members had an equal voice, and part of this involved a commitment to enabling the participation and perspectives of organizations that are particularly under-resourced, such as sexual violence services and those supporting women from minority communities.

One example illustrates these processes. During 2006 and 2007, how to respond to forced marriage was a policy issue, with proposals for both a specific criminal offense and a civil protection order on the table. EVAW members reached a consensus to support the civil protection order, paying particular attention to the arguments from members working in affected communities. This was also the outcome of the political process, with legislation passed in 2007.

Consultation with members has acute resonance, since approaches to VAWG in England, Wales, and Scotland and Northern Ireland have specific trajectories. Argumentation that might prove effective in discussion with the Westminster government does not necessarily transfer across to the Welsh Assembly or Scottish Parliament, where histories of support and differing legal frameworks inflect what policy makers are likely to heed. Finding ways to accommodate nuances within an overarching campaign premised on a clear policy goal required careful negotiation, and has not always proved possible or relevant. Some EVAW campaigns have been focused only on Westminster or England, while others have been UK wide. Recognition of members' situated knowledge about local contexts was a basic building block of the coalition work. It was also essential for specialized organizations working with black and minority ethnic women, which have been core and active members of EVAW. Weldon (2011) notes that social movements are strengthened by recognizing intersections of marginalization, and thus in turn government responsiveness to VAWG is enhanced.

A recent project addressing these intersections is a partnership project between EVAW, Imkaan (a black feminist organization working on VAWG), and Object (who campaigns against sexual objectification), challenging sexism and racism in music videos.[3] Moments of change also have been created from members' expertise and concerns: An influential joint contribution to the high-profile Leveson Inquiry by EVAW, Imkaan, Object and Equality Now on media sexism and VAWG representations in newspapers,[4] and the successful campaign to criminalize the possession of rape pornography, led by Rape Crisis South London.[5]

Finally, and most significantly, epistemic communities are distinguished from interest groups by their highly specialized expert knowledge (Dunlop 2009). As the above examples show, multiple forms of expertise exist among EVAW members: Campaigning tactics; legal knowledge; communications; and academic research skills. The bedrock, however, is knowledge accumulated from decades of supporting survivors of violence and abuse, that we now recognize through the term "practice-based evidence" (Coy *et al.* 2011). This framing in itself emboldens member organizations that their insights are more than "anecdote." It also exposes the parallel processes of silencing and speaking: Just as many survivors find it difficult to have their voices heard, women's organizations that represent them are often dismissed as offering only "anecdata" inferior to an elitist conception of academics as "knowers."

EVAW provides a platform to collate and distil practice-based evidence into argumentation and campaigning: Much of the coalition's engagement with policy makers is this form of "knowledge work" (Freeman 2007). There is also crucial internal knowledge work: The rich mix of organizations within EVAW creates a reciprocal exchange where, for example, trade unions widen their knowledge of VAWG beyond the workplace.

Joining the dots: an integrated violence against women and girls strategy

When EVAW launched, the then government had introduced a range of measures to address DV, including the first national action plan. That these initiatives emerged through the Home Office meant that they were almost exclusively focused on enhancing criminal justice responses: New laws, special fast-track courts, training for prosecutors, and support for survivors linked to reporting and pursuing prosecution. Investment in services was mostly limited to the statutory sector, with new forms of provision emerging (e.g., independent DV advisors and Sexual Assault Referral Centres) that looked superficially like the long-called-for mainstreaming of responses to VAWG, but in reality often led to the marginalization of local specialized women's services. Other forms of VAWG were overlooked, with sexual violence limping into place in 2007 in the form of another action plan, disconnected from the DV plan, legislation on female genital mutilation in 2003, and funding for a specialized service for trafficked women the same year. These developments signaled a willingness to engage with the scale and scope of VAWG that was cautiously welcomed by the women's sector. Nevertheless, there were significant gaps. Chronic under-investment in the women's sector had resulted in no secure funding for rape crisis centers, which had halved in number over the previous two decades. Specialized support services for minority women were struggling against the political agenda of community cohesion that privileged the viewpoints of male community leaders (Dahliwal and Patel 2012), and an array of strategies on different forms of VAWG, which barely referenced each other, meant that their implementation at local levels was paralyzed. Prevention—the radical notion that VAWG was not inevitable and could be interrupted—remained a vision shared only by feminists.

After four *Making the Grade?* reports[6] which exposed failings in specific government departments, EVAW shifted to a different tactic—setting out a template for what an integrated strategy might look like, developed by academics in consultation with the specialized women's sector around the UK (see Coy *et al.* 2008). This template was built around the twin, intertwined pillars of gender equality and human rights principles, and identified how addressing VAWG was core business for each government department. The oft used "3 Ps" (prevention, prosecution, and protection) were extended to six: Perspective, policy, prevention, provision, protection, and prosecution. The current approach was failing to join the dots across forms of violence and government departments, with almost all recent initiatives flowing from the emphasis on prosecution, leaving provision narrowly located in the statutory sector, policy piecemeal, protection limited mostly to civil law remedies, and perspective and prevention blank. Without a perspective that included gender equality and human rights, there was no framing for policy and no imperative to develop preventative action.

In setting out a template for change, the document reiterated the United Nations (UN) definition of VAWG as: "directed against a woman because she is a woman or that affects women disproportionately" (UN 2006: para 6). Perhaps one of the most under-reported but far-reaching victories for EVAW is the adoption of this definition throughout central, and some progressive local, governments (e.g., GLA 2010; EVAW's lobbying in the London Mayoral elections was crucial to embed a commitment for a VAWG strategy across the candidates).

In late 2009, the Westminster government launched a VAWG strategy, adopting the two foundational principles of gender equality and human rights (Home Office 2009). This followed the adoption of an integrated approach in Scotland. A change of government at Westminster in May 2010 could have signaled the loss of the VAW strategy, yet provided what Karen Beckwith (2007: 327) has identified as a "political opportunity." Weldon (2011) argues left and right political affiliations are often poor indicators of responsiveness to VAWG. This proved accurate, with early support within both the Conservative and Liberal Democrat parties while Labour appeared reluctant. In the run-up to the election, EVAW had identified sympathetic individuals within the Conservative party, and lobbying them culminated in a commitment to an integrated VAWG strategy in 2007, should they be elected to government. Despite different engagement with the concept of human rights (and arguably with gender equality), the strategy (Home Office 2010) and subsequent annual action plans have again retained these two key principles. In 2010, the domestic abuse strategy in Wales was extended to cover all forms of VAWG (WAG 2010). Local VAWG strategies have also proliferated. The Crown Prosecution Service was the first Westminster government department to have a VAWG strategy, and has continued to publish yearly progress reports.[7] With carefully crafted arguments, rooted in international human rights obligations and members' expertise, EVAW succeeded in shifting public policy toward its campaign aims: the sharing of good practice; for VAWG to be understood as cause and consequence of gender inequality; an integrated strategic approach to VAWG; and raising awareness of its scale and extent.

The map of gaps research: linking strategic approaches to support for survivors

One of the core arguments for developing an integrated approach to all forms of VAWG was its potential as a lever to ensure that survivors have equitable access to support provision (Kelly and Lovett 2005; Coy *et al.* 2008). Under the range of international instruments which require governments to adopt integrated strategies, are linked obligations for support in the aftermath of violence.

EVAW members were acutely aware that specialized support for women from minority communities and sexual violence survivors were under-resourced. Significant swathes of the country appeared to have no services, and until 2010, just one rape crisis center covered London. Parallel to campaigning on the basis of international obligations, EVAW commissioned research that mapped the presence of specialized VAWG organizations across UK regions (DV services including shelters, perpetrator programs, specialist courts, rape crisis centers, organizations supporting survivors of female genital mutilation, services for minority women, trafficked women and those involved in prostitution). This unique project—Map of Gaps—used geographic information system software to produce color-coded maps of VAWG services, with red as a danger sign of no specialized support. Regional proportions of services were compared to population figures and extrapolations of prevalence data to bring these red areas to life: In each were potentially thousands of victim-survivors. One third (30 percent) of local authorities were found to have no specialized support organizations; this rose to over three-quarters (78 percent) for services for survivors of sexual violence, and nine in ten (89 percent) for women from Black and minority ethnic communities (Coy *et al.* 2007). Crucially, the rapidly dwindling number of rape crisis centers in England and Wales was contrasted to Scotland, where ring-fenced funding for each center had led to their expansion.[8]

This first report (Coy *et al.* 2007) was co-badged by the newly established Equality and Human Rights Commission (EHRC), and explicitly linked the need for access to specialized support in the aftermath of violence, with obligations on gender equality. The second report (Coy *et al.* 2009), which updated the findings and explored the impact of new funding regimes, was funded by the EHRC. A campaign website accompanied the report, where it was possible to examine provision in specific areas and write directly to politicians. Less publicly, but no less significantly, the EHRC wrote to all local authorities that were identified in the updated report as having no specialized services, and asked them to demonstrate how they were meeting obligations under legally binding equality duties. This audacious action was greeted, predictably, with defensive sound and fury about methodological flaws. Yet several local authorities were ultimately judged to be in breach of equality legislation, and proceedings initiated by the EHRC against them. Map of Gaps shows connections between EVAW members highlighting funding gaps, research that documented a postcode lottery of support for survivors, to local governments being held legally accountable for failing to resource this provision. The stark findings about the paucity of support for survivors of sexual violence also contributed to political commitments to centrally fund rape crisis centers. Perhaps more than any other project, *Map of Gaps* demonstrates that the epistemic community of EVAW, blending the expertise of women's organizations and researchers, had evolved into "a major means by which knowledge translates into power" (Cross 2013: 138).

While epistemic communities cannot control how their knowledge is directed (Freeman 2007), EVAW can claim to have, over time, institutionalized learning from the practice-based evidence of women's organizations in the process of policy formulation. The development of a sub-committee focused specifically on prevention of VAWG sought to further ingrain these engagements between specialists and policy makers.

The prevention network: an epistemic community within an epistemic community

The launch of an integrated VAWG strategy marked a momentous milestone for women's movements and feminist campaigns in particular. In the current approach, prevention of VAWG is said to be "at the heart" (Home Office 2010: 3–4); indeed, the first guiding principle of the strategy is to "prevent such violence from happening by challenging the attitudes and behaviors which foster it and intervening early where possible to prevent it" (Home Office 2010: 3). EVAW had already developed a policy goal on prevention, and a logical next step was to engage with this policy conversation.

The prevention network was established in 2010, launching with a report which encapsulated the core message of the campaign in its title, *A Different World is Possible* (EVAW 2011a). Ten areas of action were identified, offering ways of thinking about prevention which moved on from vague hopes and intentions, to thinking about more targeted approaches to interrupt specific pathways to violence perpetration drawing on recently published research for the European Commission.[9] Again EVAW showcased the accumulated expertise of community projects, including member organizations, with an accompanying report which profiled 15 innovative projects working on prevention with young people in schools, the community, and the media (EVAW 2011b). This was another distillation of practice-based evidence into a specific policy goal: For prevention initiatives to be delivered across a range of youth settings, preferably by specialized organizations who bring a gender analysis to their work. In a sense the network comprises an epistemic community within an epistemic community—linking longtime EVAW members with those working on anti-bullying.

Through the prevention network EVAW stepped boldly into "the moving picture" (Dunlop 2009: 299) of political priorities. With a more diffuse overall goal to ensure that VAWG prevention remained on the policy agenda, campaigning opportunities have had to be winnowed out from broad agendas. Some doors have gradually blown shut, and others have provided new openings. The "contemporary fascination" (Walby 2011b, cited in Coy and Garner 2012) with sexualized popular culture is one of these.

The Westminster government has commissioned two reviews into sexualization, the first by the previous Labour administration (Papadopolous 2010) and the second by the current coalition government (Bailey 2011). Both were linked notionally to VAWG strategies, yet differed in framing and emphasis. The Papadopolous (2010) review was based on an explicitly gendered analysis, and drew on contributions from specialized women's services, who recognized sexualized popular culture as a "conducive context" (Kelly 2007) for VAWG (Coy and Garner, 2012). In contrast, in the Bailey (2011) review, VAWG and gender equality disappeared, replaced by a manifesto commitment to a more "family friendly" society, parent power, and corporate responsibility. Both reviews endorsed the notion that the problem with sexualized popular culture was age-appropriateness and the premature imposition of sexuality on children (Coy and Garner 2012). In response to the Bailey review, EVAW pointed out that recommendations would be far more effective if rooted in both children's rights and implications for gender equality. While the political agenda on sexualization was not perfectly aligned with EVAW's perspectives, specific actions and policy changes have been supported by EVAW because of their potential to deliver on the VAWG strategy.

Since then, EVAW has burrowed deeply into policy conversations on addressing sexualization as a conducive context for VAWG, invited into discussions at the highest level of government about how to address the intrusion of pornography into young people's lives. A consistent element here has been that debates about sexualized popular culture should take account of questions and enquiries that are underpinned by the practice-based evidence of women's organizations (Coy and Garner 2012).

The prevention network also has adapted the methodology of *Making the Grade?* reports. In 2012, prevention initiatives in the VAWG strategy and action plans and the UK government's 7th Periodic State Report to the UN Committee on the Elimination of Discrimination against Women were graded against the ten key areas of action set out in EVAW's vision for prevention (2011). Analysis and scoring was carried out by Prevention Network members: 1–3 for little evidence of work being carried out, 4–6 for some evidence, and 7–10 for strong evidence. The overall score for the Westminster government was just 24 out of 100 (EVAW 2013a). This policy-oriented report has an activist companion in the Schools Safe for Girls campaign, which has led to the opposition Labour party announcing a commitment to make addressing VAWG in sex and relationships education compulsory.

Yet this latest report also highlights the ongoing challenges in reshaping public policy on VAWG: Despite the momentous shift toward an integrated approach, many government departments have yet to translate their symbolic commitments into concrete actions, leaving many gaps in central policy and on the ground at local levels.

Social media: new challenges for old issues

No account of EVAW's evolution as an epistemic community—a "professional [network] with authoritative and policy-relevant expertise" (Cross 2013: 137)—would be complete without a brief discussion of the coalition's newest development: addressing VAWG in social media.

Engagement in the very public spheres of social media is a key avenue for galvanizing support and indirectly shaping public policy (Weldon 2011). Perhaps the most illustrative example is the case of Ched Evans, a footballer convicted in 2011 for raping a young woman. Upon his conviction, an avalanche of hatred directed toward the woman followed, primarily from football fans who abused her on Twitter, fan sites and elsewhere and repeatedly named her in breach of the lifelong protection of anonymity afforded to rape complainants. By reacting quickly on Twitter, making reports to the police about this illegal and abusive activity, and passing on screenshots of tweets to the relevant police force, EVAW led a call for action, resulting ultimately in the conviction of ten people. EVAW has since held a roundtable on VAWG and social media, jointly with the *Guardian* newspaper (EVAW 2013b), and see this as an ongoing area of engagement with policy makers about the challenges of addressing women's safety online.

Conclusion

EVAW brought a blend of "practice-based evidence" from organizations with decades of working with women and girls, academic analysis, and campaigning skills to bear on policy on VAWG. This was achieved through the development of an epistemic community amongst members, which included building consensus, extensive engagement face-to-face and through virtual communication methods, and coordination which reached fruition through a "common policy enterprise" (Haas 1992: 3), a process which has continued in the development of a framework for prevention. In building a coalition linking a broad range of organizations, EVAW transformed a single-issue campaign into one linked to gender equality in the home, public space including online spaces, workplaces, and education, and can claim to have enhanced government responsiveness to VAWG in deep and far-reaching ways.

Notes

1 We use this term to refer to the government for England and Wales, since legal and policy frameworks for certain matters differ across nations and regions of the UK.

2 For a full list of members, www.endviolenceagainstwomen.org.uk.
3 See www.rewindreframe.org.
4 The Leveson Inquiry examined the culture, practices, and ethics of the media. See www.levesoninquiry.org.uk.
5 See the webpage "Success for rape crisis campaign to close the rape porn loophole" at www.rapecrisis.org.uk (accessed 25 May 2014).
6 Three scored the Westminster government, and one focused on Northern Ireland.
7 See http://www.cps.gov.uk/publications/equality/vaw.
8 When the current government was elected, they announced ring-fenced funding for rape crisis centers in England and Wales, and a number of new centers have since opened.
9 The model which was adapted can be found online at http://ec.europa.eu/justice/funding/daphne3/multi-level_interactive_model/understanding_perpetration_start_uinix.html (accessed 25 May 2014).

References

Bailey, R. (2011) *Letting Children be Children: Report of an Independent Review of the Commercialisation and Sexualisation of Childhood*, London: Department of Education.

Beckwith, K. (2007) 'Mapping strategic engagements of women's movements', *International Feminist Journal of Politics*, 9: 312–39.

Coy, M. and Garner, M. (2012) 'Definitions, discourses and dilemmas: policy and academic engagement with the sexualisation of popular culture', *Gender & Education*, 24: 285–301.

Coy, M., Kelly, L. and Foord, J. (2009) *Map of Gaps 2: The Postcode Lottery of Violence Against Women Support Services in Britain*, London: End Violence Against Women Coalition and Equality and Human Rights Commission.

Coy, M., Kelly, L. and Foord, J. (2007) *Map of Gaps: The Postcode Lottery of Violence Against Women Support Services in the UK*, London: End Violence Against Women Coalition.

Coy, M., Lovett, J. and Kelly, L. (2008) *Realising Rights, Fulfilling Obligations: A Template Integrated Strategy on Violence Against Women for the UK*, London: End Violence Against Women Coalition.

Coy, M., Thiara, R., Kelly, L. and Phillips, R. (2011) *Into the Foreground: An Evaluation of the Jacana Parenting Programme*, London: CWASU.

Cross, M.K.D. (2013) 'Rethinking epistemic communities twenty years later', *Review of International Studies*, 39: 137–60.

Dahliwal, S. and Patel, P. (2012) 'Feminism in the shadow of multifaithism: the implications for South Asian women in the UK', in S. Roy (ed.), *New South Asian Feminisms: Paradoxes and Possibilities*, London: Zed Books, 169–88.

Dunlop, C.A. (2009) 'Policy transfer as learning: capturing variation in what decision-makers learn from epistemic communities', *Policy Studies*, 30: 291–313.

EVAW, End Violence Against Women (2013a) *Deeds or Words? Analysis of Westminster Government Action to Prevent Violence Against Women and Girls*, London: EVAW.

EVAW, End Violence Against Women (2013b) *New Technology: Same Old Problems. Report of a Roundtable on Social Media and Violence Against Women and Girls*, London: EVAW.

EVAW, End Violence Against Women (2011a) *A Different World is Possible: A Call for Long-term and Targeted Action to Prevent Violence Against Women and Girls*, London: EVAW.

EVAW, End Violence Against Women (2011b) *A Different World is Possible: Promising Practices to Prevent Violence Against Women and Girls*, London: EVAW.

Freeman, R. (2007) 'Epistemological bricolage: how practitioners make sense of learning', *Administration & Society*, 39: 476–96.

GLA, Greater London Authority (2010) *The Way Forward: Taking Action to End Violence Against Women and Girls*, London: GLA.

Haas, P. (1992) 'Introduction: epistemic communities and international policy coordination', *International Organization*, 46: 1–35.

Home Office (2011) *Call to End Violence Against Women and Girls: Action Plan*, London: Home Office.

Home Office (2010) *Call to End Violence Against Women and Girls*, London: Home Office.

Home Office (2009) *Together We Can End Violence Against Women and Girls*, London: Home Office.

Horvath, M.A.H and Kelly, L. (2007) *From the Outset: Why Violence should be a Priority for the Commission for Equality and Human Rights*, London: EVAW.

Kelly, L. (2007) 'A conducive context: trafficking of persons in Central Asia', in M. Lee (ed.), *Human trafficking*, Cullompton: Willan Publishing, 73–91.

Kelly, L. And Lovett, J. (2005) *What a Waste: The Case for an Integrated Violence Against Women Strategy*, London: Women's National Commission.

Papadopoulos, L. (2010) *Sexualisation of Young People Review*, London: Home Office.

UN, United Nations (2006) *Secretary-General's In-depth Study on All Forms of Violence Against Women*. Online. Available at www.un.org/womenwatch/daw/vaw/v-sg-study.htm (accessed 25 May 2014).

WAG, Welsh Assembly Government (2010) *The Right to Be Safe*, Cardiff: Author.

Walby, S. (2011) *The Future of Feminism*, Cambridge: Polity Press.

Weldon S.L. (2011) *When Protest Makes Policy: How Social Movements Represent Disadvantaged Groups*, Ann Arbor, MI: University of Michigan Press.

Section VI: Preventing male violence against women

Questions for critical thought

1. Among the range of bystander interventions, which do you think will be most effective? Explain why.
2. Do you think online bystander training can be an effective way to change behavior? Why or why not?
3. How does social inequality and disadvantage challenge efforts to prevent sexual and intimate partner violence?
4. Talk with male violence prevention leaders in your local area about their programs and goals. To what extent do they work collaboratively with local, national, and international women's and anti-violence movements and advocates?
5. Are there identifiable "epistemic communities" on violence against women in your local area? How do they compare to Ending Violence Against Women in the United Kingdom in terms of goals, objectives, and political action?

Further reading

Chamberlain, L. (2008, March) *A Prevention Primer for Domestic Violence: Terminology, Tools, and the Public Health Approach*, Harrisburg, PA: VAWnet, a project of the National Resource Center on Domestic Violence. Online. Available at www.vawnet.org (accessed 25 May 2014).

Nation, M., Crusto, C, Wandersman, A., Kumpfer, K., Seybolt, D., Morrissey-Kane, E. and Davino, K. (2003) 'What works in prevention: principles of effective prevention programs', *American Psychologist*, 58: 449-56.

Ricardo, C., Eads, M. and Barker, G. (2012) *Engaging Boys and Young Men in the Prevention of Sexual Violence: A Systematic and Global Review of Evaluated Interventions*, Pretoria: Sexual Violence Research Initiative.

VicHealth, Victorian Health Promotion Foundation (2007) *Preventing Violence Before it Occurs: A Framework and Background Paper to Guide the Primary Prevention of Violence against Women in Victoria*, Melbourne: VicHealth.

Whitaker, D.J., Baker, C.K. and Arias, I. (2007) 'Interventions to prevent intimate partner violence', in L.S. Doll, S. Bonzo, J. Mercy and D. Sleet (eds.), *Handbook of Injury and Violence Prevention*, New York: Springer, 203-21.

Media

Hip Hop: Beyond Beats and Rhymes, 2007 [DVD]. Hurt, B. (dir.) USA: God Bless the Child Productions.

Tough Guise 2: Violence, Manhood and American Culture, 2013 [DVD]. Earp, J. (dir.) USA: Media Education Foundation.

Violence & Silence: Jackson Katz, PhD, at TEDxFiDiWomen, 2013 [video]. Online. Available at www.youtube.com/watch?v=KTvSfeCRxe8 (accessed 25 May 2014).

Websites

Green Dot: A comprehensive approach to violence prevention that capitalizes on the power of peer and cultural influence across all levels of the socio-ecological model. The website includes information on the Green Dot curriculum, training, and implementation sites.
www.livethegreendot.com

Prevention Innovations: Collaboration between researchers and practitioners that develops, implements, and evaluates programs, policies, and practices that will end violence against women.
http://cola.unh.edu/prevention-innovations

Raising Voices: This is a non-profit organization working toward the prevention of violence against women and children by influencing the power dynamics shaping relationships between women and men, girls and boys, and adults and children.
http://raisingvoices.org/about/

SCREAM Theater: Peer educational, interactive theater programs that provide information about interpersonal violence including sexual assault, dating violence, same-sex violence, stalking, bullying, and peer harassment.
http://vpva.rutgers.edu/scream-theater-and-scream-athletes

The End of Sexual Violence and Domestic Abuse?: A resource list of local, national, and international organizations working toward ending sexual violence and domestic abuse.
http://blog.ted.com/2013/05/29/the-end-of-sexual-violence-and-domestic-abuse-a-resource-list-of-organizations-working-toward-this/

The Men's Program by One in Four, Inc.: A non-profit organization dedicated to the prevention of rape by the thoughtful application of theory and research to rape prevention programming. The website provides presentations, training events, and technical assistance to men and women, with a focus on single-sex programming targeted toward colleges, high schools, the military, and local community organizations.
www.oneinfourusa.org

Virtual Knowledge Centre to End Violence Against Women and Girls: A useful website for step-by-step programming guidance, resources for implementation, lists of expert organizations, and descriptions of training and ongoing programs.
www.endvawnow.org

Index

Entries in **bold** denote tables and boxes; entries in *italics* denote figures.

ablism 150
Aboriginal and Torres Strait Islanders: men 238–9; women 53, 56, 78–82, 238
abortion, forced 32
abuse, overlap between forms of 131
adolescents 173, 211–13
adversarial legal systems 4, 49, 51, 68–9, 96
advocacy, in primary prevention 214–15
AFL (Australian Football League) 216
African-American community 237
Alberta, TROs in 56–7
alcohol: addressing use of 214; attempted intercourse by 24; rape facilitated by 12, 109; use by abusers 177, 179, 202; victim's use of 97, 107, 111, 119
allies, potential 221
American Indians and Alaskan Natives (AIAN) 26–7
Amnesty International 244–5
androcentrism, in research methodologies 7, 10
anger management programs 174, 190
anti-social personality 201
arrest: authorization for 50; in DV cases 48–9, 60–1; mandatory *see* mandatory arrest; police decision to make 94–5; policies promoting *see* pro-arrest policies
athletes, at risk of perpetration 213, 224–5, 240
attachment disorders 179
Australia: breaches of DVOs in 81–2; family law in 80–1; indigenous communities in 238–9; legislation on DV/IPV in 82–3, 85; police and justice responses to DV in 52–5, 61; use of protection orders in 77; *see also* DVOs
Australian and New South Wales Law Reform Commissions 82, 84
Australian Capital Territory (ACT) 53–4

batterer intervention programs: in Canada 56; in United States 176, 197; use of term 180n1; *see also* perpetrator programs
behaviorally specific questions: acceptance as methodology 7, 14, 31; effects on incidence estimates 22–3; in NCVS 25–6, 28; NISVS use of 20; for perpetrators 228; in SES 9–10;
behavior change programs 171, 174, 177; *see also* perpetrator programs
Black and minority ethnic (BME) women: and EVAW 247; issues confronting 150; services for 146–7; use of term 151n1; VAW among 142–5; *see also* ethnic minority women
boys: education against VAW 240–1; teenage 192, 240; victimization of 124, 239
Bringing in the Bystander 222–4
bullying, activism against 212, 222, 251
Bureau of Justice Statistics (BJS) 23, 28
bystander intervention programs: formats of 227; efficacy of 214, 222, 224, 227, 229; impact on disclosure 228; in colleges 222–5; evaluation of

226–30; men's involvement in 239–41; online 256; in younger populations 225–6; use of term 214, 221

Canada: immigrant communities and DV in 155–6, 163; police and justice responses to DV in 55–7, 61, 195–6; violence against WWD in 148
Canadian Advisory Council on the Status of Women 195
caregivers, violence against WWD 148–9
Cedar Project 136, 139
child abuse 27, 105, 179, 239
Centers for Disease Control and Prevention (CDC) 19, 27–8, 226–7
child protection: in CIFSR model 157; and DV work 82, 132, 136; referrals to perpetrator programs 175, 184
children: in Australian family law 80; health and safety of 192; in IPV situations 72, 131, 133; rights of 163; in victimization surveys 27; violence prevention among 212–13
Children and Family Court Advisory and Support Service (CAFCASS) 192, 193n4
child support payments 82
civil protection orders: in Australia 53, 77; in Canada 56–7, 61; in Europe 59–60; EVAW support for 247; penalization of breach 49–50
Coaching Boys Into Men (CBIM) 225–7
coercive control: and entrapment 12; intersectional approaches to 144, 150; long-term patterns of 47; and violence 83–4, 202, 216–17; *see also* controlling behaviors; terrorism, intimate
cognitive-behavioral skills training 212
cognitive behavioral therapy (CBT) 175
collectivist communities 154–7, 161, 163–5
college women: prevention programs among 212–13; surveys of 20, 22
colonization, trauma of 78–9, 238–9
community-based perpetrator programs 171, 184–5
community education programs 210–12, 215, 218
community engagement and mobilization 214–15
conceptualization, and measurement 20
Conflict Tactics Scales (CTS) 8, 12, 216
consent: building norms of 213; confusion around concept 107; inability to give 9
controlling behaviors: coercive 8–9, 12, 83 (*see also* coercive control); and DV 198, 200–1; eliminating use of 184; as precursors 228
Convention on the Elimination of Discrimination against Women (CEDAW) 118
coordinated community responses 174–5, 178–80, 183–5, 188, 204n5
Coordinated Organization Response Team (CORT) 159, 161, 163–4
Coordinated Prosecution model 196
Council of Europe: expansion of 62n5; standards on responses to DV 47, 57–8
court systems 51
crime: categories of 25; governing through 67, 74; unreported 67–8
crime victimization surveys 8
criminal damage 78, 81
Criminal Injuries Compensation Authority (Norway) 120, 122–3
criminal justice: apparatus of control in 67; deterrent effect of 48, 60, 68, 70–1, 187; influence of rape myths on 96; perpetrator programs within 174–5, 177, 185, 197; responses to DV 48; responses to IPV 66–7, 69–71, 77–80, 84–5, 195–6, 202–3; responses to sexual assault and rape 93–4; social context of 110; and unreported crime 68; and victims 72–3, 98–100, 117–18
Criminal Procedure Act (Norway) 117–19, 121, 124–6
cross-cultural disconnection 158
Cross Cultural Learner Centre 160–1
cross-disciplinary work 138–9
cross-DVOs 78, 80–1, 83, 85
Crown prosecutors 51, 55–6, 249
Culturally Integrative Family Safety Response (CIFSR), xxiii 156, 159, 164
cultural privacy 144
cultural sensitivity 154
Culturally Integrative Family Safety Response (CIFSR) 156–7, 159, 164
culture: and attitudes to state intervention 60, 62, 237–8; and engaging men 238; intersection with

VAW 144–5, 147; and violence prevention programs 217–18
cyberstalking 36–8, **37**
cycle-of-abuse theory 192

Dade County Domestic Violence Court 179
data collection: improving 15; technological methods of 42; women-centered practices of 7
dating violence: and bystander intervention programs 225–6; education programs for 132–3, 210–11
de-criming 95, 106
defense lawyers 108, 119, 124–5
defensive violence 83
Demographic and Health Surveys (DHS) program 11
depression, among abusers 179, 198
detention without charge 54, 78
disability, constructions of 143
disabled women *see* WWD
diversionary programs 175
Domestic Abuse Prevention Project 137
domestic violence (DV): against WWD 148–9; in Australia 52–3, 82–3; in Canada 55–7; in collectivist communities 154–8, 164–5; disclosures of 133–4; as distinct from VAW 245; in ethnic minority communities 145–6; etiology of 198; in Europe 57–60; forums 131; historical perspectives on 48; media campaigns against 229; men's rights perception of 237; multi-agency responses to 131–2, 137–8, 154; in Norway 117, 119, 125–6, 126n8; organizations specializing in 131–2, 134, 138–9; police and justice responses to 47–8, 50–1, 61–2; prevention programs for 132–3; risk factors for immigrant families 159, 161–4; specialized prosecution units for 49–50, 57, 61–2; trauma resulting in 161; typology of 203–4; use of term 77, 204n2; victim support in 135–6
Domestic Violence, Crime and Victims Act 2004 (UK) 58
Domestic Violence Court (DVC): Dade County 179; Ontario 196–7, 199, 203, 204n3
domestic violence orders (DVOs) 77–82, 84–5
domestic violence perpetrator programs (DVPPs) *see* perpetrator programs
drugs: attempted intercourse by 24; perpetrators' use of 179, 202; rape facilitated by 12; victim's use of 97, 111, 119
due diligence principle 58, 61
Duluth Abuse Intervention Program (DAIP) 174, 178, 198–9, 204
DV services: and child protection 132–3; culturally sensitive 154–6; multi-agency work of 131, 138; publicizing to WWD 150; reviews of 137

Early Intervention Program 196–7
eco-map 161, 164
economic abuse 85
education, violence prevention 210–13, 218; workforce 215; athletes 216
education professionals 132–3
elder abuse 27
emergency protection orders *see* TROs
emotional abuse 8, 10, 85, 190, 211, 241
emotional disorders 212
empathy: institutional 136–7, 139; programs promoting 192, 211
End Violence Against Women (EVAW) coalition: advocacy for integrated strategy 248–9; as epistemic community 246–8, 251, 253, 256; founding of 244–5; research reports from 245, 250; and sexualization 252; and violence prevention 251
EngenderHealth 215, 236
England and Wales: definition of DV in 133; EVAW activism in 245, 247; information sharing in 135; perpetrator programs in 184; reviews on sexualization in 252; specialized DV courts in 61; use of term 253n1; VAW strategy in 244, 249; victim support services in 250, 254n8
entrapment 12
epistemic communities, use of term 246–7
Equality and Human Rights Commission (EHRC) 245, 250
Equality Now 247
ethnic minority women: access to justice for 53, 57; cultural support for violence against 145; organizations of 247; prevalence of violence against 144; and pro-charging policies 56; specialized

services for 248, 250; *see also* black and minority women
European Union (EU): expansion of 62n5; prevalence of sexual harassment in **37**; prevalence of VAW in 32–5, **33–4**
European Union Agency for Fundamental Rights (FRA) 15, 31–2, 35, 38–9
Europe, police and justice responses to DV in 57–9
exclusion orders 52, 54, 60
Experience Sampling Method (ESM) 15
experimental design 218
expert witnesses 120
expulsion orders 59, 61

faith groups, providing VAW services 147
families: ideological reluctance to intervene in 70; in immigrant communities 155, 159–62; remaking relationships within 189
family conflict 8, 161, 217
Family Justice Center model 137–8
Family Law Act (FLA) (Australia) 80, 83–4
Family Law Court (Australia) 84
family screening 161
family violence, use of term 58, 77, 84
female genital mutilation/cutting: surveys on 11, 32; UK legislation on 248; as VAW 3, 145–6; and victim lawyer system 118
feminism: advocacy campaigns by 215; and BME women 142, 145–6; and epistemic communities 246; perspective on VAW 9, 172–3, 184; professionalization of 57; on role of men 233
feminist: contributions of researchers: 5, 7, 9–10
financial control 69
fines 59, 77, 82, 174
Finland: perpetrator programs in 172; victim lawyers in 117
forced marriage: criminalization of 147; EVAW's response to 247; surveys on 32; as VAW 3, 144–6; and victim lawyer system 118
forensic evidence collection 97–8
Fornærmedeutvalget (Victim's Committee) 118

Four Aspects Screening Tool (FAST) 161–2, *162*
fraternity members 224

gay and lesbian perpetrators and victims 185
gender: and IPV 8, 83–4, 217; relationship with culture 143–5
gender-based violence: as distinct crime 58–9; ecological framework of 34; links to HIV and reproductive outcomes 236; *see also* VAW
gender equality: in marginalized cultures 238–9; men's interest in 235; in relationships 184; in VAW strategy 244, 249–50, 252
Gender Equality Duty 245
gender inequality: institutions reinforcing 1–3; VAW as maintaining 83, 172, 236
gender norms: challenging 240; enforcing 12
genogram 161, 164
girls, violence against, see VAW
globalization, and VAW 2
global South 143–4, 238
Green Book initiative 137
Green Dot program 224–6

health services 133–4, 179
HIV 235–6, links to gender-based violence 236
homeless youth 212
honor-based violence 144–6
House of Ruth 197
human rights: global framework of 57; in VAW strategy 244, 249

Imkaan 247
immigrant women: access to services 157; discourses about 143; experience of DV 155–6; interventions for 159; legal status of 72, 144, 150; social challenges for 163; *see also* black-minority women, ethnic-minority women
incest 117–18, 121, 126n7
Independent Domestic Violent Advisors 58
Indigenous Australian women: 78–82, 238, *see* also Aboriginal and Torres Strait Islander women

individualist cultures 154–5
inequality, as root of violence 219, 256
information processing biases 96
informed consent, graduated process of 27
injunctions 51–2
Institute on Domestic Violence 237
institutionalization, and WWD 149–50
institutionalized learning 251
integrated support services (ISS) 184
interACT 223, 227
interagency training 137, 139
International Men and Gender Equality Survey (IMAGES) 13–14
International Violence Against Women Survey 35, 94
Internet: harassment and stalking via 36, 38; surveys over 42
interpretation services 147, 155
intersectionality 142–3, 146
intervention, levels of 132
Intervention with Microfinance for AIDS and Gender Equity (IMAGE) 215
interviewers, training of 7–8
interviews, safety precautions in 7
intimate partner sexual assault (IPSA) 100
intimate partner violence (IPV): and adversarial justice 69; against WWD 148; civil responses to 78–9, 82–3, 85; claims of gender symmetry in *see* gender and IPV; correlates of 13, 179–80, 213; criminal justice paradigm of 66–7, 73–4, 172, 174; debate on definitions of 82–3, 216; explanatory frameworks for 172–3; fines for 82; perpetrator programs for 171–2, 174–80, 180n1; primary prevention of 73, 210, 212–15; protective orders in 56, 77; punishment for disclosing information on 27; recidivism in 71, 177; relationship of victim and offender in 69–70; restorative justice approaches to 79; in series victimizations 23; sources of information about 228; surveys on 8–10, 14; typology of 84, 200–2, 206; unreported 68
intimate terrorists *see* terrorism, intimate
intoxication: of offender 111; of victim 95
investigative/inquisitorial legal systems 4, 49
The Iramoo Zone 239

Islam 157–8
Istanbul Convention 31–2, 35, 39, 58

justice system *see* criminal justice

knowledge work 248

language barriers 72, 139, 150, 155–6, 178
learning disabilities 178
legal systems, diversity of 49–50
legislative reform 82–83, for prevention 216
low-income countries 217

Making the Grade? reports 248, 252
male peer systems 241
mandatory arrest: deterring reporting 203; in Europe 58; and police discretion 70; research questioning 84; in the US 48, 50, 60; *also see pro-arrest*
mandatory charging 197f, 200; *also see pro-charging*
mandatory prosecution 195, 197, 200, 202–203; *also see pro-prosecution*
manhood 234–6, 238, 240
Map of Gaps 250–1
marriage, forced *see* forced marriage
masculinities 235–7, 241
memories, fragmented 95
men: in bystander approach 221–2, 239–41; education programs for 214; engaging in action against VAW 215, 233–9, 256; impunity for sexual coercion 107; intra-psychic reasons for violence 197–8; in minority communities 144, 158, 162–3; surveys of 13–14; as victims 132
Men Can Stop Rape 236; ‘My strength is not for hurting’ 213
MenEngage 241–2
Men of Strength (MOST) clubs 213
Men’s Project, The 223–4
men’s rights movement 237
mental health services 135, 138
mental illness: of abusers 179, 202; effect on families 162; of victims 105
minoritization processes 143
misogyny 13, 111, 234, 238
mobile phones use of for harassment or stalking 36, 38; to improve survey methodologies 15
motivational interviewing 175

multi-agency assessments 191
multi-agency meetings 137
multi-agency responses: culturally sensitive 164; in Europe 57–8; factors promoting 138–9; legal foundation of 60; mainstreaming of 145
Multi-Agency Risk Assessment Conferences (MARACs) 135, 191
multiculturalism 142–3, 154
multi-faithism 143, 147
music videos 111, 247
Muslim communities 156–8, 164
Muslim Resource Centre for Social Support and Integration (MRCSSI) 156–7, 159–60, 162–4
MVP (Mentors in Violence Prevention) 222, 236, 240

narrative therapy 175
National Crime Victimization Survey (NCVS): definition of rape in 19–20, 26; crime context of 24–5; protecting respondents to 27; question wording in 20, 28; sampling in 24–5; screening questions for **21–2**; victimization in 23
National Intimate Partner and Sexual Violence Survey (NISVS): definition of rape in 19–20; data collection in 15; health context of 24; incidence and prevalence in 24; protecting respondents to 27; question wording in 20, 28; sampling in 25; screening questions for **21–2**
National Violence Against Women Survey (NVAWS), on reporting of rape 24, 93–4
National Women's Study (NWS) 10
New Directions Program 195–202
New South Wales, multi-agency work in 135, 138 new technologies: harassment and stalking via 12, 14, 38; and survey sampling 15
New Zealand: law reform efforts in 113; prominent rape cases in 104–6, 108–10
non-contact, imposing 59–60
non-partner violence 34
Norway: compensation for victims in 122–3; responses to rape complaints in 118; rights of victims in 117–20; terrorist attacks in 123–4
nurses, forensic 97

offenses, categories of 49–50
Ohio University 223–4
one-stop centers 137–9, 166
Ontario, police and justice responses to DV in 57, 196–7, 203
organizational development 215–16
Ottawa, Domestic Violence Court in 196–7

parenting: education 212–13; positive 191, 213; shared 80, 191
Parivartan 225
participatory research 14
Partner Assault Response (PAR) program 197, 202–3
partner safety contact 176, 180
pathological violence 202
patriarchy: 111; challenges to concept of 113
pedagogy 218
perpetrator programs: accreditation for 184; in Australia 54–5; in Canada 195–6; challenges for 178–80; development of 171–3; diversity of participants 198–9; evaluation of 176–8, 183, 185–6; indicators of success in 189–93, 206; multi-agency support for 136–7; names for 180n1; organization of 174–6; service provider attitudes to 186–9; standards of practice for 176; voluntary clients of 197; *see also* behavior change programs
perpetrators: detailed information on 191; effectiveness of work with 132, 186, **187–8**; enhancing awareness of 191–2; extended detention of 61; in relationship with victims 72, 96, 107; social worker attitudes to 187; typologies of 178–9, 198–200, 203
perpetrator–victim binary 239–40
physical aggression: precursors to 228; reducing 227
plea bargaining 48–9, 51, 60, 96
police: attitudes to perpetrator programs 188–9; in CIFSR model 157; discretion of 49; occupational culture of 110–13; perceptions of victim responsibility 105–7, 109–10, 128; power to lay charges 51, 61; rape by 108; responses to DV/IPV 47–8, 62, 70, 85; responses to rape complaints 93, 95–6, 99, 104–5; safety strategies of 50–1, 54, 59–60;

specialized DV units of 56–7; and third-party protection orders 53–4, 78; and victim lawyers 120
police bans (PBs) 52, 54, 57, 59–61
Police Family Violence Orders (PFVOs) 53
police holding powers 54, 61
policy reform 216, 246
poor communities 237–8
popular culture, sexualized 252
pornography 36, 111, 113, 252
positivism 177
postcode lottery 149, 245, 250
post-traumatic stress disorder (PTSD) 156, 160
poverty 2, 212–13, 239
Power and Control Wheel 199–200
practice-based evidence 248, 251–3
prison: as deterrent 189; perpetrator programs in 175
prison sentences: suspended 59
pro-arrest policies: feminist activism for 174; lack of in Europe 62n7; and police discretion 70; in UK 58; in United States 48, 50, 55; *see also mandatory arrest*
pro-charging policies: 58; victim opinion of 55; *see also mandatory charging*
pro-prosecution policies: in Canada 55; in the UK 58; *see also mandatory prosecution*
Project Mirabal 183, 185–6, 188, 192–3
Promundo 236
prosecution: appealing decisions to drop charges 120; decision to proceed with charges 96–7; of DV cases 49, 51, 61–2; no-drop policies 50–1, 60, 84; and protection orders 53
prosecutors: attitudes to victims 98; meeting victim lawyers 121; *also see public prosecutors*
protection orders 45; counter-applications to 80; criminalizing breaches of 58; enforcement of 56; police applications for 53–4; use of term 51–2; *see also* civil protection orders; emergency protection orders
psychological abuse and violence 10, 69, 88, 177, 228; criminalizing 32, 59–60; and criminal justice 69; surveys on 10, 12, 33, 35
public prosecutors 49–51, 61, 118, 125; *also see prosecutors*

Queensland: legislation on DV/IPV in 83; mandatory investigation in 78; protection orders in 54, 81, 85

race anxiety 144
racialization 143
racialized oppression 80
racism: and men of marginalized communities 238–9; and responses to VAW 144, 146–7, 150
rape: accusations dismissed as false 93, 96, 105; case attrition in 128; cultural stereotypes about 95 (*see also* rape myths); debate on definitions of 19–20; men speaking out on 240; police data, on SV 19; police reactions to reports of 104–5; self-reporting of 26; surveys measuring 8–10, 23–4; underreporting of 94
rape crisis centers 1, 248, 250, 254n8
rape myths: education against 211, 222–4, 227; examples of 96; influence on juries 97; influence on police 105; and IPSA 100; victim-blaming 107, 110–11
rape pornography 247
rape prosecutors, specialist 97
'real rape' 97, 105
recidivism 71, 177
re-education, in perpetrator programs 198
referral pathways 134, 138, 175–6
refuge accommodation 146, 150, 171
Regional Coordinating Committee to End Violence Against Women 195
relationships education 73, 132–3, 213; improved 189–90
repeated violence 58
research methodology, innovation in 14–16
resistance, violent 9
retribution 49, 67
risk assessment: multi-agency work on 57–8; in perpetrator programs 176, 178; in SIP 159, 161; for WWD 150
risk management: and criminal justice 67; multi-agency work in 191

'safe at home' strategies 53–4
Safe Dates program 211
Safe Integration Assessment 162

safety, of survey respondents 24, 26, 33
safety notices 54
safety of victims: criminal justice responses to 54–5, 59–61, 82, 85; and deterrence 62; multi-agency work for 57; and perpetrator programs 171, 174, 176–8, 180, 184, 190; and victims' voice 72–3
schools: bystander interventions programs in 226; violence prevention in 211–12, 217
Schools Safe for Girls campaign 252
school violence 23, 222
Scotland: perpetrator programs in 185; rape crisis centers in 250; VAWG strategy in 244–5; victim support in 136
screening questions **21–2**
The Second Step 227
secular spaces 147
self-defense 211, 213
separation-instigated violence 9
series victimizations 23–4
service providers: competition for funding between 247; and immigrant communities 157–60; resources for 32; stopping cyberharassment 38
sex, social norms around 235
sexist abuse 234, 238, 241
sexual assault: case processing decisions in 94–5, 99–100; decision to prosecute 97; integrative model of 223; prevention programs for 211–13; skepticism towards allegations 96, 107; specialist investigators in 104; surveys on 9–10; underreporting of 93–4; victim empowerment in 98–9; *see also* sexual coercion, sexual violence
Sexual Assault Nurse Examiners (SANE) 97–9
Sexual Assault Referral Centers 248
sexual coercion 228; *see also* sexual assault, sexual violence
Sexual Experiences Survey (SES) 9–10, 19–20
sexual harassment: and bystander intervention programs 225; improving attitudes toward 215–16; in Istanbul Convention 32; men speaking out on 240; reporting 38; surveys on 10, 15, 35–8, **36–7**; and violence 34–5, 42, 228
sexualization 252
sexual violence (SV): barriers to progress in 112–14; bystander approach to 214, 222; debate on definitions of 8, 216; in ethnic minority communities 145–6; measuring 19; men's rights arguments on 237; police responses to reports of 104, 107, 111, *see also* sexual assault, sexual coercion
Safe Integration Program (SIP) 159–63, *160*
situational couple violence 9, 199–203, 217
social isolation 72, 148, 163
social learning theory 172–3
social marketing campaigns 213–14, 229
social media, VAW in 12, 253
social network analysis 228–9
social norms: and bystander intervention programs 214, 222–3, 226; changing 14, 215, 234–6; diversity of 11, 15; research into 9
social workers 134–5, 159
Sonke Gender Justice 235–6
South Africa 14, 211, 213, 235
space for action 144, 190
Spain 35, 58–9, 61, 172
specialized DV courts: in Australia 54–5; in Canada 56; in Europe 57–9, 61; legal scope for 49–50; level in legal system 51; and recidivism 71
spectrum of prevention 209
stalking: as breach of DVO 81; and bystander intervention programs 225, 229; criminalization of 58; in Istanbul Convention 32; reporting 38; surveys on 35–8, **37**; as VAW 7, 12; *see also* cyberstalking
statutory agencies: intervention duties of 60, 62; intervention powers of 131
Steinhauer Parental Capacity Assessment 161
Stepping Stones programs 215
sterilization, forced 32
stranger rape 105
stranger violence 8
Students Challenging Realities and Educating Against Myths (SCREAM) 227
Students Educating and Empowering to Develop Safety (SEEDS) 224
subpopulations, coverage in surveys 26, 32
substance abuse programs 179

suicide, threatening 201
super diversity 143
surveys: classification of incidents in 25–6; compared to police statistics 68; context of 24; cross-national comparisons of 11, 31–2, 42; feminist critique of 8–10; Internet-based 15; multi-mode designs of 38; protecting respondents 26–8; question wording in 20, 22–3; reference periods of 25; repeating over time 39n5
survivors: interventions for 132, 135; representation of 137; voices of 150–1; *see also* victims
systemic change 234

talking therapy, rational 175, 178
Tasmania: family violence legislation in 85; police and justice responses to DV in 53–4
temporary restraining orders (TROs) 52, 56
terrorism, intimate 199–203
test-retest effect 23
theater, in bystander intervention programs 223, 227, 230
Theater of the Oppressed 230n1
Toronto Star 196
Towards Better Practice (TBP) 135, 138–9
trade unions 244, 248
transsexual perpetrators and victims 185
trauma: historical 238–9; migration-related 156, 159, 161, 164; neurobiology of 95
trials: attacks on victims in 108; proper functioning of 69; victim lawyers in 117, 119–21, 123
trust, building 156

unfounding 95–6, 99
United Kingdom (UK): advocacy on VAW in 247; disability and VAW in 149–50; encouraging police action in 61; experience of BME women in 142–3; government strategy against VAW in 244; multi-agency work in 131–2; perpetrator programs in 183–5; police safety strategies in 59; powers of arrest in 50; rape prosecutions in 97; restorative justice 79, 203; services for BME women in 146–7; stalking as offense in 58
United Nations (UN): Committee on the Elimination of Discrimination against Women 118, 252; definition of VAW 249; Guidelines for Producing Statistics on Violence against Women 39; model survey module 11; research on VAW 236
United States (US): DV policy development in 48–9; evaluation of perpetrator programs in 185; multi-agency work in 131, 137; police and justice responses to DV in 60, 70; police response to rape complaints in 93; Virginia Standards for Batterer Intervention Programs 176
University of Kentucky 224–5

VAWG (Violence Against Women and Girls) *see* violence against women (VAW)
verbal abuse 8–9, 216
victim empowerment 48, 58, 60–61, 62n2, 91, 98–9, 128, 143, 146, 215, 230, 242
victimhood, collective 143
victimization: classifying 28; incident rates of 23–4; measurement of in bystander program evaluations 228; primary prevention of 209 (*see also* violence prevention); as process in everyday life 69
victim lawyers: challenges for 123; and defendants' rights 125; entitlement to 118; multiple 124–6; role of 119–22; use of term 117, 126n1
victims: assessments of credibility 95–6, 98, 100, 105; distrust of criminal justice 119; effects of trauma on 95, 110; expectations in disclosure 133; hopes and goals of 72–3, 77, 193; involvement in perpetrator programs 174, 176; in multi-agency work 135; policies to protect 50, 57–8, 60–1; reluctance to prosecute 147; responses to specialized courts 56; responsibilities in prosecution of 51; role in criminal justice 69, 118, 121; sense of self 190; willingness to report 68, 94; *see also* survivors
victim support: in Australia 53–4; in differing legal contexts 4; equitable access to 250; multi-agency 135–6; *see also* victim lawyers
Victim/Witness Assistance Program 196